KILLING FOR LAND

Killing for Land in Early California

—

Indian Blood at Round Valley
Founding the Nome Cult Indian Farm

Frank H. Baumgardner III

Algora Publishing
New York

ISBN: 0-87586-364-7 (softcover)
ISBN: 0-87586-365-5 (hardcover)
ISBN: 0-87586-366-3 (ebook)

Library of Congress Cataloging-in-Publication Data —

Baumgardner, Frank H.
      Killing for land in early California: Native American blood at Round
Valley, 1856-1863 / Frank H. Baumgardner, III.
          p. cm.
      Summary: "This is a history of the clash between the White settlers and the
Native Americans in what is now an affluent county in California. The frontier
wars gave land and gold to Whites and reservations to the Native Americans.
Eyewitness accounts and extensive research show the conflicting roles played
by the Army, State Legislature and the US Congress."
      Includes bibliographical references and index.
      ISBN 0-87586-365-5 (hard cover: alk. paper) — ISBN 0-87586-364-7 (soft :
alk. paper) — ISBN 0-87586-366-3 (ebook)
      1. Indians of North America—Land tenure—California—Round Valley. 2.
Indians of North America—Wars—California—Round Valley. 3. Indians of
North   America—California—Round   Valley—Government   relations.   4.
Frontier and pioneer life—California—Round Valley. 5. United States—
Politics and government. 6. United States—Race relations. I. Title.

      E78.C15B35 2005
      323.1197'0794'09034--dc22
                                      2005003571

Cover photo: Round Valley, CA. Photographer Frank H. Baumgardner III.

Printed in the United States

For all victims of the West's frontier violence.

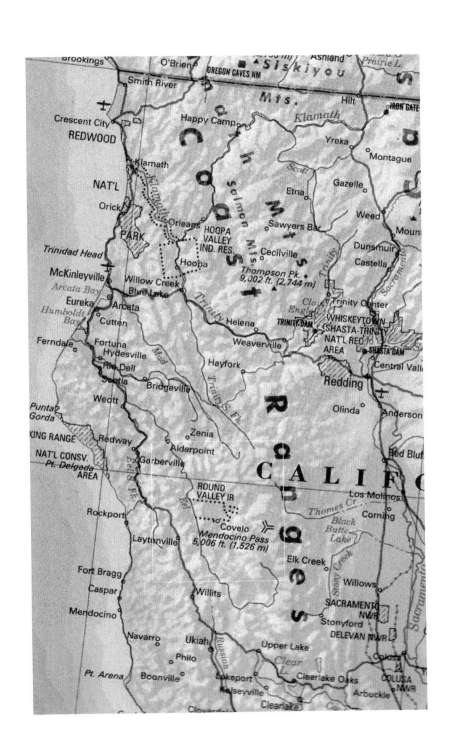

ACKNOWLEDGMENTS

Many individuals have helped me research and write this book during the past seven years. I'd like to give special thanks to Mr. and Mrs. Robert (Robert and Lila) J. Lee, Head of the Photo Collection, Mendocino County Historical Society, and Curator, Held-Poage Historical Research Library, respectively, in Ukiah, California, and to Ms. Linda Christy, Curator at the California Archives, Sacramento, CA. Thanks also to all the other members of Held-Poage Library's fine staff, especially Mr. Ed Bold, Ms. Janice Pollard Hague, and Mr. Phil Carnahan, for their hospitality, understanding and patience. It was Lila Lee who suggested that Round Valley's history had not been written.

Special thanks also to all five archival staffs as well as the U. C. students at the Main Library and Bancroft Library, the California State Archives, the California State Library, California History Room, the Pioneer Society of California, and the National Archives, Washington, D.C. and San Bruno, CA. In January 2000 Mr. Bob Schmidt, Archives Listserve Coordinator at Miami (of Ohio) University confirmed that John B. Weller attended Miami from 1825 to 1829 but did not graduate. Thus, he is not listed in the university's graduate catalog.

Most others are individually named in the footnotes. I would be remiss without thanking, in particular, Mr. Floyd Barney of Covelo, CA, who is an author himself. Mr. Barney took time out from his own busy life and schedule to read parts of the manuscript, to provide me with a very useful timeline of Round Valley events and to give a poignant critique of the first draft of this book.

Thanks also to Edicetera, in Berkeley, for help in preparing the manuscript, and, especially to Patricia Heinicke, Jr., and to Algora Publishing for help with the final product.

Several friends and relatives helped me keep sane at several points where there seemed to be no chance of ever publishing this book. This group includes my friend Janis M. Valderrama, who is the great great granddaughter of Jasper O'Farrell, Suzanne Wargin, Carol Cunningham-Ruiz, and last, but by no means least, my wife, Jeannette, who proofread several crude early versions of this book. My "history" is one reason why she has had to repeat so very many things to me over our years of marriage. I would also like to credit my father and mother who kept the faith.

The author alone takes full responsibility for the accuracy of this work. Any mistakes made herein are mine alone and I apologize in advance if anything herein offends anyone. Such errors as there may be are not made with any conscious hurtful intent on my part but I have tried to simply accurately describe what happened.

Sebastopol, 2005

MAIN CHARACTERS

1. Frank and Pierce Asbill: Two Euro-American brothers who discovered Round Valley, May 1854.
2. Thomas J. Henley: California's second Superintendent of Indian Affairs, 1854-59.
3. Simon Peña Storms: Founder and the first Agent in Charge, Nome Cult Farm (Round Valley Indian Reservation), 1856-59.
4. Lt. Edward Dillon: 6th Infantry, U.S. Army, platoon commander stationed at Nome Cult Farm, 1859.
5. Judge Serranus C. Hastings: Rancher, developer and anti-Native American agitator in Eden and Round Valleys, 1859-63. Founder and primary benefactor, Hastings Law School, San Francisco, CA, first Chief Justice, California Supreme Court.
6. Captain Walter Jarboe: Commanding Officer, Eel River Rangers, summer and fall, 1859. Commander in chief of the militia forces in Mendocino County during the Mendocino War, 1859.
7. Gov. John B. Weller: Fifth Governor of California, 1858-60.
8. Gov. John G. Downey: Seventh Governor of California, 1860-62.
9. Senator David C. Broderick: Democrat, U.S. Senator from California, 1857-1859.
10. Senator (Dr.) William ("Duke") Gwin, U.S. Senator from California, 1850-1858.
11. Senator Henry Wilson: Republican, Massachusetts. He led the opposition in the U.S. Senate to a bill which would have given the California Legislature independent control of all of its Indian reservations in 1859-1860.
12. Major General John E. Wool: The U.S. Army's commander in chief in California, 6th Infantry, Benicia, California, 1857-58.

13. Gen. William Kibbe: California Militia's commander in chief of the War with the Win-toons of the Klamath and Mad River Expedition, and Hoopa Valley Campaign.
14. Tom-ya-nem: Chief of the Concow Tribe, 1861-62.
15. State Senator Jasper O'Farrell: Senator from Sonoma and Marin Counties, Member of the Select Legislative Committee to Investigate the Mendocino War, spring 1860.
16. State Assemblyman Joseph B. Lamar: Assemblyman from Mendocino County. Chairman of the Select Committee to Investigate the Mendocino War, spring, 1860. Authored the Minority Report.
17. Lt. A. (Augustus) G. Tassin: Army scout and writer for the Overland Monthly, a monthly national magazine featuring geographical and general feature articles on the West in the late nineteenth century.
18. Capt. Charles D. Douglas: Commander of Company F, 2nd Infantry, U.S. Army in Round Valley from December 12, 1862 through the spring of 1863. Capt. Douglas established Fort Wright. He also conducted a General Investigation of Indian Affairs following the Wailaki Massacre at Upper Station a part of Round Valley Reservation.

TABLE OF CONTENTS

PREFACE

As an elementary school boy in the 1950s, this writer looked forward each week to a Western movie at the Saturday matinee. For my quarter admission fee to the show, I wallowed in the adventures of the cowboy stars of the time, popular heroes like John Wayne, Gary Cooper, Richard Widmark and Randolph Scott, as they re-conquered the continent once again for me every seven days. Against them were arrayed huge numbers of ruthless and fierce Native American warriors. Little did I know then that I was absorbing the myth of the Hollywood "wild Indian." But this myth, like a lot of others in American frontier folklore, was based on an earlier historical prototype in the Euro-American mind. Fears of being killed by "hostile Indians" did actually interrupt the sleep of the Euro-American immigrants to California in the 1840s and 50s.

Hollywood usually portrayed all Native North Americans as stereotypical Plains Indians. Made up of a composite of the most warlike armed Indian males, from tribes like the Sioux, Apache, Cheyenne, and Comanche, this image calls for an almost superhuman warrior, always well armed, vicious and shooting an unlimited supply of arrows or bullets. Indians in the movies were able to ride horses bareback at incredibly rapid rates over almost any terrain. As revealed by research of sources from this period the reality of the Northern California Native American is something quite different.

True Native Americans were generally peaceful, although they occasionally fought other tribes over boundary disputes or hunting rights. The California tribes like the Yuki, Pomo or Concow were accustomed to outdoor living, hunting for game as well as fishing and food gathering. Their lives were at a survival level where few individuals had any reason to travel outside of a tribal circle of ten to twenty miles in radius except to trade with other tribes.

Native American history is based on rare, now almost totally forgotten, survival stories of another sort. For example, in 1859 the Pit River tribe was forcibly relocated from ancestral homelands near Alturas, Modoc County, California to Round Valley two hundred miles southwest in northeastern Mendocino County. After trying to survive there for approximately a year, a Shasta Native American father and his young daughter "Jit-sic-wick" left Round Valley late one night in 1860. Traveling by night and hiding in brush by day, the pair at last reached their homeland using the beautiful and majestic peak of Mount Shasta as their only guide. The young girl held on tightly to her father's waist when he swam across many icy-cold creeks and rivers to eventually reach their destination.

Before the conquest by Euro-Americans, Indian tribes spread out like the Milky Way across the vast black sky of the great western region that in 1850 became the state of California. Like the stars on a clear night, most tribes flourished independently here, free and self sufficient for thousands of years. California Native Americans had a complex civilization. Some tribes thrived while others disappeared like burned out novas. Within and around Round Valley, Yuki was one star, Wailaki another, Nomlaki, Wintun, Pomo, Shasta, Hoopa—all were stars that made up a huge constellation filling the northern part of the state. By far the largest Round Valley tribe was Yuki—until the 1850s.

To the Yuki, Round Valley, located in remote northeastern Mendocino County, was like the vastness of outer space. Before the 1840s there seemed to be no boundaries to this place, despite a high rim of the surrounding Mayacama Mountains, a segment of the great California Coastal Range. The Yuki (or "Ukom n'on" valley people, as its most numerous subdivision was called), had no reason, except occasionally to trade, to venture out of the valley. They lived comfortably on clover, seeds, acorns, berries, and small animals that co-habited their home valley's large and grassy floor. Salmon and other fish filled the valley's creeks and streams that empty into the Middle Branch of the Eel River outside the valley's large but relatively flat broad surface.

Almost like an invasion by aliens from another galaxy, the Euro-American conquest of California, especially after 1846, happened very suddenly. The immigrants, accompanied by African-Americans and a few other ethnic groups, some with long-range weapons, like Hawken or Sharps breech-loading mountain rifles, had the power to annihilate entire Native American tribes. With the expansion of Euro-Americans into the Far West by the 1850s, the mountain rifle began replacing less powerful and less accurate muskets. Ultimately, after the so-called Mendocino Indian War, 1858-60, whites seized control of much of Round Valley's land and bounty.

Hopes of becoming better off than they were in the Midwest were what drove many like James Short, his wife Delilah Armstrong Short, and their two sons J.G. (James Green) and J.S. (John Stewart), then in their late teens, to emigrate from Illinois to California. Two letters that were written during the fall of 1860 give the reader an idea of some of the realities of wagon train travel as well as providing vivid pictures of the character of the third agent in charge at Round Valley Indian Reservation.

TWO FIRST IMPRESSIONS OF CALIFORNIA

J. Green ('Green') Short wrote the following note to his first cousin, J. L. ('Link' or 'Lincoln') Short on September 24, 1860 from Summit Lake (Donner Lake?), California. His homesickness pervades almost every line of his letter, which begins:

Dear Cousin:

It is with pleasure that I send you these few lines to let you know that I am well at present, and hope these few lines may find you the same.

We got here safe and sound on the 10th of this month. The cattle all looks well, and the best ones cattle is not worth anything out here. You can buy a good cow for 25 to 30 dollars. Horses is a good price, and I can get 200 dollars for that mare I got of Mat. Father [James Short] says if he can sell his cattle he is coming back to Illinois to see old Aunt Delila. I am coming back as soon as I can get back.

Link tell Babe [Rice Short, brother of James Lincoln] that if he had 'Britches' [probably a horse owned by James Lincoln] out here he could make his pile on him. Well Link I want you to tell me all the news, and how you get along with the girls. And tell me when you are going to get married. I expect that you are married now. Tell Babe that he must not run after the girls too much.

Babe I want you to write to me, (and) tell Aunt Sally and Cy I would like to see them very much. Tell Aunt Betsy that I would like to see her and all the rest.

Tell Jane [not identified] I want her to write to me, and tell the boys to write. I would like to be back in Illinois again. I am getting tired of California, times is so hard. Give my love to all now. Link I want yo to write to me as soon as you get this. I have nothing more to write at present. It is getting dark now [and] I must bring my letter to close. Direct your letters to Jackson, Amador County, California.

So no more at present.
but I remain your affectionate cousin.
J. G [Green]. Short[1]

We might readily imagine an unkempt teenager, Green Short, his youthful body hunched over a crude table, perhaps on Summit Lake's narrow shoreline or in some nearby clearing trying to finish his letter to his cousin back in Illinois before nightfall prevented any further efforts. Green Short's letter urged his family to write to him soon. He was lonely and completely isolated from the life he had known back in Illinois. The position he was now in was one that many others in the wilds of the High Sierras shared in that long ago fall of 1860.

Miss Mary Smallwood, another 1860 immigrant to this recently admitted state, who also entered via the California Trail, expressed somewhat different sentiments about moving to the Far West. Like Green Short, Mary Smallwood thought it made very good economic sense for ordinary Euro-American Midwesterners to make the long, sometimes dangerous journey across the plains and the Rocky Mountains to the West:

> Dear Friends:
>
> I enbrase [sic] this opportunity of writing you a few lines to let you know that we are still alive and well, and hope these few lines may find you all enjoying the same blessing.
>
> We all landed at Mother's the last day of August and found all well and doing well. Mother looks as young as she did when she left the states. I never had but three days sickness on the road. Jo and the children kept well the whole trip. We never got with Uncle Jimmy [James Short] until a way out in Iowa. We only traveled with him about four weeks.
>
> He and Hartmon left us [as] they thought we did not travel fast enough. We never saw anything more of them until we got in. They came to Mother's after we got there about the 10th. Aunt got sick during after they left us on the road, and was sick nearly all the way across. She first had the fever and the doctor broke that up, and she took the chills. Aunt looks very bad and has the awlfulest cough you ever heard.
>
> I heard from her since they left, and she was very sick again. They are about one hundred miles from Mother's up in the mountains amongst the Indians, where he is. ["He" apparently refers to James Short.] Betsy and Greene and Stewart [James Short's three children] was with him. And Rolston went also to the mountains with them.
>
> One of Uncle Jimmy's grey horses died on the Humbolt, and the rest have been in a bad fix as they only beat us in by one week. We lost one yoke of our steers, and one cow on the road which was all the bad luck we had.
>
> We yoked up cows and drove them on as merry as you please. It is nothing of a trip if you will only be patient. There were several women in our train. One sixty

---

1. Josephine S. Lynch, *Short, An Early Virginia Family*, (Richmond, Virginia: Whitter & Shepperson, 1970), 375.

years old and another fifty. They stood the trip fine, and they were never sick a day. I tell you that I would not dread to start across the plains again half as bad as I did before I crossed it.

I would like to see the folks back there, and [from] what I have seen, this part of the world does pretty well. I can't tell exactly how I like it yet but think I will like it very well.

They say times are dull. Hogs are from three to four cents gross weight, chickens from five to six dollars a dozen, turkeys one dollar apiece, eggs six bits a dozen. Mammy sent off a wagon load of chickens and turkeys yesterday. You and Cy had better come out here. You would get rich in a year or two. Now Sally I have told you all I know to tell.

Oh I forgot to tell you about Uncle Jim and Lily getting jealous of Betsy and David Hartmon, and they left the Hartmons not long after they left us (on the road) so Betsy told us.

I must quit as it is getting late. Give my love and respects to all enquiring friends.

To Sarah Hohamer

Mary Smallwood
Princeton P.O.
Colusa County, California[2]

Colusa County is about fifty miles north of Sacramento. In this revealing letter to her friend Sarah, Miss Smallwood made several comments that describe "Uncle Jimmy" (James Short's) personal traits. Possibly because he was anxious to get into the gold mines in the High Sierras, Jim Short had left the slower moving wagons behind (not once but twice), thus abandoning his responsibility. Despite losing one of "Uncle Jim's" horses, one cow, and one yoke of steers by 1860, wagon train travel across the plains, deserts and mountains was usually a little less dangerous than it had been in the 1840s and 50s. Note also the novel way that Miss Smallwood's group pulled their wagon when they had lost "one yoke of our steers." While he may well have been an able leader when he paid attention to his job, James Short could also be narrow-minded. It was due to this tendency of Supervisor Short to lose sight of his responsibilities, especially during a crisis, that many Native Americans' lives would be unnecessarily lost near Round Valley in 1861-62.

As we will see, many of James Short's actions as supervisor of the reservation were rash and at times dangerously irresponsible. Soon after this letter was written, in early 1861, Short, together with his two sons, Green and Stewart,

---

2. Lynch, *Ibid.*, 373-4.

moved away permanently from High Sierra gold country nearly one hundred miles west to Round Valley. Fortunately for his family, Short had an old friend, President Abraham Lincoln, who appointed him to be the new supervisor (or agent) at Round Valley Indian Reservation (Nome Cult Indian Farm).

In the end, after over five years of bloody losses, the California Native American tribes ended up with only broken promises in eighteen worthless unratified treaties. They had no way of knowing that they had been simultaneously betrayed both by the U.S. Congress and the California State Legislature. Ultimately, by 1876, ownership of most of the valley's best farmland went to individual Euro-American ranchers. The subject of this book is how all these events came to pass.

Today, historians note that a vast gap existed between the two cultures. It was a yawning gulf that adversely affected relations in hundreds of ways. Native Americans were hardly "savages." Before the Euro-American invasion of Northern California they had lived under a well-developed system of customs, beliefs, and laws. Many commonly thanked the Great Spirit for each day they were alive. Each was personally bound by his or her promise, so it was imperative not to give it unless one could keep it.

The first California and Nevada Superintendent of Indian Affairs was the explorer Edward ("Ned") F. Beale, an ex-Navy officer and Mexican War veteran who had carried out dangerous missions under Commodore Stockton. Beale came from a distinguished family of American patriots. He was at once a dedicated public servant and a visionary reservation planner.

From 1845 through 1853, Edward Beale made six transcontinental trips, really exploratory expeditions like the travels of John C. Frémont. Beale was appointed to the Office of Indian Affairs post in charge of all the Native Americans in California and Nevada in late 1853. Beale's California Native American reservation plan was adopted by the Pierce Administration. Soon Congress also approved it. Superintendent Beale planned to create a number of large self-sufficient Indian reservations where the Native Americans would learn to farm while being protected by the US Army. In theory it would have been efficient, economical and a positive life-saving scheme, equally beneficial to both the settlers and Native Americans alike. But theories in the West often simply failed. Beale served for two years before he was replaced in 1854 by Thomas J. Henley.

All of the western tribes were lumped together, as if they all were the same great tribe: the "Indian Savage." News stories and bulletins of the time referred to guides or employees who happened to be Native American as "boys." Generally, California Native Americans were looked upon by most whites as inferiors who were capable of little, partly because very few of them could speak or understand very much of the English language. Almost none of them could write English. Many Euro-Americans believed that the wild Indians would kill livestock, or rape their women, or possibly kill and scalp entire families.

To understand the violence of this period, readers might try to remember that there were tremendous fears and misunderstandings on both sides, both before and after the Mendocino War. One key factor of Beale's plan for reservations in the West was the principle of separation of the Native Americans from Euro-Americans.

The simple aboriginal peoples, who commonly went about nearly naked except for deer or elk skin robes, loincloths, and occasionally moccasins, seemed to the Euro-Americans to be little more than animals obstructing their plans for land development. The Native Americans' practice of occasionally killing whites' livestock for food, widely referred to as "depredations," raised the possibility of war. If war did come, it would not be a European sort of conflict where organized units of large numbers of trained, well-armed men contended on battlefields. European nineteenth-century rules of warfare, with formal war declarations, the delivery of terms of surrender and the concept of equal treatment for prisoners, would be completely absent in Northern California.

By the early 1850s, reports about Round Valley from Euro-American mountain men had created a vague image of a great open valley, a somewhat idyllic pasture, high up in the coastal mountain range. Fighting between the two traditionally contending cultures over the land would soon begin, as a few powerful leaders like Judge Serranus C. Hastings well understood. As in the past, in the case of the Black Hawk War of the 1830s in Illinois and Iowa, racial conflict further complicated an already tense situation. Ultimately the Euro-Americans would use minor incidents or clashes as a pretext for stealing even more Native American land.

The initial phase of this bloody race war lasted for seven years, 1856–1863. The Yuki tribe possibly suffered more deaths, or at least more deaths proportionally, than any other tribe in Mendocino County. According to the great anthropologist A. L. Kroeber the Yuki originally numbered about two thousand. By about the middle of the next century (1940), the Yuki were very close to extinction. By this time there were fewer than two hundred living Yuki Indians. By contrast, the Euro-Americans lost fewer than ten settlers during the seven-year period in the Mendocino War, according to notes made by historian Estle Beard and left at Held Poage Library in Ukiah.

After surviving a bitterly cold winter at Fort Weller, a fort near present-day Willits, one platoon of nineteen Army soldiers of the 6th Infantry arrived in January 1859 at Round Valley. This unit was reassigned elsewhere one year later. Following a period of more intercultural bloodshed from 1861 through the winter of 1862, a company-sized US Army unit ultimately stopped the violence. What remained of peace following this ugly race war, for Native Americans and Euro-American settlers alike, were strong antipathies, memories of terrible events of shootings and killings, and a coldness, an almost complete lack of mutual understanding.

Due in part to the passage of nearly one hundred fifty years, as well as scanty documentary evidence from this period, when most Americans think of the settlement period they see it as a kind of blurred image where a roughly equal number of crimes were committed by two sides. Moreover most of us believe that the decrease in the Native American population was *mostly* due to diseases like smallpox some of which the Euro-Americans brought with them.

This book presents a different thesis. It describes the years 1856–1863, the start of this tragic and unequal fifty-year conflict. The first two years of the period were essentially peaceful. The few nonviolent Euro-American settlers and local Native American tribes lived in relative harmony and cooperation. The first bloodshed did not escalate into unlimited war.

According to a few ranchers, local Native Americans began taking their livestock. Starting in the midsummer of 1859 near Round Valley a vigilante militia unit, named by its captain the "Eel River Rangers," started to kill Native Americans. Walter S. Jarboe was this so-called captain's name. Late in 1859, the state's highest politicos in Sacramento began to ask questions about why violence had broken the peace in the vicinity of this isolated valley in rugged northeastern Mendocino County. In early 1860, Gov. John G. Downey appointed a joint state legislative committee consisting of five California legislators to record Army officers', reservation officials', settlers' and Native Americans' personal depositions about their own personal roles in what was called "the Mendocino Indian War."

These depositions (testimonies or affidavits) were sworn eyewitness statements and settlement accounts as reported by inhabitants. Most of the ranchers lived either in Round Valley or its immediate vicinity. As valuable to historians as fossils are to biologists, the depositions are fascinating, rare vignettes of a long-gone California past. They give us clear personal insights into a California frontier war in the late 1850s that gave rise to a stable and permanent ranch economy for the Euro-Americans and a reservation system for the few surviving Native Americans.

Despite a small majority of nineteen settlers (out of just over thirty depositions closely reviewed) who testified that they thought that Native Americans killed livestock for food, Round Valley's settler opinion split almost fifty-fifty over whether they thought a citizen-militia force should be established to protect settler property, mainly livestock.

In stark contrast to all the other depositions, the Native Americans' depositions were either lost or destroyed. The reasons for their disappearance are still mysterious. Much of the following story is told by the ranchers, farmers, or their Euro-American settler employees in their own words from their 1860 depositions to the "Select Committee" of the 1860 California Legislature.

So complete and absolute was the Euro-Americans' military victory in 1859-1860 that the Yuki culture and way of life were nearly completely destroyed. Native American hatred for Euro-Americans was sublimated so completely, driven so deep into Native American psyches and souls that their emotions were nearly indiscernible to Euro-Americans in the 1850s down until the 1890s. The Progressive movement brought minor reforms yet deep wounds are still present today. The bitterest of hatreds has been allowed to fester internally for more than one hundred twenty five years. These were passed on to each succeeding generation.

To California's first great ethnologist-anthropologist, Stephen Powers, California's frontier wars were simply part of a much broader racial and political struggle for land and power that had started in the early 1600s on the North American continent.

By 1763, the French and Indian War (or the Seven Year's War, as it usually was known in Europe) between France and Great Britain ended up with the almost total victory for one side. The British, their Native American allies, and Euro-American colonial (militia) officers and troops, such as Lt. Col. George Washington of Virginia and others, were now free to settle in many new areas of the continent. With victory in the Mexican War, this area expanded to include most land west of the Mississippi River.

It was during this first great North American conflict, as well as earlier Indian wars such as King Phillip's War and the Pequot War, that Euro-American militia units developed a unique style of warfare in which farmers and settlers made up large parts of eventually victorious forces. Euro-American militia units that fought and won the later so-called "Mendocino War" about a hundred years later were really not very different from the deerskin hunters, escaped convicts, and other outcasts from all the aristocratically-controlled North American British ex-colonies—the Regulators of North Carolina, for example. Many, possibly most, of the leaders of the earlier conquest by the United States of Hispanic California from 1846–1848 in the Mexican War had been born in Southern states like Virginia, North Carolina, Tennessee, Kentucky, and Texas. Lt. Colonel (Senator and then later General) John C. Fremont from Virginia, Zeke (Ezekiel) Merritt from North Carolina and Captain Isaac Messic from Texas are three examples. While immigrating here twelve years later in 1860, James Short also hailed from Virginia, by way of Illinois.

The dual legacy of manifest destiny and settlement of Western states like Oregon, California, Nevada, and Colorado by a united Euro-American majority continues to haunt interracial relations today. Those ethnic wounds caused by wars such as this one, then dubbed by participants as "The War of the Wintoons," "General Kibbe's War," or "The Mendocino War," as it was known locally in Mendocino County, left a tragic legacy today. They are buried deeply in the nation's collective unconscious mind. Sometimes they surface to prevent any real interracial hope or progress.

This book claims to be neither a definitive military history nor, strictly speaking, regional history. In fact, it is some of each. Hopefully, it is a generally accurate narrative summary of what happened and how and why a deadly conflict raged that lasted over five years and was so very deadly to one side. It is also to put the valuable depositions into print for the general public to read.

I began this book after conducting regional research at five locations: in Sacramento at the state archives and the state library, at Held-Poage Historical Research Library in Ukiah, at Bancroft Library at UC Berkeley and at the National Archives in San Bruno. I also visited the National Archives in Washington for materials on Fort Wright. I do not feel qualified to tackle the broader questions raised by such excellent scholars as Robert F. Heizer, Albert Hurtado, Estle Beard and Lynwood Carranco, James Rawls, Jack Norton, George Harwood Phillips or others who have painted California history with such broad strokes upon their historical canvases that we may lose sight of the importance of eyewitness accounts of direct participants, on-the-spot reports, news articles on events and memoirs.

Ralph Waldo Emerson concluded a 1841 essay entitled *History* with the following sobering sentence: "I am ashamed to see what a shallow village tale our so-called History is."[3] This story, like the history Emerson referred to, is frequently depressing. At times, it is even tragic. Yet, it is never dull. I believe the great American poet and philosopher would have agreed that there are many valid reasons for studying Round Valley. Probably most of the actual Euro-Americans new to California in the 1850s and 60s favored the Office of Indian Affairs' Indian removal-reservation plan. For California indigenous people the only alternative was extermination.

Some might try comparing the mistreatment of the Native Americans on California's nascent reservations through the nineteenth century with the holocaust of Adolph Hitler's Nazis of the 1940s, Serbia's so-called "ethnic cleansing" in the late 1990s, or the situation in the Middle East that preceded the September 11, 2001 attacks on this country. As almost any history student, professional historian or history buff well knows, such comparisons inevitably are at least partially fallacious for many reasons. Probably most Euro-Americans along the California frontier in this period would have resisted the idea that they wanted to exterminate the Native Americans. This is not to deny, however, that there certainly was a significant minority of Euro-Americans led by people like Walter Jarboe who might have consciously supported such an approach. Fortunately for the Yuki and for all the other Northern California Native Americans at this time, machine guns, poison gas, nuclear weapons, cluster bombs deliberately used on civilians, guided missiles, two-thousand-pound "daisy cutter" bombs or civilian aircraft fully loaded with hundreds of thousands of pounds of aviation gasoline were far in the future.

Regarding terminology used in this work, I would be remiss without mentioning the use of the words Indian and Native American. Some of my earliest boyhood readings about Native Americans were the characters in John Fenimore Cooper's *Deerslayer* series. When I first read about American pioneers in the fourth or fifth grade, "Indians" was the term of choice by textbook authors. In the 1970s, it suddenly was found to be offensive. Readers will please note that I use both terms here, but have tried to use Native American, and have avoided the word "white" when "Euro-American" will do better. I am aware that how we use words is a vitally important subject that should be freed from old and hurtful racial stereotypes and constraints.

---

3. Ralph Waldo Emerson, "History," from Emerson's first book of essays, published March 1841, as quoted in *The Portable Emerson*, edited by Carl Bode in collaboration with Malcolm Cowley (New York: Penguin Books, Viking Penguin Inc., 1974) copyright renewal from 1946 by Viking Penguin Inc., 137.

INTRODUCTION

For tens of thousands of years after their ancestors' arrival on the North American continent from Asia and long before the Gold Rush in 1848, the Yuki like other northern California tribes maintained its own distinct culture. In the Round Valley region the Yuki tribe consisted of five distinct subdivisions: Ta'no'm (slope people), Witukomno'm (sited at Eden Valley) and Ukšišmul-háñtno'm (sited at Coal Mine Creek), Ukomno'm (valley people), Huititno'm (middle-ridge people) and, finally, Sukšaltátamno'm (nicely-shaped pine tree people). In addition to these five main Yuki subdivisions, the Onkolúkomno'm (ground in another valley people) lived apart from the others "at the headwaters of the South Fork of the Eel River,"[4] isolated from all the other Yuki tribelets by a four thousand foot ridge. Partly because they were separated from the other groups, there are no survivors of the Onkolúkomno'm. Besides these six Yuki groups just listed, there were also two smaller ones. The Lalkútno'm lived from the outlet of Round Valley to the Eel River. At the valley's outer edge about two miles from the Lalkútno'm lived a final Yuki group, the Ontítno'm (tableland people). East of Round Valley lived various Wintun, north were Wailaki, Lassik, and southeast were various small tribes of Pomo.

Also, according to Prof. George M. Foster's 1944 study, the Yuki had a Creation myth:

---

4. George M. Foster, *A Summary of Yuki Culture*, Anthropological Records 5:3, (Berkeley and Los Angeles, University of California Press, 1944), p. 160.

In the beginning, there was only water, upon which floated a down feather. As Coyote (hulk'oi) looked on, this feather emerged in human form—Taikomal, taking from his body material for sewing, he proceeded to make the world, somewhat in the manner of a coiled basket, while Coyote helped by running errands. The earth in order, mankind was created by giving life to sticks, the largest becoming men, smaller ones women, and the smallest, children. Then he brought the powerful Ghost Dance to man, but the real ghosts were so powerful that the initiates could not survive the test. So, disguised human beings were substituted for real ghosts. Various other incidents occurred: the placing of other tribes in their habitat, teaching them their languages and ways of doing things, and the introduction of death through Coyote's desire that his dead son should not be resurrected.[5]

When Taikomal got angry with his people he might send great thunderheads. People would say, 'ká'-ahik ([he's] looking out [at us]).' Then the Yuki would become uneasy. Sometimes special doctors (mitš-lamšími) would step in "pleading, 'Please stop. My people are afraid! Why are you doing this?'"[6] As was noted by Professor Foster, Taikomal's omnipresent and omnipotent qualities dovetailed into Judiasm's and Christianity's concept of God or of the Supreme Being who made man in His own image. This point explains, in part at least, why the Pentecostal Church in the 1940s had such a strong following among the modern Yuki representatives whom Dr. Foster interviewed as he prepared to publish his study on Yuki culture.

A glance at the California map depicting the "Disposal of the Dead" by Dr. A. L. Kroeber, *Elements Of Culture In Native America* (1922), shows that cremation was nearly as common as burial of bodies as a method of disposing of dead bodies. However, the Yuki as well as most Wintun and "Northwestern Maidu of the foothills"[7] generally buried their dead instead of cremating them. Perhaps if the Round Valley settlers in 1859 had known this fact about the Yuki culture, they would not have so quickly destroyed a Yuki rancheria they assumed was responsible for killing John Bland. His charred body indicated an attempt at cremating his remains; this might well have led Captain Jarboe and the other Eel River Rangers to make the more likely conclusion that it was not Yuki but Pit River Indians that had killed John Bland.

The Yuki territory in northeastern Mendocino County was about 1,100 square miles. It varied in altitude from 1000 feet to 7500 feet at the top crest of the Mayacamas. It consisted of a very large, forty-mile square valley, Round Val-

---

5. Foster, *Summary of Yuki Culture:* 204.
6. Foster, *Ibid.,* 204.
7. A.L. Kroeber, *Elements Of Culture In Native California,* 13, 8, University of California: Publications in American Archaeology and Ethnology, 295.

ley, together with six smaller valleys around it. In addition as Dr. Foster described it: "Yuki territory is a jumble of mountains, cliffs, swift streams, falls and cataracts, mountain meadows and oak groves, pine forests and rocky summits—as beautiful to the civilized eye as to the eye of the Indian, to whom it was a paradise of game and fish."[8]

Yuki men and women were village folk. Again, as was first described by Dr. Foster, one Yuki might say, "I am Witukomno'm." Just as an American citizen might say, "I am American."[9]

It is also important to recall that the unique kinship that the Yuki felt for their Round Valley homeland came about not so much from one "surveyor's precise marks" as from what Professor Foster described as the "phenomenon of drainage." Here, he was talking about watershed boundaries. Round Valley villages, like Native American rancherias and villages throughout California, were located beside creeks and streams within the valley.

During the Mexican period, 1769-1845, there was little contact between the Yuki and Hispanics. Alta California did not extend that far north. In the first half of the 19th century, Euro-American mountain men, hunters and trappers penetrated the area and moved on.

In early 1852 President Millard Fillmore sent a team of three federal Commissioners out to California. Redick McKee of Virginia, Colonel George W. Barbour of Kentucky, and Dr. O. M. Wozencraft of Louisiana were the three federal Commissioners appointed to negotiate treaties by the president.

As anthropologist Robert F. Heizer noted in his Introduction to *The Eighteen Unratified Treaties of 1851-1852 Between the California Indians and the United States Government*: "Between April 29, 1851, and August 22, 1852, a series of eighteen treaties 'of friendship and peace' were negotiated with a large number of what were said to be 'tribes' of California Indians...[10] and the United States Government." The treaties directly affected 139 tribes that represented about 25,000 Native Americans. The three Commissioners did not make an actual treaty with the Yuki.

The treaties made with two other tribes who lived closest to Round Valley were Treaty O, "Treaty made and concluded at Camp Lu-pi-yu-ma, at Clear

---

8. Foster, *Summary Of Yuki Culture*, 157.
9. Foster, *Ibid.*, 157.
10. Robert H. Heizer, Introduction, *The Eighteen Unratified Treaties Of 1851-1852 Between The California Indians And The United States Government*, Archaeological Research Facility: University of California, Berkeley, CA, 1972, 1.

Lake, State of California, August 20, 1851, between Redick McKee, Indian Agent on the part of the United States, and the Chiefs, Captains and Head men of the Ca-la-na-po, Ha-bi-na-po, Etc., tribes of Indians," and Treaty P, "Treaty made and concluded at Camp Fernando Feliz, on Russian River, in the state of California, August 22, 1851, between Redick McKee, Indian agent, on the part of the United States, and the Chiefs, Captains and Head men of the Sai-nell, Yu-ki-as, Etc., Etc., Tribes of Indians."[11]

From a reading of these treaties we learn about the promises that the Commissioners made. For example, Treaty P stated that in return for the Native Americans' agreement to "remove with their families and property from the lands they now occupy, on Russian River, to the Indian reservation on Clear Lake"; the Sai-nell, Yu-ki-as, Mas-su-ta-ka-ya and Po-mo would receive in return "one hundred head of beef-cattle, and two hundred sacks of flour, equal to ten thousand pounds, and a like quantity of the same for two years after their said removal and settlements....etc." and "for their permanent use besides the provisions, clothing etc. given them at this camp, such brood stock, farming implements, mechanics, instructors in agriculture and learning, as their numbers may, when ascertained, entitle them to, upon a fair and just equality with the Indians now residing at Clear Lake,...."[12] The Commissioners did their jobs efficiently, as the map showing "Areas supposedly ceded by Indians in the 1851-52 treaties...."[13] indicates. A major stumbling block to ratification was the fact that the treaties had set apart about 11,700 square miles of prime California real estate for the Native Americans. This amount of land was so great that Congress was deluged with petitions and letters from settlers in California protesting the treaties. Thus, unfortunately for the Native Americans, the Senate not only refused to ratify any treaties but on July 8, 1852 put all the treaties on file "under an injunction of secrecy which was not removed until January 18, 1905."[14]

This was like putting all eighteen treaties into a locked box and burying it for over fifty years. By so doing the Senate made sure that only social scientists, ethnologists, anthropologists or a few historians would one day puzzle over the meaning of these documents. As far as having any practical value to the indigenous people of California in the 1850s and throughout the nineteenth century, the treaties were an almost total fraud. Even worse than that, it is possible that

---

11. Heizer, *Ibid.* "Treaties O and P," 81 to 91.
12. Heizer, *Ibid.* from "Treaty P," 89.
13. Heizer, *Ibid.* Map 1, "Areas supposedly ceded by Indians in the 1851-52 treaties...etc." 7.
14. Heizer, *Ibid.* Introduction, 1.

they raised false expectations among other tribes like the Yuki, the Nomlaki, the Pomo in Round Valley, or even the Wailaki, Hoopa, or Wappo, who may have gotten word of these treaties.

No written records of the Yuki tribe exist from the early 1850s or earlier than the Euro-American takeover. Throughout this time, Yuki patterns of daily life continued undisturbed, just as they had for eons before.

Chapter 1. The Yukis Meet White Men

1. Justices of the Peace shall have jurisdiction in all cases of Complaints by, for, or against Indians, in their respective Townships in this State,...

6. Complaints may be made before a Justice of the Peace, by white persons or Indians; but in no case shall a white man be convicted of any offence upon the testimony of an Indian.
—An Act for the Government and Protection of Indians, The California Indian Indenture Act, April 22, 1850.

A brief but decisive frontier war throughout northern California and more specifically in Mendocino County occurred between 1858 and 1860. This bloody two-year period that the Euro-Americans originally termed the "War with the Win-toons" or, in Mendocino County, "the Mendocino War," should be recognized for what it really was: a genocidal struggle between two peoples of vastly different cultures over control of the entire northern half of California. Relatively tiny forces of briefly trained but well-armed volunteer Euro-American militiamen defeated all the bands of Native Americans they encountered. Many northern California tribes fought including the Yuki, Wailaki, Cancow, Yana, Maidu, Paiute, Pomo, Redwood Creek, Hoopa, Pit River, and Wintun (or "Win-toon").

Getting at the truth regarding intercultural events, especially those involving violence between the invading Euro-Americans and California Native Americans, is a particularly difficult task for two reasons. The first and most obvious reason is that the passage of more than 125 years means there is some scarcity of good source material. Most settlers left little or no records that survive today. Most California Native Americans followed the oral traditions of their native culture. Almost none of them wrote down their stories, either in their own Indian dialect or in English.

The second problem in getting a clear picture about this period is that, in part at least, historians as well as just about everyone else have had their minds prejudiced by the Hollywood image of the American Indian. According to the mold Native Americans were ruthless, rampaging savages who attacked "Home On the Prairie" settlers as they were innocently trying to establish a small farm or homestead. Mention the word "Indian" and what comes to mind is a youthful warrior on horseback carrying a weapon in one hand while deftly guiding his mount at a gallop across the Plains. In other words, we think of a Sioux, Apache, or Comanche brave in a loincloth with a string of white scalps, attacking an almost defenseless wagon train. Such images, while they may excite today's moviegoers just as they entertained dime novel readers in the late nineteenth century, bear almost no likeness to reality, especially as regards the Native Americans who lived in California in the 1850s.

Simply by reading the actual reports and letters from this conflict, the reader will be able to learn some of the facts about what really happened in Mendocino and in other northern California counties between 1858 and 1860. The reader is the best judge of who is telling the truth and who is exaggerating. One of the reasons to study history is so that we can first locate and fully describe the past, and then, hopefully, to treat these still terrible scars so that all can learn, reconcile and move on. In order to do this, we must forgive each other. We must not repeat the mistakes of the past.

"Nearly the Whole Number Destroyed": Patterns of Violence in Northern California

Round Valley is located about twenty-five miles inland from the rugged northern coast of Mendocino County California. For a long time it was overlooked by European and Euro-American explorers and settlers. In 1821, the Hispanic discovery party of Captain Luis Arguello and Father Blas Ordaz explored only as far north as the Russian River. Both Jedediah Smith in 1828 and Christopher (Kit) Carson in 1846 bypassed Mendocino County far to the east on their separate ways toward Oregon. Even today, a casual look at Round Valley's location on a state road map reveals its remoteness and explains why development and settlement were slower there than in many California villages and towns.[15]

Most of Round Valley consists of a huge bowl or a large, flat upland valley, measuring roughly six by eight miles. It contains fertile and generally moist top-soil, irrigated frequently by creeks and streams, which flow, in general, from south to north. Most of these streams eventually reach the Pacific by way of the Eel River.

In the 1850s, the best way for a non-Indian to reach the valley was by horseback, mule team, or simply by setting out on one's own two feet across steep, rugged trails many miles long. Because most Euro-Americans were new-comers, they had to depend upon Native American guides to help them traverse through a few passes in the steep Coastal Range westward either from Red Bluff or, even farther to the east and southward, from Sacramento. The approaches to the valley from Fort Bragg, Mendocino, or Eureka inland from the Pacific Coast also were dangerous. The way was impeded by a four-hundred-mile-long by thirty-mile-wide stretch of almost impenetrable redwood forest and difficult fords across fast-moving branches of the Eel River. In 1854, the route taken by the Sam Kelsey party, which included the Asbill brothers, Frank and J. Pierce, was to travel up from Sonoma in Sonoma County—a rough trail because no roads existed.[16]

If there had been an imaginary protective shield around all of Northern California's Native Americans up until 1848, the Gold Rush of 1848–1849 over-came this barrier to the massive Euro-American invasion. On the day the Asbill brothers "discovered" Round Valley in May 1854, their party encountered a large group of Native Americans. A brief firefight broke out. Approximately forty

---

15. Round Valley is still somewhat difficult for a visitor to reach unless one can fly a private aircraft. The nearest town is Willits, located approximately forty-two miles southwest of the valley along a tortuous road. One can get to Round Valley by auto by driving north on Hwy. 101 from Willits. At the junction of California Highway 162 and 101 at Longvale turn right and follow Hwy. 162 through rugged terrain until reaching Dos Rios. The actual reservation property is just north of Covelo in the central part of the valley.

16. The first road between Round Valley and Ukiah, approximately seventy miles south and west, wasn't completed until 1869, according to the first early twentieth century Mendocino County local history by Lyman Palmer. Weaverville, the site of several gold mines, was located over seventy miles northeast from Round Valley, over mostly rugged terrain. Supplies for the valley would come through the mountains from Weaverville by mule train or Indian carriers. Weaverville and Round Valley were interdependent in many ways. A small number of Round Valley Indians became hard-working guides and mule drivers in the pack trains between Round Valley and Weaverville.

Native Americans, probably mostly Yuki, were killed according to Frank Asbill's account.

"THEIR OWN NAME FOR THEMSELVES": THE ORIGINAL INHABITANTS

A great many different Native American communities were represented in frontier California. In Round Valley, people from a number of different tribal groups lived together up until the time of the valley's discovery by Euro-Americans in 1854. Settlers and ethnologists classified many of these groups, or tribelets, as Yuki. In the Round Valley area the most numerous Yuki subdivision was called Ukomno'm, meaning "valley people" or "west place." The Yuki were traditional enemies of both the Wailaki to the north and the Nomlaki to the west. It was the Nomlaki, a Wintun tribe that generally lived on the western side of the coastal range, who called them "Yukie," or "enemy."

Before Euro-Americans came to Mendocino County, California's Native Americans depended on territorial markers such as ridges, streams, tall trees, boulders, and outcroppings to mark separate territories. Wars between tribes were rare in California, as each tribe's territory was small and well known by outside contiguous tribes. Most of Mendocino County's Native Americans, such as the Yuki and Pomo, at first aided the Euro-Americans in exploration and settlement.

One of America's first anthropologists to study and to write about California Native Americans was an ethnologist named Stephen Powers. Powers grew up in rough and tumble pre-Civil War Ohio. During the Civil War he was a full-time war correspondent who covered many of the largest battles. The war honed Power's skills, both as an observer of the human condition and as a journalist and writer.

In his classic book entitled *Tribes of California*, originally published in 1877, Powers noted that there were at least four separate tribes that were called "Yuki" by their original neighbors and later by the invading white settlers:

Their own name for themselves is U-kom-nom (meaning "in the valley"), and for those on South Eel River speaking the same language, Huch'-nom (meaning "outside the valley"). Those over on the ocean are called Uk-ho'at-nom ("on the ocean"). It is possible that the word *ukum* was corrupted by a neighboring tribe, the Wintün, into *yuki*, their present name.[17]

Whether justified or not, throughout the nineteenth century the Yuki tribe often was singled out for criticism both by their fellow Native Americans and Euro-Americans. Other Native Americans charged that the Yuki of both genders tattooed their faces. Some even went further charging the Yuki with cannibalism. Most anthropologists now believe that only Yuki women and generally not the Yuki men tattooed. Reputable anthropologists also say the Yuki did not practice cannibalism.

In the mid-nineteenth century the Yuki were rumored to be more aggressive or warlike than some of their neighbors like the Pomos, Nomlakis, or a few others. These more passive Northern California tribes were fearful of the Yuki who attacked en masse. They may have given them a tag as "cannibals" as a way of getting even with them or to reflect how they felt about their aggressive tendencies.

Regarding the Yuki, Powers maintained:

> The Yuki had few friends among their neighbors, except the Wailaki, and they had more intercourse with them than with any others, although they occasionally fought each other with a hearty good-will. They joined territories about half-way between Round Valley and North Eel River, and they intermarried, giving rise to a progeny called Yuki-Wailaki. The Yuki were unrelenting enemies of the Nóam-lak-ki [Wintūn], and often fought them on the summit east of Round Valley. They would climb trees up there and wait for hours for a Nóam-lak-ki to come along, when they would imitate the grouse, the California quail, or some other choice game-bird, and so lure them within arrow-shot. They were also especially bitter against the whites, and seized an early opportunity to kill any of their squaws who went to live with them.[18]

Native Americans saw warfare as a means to an end, a temporary state of peace or possibly settling a dispute thus making a possibly short-lived truce between tribes. Usually tribes did not fight unless there were the most serious disagreements among neighbors such as over territorial boundaries or hunting grounds. Their battles rarely lasted more than one day. Native Americans usually removed their dead from the battlefield soon after a battle. They buried dead warriors in graves in a prescribed manner, usually in a sitting position. Cremation was rare in the Yuki culture. According to Stephen Powers, it meant that the dead person's life appeared to most tribal members or the chief as unworthy in some way.

Yuki dominance in war may have been due to one seemingly unlikely factor: better home ventilation. Coastal Indian tribes like the Yukis and Wailakis used wood to build their lodges, while Sacramento and San Joaquin Valley and

17. Stephen Powers, *Tribes of California*, with an Introduction and Notes by Robert F. Heizer, (Berkeley: University of California Press, 1976), originally printed in Washington, D.C., Government Printing Office, 1877, 128 ff.
18. Powers, *Ibid.*, 129.

High Sierra Native Americans like the Wappo, Pomos, and Maidu made lodges from "thatch and earth," which made for a more smoky domesticity. Almost certainly, better eyesight developed in smokeless Yuki homes.

Powers used all of his considerable wartime skills in observation and journalism to describe most of the hundreds of California Native American tribes that still existed in the early 1870s. In his chapter on the Yuki tribe, Powers described their quality of self sacrifice, bravery in battle and strong emotion when aroused by injustice:

> As the Yuki were so often involved in war, martial matters necessarily engaged a great deal of their attention, and occupy a large part of their conversation. Their customs and usages in this direction were quite elaborate. Mrs. Dryden Laycock, one of the pioneer women of Round Valley, described to me a Yuki war-dance, that she once witnessed, which was a fantastic and terrible spectacle. The warriors to the number of several hundred assembled behind a small hill where they stripped themselves naked [though their aboriginal costume consisted of little else but breech-cloths]; then they smeared their bodies with pitch or some other sticky material, and sprinkled on white eagle-down from tip to toe. On their heads they put bushy plumes and coronals of larger feathers. Then, seizing their bows and arrows, and slinging their quivers over their shoulders they rushed over the brow of the hill and down upon the plain in a wild and disorderly throng, uttering unearthly yells and whoops, leaping, brandishing their weapons above their heads, and chanting their war-songs. Before a battle takes place the heralds of the two contending parties meet on neutral ground and arrange the time and place of the conflict. The night before going out they dance all night to inflame their courage. If the warrior possesses a wide elk-skin belt he ties it around him to protect his vitals, but otherwise he is quite naked. About three hundred arrows to the warrior is the complement of ammunition for a raid. The Wailaki, on the other hand, wear shields of tanned elk-skin, which are very thick and tough, and proof against arrows. The body of the skin is tough, and is left wide enough to shield two or three men. It is worn on the back, so as not to incommode the warrior in battle, and when he sees an arrow coming he turns his back to it, and two or three of his friends, if they choose, screen themselves behind his shield, at the same time shooting over it or around the sides of it. If the shield-bearer sees an arrow coming so low that it may strike him in the legs, he ducks. They time their march so as to be at the battlefield at daybreak. If a Yuki falls and stumbles on the march, or is stung by a yellow-jacket, it is a bad omen; he must go home, or he will be killed....
>
> During the battle they simply stand up, in masses in the open ground amid the chaparral, and shoot at each other until they "get enough," as one of them expressed it; then they cry quits and go home. If any dead are left on the field both parties return afterward and carry them away and bury them [they burn only those whom they do not honor, though this rule is not invariable]; but a pioneer states that he has seen Yuki dead left on the field, a prey to beasts and birds.[19]

Native American soldiers might have been pleased to hear that Mrs. Laycock thought their preparation "fantastic and terrible," for that was no doubt its

---

19. Powers, *Ibid.*, 129, 137–138.

intent. As this description points out, the Native Americans were accustomed to battles announced well in advance, prepared for by one or more nights of dancing and then fought out on some neutral ground. However well this practice worked before the introduction of firearms, it was violated repeatedly by Round Valley's white settler militia units when they raided Yuki rancherias in early morning attacks starting about 1858. Ultimately, attacks by whites took a serious toll both on Native American morale and on numbers of healthy warriors still well enough to go into battle. More recent scholars, such as Alfred L. Kroeber, Robert F. Heizer and P.E. Goddard, have noted that, as in the case of other warring tribes like the Sioux of the Great Plains and the Apache in Arizona, the Yuki made training for war a constant part of life.

Many Native Americans helped white newcomers to adjust to their new lives on the California frontier and understood some of the problems they faced. There are countless stories in the literature from this period of Western history of Native Americans who guided settlers through bitterly cold conditions or vast dry deserts to safety and of Native Americans who provided food to individual Euro-American settlers when they were sick or starving. As some historians have noted, most Native Americans also tolerated great abuses before taking any action in self-defense. Round Valley Indians were no exception.

Powers told the following story describing the Native Americans' remarkable memory regarding features of Mendocino County's terrain in a chapter of his study of California Native Americans. The chapter of Powers' book, *Tribes of California*, was titled, "The Yu'-Ki:"

> A veteran woodman related to me a small circumstance which illustrates the remarkable memory of savages. One time he had occasion to perform a piece of labor in a certain wood where water was very scarce, and where he was grievously tormented with thirst. He remembered to have seen a little spring somewhere in that vicinity, and he considered it worth his while under the circumstances to search for it two days, but without success, when there came along a Yuki woman, to whom he made mention of the matter. Although she had not been near that place for six years, and, like himself, probably had never seen the spring but once, yet without a moment's hesitation or uncertainty, she led him straight to the spot. Probably there is no other thing in this country, so arid through the long summer months, of which the Indians have better recollection than of the whereabouts of springs.[20]

This account is only one of numerous reports from this period of incidents where Native Americans helped mountain men and settlers.

---

20. Powers, *Ibid.*, 134.

A "JUST AND EQUITABLE TITLE": AFTER THE WAR WITH MEXICO

A fierce three-month Congressional debate took place in the late summer of 1852 over California land claims and the results of the U.S.-Mexican Treaty of Guadalupe Hidalgo. California's first-term Senator John B. Weller was an active participant. Weller had served as a volunteer officer in the Mexican War, helping to enlist and lead an Ohio regiment under General Taylor. He rose through the ranks to a relatively high rank of lieutenant colonel. At the war's crucial Battle of Monterrey, Weller's commanding officer was badly wounded. Then Captain Weller became commander of his Ohio regiment, the so-called "Butler's Guards," named after Butler County, Ohio.

After the Mexican War ended in 1848, Weller served on the joint Boundary Commission that drew the border between Mexico and the United States. He was probably more unpopular than other Americans with the Mexican Government because he insisted that El Paso be a part of Texas, thus within the United States. After performing this duty for the national government and a brief period practicing private law in California, Weller returned to Washington. Prior to the Mexican War, he had been a two-term representative from Ohio. In 1852, Weller took office as one of California's two senators. He was to play a fateful role in the Win-Toon/Mendocino War of 1858-60.

The Thirty-First Congress did not discuss the nearly twenty treaties its commissioners had made with California's tribes and tribelets in 1850–1851. Although four years had passed since Marshall's discovery of gold, relations between white immigrants and California's Native Americans were in a state of almost complete anarchy. But whatever happened to Native Americans on California's new reservations, many white Californians were more concerned about their titles to the land they worked and lived on.

In a speech to Congress on August 2, 1852, Weller focused on defense of The Treaty of Guadalupe Hidalgo as well as subsequent congressional legislation that provided for the eventual confirmation of Hispanic land grants:

> . . . I can readily imagine that a claim may be presented to the board of commissioners, which is incomplete, in which the grantee may not have performed all the requirements of the Spanish and Mexican laws; but that person may have a just and equitable title through the occupation, improvement, and enjoyment of that which is covered by the original grant.
>
> I believe that after a grant has been made to any person—no matter what may be the extent of that grant—if he has taken possession in good faith, and enjoyed, improved and occupied it, thus substantially complying with the terms of the grant,

he is entitled to have it confirmed. The Government of the United States should do what justice and honesty would have required from the Mexican Government.

If that Government, under the usages and customs which prevailed, would have been required to secure the land to the grantee, then our Government is bound to respect it. The extent of the grant cannot affect the question.[21]

Sen. Weller's speech, as well as those of other senators at this time, tried to establish land grants originally made in Alta California to individuals before the Mexican War.

Sen. Weller was a pro-Southern Democrat. Sen. Weller was opposed to abolition. During and after the Civil War he opposed the North. There is little record that as senator, he had any view on California's Native Americans other than to support the policy as established by the federal Office of Indian Affairs and to assist any settlers in alleged physical danger from what the settlers termed were "Indian depredations."

The Congressional debate about land grants quoted above took place about six years before John B. Weller took office as the fifth popularly elected governor of California.[22] One can clearly see how committed Weller was, as a lifelong middle-of-the-road Democratic politician, to the principle of landowners' rights and privileges. He would soon be making many decisions as California's governor to use militia forces to defend Euro-American farmers and settlers.

"THE FOUNDERS OF HUMAN CIVILIZATION": THE SETTLERS

Despite its isolation and lack of both transportation and communications, Round Valley had a small but growing Euro-American population after 1856, the year the Nome Cult reservation farm was established in the valley. Probably even before then, John Lawson and Benjamin Arthur had driven a herd of hogs up into the valley. Charles Brown was another early settler, arriving in 1856. According to ethnologist-historian, Professor Virginia P. Miller, the white population grew

---

21. See "Remarks of Hon. Mr. Weller, of California on the Mexican Boundary Commission: The River and Harbors Bill, The Fugitive Slave Law, and California Land Titles" delivered in the Senate of the United States. Aug. 2, 1852, F786.W4, Bancroft Library, University of California, Berkeley, CA.

22. There were six different military governors of California. They were followed by popularly elected governors, of which Weller was the fifth. Milton G. Latham would have been the sixth governor had he not bowed out to accept the legislature's appointment as senator.

from eleven in 1856 to twenty-four in 1857. Some of these early settlers fenced in "several thousand acres apiece," according to Professor Miller.[23]

Early valley settlers built cabins or small houses and simultaneously cleared plots and built fences so that they could eventually make a land claim to the government. Some of the more prominent local white settlers who later became leaders in the Mendocino War arrived in the valley in 1856–1857. This list of settlers includes John Owens, J.H. Thomas, T.D. (Dryden) Lacock (Laycock), C.H. Eberle, George White, S.P. Storms, and C. (Charles) H. Bourne. White and Bourne introduced a herd of cattle to the valley.

By 1858, much of the valley's more fertile acreage outside of the reservation was split up into private ranches or farms. By this time, Dr. Melendy, Jesse Holland, Col. Davis, and Dan Stevens and his family had arrived, further increasing the number of white settlers living off the reservation. As more male settlers arrived, a few were married to either Caucasian or Native American women.[24] These early couples started families there. According to a family source, Henry (or Harry) Storms was the first Euro-American child born in Round Valley who survived.[25] Other aspects of civilization, such as a police force, courts, lawyers, and a postal service, all came later. The home of J. H. Thomas, built in 1857, was later used as a store, saloon, and dance hall. This was located southwest of the present Round Valley airport in an area later called Stringtown. Starting in the summer of 1858, Jesse Holland began carrying the mail. Settlers had to subscribe and either paid the costs of this local form of the "pony express" or got no mail service.[26]

In 1859, a local court began holding sessions and the job of constable for the Round Valley Township was filled for the first time by Doc Jeffers. One year later, the job was shared by J.R. Shannon and Ben Burch, or "Birch." He was the

23. See Virginia P. Miller, *U Komno'n: The Yuki Indians of Northern California* (Socorro, N.M.: Bellena Press, 1979), 46–47.
24. Many California historians of the period 1840–1860 agree that many of Euro-American settlers who immigrated to California were young men, many of whom had left their wives or sweethearts back East or as far away as Europe or South America. Whether these newcomers were ranchers or ranch hands working to develop ranches in Mendocino County, gold miners in the Klamath River area or in the Sierra Nevada or young clerks in newspaper offices there were few eligible young women from whom to choose possible spouses. For this reason and others, many Euro-American men chose Native American women to be their wives or lovers.
25. See also *The History of Mendocino and Lake Counties* (1914) by Aurelius O. Carpenter and Percy H. Millberry. Harry Storms was born to the reservation's first Subagent, Simmon P. Storms, and his wife Sarah.

same man who would lead one of Capt. Walter S. Jarboe's detachments in raids on Native American rancherias during the Mendocino War in 1859.

"EXPENSIVE WARS AND BARBAROUS DEVASTATION": THE EFFECT OF WHITE SETTLEMENT ON NATIVE PEOPLES

Once Euro-Americans arrived on the scene, many Native Americans, individually, in tribes or in smaller units called "tribelets," began to suffer from almost constant oppression and humiliations. In the long and the all-too-often tragic history of unnecessarily bitter racial conflicts between Euro-American settlers and Native Americans throughout North America, the complexity of Native American tribes in California presented the settlers with unique problems not confronted elsewhere. The diversity of the tribes made Indian Affairs Department policy-making especially difficult here.

In response to California's statehood and many reports of conflicts in Northern California, federal Commissioner Redick McKee traveled to northern California in 1851. McKee's mission was both to explore and investigate but also to make treaties with the California Native American tribes. Part of the later confusion and turmoil in relations with the aboriginal people in California stemmed from the fact that Congress failed to ratify any of these treaties. The records and reports left by Commissioner McKee are invaluable sources. McKee's recording secretary was George Gibbs, who wrote a report in the form of a diary of McKee's journeys in northwestern California. The following passage is from Gibbs' journal on Monday, September 29, 1851:

> We too often give a general character to savage races, derived from a few, and those most probably the worst of their nation; forgetting that there may be as great diversity of disposition among them as among ourselves. Thus the majority may be well disposed, and yet implicated in crime by the acts of a very few; for knowing by experience the indiscriminate manner in which punishment is meted out, they are driven in self-defense to abet or defend them. But besides this, a constant source of provocation is to be feared from such of the whites as, transiently passing through their country, offer them insult and violence, without perhaps, endangering themselves; but probably quite innocent persons. A population drawn together, like that of

---

26. The valley's isolation was underlined by this lack of regular mail service in the early years of Euro-American settlement. News of President Lincoln's election, for example, was brought not by the mail, but by two reporters from Ukiah, who hand-carried the news to Round Valley. The first person to have a government contract for mail service was Charles H. Eberle in 1870.

California, necessarily contains reckless and unprincipled characters, too many of whom regard the life of an Indian as of no more account than that of a dog; and who, in murdering them without provocation, give cause for reprisals which have sacrificed many innocent lives and brought about expensive wars and barbarous devastation. [27]

Both McKee and Gibbs were open minded men who tried to understand the many problems generated by contacts and conflicts between the Native Americans and Euro-American immigrants to California. In this vein one of the observations Gibbs made was that "reckless and unprincipled characters," those few who always played a negative role on the frontier, would soon become a serious problem, not only to the Native Americans but also to everyone living in the growing new state.

The admission of California to the Union in 1850 did little to change this. As noted by numerous Euro-American writers on California history, including Robert Glass Cleland in 1922, California's first legislature in 1849, the "Legislature of a Thousand Drinks," was concerned mostly with "the protection of frontier counties from Indian depredations."[28] Almost all of these early lawmakers appear to have had almost no concern for the safety or the welfare of individual Native Americans. They were far more preoccupied with the questions of setting California's borders and choosing the first two senators for this new American state. Whatever we may think today of the actions of the state's first lawmakers,

---

27. For the sake of a frame of reference, the Win-Toon/Mendocino War was only one of many Euro-American-Native American conflicts going on about this time. For instance, 1858 was the year that the last Seminole guerrillas surrendered to U.S. troops and finally quit fighting. 1858 was also the year of the Utah War between Indians and Mormons in Wyoming, Nebraska, and Utah. Here the Indians attacked white wagon trains of both Mormons and other Euro-Americans to retaliate for the theft of Indian land and incidences of terror. (For instance, in September 1855, eighty-six Sioux Brule people were killed in a massacre inspired by the "theft" of a sick cow, which had been abandoned by a Mormon wagon train.) McKee's 1851–1852 expedition traveled up the Sacramento Valley far to the east of Round Valley. This seems certain for two reasons: geography makes the journey far easier this way, and Gibbs' *Journal* made no mention of Mendocino County. If one wished to travel from Sacramento to other towns of northern California like Union or Eureka, there was no reason to take on the formidable Mendocino coastal mountain range, the Mayacamas. Far better to use the wide open Sacramento River Valley north and then continue up California's San Joaquin Valley to Red Bluff to the Oregon border. See entry for Monday, Sept. 29, 1851, *George Gibbs' Journal of Redick Mckee's Expedition Through Northwestern California in 1851.* Edited and with annotations by Robert F. Heizer (Berkeley: Archeological Research Facility, Department of Anthropology, University of California at Berkeley, 1972).

what is significant is that California's Native American population was being rapidly reduced in both health and numbers as the prisoner of war camps or "reservations" like Round Valley and Mendocino began operations.

By contrast to the Native Americans' status frontier law tended to fully support the rights of ranchers, miners and settlers. California's takeover by predominantly Caucasian Euro-Americans did little to improve the legal status of the Native Americans. An American twist was simply added to the Hispanic system. Native Americans had to be very good workers or they could be killed. If Indians found off the reservation or outside the protection of their employer were to be allowed to live, they had to have proof of employment and proof of ownership of all property they carried. They must not even appear to have anyone else's property, especially horses. If they were caught driving horses without proof of ownership by white settlers after 1847, they could be tried in county courts. If found guilty by the generally all-Euro-American juries in these courts, they were hanged as soon as possible for horse stealing. It was important to many of the settlers to set an example to other Native Americans.

This sort of practice took the lives of countless Indians. The harsh rules may have taken hold in California in part due to an early edict of Lt. William T. Sherman, later of Civil War fame, who was destined to become one of the North's more brutal generals. During the Mexican War, Sherman issued a racist, wrongheaded proclamation that made it legal for whites to try and then execute Native Americans found with horses they could not prove belonged to them.[29] Later this edict was generally applied in various instances in Northern California.

In this kind of racist environment it took little effort for some determined and unscrupulous individuals, those like Judge Serranus C. Hastings and others,

---

28. This historic first California State Legislature of what was later called "The American Period of California history" was the only one held at San Jose rather than Sacramento. This Thousand Drinks Legislature was composed of sixteen senators and thirty-six assemblymen; the name came from Senator Thomas J. Green, "late of Texas," who supposedly repeatedly made the motion to adjourn "and take a thousand drinks." On a more serious note, this session also dealt with the problem of local lawlessness as well as electing to Congress the two first California senators, John C. Fremont and Dr. William ("Duke") Gwin. See John Glass Cleland, Ph.D., *History of California: The American Period* (New York: The MacMillan Company, 1923), 343–344.

29. See Gary Garrett, "The Destruction of the Indian in Mendocino County," unpublished MA thesis, History, Sacramento State College, July 22, 1969, 26.

to organize local protest rallies of predominantly white settlers of the Round Valley area to produce some reaction against the Indians from the governor.

Euro-American settlers entered California in ever greater annual numbers after 1850. As a result, disputes, armed conflicts and violence between the Native Americans and settlers and hunters were almost inevitable. In addition to armed conflicts, the Native Americans in Mendocino County were already frequent victims of white kidnap rings by the mid-1850s. Many Indian families were destroyed by the kidnapping of women and children by whites in this period. Professor Sherburne Cook, historian and anthropologist in the 1940s, estimated that "between three and four thousand Indian children were kidnapped and sold in the period from 1852 to 1867."[30] The California Constitution and the state's Indian codes made it very easy to enslave Indians, especially women as well as both young boys and girls.

Turning from hunting deer for their skins to a more profitable trade of kidnapping Indian children even the co-discoverers of Round Valley, Frank and Pierce Asbill briefly led a kidnapping ring. Such criminal rings enticed their young victims with alluring tales of "the land of bread and syrup" they described as just beyond the mountains to the east. In Sacramento or in the mining camps, Indians were often auctioned off as house servants, miner's helpers or field hands.

Violent meetings between Euro-Americans and Native Americans in the region continued as a pattern, as would a parallel less influential custom of friendship and cooperation. Determined Euro-American newcomers discovered numerous routes over the coastal mountain ranges to get into Round Valley or elsewhere in Mendocino County. Forces released by the Gold Rush and land hunger rapidly changed the valley's quiet status quo. More and more white settlers immigrated to California and the West. Even before the Euro-Americans first entered Round Valley, the pattern of violence was established some seventy miles to the north.

In 1852, the so-called "Natural Bridge Massacre" had ended the lives of approximately one hundred and fifty Native Americans. Discovery of the dead body of a Weaverville settler, a butcher by the name of Anderson, about six miles from Weaverville shocked local settlers into action. Anderson's corpse was

---

30. Sherburne F. Cook, *The Conflict Between the California Indian and White Civilization*, Ibero-American Series, Vol. 23, (Berkeley: University of California Press, 1943), pp. 60–61, as quoted by Gary Garrett, *Ibid.*, 57–58.

found with numerous arrows in it. Anderson's throat was cut. At about the same time, a party of white men composed of "George Butler and Jacob Turner, with two other men" disappeared on "Winter Creek about eight miles from Weaverville on a prospecting trip."[31] A group of thirty-six vigilantes rode after the Native Americans whom they thought were the ones responsible for Anderson's killing and also the prospectors' disappearance.

After 1856 this would become a more frequent scenario for attacks on Native American rancherias near Round Valley. As was first noted by the *Shasta Courier*, men who had fresh personal memories of Mr. Anderson made up the posse. These angry vigilantes showed little mercy to the rancheria inhabitants that the armed settlers deemed guilty:

> A Rancheria of 150 Indians, including women and children, was attacked, and nearly the whole number destroyed....
>
> On Thursday afternoon, April 22, 1852, the scouts discovered the Rancheria in a small valley at the base of three mountains on the south side of the South Fork of Trinity River. At midnight, the company started from their encampment.
>
> Captain [earlier in the article he is referred to as "Sheriff." It is unclear if he was actually a sheriff of Tehama County]. Dixon, divided his force into three parties so as to come upon the Indians from different quarters and surround them. When the day broke, all parties were in desired positions and, the signal being given, the attack commenced. Each rifle marked its victim with unerring precision, the pistol and knife completed the work of destruction and revenge, and in a few minutes all was over.
>
> Of the 150 Indians that constituted the Rancheria only two escaped and these were supposed to be dangerously wounded; so that probably not one of those engaged in the murder of the unfortunate Anderson now remains alive. Men, women, and children all shared the same fate, none were spared except one woman and two children, who were brought back prisoners.[32]

While the body count in this engagement was possibly inflated in this news article, what is most important about this attack is the methods and mood

---

31. Floyd Barney sent the newspaper excerpt from *The Shasta Courier* that is quoted below here. The article, "Tales from the mountaineer," was first printed on April 24, 1852 in the *Courier*. The copy of the reprinted acticle was authored and reprinted by Jake Jackson in 1984. I received the article on March 29, 2000.
32. *Ibid.*, following the article quoted here, Mr. Jackson included the following statement: "The above article claims the only survivors were one Indian woman and two children who were brought in as prisoners. Again, I believe the *Courier* correspondent possibly was misinformed at the time of writing. In 1898 the Old Settlers Society of Trinity County called on their members, several of whom had taken part in the massacre, to write their version of the episode." Possibly there were more survivors.

of the Euro-American force that acted in revenge. Such motivations, methods and results later became familiar occurrences in the Win-toon/Mendocino War.

This article also sets a pattern repeatedly seen in accounts of similar raids. These pro-settler accounts seldom question the methods of summary execution used by the attackers, although eventually most news articles carefully pointed out that the lives of women and children were usually spared. Other accounts give a different, more critical perspective, questioning both the vigilantes' motives and methods, and whether or not they strove for a nonviolent solution. Both perspectives will be represented in the following chapters through eyewitness accounts of the participants.

About ten years after the Natural Bridge Massacre, a Euro-American settler and kidnapper named George Woodman lived in Long Valley, approximately ten miles to the west of Round Valley. Woodman regularly raided the Native Americans in Round Valley. Finally, in 1862, Woodman became one of the few Round Valley Euro-Americans ever prosecuted for kidnapping Indians. Both he and his partner were found guilty in court and received a ludicrously low fine of $100. The case was closed when Woodman paid the fine. Both men were released from custody without serving any time in prison.

How awful such practices must have seemed to California Indians. We might imagine by an example from their beliefs, as depicted by Powers in this description of an ogre from Pomo legend:

> The Cahto Pomos believe in a terrible and fearful ogre, called Shillaba Shilltoats. He is described as being of gigantic stature, wearing a high-sugar loaf head-dress, clothed in hideous tatters, for small boys. He is particularly useful to administration of his household affairs, and especially in the "taming of the shrew." When the squaw gets so vixenish that he can not subdue her in any other way, he has only to shout into the wigwam—with his eyes judiciously dilated and his hair somewhat tousled—and to vociferate, "Shillaba Shilltoats! Shillaba Shilltoats!" when his squaw will scream with terror, fall flat upon the ground, cover her face with her hands—for that squaw dies who is ever so unfortunate as to look upon this dreadful ogre—and remains very tractable for several days thereafter. The children will also be profoundly impressed.[33]

To local tribes, some of whom were destined to be among the first residents at the Round Valley reservation called Nome Cult Farm, all whites were strangers who frequently killed Indians and kidnapped women and children. For

---

33. Stephen Powers, *Tribes of California*, "Contributions of North American Ethnology," No. 3, Washington, D.C., Government Printing Office, 1877, as quoted by Lynwood Carranco and Estle Beard, *Genocide and Vendetta: The Round Valley Wars of Northern California*, (Norman: University of Oklahoma Press, 1981), footnote #20, Introduction, 11.

them, Shillaba Shilltoats may have taken the menacing form of Euro-American, buckskin-clad ranchers and icy-hearted settlers who stood in the way of peaceful progress in reservation living. To Round Valley's Native Americans Frank and Pierce Asbill and others like them were real-life monsters.

CONCLUSION

Upon his "discovery" of Round Valley in May 1854, Frank Asbill placed the number of Round Valley Indians at about twenty thousand. He was impressed by the large number of Native American campfires visible to his party at night. The actual number residing there before 1854 will probably never be known; it is doubtful there were actually as many as twenty thousand. In any case, by 1856 there were approximately twelve thousand Native Americans living either in the valley or in the neighboring hills and mountains.[34] These people, who had lived in the region for untold generations, would soon face a disaster experienced by Indians all over the state.

In his *Indians of California: The Changing Image*, Professor James J. Rawls describes this disaster succinctly: "During the first quarter century following the American occupation of California in 1846, the state's Indian population declined from an estimated 150,000 in 1845 to less than 30,000 in 1870." Writing in the 1940s, former biologist turned cultural historian and ethnologist of Native Americans, Sherburne F. Cook stated, "The general Indian (California) population was roughly 80,000 in 1848 and 15,000 in 1880."[35] Whether we use Professor Cook's lower estimate or the slightly larger number posited by Professor James J. Rawls, one has to admit that these losses are staggering in extent.

Professor Cook argued that it was starvation and the elimination of food supplies by the invading Euro-Americans that caused some of the worst problems for Native Americans. Furthermore,

> The basic point is that the Indians, faced with the clear prospect of starvation, attacked the race responsible for his condition. The attempt was abortive in the long run, but for a period, until utterly defeated and exhausted, the Indians instinctively demonstrated the primitive, automatic struggle for *Lebensraum*. I think it may

34. See Aurelius O. Carpenter and Percy H. Millberry, *History of Mendocino and Lake Counties*, (Los Angeles: Historic Record Company, 1914) 33 and 93.
35. James J. Rawls, *Indians of California: The Changing Image* (Norman: University of Oklahoma Press, 1984), 171; Sherburne F. Cook, *The Conflict Between the California Indian and White Civilization* (Berkeley: University of California Press, 1976), 132.

be maintained with assurance that the Indian wars and difficulties in California up to 1865 had as their basic cause the dislocation and depletion of the aboriginal food supply.[36]

Dr. Cook also noted that Native American attacks on livestock as a way of obtaining meat did not originate only after 1848 when Euro-Americans flocked into California.

> The details of this process may be read in the accounts of Indian troubles of the mid-nineteenth century. When the Indian turned to the white man for food, he found one admirable source ready at hand, livestock. The problem of stock-raiding, to be sure, was one which existed since earlier Spanish times. It had been the cause of great difficulty between the heathen tribes and the Mexican immigrants, and no essentially new features were introduced by the coming of the Americans.[37]

Certainly the habitat required for the traditional Native American lifestyle was being disrupted and this process had been going on at least since the arrival of the Spanish. But as this study and others make clear, the decrease was also partly due to genocide.

Most of the Euro-American settlers who had moved into Round Valley starting as early as 1856, including leading California state leaders like Mendocino County's Assemblyman Joseph B. Lamar, Supt. Thomas J. Henley, Subagent Simmon P. Storms, and Judge Serranus C. Hastings, enthusiastically endorsed Sen. Daniel Webster's ethic as expressed in the words: "When tillage begin, other arts follow. The farmers, therefore are the founders of human civilization." If there was any general belief that welded the settlers into a unit it was this one. This agrarian concept, accompanied by a strong faith in the success of the agricultural effort was the prevailing idea of the era. It is also the key to our understanding of the course of events in Round Valley.

All too often this belief came into direct, even violent conflict with the daily life of the native population, as the predominantly white settlers attempted to oust the Native Americans from their homes by force, even if it meant killing them outright. Sometimes this took place by relatively more expensive large state expeditions like Gen. Kibbe's, or by smaller private bands of state subsidized militia and vigilantes, such as the Eel River Rangers headed by Walter Jarboe.

General Kibbe's militia campaigned throughout most of 1859 in the extreme northwestern corner of the state along the Hoopa and Klamath River

---

36. Cook, *The Conflict*, 290–291.
37. *Ibid.*, 292.

valleys as well as in the Trinity River area and far to the south near Red Bluff in the north central San Joaquin, or Sacramento River valley. Native American resistance was seriously affected as many Native American tribes were driven permanently away from their homelands.

Simultaneously to General Kibbe's War with the Wintoons, local Mendocino County militia units such as those commanded by Captains Jarboe, Farley, Laycock or others attacked Native American rancherias in many previously unexplored mountain areas of the county but especially near Round Valley. Many of these Native Americans were killed, wounded or captured. Most who survived the massacres were either shot or forcibly marched to either Mendocino Reservation or Round Valley (Nome Cult Farm) Reservation. Many tribes were simultaneously subjected to very severe pressure due to poor and inadequate food supplies, diseases and exposure.

All these factors coalesced in the late 1850s producing a period of bloodshed for the native peoples. This tragic story began with the establishment of Nome Cult Farm in Round Valley in June 1856.

Equally important to the reader's understanding how events unfolded at Nome Cult Farm is learning a little of the role of regular Army units in northern California up until 1859. At the end of the Mexican War the Army dispatched the 3d Artillery and the 2d Infantry around Cape Horn to California. Brevet Lt. Col. Robert C. Buchanon, commander of Companies B and F, 4th Infantry, established Fort Humboldt at Bucksport in January 1853. Fort Humboldt in the northwestern corner of California was a key fort in the Humboldt Bay region.

In response to an appeal in the spring of 1858 by Supt. Henley, in early May 1858 three officers of Company B, 4th Infantry, First Lt. Joseph B. Collins, Lt. Charles Rundell and Asst. Surgeon La Fayette Guild and thirty eight regular soldiers left Ft. Humboldt on May 12, 1858. Henley asked for help in keeping the trail from Mendocino Reservation to Nome Cult Farm free of Native American attacks. The unit had a hard time keeping on the trail but was twice aided by unknown tribes of Native Americans. At last on June 6th Lt. Collins' detachment arrived at Round Valley.

While it was first planned that this unit would remain on station in Round Valley through the summer of 1858, the force hastily returned to Fort Humboldt on July 2nd. One certainly has to wonder at the fitness of these soldiers who had to march one hundred and fifty miles down to Nome Cult and back again very rapidly through some of the West's most rugged terrain. Most of the local tribes kept their distance away from these mounted and well armed blue coats.

Lt. Collins thought the Native Americans at the reservation seemed to have enough to eat at that time. Although it is unknown which tribe provided the two guides that knew the last part of the trail into Round Valley from the north, the fact that they were clad in deerskins leads me to suggest that they were Wailaki. The Wailaki inhabited the region north of Round Valley. First Lt. Collins commented on housing for the Native Americans at Nome Cult Indian Farm, "indeed I have seen much worse [quarters] in this country occupied by our officers and men."[38]

---

38. First Lt. Joseph B. Collins to Col. Mackall, June 9, 1858, RG 393, as quoted by William F Strobridge, Regulars In The Redwoods The U.S. Army in Northern California 1852-1861, (Spokane: Arthur Clark, Co., 1994), 170. Prof. William F. Strobridge described how the regular Army's units were deployed in northern California.

Chapter 2. The Establishment of Nome Cult Farm

About three hundred died on the reservation, from the effects of packing them throughout the mountains in the snow and mud; They were worked naked, with the exception of deer skin around their shoulders...
They usually packed fifty pounds if able; if not able, a less load.....
> —Benjamin Arthur, Deposition taken February 28, 1860, Indian War Files as quoted by Gary E. Garrett, "The Destruction of the Indian in Mendocino County 1856-1860," unpublished MA thesis, History, July 22, 1969, Sacramento State College (now California State University), Sacramento.

In 1854, the Pierce Administration replaced California's first Superintendent of Indian Affairs, Edward Beale, with Thomas J. Henley, who was unqualified in almost every way for the office. When Henley took over, there was only one reservation operating in the entire state, at Tejon, south of Bakersfield. Supt. Henley then set up two new reservations: one at Nome Lackee in western Tehama County and another at Mendocino on the Pacific Coast near Fort Bragg. Each began as the Indian Affairs Department's standard size of twenty-five thousand acres. The Nome Lackee Indian Reservation (now defunct) was started in 1854 east of the Mayacama Mountain Range and southwest of the town of Red Bluff, about sixty miles northeast of Round Valley.

The Mendocino Indian Reservation, established in 1854, was located about forty air miles south-southwest of Round Valley, just south of land that later became the town of Fort Bragg. It stretched "along the coast from Hare Creek, a small stream about a half mile south of the Noyo River, northward, to about a mile north of Ten Mile River and about three miles inland."[39] Various tribes of California Native Americans lived south and west of Mendocino Reservation. Although both Mendocino Reserve and Nome Lackee were closed before 1870, the Office of Indian Affairs started two more reservations, the Hoopa Reservation in 1867 at the Klamath River, and Kings River near Fresno by 1870.

Congress authorized only five reserves in the state. By the summer of 1856 Henley had reached this number.[40] Furthermore he had already spent almost all the funds allocated to him by the Indian Affairs Department for the year. Yet he needed another location to support the two other struggling Northern California reservations at Mendocino and at Nome Lackee. Indian Affairs employees also needed a safe place to rest pack mules and horses along the long and difficult trail from the Sacramento Valley to the Mendocino Reservation.

To solve this dilemma, in June 1856 Henley sent Simmon P. (Peña) Storms to Round Valley to start a farm there. Originally this new establishment was not to be a full reservation but just a farm and holding or resting station for the Mendocino Reservation.[41] In June 1856, U komno'm Native Americans, the peaceful branch of the Yukis in Round Valley, sighted a small party of armed Euro-Americans and Native Americans led by Storms entering Round Valley from the east. A great change was about to happen in the valley.

The Yukis recognized some of the Native Americans in the group, but others in this discovery party were like no white men they had seen before. These men were not interested in capturing Native American children for sale. Nor were they just settlers, traders, mountain men, or even hunters seeking hides or pelts. The mixed exploration party of whites and Native Americans originated east of the Coastal Mountains at Nome Lackee Reservation in the upper Sacramento Valley. Acting boldly in his post as California Superintendent of Indian Affairs and on the advice of Judge Montgomery Peters of Yreka.[42] Thomas J. Henley had sent Storms, formerly an Indian trader, language interpreter and Subagent at Nome Lackee Reservation, into the pristine eight-mile-wide saucer-shaped valley to found a new Indian farm.

Born in 1830 in Venezuela, Storms' mother immigrated with him to the United States, first settling in New York City. The Storms family moved next to

---

39. Bonni Grapp, *Footprints: An Early History of Fort Bragg, California and the Pomo Indians* (Fort Bragg: n.p., 1967), pages unnumbered, 2. Copy at Regional Books Section of the Jean and Charles Schulz Information Center of Sonoma State University, Rohnert Park, CA. Local facts provided by Mr. Floyd Barney in conversation on March 20, 2000. The Noyo or Mendocino Reservation was closed in 1864. All of its living Native American residents were relocated to Nome Cult Farm, which was renamed Round Valley Indian Reservation, which name has persisted to the present.

Boston Massachusetts. Young Simmon spent his childhood in Boston. In 1849 at age nineteen Simmon left his mother and the possibility of learning a profession or trade in New England.

At first he was determined to strike it rich in the gold mines of California's High Sierra. After a short stint as a miner, Storms began to make his living as a rancher and an Indian trader working with the local Native American tribes, like the Paiute of Nevada and the Maidu of Nevada County. Unlike most other 49ers, Storms had a remarkable innate facility for learning new languages. Despite his youthful good looks, Storms suffered from tuberculosis.

By the early 1850s Storms helped with the Office of Indian Affairs with the transfer of the Maidu Indians from Nevada County in the High Sierra's to Nome Lackee Reservation in the western Sacramento Valley near Red Bluff. There he assisted Supt. Henley and Nome Lackee's first subagent Henry L. Ford as a key interpreter. He was also one of the reservation's first overseers.

Tough, shrewd, fluent in numerous Indian languages, by 1856, Storms had become a well-known frontiersman and Indian Affairs Office employee. He sought an opportunity to exploit the rashness of his boss, Supt. Henley, and the funds of the Indian Affairs Department. Although he did not know about Hen-

40. Henley's 1856 report to Washington, written after the establishment of Nome Cult Farm in Round Valley, gives us an idea of the number of Native Americans on each of the state's five reservations in 1856.
"The number of Indians now collected and residing upon the reservations is—

At Klamath	2,500
At Mendocino	500
At Fresno	900
At Tejon	700
At Nome Cult valley [attached to Nome Lackee]	3,000
At Kings River [attached to Fresno]	400
Making in all	10,000

"The number of Native Americans not connected with the reserves cannot be correctly estimated." From Stephen R. Holman, *Round Valley Indian Reservation*, pp. 34–35.
The final sentence demonstrates a frustrating fact for historians of California history. That is, during this whole period the so-called "wild Indians," or those who were still free, were very often not being counted by the federal or state governments. In the 1850s there was no government or private authority fully capable of doing it. Thus, while they were shot at and killed by settlers their existence went completely unconsidered in all future plans for expansion or reduction in funding for the California Indian Affairs Department.
41. The original farm was south of a walnut orchard presently at the corner of Barnes Lane and Highway 162 that one sees on entering Covelo from the south. The orchard is on the right of Highway 162 heading north into Round Valley and Covelo.

ley's shortage of funds, Storms sought a way to use his influence to feather his own nest and sustain the development of the new reservation.

In his first report to Henley after his June 14, 1856 arrival at Round Valley, Storms had good things to say about the valley's resources:

> On the 13th we made an early start; travelled up the divide to the summit & arrived there about noon; stopped & took dinner etc.—from the summit we had a fine view, of the Sacramento Valley to our East, and of Longs Valley to the West, beyond which as far as the Eye could [see]. nothing was to be seen but Mountains, which appeared to be rugged and broken, the area to the North & South, found but little snow on the summit & but little timber. About 1 p.m. we started for the Valley in our West (?) [parentheses in original] which appeared to be about 20 miles distant. We kept down a divide between two small streams—on getting to the forks, found the river much larger than I expected, in fact quite a large one. We supposed this to be "Big River" [the Eel River]. We camped near the forks all night—saw a great many Indian signs on our way down, but only one Indian & he happening to be acquainted with the Indians who was with our party. They xxxxxxxxxxx [illegible, may say "expressed"] appeared much pleased at meeting. I found the West slope of the Mountains timber—about the same as the East. [Earlier in this report Captain Storms stated the Eastern slope was "heavily timbered & game in abundance."] This river instead of running through the valley runs about three miles East of it—then two miles south of it—in a westerly direction towards the Coast saw a great many fish in it the weather cool....

Next, Storms' report describes his first impression of Round Valley and its possible eventual use as an Indian reservation.

> On the 14th we got an early start and arrived at the Valley a little after sun rise—this day as well as the 15th, 16th & 17th we spent in exploring the Valley, and getting all the Information I could in regard to the Indians, their Numbers, habits, xxxx &c. On the first day of my arrival I was satisfied in my own Mind, that of all the places I have ever seen, this was the place for an Indian Reservation. And accordingly I laid claim to the Valley in the name of the Government for that purpose. In the afternoon I called my party around me and christened it "Nome Cult" Valley.[43]

It was clear from this report that Storms thought he was claiming the entire valley as land for a national Indian reservation. Yet, because of the federal restrictions on reservation development, Henley had already limited Nome Cult to farm status. He made this clear in his 1856 report on Storms' work to Commissioner Manypenny:

---

42. Judge J. Montgomery Peters, district court judge in Yreka, wrote a letter to Henley in June, 1855, which stated, "I would suggest what is known as the Round Valley on the headwaters on one of the branches of Eel River as a suitable place to establish a reservation for the Indians." As quoted by Lynwood Carranco and Estle Beard, *Genocide and Vendetta*, op.cit, 50–51.

... Attached to Nome Lack [Nome Lackee] a farm has recently been established at Nome Cult valley. This valley is located in the coast range of mountains about forty miles east of Cape Mendocino, and there are in the vicinity about three thousand Indians. The farm is placed in charge of three of the employee's from Nome Lacke. The Indians are now engaged, under the direction of the persons in charge of them, in collecting acorns, manzanita berries, and other wild food for their winter supply, of which there will be plenty for their subsistence until the crops can be produced for their support.[44]

A farm would seem more palatable to Congress than a reservation when it came time for the required Department of Interior and Congressional funding and authorization. A farm designation meant five thousand acres or less, while a reservation was twenty-five thousand acres or more. This was just the beginning of what would later become a great difference of opinion between Nome Cult's leaders, on the one hand, and Superintendent Henley and his superior officers in the Office of Indian Affairs in Washington, D.C., on the other.

Another conflict that soon faced Nome Cult was the growing presence and demands of the Euro-American settlers. Perhaps Storms did not know about the early settlers who were already living in Round Valley, such as Charles Bourne, who had built the first cabin in the valley. Or possibly he simply chose not to report on individual settlers to Superintendent Henley. Whatever Storms' intentions were for developing a thriving reservation, Euro-American settlers, ranchers, and cattle traders like Judge Hastings and others also knew about the potential of Round Valley. Euro-American settlers, whether or not they were physically present in the valley, felt that their claims preceded the government's claim. By and large, the settlers viewed the local indigenous people as simply in the way of clearing the land for ranching success.

---

43. Subagent Simmon P. Storms to California's Superintendent of Indians Affairs Thomas J. Henley, June 29, 1856, carbon copy of this report from the National Archives, Microfilm Series 234, Frames 47–76, in the Round Valley file, Estle Beard Collection of the Held-Poage Historical Research Library, 603 W. Perkins St., Ukiah, CA.
The name "Nome Cult" meant "west home" in the Wintu language. Storms used the name the local Indians were called, "Nome," or "Nom," to name the reservation he was starting in the valley. The Anglo name, "Round Valley," was the first name that Frank Asbill had used in his discovery notes two years earlier in 1854. After 1870 the name "Nome Cult Farm" was dropped and "Round Valley Indian Reservation" became the commonly accepted name.

44. See Stephen R. Holman, *Round Valley Indian Reservation: A Study in Ethnocentricity*, Committee on the Study of History, Amherst, Massachusetts: Teacher's Manual, 1970, 34–35. Actually this "stock resting station" of Nome Cult Farm was the largest operating California reservation in the year 1856, with as many as 3,000 Native Americans present.

An unusually versatile leader, Storms had had experience as an interpreter, even as a showman, running a "bull and bear" circus near Sacramento, and as a key mediator between the Indians and the predominantly Euro-American community. Doubtless in his time he had come across countless western frontier valleys. So the sense of genuine awe he expressed at the astounding beauty and abundance of nature he saw at Round Valley is especially significant:

> I have visited many valleys in all parts of the country, but have never [seen] anything that will compare with this. As near as I can judge it is 8 or 10 miles long by 6 or 8 miles wide—and about Midway between the Nome Lackee Reservation and the coast—the distance from Reserve being about [50?] miles there are several small streams running through the Valley, all of which empty into the River south of it, in those streams or creeks there is an abundance of [timber?], and the finest I have , oak, & [Willow?], I found oak trees that were from 60 to [70?] feet without a limb and 4 to 6 feet through—the principle [sic] grasses in the Valley are timothy & clover there also a great variety of the names of which are unknown to me. On riding through the Valley the grass was up even with our horses backs & it was often difficult to get through it, it is of the same height over nearly the whole Valley with the exception of a narrow strip on the West side, there the soil & but little grows, in the other portion of the Valley the soil is of the best, well adapted to raising vegetables of all kinds & grain, the land there does not bake & there is but little clay in the soil. While we remained we had many heavy dews, which would wet our blankets about through, vegetation has not yet commenced drying up & from appearances I should judge it is green year round—I found amount of Currants, Blackberries, Strawberries, Grapes, with plenty of Manzanita berries & acorns. The mountains which extend down to the Valley are covered with the [best?] of grass & timber, And within one fourth of a mile from the Valley there is as fine a Sugar pine as I have ever seen xxx [x's in original] & no trouble to get at them.[45]

Storms was genuinely awed by the beauty of this large upland valley. While he may have also been moved by the high atmosphere and the exhilaration of a hard climb after a trek across the hills and mountains, he nevertheless was completely swept away by the natural beauty of a great, unknown valley.

Storms then asked Henley to send tools as "there are plenty of hands to work," referring of course to the local Native Americans. He described his initial meeting and experiences with local Native Americans, whom he identified in their current terminology, as "U kom no'ms, Cahtos, and Cahto-Pomos."

According to this first report, the Round Valley Native Americans' reaction was to run away. Still, their curiosity was also aroused. Soon their interest in this party of Native American scouts and Euro-American men overcame their fears. The Yuki sent representatives to talk to Captain Storms.

---

45. Simmon P. Storms to Thomas J. Henley, June 29, 1856, carbon copy of a letter, Held-Poage Historical Research Library, 603 W. Perkins St., Ukiah, CA.

As we came into the Valley, we saw some Indians coming towards us, as soon as they saw us they started off like so many deer. We kept on our course to a grove of timber and there was collected on a small knoll North of us two hundred Indians— I sent my interpreter to tell them to come over where I was. When they saw him approaching, many of them ran off, but as soon as he commenced talking with them, they came back, in a few minutes he returned with six Indians, one of whom I afterwards learned was their head chief. When he came up he offered me his Bow & Arrows. I told him to keep them. I then told him I was sent over by the great Captain to see them and have a talk with them & to settle among them & teach them how to work &c. He appeared much pleased. I told him that I wanted him to get his head men together & meet me the next day—that I might talk with them, during the day the Indians were coming and going all the time, as soon as they found we did not wish to molest them—I found these Indians about the same as all the California Indians which I have seen. The most of them have deer skins—but no other clothing. I find there has been a number of squaws and children taken away by white men, which is the principle [sic] reason of there being so much [fear?] of the whites. When we first went in the valley some of the Indians stole two & [illegible], I told them it was very wrong to do so and the old chief made them return all. After that they never attempted to take anything again. I saw among them a number of shells which they said came from the coast, & that they could get there in two sleeps, & that white men were living there. The next morning [illegible] a band of about two hundred came into camp, but few had their Bows & Arrows. I then explained to them the object of my visit, with which they appeared much pleased and when the interpreter told them how the Indians on Nome Lackee Reserve lived, they seemed delighted & said they would all work at anything I wanted them to do, if I would only protect their squaws and children. I told them that hereafter no one should molest them; that I intended to leave men to look out for them while I went back for tools &c to work with, &c. if any men came into the Valley to trouble them to let my men know it & they would stop them. The old chief told me he would like to go to Nome Lackee with me & see the place / he & one other came over with me/ I then gave them the presents I had for them. I was very careful not to make any promises, but such as I knew I could carry out—I think that in the Valley and in the low Mountains around, there are at least five thousand Indians, & that the Valley can be made to support twenty thousand or more. it is the best place for Indians I ever saw. I did not see a sick Indian or one afflicted with the venereal. I think they are generally a better looking set of Indians than those at the Nome Lackee Reserve. Most of the squaws tatoo [sic], the men do not.[46]

It is worth pausing here to examine several points made here by Storms. He notes that the Round Valley natives did not have venereal diseases. He describes the Yuki leader as "much pleased" at his proposal. He states that the Yukis "seemed delighted." The "chief" sought a better life for his people. If this meant establishing a new reservation, then it was certainly acceptable to him. In his own right Storms was pretty confident and full of inflated hopes about the chances of supporting up to "twenty thousand" Indians in Round Valley.

---

46. *Ibid.*

Storms's optimism echoes that of his former boss at Nome Lackee, Agent Edward A. Stevenson. Stevenson's report was sent to Superintendent Henley at about the same time, on July 31, 1856. Stevenson's report must have added to the department's general confidence in the promise that lay in the establishment of Indian reservations in California. On the good innate abilities of Native Americans in learning how to farm, Agent Stevenson wrote:

> I arrived at and took charge of the reserve on the 16th of January, 1856; a large crop of grain was put in during the winter, consisting of about eight hundred acres of wheat, forty acres of barley and a large lot of vegetables; which, I am happy to say, have all yielded an abundant harvest. The Indians are quiet, contented and happy; they work cheerfully and well in all branches of labor, particularly agricultural; they are quick to acquire a knowledge of it; many are excellent hands with the cradles, sickles, etc., and have, with the aid of a few white persons as overseers and directors, harvested all the wheat [about 16,000] bushels and other crops, and have cut and put up about two hundred and fifty tons of hay of the best quality.
>
> The reserve will now be able to produce sufficient breadstuffs for about five thousand Indians. The number is now increasing daily, as they are beginning to understand the liberal policy of the government towards them.
>
> There are now on this reserve about two thousand Indians of four different tribes; the Nome-Lackes, Nome Cults, Niv-mucks, and Wye-Lackes [Wy-lackies]; of these, the first named is the most numerous. None of them have any head or principal chief, except the Nome-Cults; they have one who appears to exercise a very great influence over them. The several tribes are located in different parts of the reserve to prevent any disturbances among them, arising out of the enmity which has always existed among various tribes in this State.[47]

Like Storms, Agent Stevenson assumed that most Native Americans would be good workers. Those whom Storms took with him to Round Valley did a good job of founding Nome Cult Farm. Also like Storms, Agent Stevenson expands upon the health of the Native Americans and progress at "his" reservation,

> There is no disease of any importance among those who have remained any considerable time on the reserve; but most of the newcomers are diseased, miserable, and wretched, and would, without assistance from government perish from the continued effects of disease and famine. Within the last ten days, about ninety Wye-lackies have been brought in; almost every one of them is afflicted; but in a few months, with proper care and medical aid, will be mostly cured. Until recently, there was a fifth tribe here [those whom Storms referred to as "Nevadas," or Maidus] but they have been removed to the Nome Cult valley [Round Valley] west of

47. Report of Agent Edward A. Stevenson to California Supt. of Indian Affairs Thomas J. Henley, July 31, 1856, No. 103, 250 of Department of Interior, Letters received by the Office of Indian Affairs, 1824–1880, on Microfilm at Held-Poage Home and Historical Research Library, 603 W. Perkins St., Ukiah, CA.

this reserve, and are now located there, under the supervision of Mr. S.P. Storms, who was formerly their overseer here. As that valley is some distance from here; it is impossible for me, at this time, to say anything of its prospects of utility, success, etc., I shall therefore reserve it for future report.[48]

Interestingly, Storms' report to Henley noted that the Round Valley natives had no venereal disease, unlike the Wylackies newly arrived at Nome Lackee Reserve. Indeed, each agent or supervisor seemed eager to describe the prosperity and health of those under his care. While this sort of undue optimism is difficult to interpret, it does seem to be the standard line of many reports of Indian Agents to their superiors. One can not help but wonder about the true conditions of the Native Americans at Nome Lackee. If Native Americans faced such desperate conditions off the reservation: unable to find adequate food, riddled by new diseases, molested by kidnappers and by random murders, the apparent readiness with which the old Indian "chief" was taken in by this disingenuous "Captain" Storms made more sense. Possibly, the Native Americans were already tired of trying to fight with these strange and hostile white men. They saw that this party was well armed and wisely chose amenability as their best first response. Unfortunately, we do not know what their real impressions were. In any case, the Yuki leader was savvy enough to request a personal visit to Nome Lackee, that had just been described to him in such glowing terms by Storms.

Captain Storms finished this unique first report to Superintendent Henley by turning to the necessary, yet relatively mundane, question of road building.

> From Taylors Ranch to the main divide a good Road can be made, with but little labour but on the West side it will require considerable work to make it a good one—With Indians I could make a good Mountain Road in six Weeks time. I would not hesitate now to take an empty Wagon over with two yoke of oxen, in five days time, with the aid of a few Indians, the distance is not over 50 miles. A good Mule can make the trip over in one day easy—a good pack load now—a good Mule now, can pack over two hundred pounds—leaving. On the morning of the 18th I left the Valley, [illegible] with three Men in charge until my return. I would have remained longer to explore the country around, but our provisions gave out & we had nothing but venison & wild onions to eat on our way back.

> The men in the valley will have to live on meat and what they can get from the Indians until I return. I xxxx [x's in the original] leave here again on Monday next the 23rd inst &c to build a house &c. On my return as I came down the Mountains, I met several parties going over to settle in the Valley—but [blank] informed them that it was reserved by the Government. They will probably go elsewhere.

---

48. *Ibid.*

All of which is Respectfully submitted by
Yours Respectfully
Simmon P. Strong [*sic*; copyist's error, "Storms."][49]

Storms' report shows Round Valley's relative isolation from the outside world. It also demonstrated how interdependent reservation employees initially were with the local Native Americans. The report also documents a widening culture gap between the latter and all the Euro-Americans that would reside in or visit the valley during the next few years, whether settlers, reservation officials, military personnel, or newspaper reporters.

As Storms' final comment to Supt. Henley indicates, there already were parties of settlers coming into the valley in search of land. He informed them that "it was reserved by the Government." He concluded hopefully, "They will probably go elsewhere."

Whether Storms knew it or not such weak attempts to slow the increasing flow of new settlers into Round Valley were far too little and far too late. He inadvertently reveals one of the ever-present and overriding problems that plagued the frontier: how to channel "Manifest Destiny" so that the poor and the innocent were not ground up or totally obliterated. Although Storms' advice to one or two immigrant parties may well have caused some to change course, it did not stop others who were determined to settle on the four-fifths of the valley that was not already earmarked by the Indian Affairs Department for the farm.

As Captain Storms and his reservation party rode on through Round Valley for the first time during this cool Mendocino summer of 1856, a fatally deceptive illusion was planted in the Native Americans' minds that peaceful coexistence with the whites and a prosperous life ahead were both possible. Indeed, there must have been times when it seemed that life at the farm could be good for all. Storms brought with him from Nome Lackee a number of Native Americans whom he knew and trusted. These were the so-called "Nevada Indians," probably really Maidu from the High Sierra region east of Sacramento in Nevada. Storms went so far as to refer to this group as "his Indians." He considered these people as close allies, even coworkers in the development of Nome Cult Farm.

Despite obstacles to reservation improvements, work progressed on Nome Cult Farm, as subsequent letters and official reports by officials like Storms, his

---

49. Simmon P. Storms to Thomas J. Henley, June 29, 1856, p. 3, letter on file at Held-Poage Home and Historical Research Library, 603 W. Perkins St., Ukiah, CA.

successor, George Rees, and others make clear. Between 1856 and 1857, Round Valley's Native-Americans, under S.P. Storms' direction, built a twelve-foot high stockade around a commissary and a few other buildings. This part of the reservation was later to be called "Lower Quarters," enclosing only a tiny part of the valley. By 1858, Nome Cult Farm had ten miles of fencing. In 1859, white militia brought the Concow tribe to the reservation. In 1860 they added the Nomelaki Tribe from Fort Bragg. In 1861 Round Valley Reservation included the Pit River tribe from the northeastern part of the state east of Redding, as well as many other tribes.

New Round Valley immigrant-settlers, including William Murphy, George White, Martin Corbitt, William Pollard, P.A. Wit, and Benjamin Arthur, continued to occupy more and more prime sections of the valley. Some reservation employees, like Superintendent Henley's sons and nephews, as well as Sub-agent Storms, started personal family ranches in the valley off the reservation. For the first couple of years after 1856, there was some sense of cooperation between the Euro-Americans and the Native Americans. This disappeared altogether with the arrival of more determined, predominantly white settlers in the valley in larger numbers. Private land claims equaled to the reservation's claim-even to take precedence. By 1860, the Euro-American population grew to about one hundred. The 1860 Census totaled ninety-six non-Native American residents. The federal Indian Affairs Department's and Congress' failure to survey the reservation earlier, and then, to enlarge it soon after the beginning of the reservation in 1856 proved to be lethal policy for the Native Americans.

Given Storms' past experience and present purpose, as well as the weaknesses and ineptitude of the Office of Indian Affairs vis-à-vis the better organized and far more vicious settlers' group, true peace and Native American security may not ever have been possible. What happened next was as profound and sad a tragedy as any before in American history. It was almost as if the Native Americans were being stealthily led down a steep mountain trail that ended with a blind fall into an abyss. Each new incident of an abuse or rape, lying about wages, beating, false arrest, fraud, or murder made it just a little easier for the ranchers and settlers to commit another outrageous crime or atrocity. As ranchers and settlers fought each other for power and increasingly scanty remaining land within Round Valley, their ugly blood lust was fueled. This racism was compounded by ignorance of Native Americans, ethnocentrism, and their own superiority complexes.

KIDNAPPING OF NATIVE AMERICAN CHILDREN

About a year before Storms' party from Nome Lackee reservation entered Round Valley to found Nome Cult Indian Farm, California's Superintendent of Indian Affairs Thomas Henley attempted to obtain a special "detachment of Soldiers to capture certain Spaniards under indictment for kidnapping Indians, which application was not granted." The request eventually went through channels to Major General John Wool, commander of the Department of the Pacific. The Secretary of War Jefferson Davis officially nixed this proposal on May 23, 1855.

Davis' letter to Secretary of the Interior McClelland continued:

> The commissioner asks that Genl. Wool may be authorized to detail a Military force whenever called on by the Superintendent to enable him to carry out in good faith the provisions of law, and the obligations of the Government to afford protections to the Indians, etc. In the particular case mentioned by the Superintendent it would seem to be the appropriate duty of the civil officers to arrest the persons under indictment, and if aid be necessary, the *posse comitatus* is their proper reliance....." [50]

In March 1856 another kidnapping case occurred. Judge R. N. Wood wrote a letter to Supt. Henley requesting a payment of five hundred dollars for the legal services of the prosecuting lawyer, Mr. William McDaniel. An attorney, McDaniel, had just successfully argued an important kidnapping case that had led to "the conviction of several persons who violated the laws of the U.S. and of California in kidnapping Indians...." [51]

Judge Wood, who was the presiding judge of the Court of Sessions of Contra Costa County, in the same letter to Supt. Henley, stated that McDaniel's work had broken up a kidnapping ring and that "Mr. M. D. is not only entitled to fair compensation but the thanks of all good citizens."

---

50. Letter from the Secretary of War Jefferson Davis to R.M. McClelland, Secretary of the Interior, May 23, 1855, as quoted by Robert F. Heizer, *The Destruction of California Indians*, Lincoln: University of Nebraska Press, 1993, 235.
51. *Ibid.*, p. 235.

Chapter 3. The Army, the Settlers, and the Office of Indian Affairs in 1857–1858: Conflicting Views of a Complicated Situation

I saw one of the squaws after she was dead, I think she died from a bullet; I think all the squaws were killed because they refused to go further. We took one boy into the valley, and the infants were put out of their misery, and a girl ten years of age was killed for stubbornness.
    —*H.L. Hall's deposition, Storms Hotel, Round Valley,*
    February 26, 1860, Indian War Files.

The Army vs. The Indian Affairs Office

Soon after Agent Storms arrived in Round Valley, some signs of trouble ahead were already obvious. Late in 1856, California Senators William ("Duke") Gwin and David C. Broderick received numerous letters and petitions from settlers throughout northern California pleading for federal troops to be dispatched to protect settler property and Native Americans on the California "military reservations." From the nation's capital, the two senators sent a request for troops to Maj. Gen. John E. Wool, the Commandant of the U.S. Army's Department of the Pacific in Benicia.

Washington, D.C., was well over three thousand miles east of Major General Wool's base in Benicia, located on the Carquinez Strait in the East Bay, in a time when the fastest overland transportation usually took over four weeks or sometimes much longer. It was as though two strange and distant nations were trying to reach a difficult agreement about very complex issues about which neither side knew much at all.

In his reply to the California senators, Maj. Gen. Wool invoked three Congressional acts and an Office of Indian Affairs directive to Superintendent Henley ("3rd March, 1853, July 31st, 1854 and 3rd March, 1855, and the instructions of the Secretary of the Interior, dated the 13th, April 1853") to vehemently deny the senators' plea for troops:

> These laws authorize five military reservations not exceeding 25,000 acres each, and appropriations amounting to at least $948,300, besides the pay of the Superintendent and three agents, for *removing, colonizing, subsisting and protecting* [emphasis in the original] Indians in California. The mode of selecting these reservations are pointed out in the instructions of the Secretary of the Interior, dated the 13th, April, 1853, as follows—"The selection of the military reservations "are to be made by you [Superintendent of Indian Affairs Henley] in conjunction with the Military Commandant in California, or such officer as may be detailed for that purpose; in which case they must be sanctioned by the Commandant. It is, likewise, the President's [President Pierce] desire that, in all other matters connected with the execution of this place, you will as far as it may be practicable, act in concert with the commanding officer [Maj. Gen. Wool] of that Military Department.[52]

Maj. Gen. Wool was unhappy with Supt. Henley for at least two reasons. First, Wool felt that Henley should have consulted more often with him. This recitation and the explanation that follows indicate that Superintendent Henley had not followed this directive to cooperate with Wool in establishing California's reservations. Second, Wool rightly believed that Henley's job performance was inadequate. Major General Wool was determined to make it clear to all what all his objections were, directly and in no uncertain terms. Using the establishment by Henley of Nome Lackee Reserve as his example, he further explained that he thought he had done all in his power that he could do, and thought he should do, to cooperate with Supt. Henley:

> The Superintendent of Indian Affairs, Colonel Henley, has called on me but once to make an examination with reference to locating a reservation for the protection of Indians in California, and that was to examine the tract called Nome Lackee. I sent an officer, Captain Keyes, with Colonel Henley for that purpose who reported favorable of it, and it received my approval.

> Nothing further on the part of the Supt. of Indian Affairs has been done to perfect the reservation. It has not been surveyed, nor the jurisdiction of the State ceded

---

52. This and subsequent quotes from General Wool's letter are from "Letter #44 Maj. General John E. Wool to Sens. D.C. Broderick and Wm. Gwin," Interior Department Appointment Papers, Microcopy #732, Roll #20, California Superintendent of Indian Affairs, 1852–1862, on file at Held-Poage Library, 603 W. Perkins St., Ukiah, CA.

to the United States. Without these pre-requisites, with my approval, as required by the Secretary of the Interior; it can no more be considered a military reservation for the protection of Indians than the City of Benicia. These remarks are applicable to all the reservations reported by Colonel Henley to the Secretary of the Interior.

Given the inadequacy of Henley's work, Maj. Gen. Wool was not about to meekly comply with the senators' request and commit soldiers to duty on California's newly established and far-flung Indian reservations. It should be noted that Major General Wool had good reason to be angry at Superintendent Henley. Although Wool does not mention it, Henley had also not consulted with Wool about establishing Nome Cult Farm.

The next paragraph of Major General Wool's reply is also significant because it presents to the civilian authorities a brief for what was, and would be for much of the remainder of the 1850s, the Army's view of its role with respect to the hostility and the frontier warfare that had become increasingly common between the Indians and white settlers here:

> California is in no sense of the word an Indian country. It is a sovereign State, whose laws extend over all, Indians and Whites, residing within her borders. Before the Military of the United States can exercise, legally control or protect the Indians from the encroachments of Whites all military reservations intended for the protection of Indians should be surveyed, the number of acres given, not exceeding 25,000 acres each, metes and bonds stated, or, approved by the United States Military Commandant, and the jurisdiction of the State ceded to the United States. Until these reservations are thus perfected the United States troops would have no right to control the actions of the Indians, so far as forcing them to remain on the reservations or punish them for infractions of the State laws, nor to exclude the Whites from entering and occupying the reserves, or even prevent their taking from them Indians, squaws and children. In all such cases, until the jurisdiction of the State is ceded to the United States the civil authority should be invoked to correct the evil.

Herein in a nutshell lay the true difficulty as Maj. Gen. Wool saw it. The U.S. Army had been requested by the senators to intervene in a situation in which the "civil authority" was too weak and too poorly organized to effectively police and keep local order. If U.S. soldiers were about to be put to such a use, under whose laws were the soldiers to act? The State of California's laws, federal laws, or the military's own laws and codes of practice and behavior?

As Maj. Gen. Wool, other American military officers, and even members of the public knew full well late in 1856, this was not at all a clear-cut situation of right and wrong in which soldiers would be comfortable that they were doing the right thing.

Major General Wool continued with an example of the ambiguous authority exercised over California Indians by the Indian Affairs Department:

> For, not long since a party of Indians left the so-called Nome Lackee reserve for their old hunting grounds. They were pursued by the agents, overtaken and brought back, but not until after, as reported, some four or five Indians were killed. No white man, it would seem, was seriously wounded. Under the circumstances, I would ask from whom did the agent derive his authority to pursue those Indians & kill them because they were not willing to return to Nome Lackee? It was a barbarous act for which he had not the shadow of right or justification.

Maj. Gen. Wool continued to make a strong and still stirring moral case against using the troops on the reservations. As he concluded this lengthy, elaborately reasoned yet eloquent reply to the California senators' call for assistance, Maj. Gen. Wool threw in one more point. Stating that while Henley's reservations contained only approximately four thousand Indians, Wool noted also that there were fifty-six thousand more California Native Americans outside of the reservations whom his soldiers also needed to watch. Moreover,

> If the liberal means placed at the disposal of the Indian Department in California were properly applied, I am sure an agent or employee would need no troops to protect them from Indians who are willing to occupy reservations. See Lieut. Rundell's report of June last and my correspondence with the War Department. By all which you will discover that very little progress has been made in California in carrying out the humane policy of the Government so liberally manifested towards the Indians.
>
> I have the honor to be
> Very respectfully
> Your Obt. Servent
> John E. Wool
> Major General
>
> To the Hon. D.C. Broderick
> & the Hon. Wm. Gwin
> Senators in the Congress
> of the United States
> Washington.
> D.C.

These were critical, basic questions regarding what role the U.S. Army should take in California. The system of military posts set up along the Oregon and California Trails was originally established by Congress just to help guide Euro-American emigrants safely across the continent. Generally speaking, federal soldiers were not supposed to go out on search-and-destroy missions aimed at clearing the Native Americans off the best land of the new states. Except in special, very dangerous circumstances, such as when a wagon train had been attacked by a band of hostile Native Americans, troops were supposed to remain at or near the military posts.

As we have seen by his reply to Senators Gwin and Broderick, Maj. General Wool listed instances of mismanagement and lack of proper planning by Indian Affairs Superintendent Henley in California. He also was upset because funds were being wasted by the California Office of Indian Affairs. Maj. General Wool pointed out that the lack of proper surveying by Colonel Henley at Nome Lackee was also another important reason not to send federal troops for duty there.

This exchange of letters between the two California Senators and Maj. Gen. Wool caused at least a two year postponement in the dispatch of an adequate number of troops to remote California reservations like Round Valley and Mendocino Reservations. It is also significant that the public was in the dark about this change in the original plan for the reservation. These letters were not publicized. To reiterate briefly, Supt. Beale's original plan had called for enough U.S. Army troops assigned to each reservation to protect reservation property, to keep order and to separate settlers from Native Americans.

Such criticisms would not soon be addressed by reform within the Office of Indian Affairs, on either the state or the federal level. The Army's role was further confused by conflicting demands of the Euro-American settlers in the region and other problems arising out of rapid unplanned settlement.

THE SETTLERS

Land speculators and large investor ranchers such as George E. White, Judge Hastings, Supt. Henley, and even to some extent, Captain Storms saw Round Valley as an almost ideal mountain valley with lush grassland seemingly perfect for grazing livestock. The settlers entered the valley at the rate of about ten new settlers per year from 1856 through 1860. Most had superior weapons at their disposal, including modern rifles, accurate pistols, and plentiful ammunition. Rightly or wrongly, these settlers soon realized that the most successful rancher there would be the one who controlled the most livestock. Ultimately this meant cattle, which were more valuable than most other livestock. The winner of the race for power, as they saw it, would be the individual who could simultaneously control both the largest acreage and the largest herds.

The reservation, or Nome Cult Farm, took up nearly the whole of the northern third of the valley. It did not take long for the rest of the valley to be claimed by white ranchers. Ironically, a few reservation employees stand out among those who profited. From 1857 on, Storms and other reservation employees tried to follow the advice of their boss, Supt. Henley, who encouraged everyone to immigrate to the valley, to start farms and build up their own personal land holdings. In 1856, and again shortly after, in 1857, new settlers like Samuel S. Davis, Martin Corbitt, P. A. Wit (or Witt), and a number of others, were encouraged to settle by Supt. Henley because there was strength in numbers. Strong, young new settlers could quickly become soldiers.

Individual settlers claimed the last large parcels of good ranch land in Round Valley by December, 1858. The southern half of the valley was almost entirely claimed by settlers by the start of the Civil War in the spring of 1861. As time went on, the Native Americans, both the so-called "wild" ones who might be a problem on settlers' land and the so-called "domesticated" ones on the reservation itself, were increasingly seen only as obstacles to this ambition.

In the case of the "wild" Indians, many settlers thought that the easiest method of removing them was to hire, or have the state hire, soldiers to kill or remove them. The reservation Indians required more overt methods. Round Valley settlers tore down reservation fences, ran their herds through freshly tilled or planted fields, or abducted Indian women for sexual uses. All of these actions were direct tactics of warfare still used today.

An even more violent tactic, killing the Native Americans outright, was accomplished in part by a campaign to fan the alarm of the public and thus get the attention of public officials. The new settlers became increasingly adept at manipulating the newspapers and making propaganda to mold public opinion and impress state authorities with images of vicious wild Indians stealing and killing settler livestock. After 1857, the hateful term "Indian depredations" became a mantra for settlers looking to justify attacks on local native peoples. From this time on, settlers repeated the term over and over again, in their own correspondence, in significant official petitions and protests to the governor, or to their state and federal legislators after alleged Indian attacks upon their herds.

The term "Indian depredations" had obvious pejorative overtones. From 1859 on, losses of settlers' stock were assumed to be caused by Indians, rather than by "natural" causes such as death from thirst, starvation, disease, or by predators such as grizzly bears, rattlesnakes, and cougars (mountain lions). The word "depredation" itself implies a life based on wanton and habitual destruction, whether it was the killing of livestock or the alleged thefts of horses, arms or items from settler houses or barns.

A key to understanding why so many Round Valley Euro-American ranchers became angry at Native Americans for their losses of stock can be found in understanding ranch methods of the mid-nineteenth century. Ranchers could not confine livestock on the range as efficiently as modern ranchers can. Barbed wire and ranch wire were still twenty years in the future in the 1850s. Brush fences were more frequently used, as split rail fencing was a labor-intensive and expensive solution to separating livestock from fields of newly planted grain, corn, or produce.

The early California rodeo method of constantly training livestock to recognize a certain place was the main method still in use throughout California farms and ranches of the late 1850s. This point about the "cattle raising" industry was clearly noted by early California settler William Heath Davis in his 1889 published reminiscence *Seventy-Five Years in California.*

> Although the cattle belonging to the various ranchos were wild, yet they were under training to some extent, and were kept in subjection by constant rodeos. At stated times, say two or three times a week at first, the cattle on a particular ranch were driven in by the vaqueros, from all parts thereof, to a spot known as the rodeo ground, and kept there for a few hours, when they were allowed to disperse. Shortly they were collected again, once a week perhaps, and then less seldom, until after considerable training, being always driven to the same place, they came to know it....

> At times, cattle strayed from one ranch to another and got into the wrong herd. Whenever a rodeo was to be held, the neighbors of the ranchero were given notice and attended at the time and place designated. If any of these cattle were found in the band, they were picked out, separated, and driven back to the rancho where they belonged. As the cattle were all branded, and each rancho had earmarks, this was not difficult.[53]

In the remote and rugged upland coastal Mayacama Range in northeast Mendocino County, the rodeo method had a number of serious flaws, one of which was the high toll taken by natural predators.

A settler by the name Samuel S. Davis was a typical small rancher in Round Valley. Davis noted in his deposition that there were a large number of remote canyons, draws, ravines, and steep cliffs in the Mayacamas, all of which created escape routes for cattle loose on a large open range such as in Round Valley. Also, given the paucity of experienced vaqueros in Mendocino County, keeping track

---

53. William H. Davis, *Seventy-Five Years in California,* San Francisco: John Howell Books, 1967, originally published in 1889, Howard A. Small, Editor, 28.

of all of one's animals could be an overwhelming job, even in the best of circumstances.

Given these factors plus the fact that there were other California areas like the lush grasslands of the San Joaquin Valley, large parts of Santa Barbara County, and many other grass-rich plains lands that were located nearer urban areas or major waterways, starting up a new ranch in Long Valley, Round Valley, or Eden Valley was a daunting job; one where stock losses and human casualties were almost guaranteed.

Certainly Native Americans may have sometimes targeted the livestock of particular settlers, especially some who, like George Woodman, conducted a business of kidnapping Indian children and deliberately destroying Indian families. But allegations against the Indians rarely considered the possibility of natural causes for stock loss, which were more common then than now. Nor did they often consider extenuating circumstances, such as starvation. Further, it was easy for settlers to exaggerate or stretch the truth about stock losses to the authorities because, according to the California Constitution (1849), it was against the law for a Native American to testify against a Euro-American in California courts or before justices of the peace. What this meant in reality was that Euro-Americans could not be convicted just on the basis of Native American testimony. As time passed, more violence and armed skirmishes occurred between Native Americans and white settlers.

As more settlers arrived and settled in the valley, Native Americans were increasingly seen as enemies of progress or, at the very least, as a liability to society. Pot shots and random murders of Indians became more frequent after 1857. Sadly, the valley's great natural beauty, initially so evident to all, faded as posses of armed men, toughs, mountain men, and even some normally peace loving settlers vied with each other for control of the land.

In the three years from 1856 to 1859, whites started to form more local militia death squads led by men like "Captain" Walter S. Jarboe, William W. Frazier, and others. Bands of armed settlers went out on raids into the mountains, laying ambushes and attacking Indian rancherias at the rate of as many as three expeditions per week. By January 1860, hundreds of Yukis a month were being killed by settlers, who were quite often expert marksmen. Despite frequent settler claims about well-armed enemy Native Americans, seldom were they armed with anything more than knives and bows and arrows.

The Yukis and other Native Americans became angry and frustrated as shots were fired at more of their rancherias. Valley lands that before 1856–1857 had been considered Yuki property were now being taken. Despite their frustrations, the Yukis rarely killed any white settlers. According to historian Estle Beard, only about seven to ten white settlers, at the most, were killed by Native Americans during the late 1850s in all of Northern California. Beard wrote this on the margin of a copy of Rena Lynn's history of Round Valley's earliest years, *The Stolen Valley*. The copy is preserved at Held Poage Library in Ukiah.

So great were the number of Indians killed in 1859 and 1860 that Storms estimated in 1860 that in the "past three and a half" years "five hundred Indians have been killed in the vicinity of Round Valley." It is probable that the actual number of Native Americans killed in that time period was far greater than that and probably will never be known. Survivors were escorted to Mendocino Reservation near Fort Bragg. Native Americans who tried to run away were shot at more frequently. Mendocino Reservation, as well as Nome Cult Farm, was a notorious death trap for Native Americans because of starvation and venereal diseases.

It must be noted that many white settlers wrongly believed that once all California's Native Americans were "relocated," that is driven by force away their home territories and onto the reservations, they were all well treated there. The opinion of this editorial, quoted by Eric K. Smith, a writer-historian from Santa Cruz, seems to have been a common one:

> One settler wrote to the *Humboldt Times* [Eureka, CA] explaining that he had seen "a number of Indians ... at present employed by some farmers in this vicinity." He responded by warning the community against "harboring or employing diggers" and remarked that "they are provided for well on the Reservation and it is to our mutual interest to have them remain there. How could one tell, after all, what kind of Indians one might meet off of the reservation?"[54]

Some settlers harbored deep anti-Native American racial feelings to begin with. Such individuals were further angered that federal funds, raised by such taxes as excises on commodities they and their families worked hard to produce, were apparently being "lavished" unnecessarily not only on supplies like grain, blankets, and other necessities of daily life for Native Americans, but also on unhealthy things like liquor, gaudy trinkets, ammunition, and guns and pistols. Such was rarely the case.

---

54. Editorial advocating better treatment of the California Native Americans in *Humboldt Times*, Nov. 10, 1860, as quoted in the recent book by Eric Krabbe Smith, *Lucy Young or T'teenetsa Indian White Relations in Northwest California, 1846–1944* (Santa Cruz: University of California at Santa Cruz Press, 1990), 21–22.

Instead of having enough food to eat and good clothes to wear, most Native Americans usually arrived at the reservations, or on so-called "farms" like Nome Cult, for example, where there were horrible living conditions, little or no food, and rules that assured only more want and drudgery.

The reservation's name "Nome Cult" was derived from a Wintun word meaning west "home" or "west place." Instead of having a safe haven there, the Native Americans actually found only more of the same conditions they experienced in the wild: starvation, abuse, assaults including rape, derision, thefts of their personal property, murder, and venereal diseases. The militia brought some tribes, like the Concow, as we shall see in the fall and winter of 1862–1863, onto reservations by force but then the same tribe was forced out in a time of severe food shortage. Reservation officials were often caught in the midst of conflicting directives with insufficient support from Washington. Almost all of the earlier agents and overseers at Round Valley were themselves guilty of corruption and theft from the very people they were supposed to be "colonizing, subsisting and protecting."

RESERVATION OFFICIALS AND THE OFFICE OF INDIAN AFFAIRS

From 1856 to 1859 the Nome Cult Reserve or Farm, which was limited to only five thousand acres or one fifth of the valley, struggled for survival. Sub-agent Storms estimated that there were only about one hundred Native Americans on the reservation who both worked and were paid in rations by employees. There were about two thousand Native Americans who made the reservation their primary home who did not do any reservation work or improvements. Almost as fast as a few of the Native Americans built new corrals, fences, and buildings on the reservation, white settlers trespassed and pulled down some of the fences. Since fencing was expensive and difficult to fashion out of raw lumber that had to be cut and brought in from some distance from the hills, some settlers stole materials from the reservation, thus from the government. Since reservation Indians generally came and went unarmed, there was little the reservation officials could do about thefts, abductions, and simple pillaging by armed outsiders. There was no local or state police force. Not until after January 1859 were U.S. Army soldiers assigned to the reservation.

Nor were those Native Americans who had been brought to the new reservation entirely content. Nearly everyone there was affected by a serious Native

American uprising in the fall of 1856. It was stopped by reservation officials aided at the last minute by white hunters, fur traders, and mountain men coming out of the hills in response to Agent Storms' appeals for help. The quick-thinking Storms, who had anticipated the outbreak, made a deal with the hunters. Since he had also prepared by storing extra ammunition brought from Nome Lackee, he gave the so-called "mountaineers" ammunition in return for meat. Fresh meat was always in high demand on the California frontier whether for reservation employees, settler use or for the Native Americans. An undisclosed and unknown number of indigenous people died in this failed uprising.

Determining the hopes and motivations of reservation officials like Sub-agent Storms is not a simple task. At the least, there seem to have been conflicting motivations, with the decision to commit to one or the other plan of action dependent on the winds of politics and fortune. We cannot deny that Storms, for one, had very strong hope that his reservation would thrive in Round Valley.

In August 1858, Subagent Storms proposed that the whole valley be set aside for the reservation. He wrote to Goddard Bailey, who was a "Special Agent" of the Interior Department's Office of Indian Affair's. Bailey was one of a small number of investigators including J. Ross Browne whose job it was to travel out from the nation's capital to the reservations to make inspections and report facts back to Washington.[55] Storms wrote:

> Nome Cult Indian Farm
>
> August 14, 1858
>
> "Round" or "Nome Cult" valley was first discovered in 1852 or 1853 by hunters, but little was known of it until 1855, when it was visited by several parties. From information gathered from men who had seen the place I was convinced that it was a suitable place for an Indian reservation, and mentioned my opinion on several occasions to Colonel Henley, Superintendent of Indian Affairs, which induced him to send me to the place with a small party in June 1856. ...
>
> When I first came into the valley there were no white people and no settlers came until the Fall of 1856. No planting was done the first year as the season was too far advanced. We erected a few cabins within an enclosure of pickets for the occupancy of the whites and a few Nevada Indians that I brought with me. We began to pack farming tools, seeds and provisions from Nome Lackee, but the winter set in sooner than we anticipated and we did not accomplish much. ...
>
> To secure the complete success of this place the whole valley should be set apart for a reservation. Past experience shows that it is not for the benefit of the

---

55. According to the deposition of another reservation employee, James Tobin (see also chapter six), Spec. Agt. Bailey eventually recommended the Interior Department cut back its appropriations to support the Round Valley Native Americans.

whites, and much to the disadvantage of the Indians, that they are allowed to min-gle together. ...[56]

Storms was badly mistaken in saying that there were no settlers there when he arrived. Sadly this claim was an error that would be repeated in official correspondence, only adding fuel to the developing conflict between the reserva-tion and the settlers.

What is omitted from the report is as interesting as what is reported. Already the Office of Indian Affairs had reports of corruption in many of its northern California reservations, so probably Storms was eager to present him-self as genuine and Nome Cult Farm as a viable operation. Here he sounds proud of his role in helping to found the farm, but he must have been uncertain about the future both for the reservation and for his own family. It seems a little odd that he mentions neither the 1856 uprising of Native Americans nor the unrest between Indians and settlers that was in full swing by this time.

Storms argued in favor of expansion of the farm:

> If this valley be taken as a reserve there will be nothing to induce men to settle within sixty miles east, seventy north, thirty west and forty south. For five months in the year communication is cut off from the Sacramento Valley by the deep snows on the mountains. I think the improvements in the valley may have cost the settlers from twenty five to thirty thousand dollars. None of the land has been surveyed.

> If this valley should be confirmed as an Indian Reservation in a few years it would afford a home for 20,000 Indians and reflect honor upon the Indian Depart-ment. The outlay required would be trifling compared with the benefits to be derived from it.[57]

The trend of settler immigration to Round Valley did not work in favor of Storms' suggestion that the reservation be expanded. By 1860 about one hundred Euro-American settlers resided in the valley most of the time.[58] What also is odd

---

56. Letter No. 109 from Major S.P. Storms, Overseer of Nome Cult Reservation to Special Agent G. Bailey, Interior Department, August 14, 1858. See the Round Valley File at Held-Poage Research Library, 603 W. Perkins St., Ukiah, CA.

57. That Special Agent Browne, as well as many others involved in constructing the Native American federal policy for California, was concerned just with short term decisions can be seen in another statement made by Browne in the same report to Commissioner Mix, "Not only did the Superintendent (Henley) fail to carry out these negotiations [talks with other California tribes to induce them to come to Mendocino Reservation], but during the past winter he suffered [permitted] the Indians who were on the Mendocino Reservation and who had been brought there at great expense, to go back to their original homes." Confusion continued. Browne to Mix, letter on September 29, 1858, as quoted in Robert F. Heizer, *The Destruction of California Indians*, Lincoln, University of Nebraska Press, 1992, p. 115.

about the whole Round Valley situation is that Storms still appears totally oblivious to the fact that the white settlers had begun organizing in opposition to both Indians in general and also to the reservation's future existence. In this report to his superiors, Storms still promotes Nome Cult (or Round Valley Reservation) much as the Chamber of Commerce might do today.

In this same letter, Storms also noted the lack of an adequate and thorough federal survey of Round Valley. Finally, he mentioned an amount in dollars that whites had spent there because there seemed to him to be some chance that the federal government might actually increase the size of the reservation after buying out all of the white settlers. Given the growing power of the settlers, it seems a completely spurious suggestion. Much later, in the 1870s, the Indian Affairs Department tried, but without any success, to buy out all the settlers.

By the fall of 1858 another problem facing Nome Cult and the other California reservations was the mismanagement and outright fraud in the activities of the California Indian Affairs Office. Indeed, as early as 1856, federal officials already had reason to be suspicious of Superintendent Henley's honesty and job performance.

Even as early as August 1856 Commissioner of Indian Affairs George Manypenny had taken time out from many other tasks to make it crystal clear to Supt. Henley to be more prudent in dispersing federal funds. It is probable that word of Henley's corruption and actual thefts of government money had already begun to reach the Indian Affairs Department in Washington.

Then as now, with regard to alleged private or public scandals, bad news traveled fast.

Henley, Esq. Thomas
Department of the Interior
Superintendent Indian Affairs
Office of Indian Affairs
San Francisco, California

58. Many of the earliest settlers should perhaps not be considered full-time residents because they were constantly moving, out on the trails between the valley and Sacramento, Weaverville, and Fort Bragg, going out with pack trains, helping other settlers get needed supplies, or selling their own "produce," in many cases, deerskins. Some, like Supt. Henley's son, Thomas B. Henley worked as a clerk at both Mendocino and Round Valley Reservations before managing the Henley ranch in Round Valley and then moving back to Elko, NV in the 1860s where he sold real estate.

August 2nd, 1856
Sir,

In accordance with the estimate submitted in your letter of the 28th June last, I have today requested the Secretary of the Interior to cause the sum of $162,040 to be submitted to Assistant Treasurer of the United States to be placed subject to your order.

This remittance exhausts the several appropriations under the control of the Department for the expenses of the service in California [pay of Agents excepted] during the fiscal year ending on the 30th of year last. ...

It is not assured, however, that because of this fact the liabilities and expenditures will for the year necessarily take up the entire amount of the appropriations, or that any disbursements for objects not entirely proper have been or will be made by you or the officers under your direction.

The usual strictness of accountability and efficiency in the application of these funds, will, of course be required at your hands.

Very Respectfully,
Your Obt. Servent, is
George. W. Manypenny,
Commissioner[59]

The worried tone of this cover letter above, and especially the warnings in the last two sentences of the communiqué, were attached to Supt. Henley's final 1856 Treasury check for reservation operations. This unusual procedure indicates that higher officials in the Indian Affairs Department in Washington, D.C. were worried about California. This kind of an official warning to a state Superintendent of Indian Affairs by Commissioner Manypenny was almost unheard of in the 1850s as is shown by reading most of the outgoing messages of that department in the years 1856-58.

More doubts cropped up in the correspondence of agents and subagents who carried out the Indian Affairs Department's policy at the reservation level. The Office of Indian Affairs had sent out special investigators, old hands like

---

59. Letter of Indian Affairs Commissioner George W. Manypenny to California Superintendent of Indian Affairs Thomas J. Henley, Aug. 2, 1856, Letter #10-29 (1853-57), July 31-Dec. 31, 1856, Roll #55, "Indian Office Letter Box," George W. Manypenny, from the Records of the Office of Indian Affairs, Letters Sent file at National Archives, Pacific Sierra Region, 1000 Commodore Sloat Dr., San Bruno, CA. In examining the large output of messages from the commissioner to the many superintendents all over the United States in 1856 to 1858, this message was the only one to include such an elaborate note of caution. Obviously, the Office of Indian Affairs had already heard a lot about Henley's misdeeds. Few federal officials at the superintendent level were ever dismissed from office.

Special Agent Goddard Bailey, to California's reservations and farms to count Native Americans in order to help the department fairly allocate future funds and to keep tabs on the job performances of its agents and subagents.

In the fall of 1858, the Treasury Department in Washington sent "Special Agent" John (or "J.") Ross Browne out to California. He went to Round Valley Reservation during the fall of 1858 in order to try to determine the actual number of Indians there. Agent Browne's report to Washington is but one more example among many in the records showing a good deal of wishful thinking on the part of the reservation and Office of Indian Affairs officials.

In his lengthy September 1858 letter from San Francisco to the Commissioner of Indian Affairs Charles E. Mix, Special Agent of the Treasury Department J. Ross Browne was not very optimistic,

> ...At Nome Cult, a few miserable Indians were brought in from Eden Valley, twelve miles distant; but the main body there are those who have always frequented and occupied Nome Cult valley [Round Valley]. The Indians of Eel river valley [probably Wailaki or other local tribes], and between Nome Cult and the Cape [Cape Mendocino] are as wild and hostile as they have ever been.

> I reiterate the opinion that no practical good has resulted so far from the reservations-not because the system of colonizing and subsisting the Indians by their own labors is impracticable, but because it has not been properly tested....[60]

Browne's report also reveals there were suspicious activities and attempts by reservation employees and others to hide the truth. When Browne asked reservation employees about the small number of Indians mustered for a count, he was told most Indians were in the hills gathering acorns. The same story was repeated so he was not ever able to get an accurate count of Native Americans living on reservations.[61]

Similar situations may also have existed at various other California reservations at this time. Browne found a number of other serious cases of outright fraud involving the theft or misuse of the government's money at Nome Cult Farm. In a lengthy and detailed report to Commissioner of Indian Affairs Mix in September 1858, Special Agent Browne praised Agent Storms before he cataloged a variety of mistakes, thefts, and irregularities, including forged vouchers:

---

60. Report of Special Agent J. (or John) Ross Browne to Secretary of the Interior, September 4, 1858. CAL Letterbox, Bureau of Indian Affairs, National Archives, quoted in footnote #10, p. 90 in "The History of Round Valley Indian Reservation," William Marion Hammond, unpublished MA thesis, U.S. History, Jan. 5, 1972, California State University, Sacramento, CA.
61. Ibid., Browne to Sec. of the Interior, September 4, 1858, CAL Letterbox

The crops at Nome Cult look thriving. Considering the means furnished the amount of work done is creditable to Mr. Storms and his assistants. I have seen no better crops in any part of California. Extensive fences have been put up, and wheat and corn produced this season in great abundance. ...

The vouchers of the employees at Nome Cult, whose accounts are rendered to this Agency, are signed in blank. The amounts are afterwards filled up. Such a practice is reprehensible and liable to abuse.[62]

When Nome Cult vouchers arrived in San Francisco, Henley could fill in any amount he needed to use for a number of private family projects. Supt. Henley, and almost certainly other reservation employees like Agents Stevenson and Storms as well, continued to use the voucher system to enrich themselves at the government's expense. Superintendent Henley was seizing the moment to take advantage of his power and of the Office's loose chain of command to steal and misuse federal money.

There was also the issue of Henley's increased stake in San Francisco real estate, which Browne's report listed as worth about $24,000 at this time. Henley's nephews and sons also had a large ranch in the southern third of Round Valley, where he "invested" some more of the federal government's funds that were supposed to go towards helping the Native Americans.

A third misuse of federal funds, documented thoroughly by Browne in the same report to Washington, was a project of transporting what Browne called "Blooded Cattle," pure-bred New York beef, by ship to the Isthmus of Panama, and across land in droves or possibly by wagon. Reaching the Pacific Ocean the cattle were loaded back on board merchant ships, up the west coast to San Francisco, from where they were to eventually be brought north to Round Valley. The purpose of this project was to improve the quality of California cattle. Despite the risk of contracting malaria or typhoid, crossing the Isthmus of Panama was the fastest route taken by many Euro-Americans to reach California.

In addition to these charges, Browne's report also gives us an indication of Agent Storms's version of the valley's history. Quoting once again from Browne's report:

---

62. This and subsequent quotes from Spec. Agt. Browne's report are from "Special Report of Special Agent J. Ross Browne in relation to Indian Affairs in California," to Commissioner Hon. Charles E. Mix, Sept. 4, 1858, San Francisco, Microcopy No. 234, Letters received by the Office of Indian Affairs 1824–81, *California Superintendency*, 1849–1880, *1880*, National Archives and Records Service, General Services Administration, 1958, pp. 5–8, "1094–7," at Sierra Records of National Archives, 1000 Commodore Blvd., San Bruno, CA.

"Nome Cult" [italics in original]

The circumstances attending the occupation and settlement of this valley, are fully set forth in the testimony of S. P. Storms. It appears ["from this," the two words are written and then lined out by the writer] that he was directed to take possession of the valley, which he did. There were no white settlers there; a few hunters came in soon after.

Regarding the white settlers, Browne was definitely mistaken. Either those he talked to had lied or perhaps he was a bit too easily impressed by the reservation's structures. Special Agent Browne tried to confirm the essential facts from the Indian Affairs Department's perspective about their view, which was Storms' view also, that the reservation had preceded any white settlers. However, there is evidence that at least four different parties, including Woodman, Lawson, Bourne, and Arthur, had started farms or ranches there before June 1856. Probably most had not yet made official land claims with the government. Later on in Round Valley's history whoever could present a valid claim to have been there first would be of critical importance as far as keeping a land claim in Round Valley.

Special Agent Browne also pointed out irregularities in the branding of cattle in the valley:

But this was not all:

I made a careful examination of a considerable number of this stock [that is, Nome Cult Farm cattle]. It is principally branded "W-" that being the Wilsey brand. [The Wilsey brothers were among the first settlers in Round Valley.] Some have the Point Reyes brand "C," but many are without brands. I noticed at least three cattle branded over the Spanish brand with the letter "W-" one of which was thus:

VC

The laws of California are very explicit about branding, and it is not usual to put one brand on top of another.

Here was yet another incidence of the California Office of Indian Affairs hanky-panky. Someone, possibly James Wilsey or some unknown reservation employee, changed the brands of government cattle. It is also possible that cattle from Point Reyes were stolen and driven north with Spanish brands. For example, State Sen. Jasper O'Farrell's estate in western Sonoma County in present-day Freestone contained similar so-called "Mexican cattle." These were hardy animals with tough meat. The probable goal of transporting cattle all the way across the nation from New York to Round Valley was to bring to market cattle that produced meat that was easier to chew than the so-called "Mexican cattle," the kind common in California.

All of these incidents of fraud were breaches of the law for which most ordinary citizens would be prosecuted and fined or even sent to prison if convicted. Yet it is one of the strangest anomalies of this period of California history that even when obviously guilty of serious crimes, many escaped the law. Probably some pioneers were simply considered by society to be above it. This was especially the case if they also happened to be federal or state officials.

Special Agent J. Ross Browne continued:

> The cattle in the valley range miscellaneously together. None of the government cattle are branded with the letters U.S. The testimony of John W. Burgess [the physician at Nome Cult Farm] shows the impolicy of this indiscriminate mixture of stock, and the attempts made to justify it.

Here in 1858 the Treasury Department's special agent noted that the identity of the true owners of Round Valley cattle was uncertain. This is vital to understanding what came later. The supposed theft, killing and consumption of Euro-American cattle by the local Native Americans was the only real grievance and charge that could consistently be made against the Native Americans. If Browne's observations were valid then we must conclude that by the end of 1858, most Office of Indian Affairs authorities including Subagent Storms were purposely ignoring some very egregious incidences of fraud and abuse of Native Americans.

Another quote from Special Agent Browne's report that followed immediately after his discussion of the age of the Spanish cattle is particularly relevant.

> Bowen testifies that Thomas Henley [Thomas Henley, Jr., Supt. Henley's son] told him his father was interested in 300 head of horses about to be brought up to Eden Valley by Judge Hastings. Storms testifies that he was requested by Mr. Henley to purchase the claim of Brizentine for the purpose of ranching these horses, and did purchase it in accordance with the instructions; that he looked to Mr. Henley for reimbursement....

It bears repeating: Agent S.P. Storms acted as a real estate agent, seeing that Supt. Henley got the title to a settler's (Brizentine's) property when Henley needed it. Timing was, and still is, a critical factor in land acquisition.

Superintendent Henley recognized that this Judge Hastings was wealthy, shrewd and, like him, cold and heartless when pursuing his own ends. What is also unique is that in this crass game involving the Office of Indian Affairs, the federal government and its Native American wards, Judge Serranus C. Hastings, a person whom none of the settlers knew, would eventually become the greatest bonanza king of this game of building private ranching empires.

THE CONFLICT CONVERGES

Who was this new player? It was not any of the Old West's famous outlaws, not the nefarious Black Bart, Jesse James, Joaquin Marietta, Wild Bill Hickok, or Doc Holliday. Nor was it any of the august leaders of the Bear Flag Revolt, even a *Californio* like Gen. Mariano G. Vallejo or John A. Sutter. It was a relative non-entity, someone who would use his own connections, pluck, cunning, and business acumen to build his own family's fortune, like the Big Four of Central Pacific Railroad fame. It was none other than the quiet and scholarly former Iowa Supreme Court Justice, Judge Serranus C. Hastings.

Hastings was born in New York State. At the age of twenty he moved to Lawrenceville, Indiana. There he studied law. Soon after that he moved to the Black Hawk Purchase territory of Iowa where he graduated from law school and began a successful law practice.

After practicing law for a time, Hastings became active in politics. When Iowa became a separate territory, Counselor Hastings was elected and served in the first territorial legislature.[63] In 1846 he went to Washington as Iowa's first congressperson. Always moving upward in Democratic Party ranks, at the end of his Congressional term Hastings was appointed the first chief justice of the Iowa Supreme Court. With news of the gold rush in 1849, he resigned from the Iowa Supreme Court and moved to California.

Hastings realized the potential for gain in Eden Valley's lush grasslands, when and if they could be cleared of its Native American population. First he dreamed of a large horse and cattle ranch there. The Native Americans, predominantly Yuki, in this small Mendocino County valley just a few miles south of Round Valley, were not as peaceful as the Pomos usually were, or as outwardly depressed as some of the other more primitive tribes of Northern California.

---

63. See the background information on Judge S.C. Hastings, Lynwood Carranco and Estle Beard, *Genocide and Vendetta*, Chapter 5, Footnote 1, 363–364. These authors, in turn, credit Allen Johnson and Dumas Malone, Editors, *The Dictionary of American Biography*, (New York: Scribner's and Sons, 1960, 387 for the facts about Judge Hastings' earlier Midwestern career as a student, successful lawyer, and politician.

Just ten miles north of Round Valley was another tribe, the Wailaki, who were not as easy to subdue or drive from their lands as some other tribes had been. Already a number of the Wailaki leaders possessed firearms. Sometimes Native Americans overcame individual Euro-American travelers out on trails and stole their weapons from them. Although most Native Americans probably could not aim and shoot as well as most Euro-American settlers and hunters, having a weapon became a status symbol. If the Native Americans were observed in the mountains to have firearms they were immediately suspects as stock killers, thieves, or at the very least, "wild Indians."

After a few incidents in which some stock was actually taken by the Wailakis or by other local tribes, Judge Hastings and Supt. Henley began hatching a new plot to remove Native Americans from their homelands and destroy the power of the indigenous residents of Eden Valley. They raised California militia raiding parties in Humboldt and Trinity Counties as well as in Mendocino County (see Chapter 5).

A necessary first step in the plan was to hold large, heated public meetings where settlers' emotions could be stirred up in racial hatred against the Indians. At each meeting some gross, even fabricated charge would be made: innocent white travelers on remote trails were being murdered by bands of "wild" Indians, or an important official's residence was burned down, or a valuable stallion was killed for spite by a local tribe of Native Americans. In California during the 1850s, such acts were not considered minor crimes in the context of frontier claims and passions. The notoriety surrounding these accusations could then be used to fuel intense hatreds and prejudices of the white populace, inciting people to make war on any tribe that stood in the way. And the best part of the scheme was that no one could be entirely sure of what had actually happened. Consciously or not, Judge Hastings was not the only one who resorted to such methods.

Chapter 4. Gen. Kibbe's "Expedition" or, the War with the Win-toons 1858–1859

The "War with the Win-toons"

While many settlers' complaints to Governor Weller and to Senators Gwin and Broderick originated in the Red Bluff area (in Tehama and Colusa Counties), a greater number of extant records from this conflict originated farther northwest. They came from small communities like Eureka and Union in Klamath, the Hoopa Valley and in Humboldt County.[64] This heavily wooded region where the annual rainfall is high was the location of much of the fighting of this almost forgotten frontier war. There was a campaign between two Euro-American militia units, Kibbe's Guard and the Trinity Rangers, and Native Americans during 1858 and 1859. This so-called war, which would only be termed a campaign today, perhaps a few battles by modern combat standards, is known as either Gen. Kibbe's War or the War with the Win-toons (or "Win-tuns," the general name for the largest tribe in Trinity County).

---

64. Like many of the towns on Humboldt Bay such as Eureka, Humboldt City, Bucksport and Trinidad, Union began during the spring of 1850 in response to a mining boom. Some of these towns were founded by private companies. The Union Company founded "Uniontown." The name was changed twice; first to Union and later to Arcata. See Owen Cochran Coy's *GOLD DAYS*, San Francisco: Powell Publishing Co., 1929, 229-232. Today there are two completely different communities with the name Union in California. The largest is Union City, a city of nearly 50,000 located near Hayward, between Oakland and San Jose. The other community is Union Hill, a town of about 400 near Grass Valley in the gold country.

On a morning in May 1859, approximately eighty California militiamen mustered out of the California militia's Trinity Rangers. There had been only one Euro-American man from this unit killed. He died when his musket misfired. Most of these men had not participated in any actions against Native Americans since December 1858. For record keeping purposes the Trinity Rangers had remained officially active during the first half of 1859. Most of the skirmishes and attacks on Indian camps thus far had occurred in November and December 1858 along the Trinity Trail, then a relatively newly-blazed route between Weaverville, sixty miles north and east of Round Valley, and Eureka, the primary seaport on Humboldt Bay.

How had this campaign started? For years, mountain men and settlers had been prepared for random violence and occasional killings of white settlers in California and the West. Over seven years before this in the Yosemite area in late March 1851 the Mariposa Battalion began its campaign to defeat the Yosemite tribe led by Chief Tenaya. The Euro-American militia successfully forced the local Naïve Americans to sign one of the eighteen unratified treaties in May 1851.

In 1858, an organized Native American military effort seemed to be under way in northwestern California. The Native American band that caused the Euro-Americans to volunteer and form militia units was primarily composed of members of three northwestern California tribes: the Hoopas, with about fifty warriors, the Redwood and Pit (or 'Pitt') River tribes, who contributed another three hundred warriors. This significant armed Indian force seemed to be a greater threat to settler safety and to commerce along the Trinity Trail than had normal up to that time.

Apparently the first incident that caused the formation of vigilante groups of Euro-Americans to hold meetings and write urgent appeals to the state government was the shooting deaths of two whites out on the Trinity Trail between Weaverville and Eureka. This came after a number of other incidents during 1858. According to historian Anthony Jennings Bledsoe in his *Indian Wars of the Northwest: A California Sketch* (1885), two men named "Granger and Cook" were killed by Indians in February 1858.[65] This event followed other random alleged cases of robbery and assault by Native American bands along roads or trails in the Eureka area.[66]

---

65. Anthony J. Bledsoe, *Indian Wars of the Northwest: A California Sketch* (San Francisco: Bacon, 1885, reprint Oakland, CA: Biobooks, 1956), 124.

Bledsoe describes another shooting of a white settler that took place on June 23, 1858.

> Two packers, Henry Allen and Wm. E. Ross, accompanied by two Indian boys, were going up to the Trinity [Lake?] with their train. As they were descending Grouse Creek Hill, not expecting danger, Ross was shot from an ambush where a party of Indians were lying. He was shot three times. He fell from his mule, and when Allen reached him he was unable to stand on his feet.... [67]

Realizing one of the whites was wounded and possibly dying, one of the two Native American so-called "boys" walked as fast as he could to Eureka. News of this apparently unprovoked attack brought the Euro-American public in both the towns of Union and Eureka and throughout the Hoopa Valley to a high fever of anti–Native American frenzy. Trinity and Humboldt Counties were incensed over the shooting of Ross coming as it had after the other shootings of Granger and Cook by Native Americans.

Readers can readily sense this urgency felt by the so-called "Yreka and Union Committees" in parts of their September 30, 1858, petition to Governor John B. Weller:

> The undersigned, Committees appointed at public meetings of the citizens of the Towns of Union and Yreka [sic], Humboldt County, on the sixteenth day of September, instant, to act on their behalf in relations to the existing Indian difficulties, have conferred with Capt. D. H. Snyder, representing the people of Hoopa Valley, Klamath County, in reference to their peculiar and exposed condition, and concur in the opinion expressed by him, that there is an urgent necessity for the establishment of a permanent military-post at that point, pending the prosecution of active hostilities at other points, until the removal of the existing Indian population from that place and the adjacent County to the Klamath Reservation, for the following reasons:...
>
> *Second*—Hoopa Valley is situated directly upon the great Northern trails leading from Union and Trinidad, to the Lower Trinity, Klamath, and Salmon Rivers, and the presence of a considerable body of Indians at that point and vicinity *at all times*, and especially in times like the present, must expose the lives and property of those engaged in the carrying trade between those places, to their assaults and depredations. Necessity, therefore, imperatively calls for their removal to a more remote

---

66. A more recent incident may put these alleged attacks in perspective. In the late fall, 2000 a botanist from the Bay Area, Paul Pierson, was lost when walking a few hundred yards in front of a party of hikers and scientists in the Sinkyone Wilderness. Now, as was the case in 1858 to 1863, a person can become separated from his or her party in many areas of the dense forests of Northern California. Disappearances of persons traveling on trails were a frequent cause of racial discord both in the Round Valley and throughout much of Northern California.
67. Bledsoe, *Indian Wars*, op.cit, 123–125.

locality, and, in the meantime, and until that can be effected, for the presence of a sufficient restraining force at that point.

Walter Van Dyke	H. W. Havens
C. S. Ricks	J. O. Craig
A. D. Sevier	E. L. Wallace
Daniel Pickard	James A. Boutell

Eureka Committee.Union Committee.
UNION, September 30, 1858.[68]

A Buchanan Democrat, Gov. John B. Weller was the fifth governor of California for one term, during 1858 and 1859. A hardworking individual, he was born in a small town in southern Ohio. He attended Miami College (now University) but withdrew to study law. He was a student of the future President Millard Fillmore. Weller was a Democratic Ohio Congressman from 1839 to 1844 before he resigned from politics. Weller took a active part in raising volunteers to fight the Mexican War. After immigrating to California, Weller's first office here was as a one-term senator from California, in 1852–1857. Weller happened to be California's governor during the most violent phase of the lengthy struggle of white settlers with California's Native American peoples throughout northern California. It is very unfortunate that many of Weller's personal state papers were not preserved, except for a very small four-page file of personal letters at Bancroft Library at Berkeley.

Weller was a man of few words. His personal philosophy, tersely expressed in a short, one sentence note to a friend, summarized a common pioneer sentiment of his time:

> Human life is too short to expend much of it in [illegible; "moralizing"?] over the Past or indulging in gloomy forebodings as to the future.[69]

---

68. Joint Petition of the Eureka and Union Committees to Gov. John B. Weller, Sept. 30, 1858, *Senate Journal, 10th Session, 1859,* 682 and 683.

69. See Gov. Weller's note on plain paper in longhand, signed "John B. Weller," May 5, 1854, John B. Weller Papers in T.W. Norris Collection at Bancroft Library, University of California, Berkeley, Berkeley, CA. Ms. Carolyn Feroben helped through the Internet in locating the whereabouts of the fifth California Governor's (John B. Weller) personal papers including his speeches in Congress in 1852 at Bancroft Library.

Gov. Weller's experience as a Mexican War officer had taught him that staff-level delays during combat were often fatally dangerous. Upon receiving the above petition from the Eureka and Union Committees, Governor Weller ordered California's adjutant general and quartermaster, William C. Kibbe, to go up from Sacramento to Weaverville to check out the facts about Native American attacks on Euro-American travelers and settlers:

[Special Order, No. 2.]
State of California, Executive Department
Sacramento, September 28, 1858.

SIR—I place in your hands an order, directing Brigadier-General Dosh, of the Second Brigade, Sixth Division, to call out, and muster into the service of the State, a company of eighty men, to clear the road between Weaverville and Humboldt Bay, of the Indians who have committed, and are still committing outrages upon our citizens. Many murders and robberies have been perpetuated, and I have received satisfactory evidence that travel over this important trail is still exceedingly dangerous....

In issuing rations, etc., you will be governed by the regulations of the United States, as nearly as may be compatible with the character of the service.... The women and children must be spared, and there must be no indiscriminate slaughter of the Indians. Humanity demands that no more blood should be shed than is indispensable to open the trail, and render travel upon it secure and uninterrupted in the future. You will take care that this order is read to the company which may be mustered into service.

Communicate with the officer in command of the Federal forces at Humboldt Bay, and endeavor to obtain his co-operation in subduing these Indians, and keep me duly advised of all your movements.

Very respectfully,
Your obedient servant,
JOHN B. WELLER.[70]

According to the scanty militia records that now exist, Brig. Gen. William C. Kibbe traveled north up to Weaverville. After he tried but failed to find out any reliable information from the local residents, Gen. Kibbe met an ex-Texas ranger who could guide him. General Kibbe went with Isaac B. Messic, whom Kibbe described as "an old and experienced mountaineer, to the country inhabited by the hostile Indians, in order to "satisfy himself fully as to number of savages."[71] The Native Americans along the Klamath River were from the Mad River and Redwood Creek tribes.

70. Special order No. 2, Gov. Weller to Brig.-General W.W. Kibbe, Adjutant and Quartermaster-General of California, Sept. 28, 1858, *Senate Journal*, 10th Session, 1859, p. 683, Bancroft Library, University of California, Berkeley, CA.

Next Brig. Gen. Kibbe and Captain Messic organized the militia (as mentioned previously above, the two units which saw most active duty were General Kibbe's Guard and the Trinity Rangers) whose members included Frank Asbill, one of the "discoverers" of Round Valley. Asbill with his close friend Jim Neafus are among a volunteer group of men who joined the Trinity Rangers in the Big Bar and Weaverville area. After Gen. Kibbe's War Asbill decided to live in Round Valley. The Trinity Rangers served in the Trinity and Humboldt County campaigns in 1858.[72]

One report, on file at the California Military Museum in Sacramento, reported on the successful conclusion to the Hoopa Valley campaign (or Gen. Kibbe's War). Based on records that were in the original California Archives up until 1940, this report states that,

> An Act was passed by the Legislature and approved by the Governor, on April 16, 1859, for payment of expenses incurred in the suppression of the Indian hostilities in that section of the State. This Act illustrates the manner in which the State appropriated money for payment to various districts, for their efforts in endeavoring to subdue the hostiles and maintain peaceful relation with the Indians.

> THE ACT

> "Section 1. The sum of fifty-two thousand five hundred and twenty-seven dollars and eighty-six cents ($52,527.86) is hereby appropriated, out of any money in the General Fund not otherwise appropriated, for the payment of the indebtedness incurred by the expedition against the Indians in the Counties of Humboldt and Klamath, during the year A.D. eighteen hundred and fifty-eight and eighteen hundred and fifty-nine."[73]

---

71. According to Carranco and Beard in *Genocide and Vendetta:* "Isaac G. Messec was born in Macon, Georgia, in 1823 but was raised in Texas, where he became a Texas Ranger." After the end of the Mendocino War he eventually became storekeeper of the San Francisco Mint, see Carranco and Beard, *Genocide and Vendetta,* footnote #58, 352–353.

72. See Carranco and Beard, *Genocide and Vendetta,* 174. The same information is covered in a summary on the "Kibbe Guard," which reported that the militia was mustered into duty on September 27, 1858, at Weaverville, CA. According to this historical summary, the unit served for three months. It was commanded by Captain Henry Hart. Second-in-command was First Lt., John B. May. See the volume entitled *National Guard of California,* Works Progress Administration, 1940,"Kibbe Guard, Sixth Division, Second Brigade, Reference Dead Letter Office File, Row 3, File 8, Location: Weaverville, Trinity County," Units 1–100, Volume 1, Unit #79, 231–232 located at The California Military History Museum, basement, 1119 Second St., Sacramento, CA.

73. As quoted in the description of the Trinity Rangers, *The National Guard of California,* 1940, Units 1–100, Vol. 1, 239–240, on file at the California Military Museum, basement, 1119 Second St., Sacramento, CA.

Despite the conclusion to the 1858 "Indian hostilities," as the campaign was termed by Gen. Kibbe himself, in reality the greater Northern California conflict between the Euro-Americans and Native Americans was far from being over. The very next year brought new claims of attacks on whites by Native Americans. By May of 1859, a new slew of petitions and personal appeals to the governor calling for militia help flooded into the executive office at Sacramento.

According to the correspondence to Gov. Weller found in Gen. Kibbe's Report on the following year's (1859) campaign, six letters from the Tehama region (three from Red Bluff, May 15, May 16, and May 27, one from Paynes Creek, May 9, and two from Tehama and Tehama County, both on May 15) described attacks upon livestock, whites, or white residences. The most serious of these 1858 Indian attacks was an arson fire that consumed a Red Bluff house built by former agent in charge at Nome Lackee Reservation, Edward A. Stevenson, on May 11, 1858. It could have been an act of retaliation for Agent Stevenson's tenure at Nome Lackee, during which there were reports of Native Americans becoming addicted to gambling and alcohol.

One hundred and seven Tehama County Euro-American residents signed an urgent message to Gov. Weller on May 15, 1859. It must have been almost impossible for Gov. Weller to ignore this plaintive appeal, which began,

> SIR—The undersigned, citizens of the county of Tehama, would most respectfully represent to your honor, that the Indians, living in the mountains, on our eastern border, have been for many months committing depredations on the white inhabitants of the valleys, by driving off and killing stock of all kinds, and within the last few days have commenced a more fearful and calamitous warfare—that of firing and burning houses at the still hours of night, while the inhabitants are asleep.
>
> We cite two instances. On the night of the eleventh instant, the dwelling of Col. E. A. Stevenson was fired by an Indian, and burned, causing the death of two women and four children, and probably that of one man; and on the night of the fourteenth instant, another house was fired and burned—the inmates previously escaping. We have heard of three other families whose domiciles have been disturbed at night by Indians within the last week; but the guard dogs have kept them at bay and given the alarm. We have unmistakable evidence that it is the work of Indians.
>
> Now, therefore, we do most earnestly pray that you take immediate steps to send us relief and protection, and your petitioners will ever pray; etc.
>
> TEHAMA, May 15th, 1859,...[74]

---

74. See Citizens' of Red Bluff Letter to Governor Weller, May 14, 1859, in the "Appendix," *General Kibbe's Report*, under "Correspondence, Senate Journal" on file at Bancroft Library, University of California, Berkeley, California.

Only a stone could remain idle while such inflammatory reports of the murders, especially the killings of white women and children, repeatedly arrived in the California governor's office. It is not possible at this distance to know for certain how many of the settlers' petitions were factual and how many were merely hysterical exaggerations. Gov. Weller acted in haste without taking time to verify the settlers' tales before ordering the use of force to dislodge the Native Americans from their homeland. As in the case of the 1858 Hoopa Valley campaign, Gov. Weller was not slow in dispatching the campaign-tested and trusty Gen. Kibbe to the scene.

An early Mendocino County pioneer, Elijah R. Potter, served with this militia. The following quotes were from his "Partial Transcript of Historical Events of Round Valley," undated (possibly about 1915–1920). This concise autobiography was found at Held-Poage Library in Ukiah.

> By 1859 the Indians in the Pitt River country became very bad; killing people at every favorable opportunity. In fact, they came five miles of Red Bluff to commit their depredations. The Governor, John B. Weller at that time, called for volunteers to go and punish them. Adjutant Gen. Wm. C. Kibbe came up to Red Bluff and organized a company of 50 men, the writer became a member. We elected our own officers. Two noted men contested for the office of Captain. One was Wm. Byrnes, who was an old Texas Ranger and noted Indian fighter; and also had the distinction of being the man who killed Joaquin Marietta (This is just one more notch in the Marietta legend). The other was John P. Jones an early day Weaverville resident, who was afterwards in the U.S. Senate from the state of Nevada. Byrnes won by three votes. I wanted to see Jones elected as I had been in an Indian fight with Byrnes in El Dorado County in 1851, and knew he was not cautions enough to be an Indian fighter. I will say nothing further on this expedition except to say that we were gone four months and that we brought away more than 1500 Indians, about half of whom were Concows and Kimshews, who were really all of the same tribe, but from different localities. The others were Pitt River and Hat Creek, more than half of whom had never seen a white man. The Concows were taken through by way of Round Valley, Eden Valley and Sherwood, there being no direct trail to the coast to Fort Bragg, which was then the Mendocino Reservation.[75]

In drafting Gen. Kibbe's orders, Gov. Weller also asked Gen. Kibbe to deliver a commission as captain to Round Valley resident Dryden Laycock, in response to petitions from that area. Laycock declined the chance to command a militia unit because he suspected he would not ever get paid. Another Round Valley area resident, Walter S. Jarboe, eventually accepted this commission as

---

75. Elijah Renshaw Potter, "Partial Transcript of Historical Events," copy by K.C. Dennis, no date (probably ca.1920), Estle Beard File, Held-Poage Historical Research Library, 603 W. Perkins St., Ukiah, CA.

Captain of the Eel River Rangers, the militia unit of the Round Valley-Mendo-cino County area (see Chapter 5).

Ascertaining the truth, as to where so-called "hostile Indians" actually were, was no simple task. The following note from a Sacramento Valley militia leader, Captain F. F. Flint, to Gen. Kibbe, reflects this confusion.

> CAMP CASS, near Red Bluff, California
> July 12, 1859
>
> SIR—
>
> I am this moment in receipt of your communication of the eleventh instant, and, in reply to your inquiries, I have to state that I have no reliable means of judging the number of hostile Indians in the vicinity. The country between Battle and Mill Creeks, and as far back as Antelope Hills, has been thoroughly examined by various detachments of my company, and, thus far, neither Indians nor signs have been met with. The settlers estimate the number at from thirty to one thousand.
>
> My company is about sixty strong, and I consider it and the orders I have received, sufficient to check the incursions of an Indians in this vicinity.
>
> I am, Sir,
> Your Obedient Servant,
> F.F. Flint[76]

This was the last communication among those on file at Bancroft Library from the militia involved in Gen. Kibbe's "Expedition" of 1858–1859 (or the Hoopa Valley Campaign of 1859). Captain Flint's unit took part in central and northeastern California battles. He was nowhere near Hoopa Valley. From this point on, the various militia units took swift, apparently victorious actions of their own against the Northern California Native Americans.

In the next message from Gen. Kibbe to the Governor Weller,[15] the conflict seems to have progressed rapidly toward an almost complete militia victory. In his summary of the campaign, a seventeen-page, handwritten report dated January 16, 1860, Kibbe outlines the conclusion of the "Gen. Kibbe's War."

> Suffice to say, that the enemy was routed from every position, whether taken to elude their pursuers or for the purpose of defense, and were finally compelled unconditionally to surrender. Out of the whole number of Indians fought, about two hundred warriors were killed and twelve hundred taken prisoner. No children were killed and but one woman during the whole campaign.[77]

---

76. Captain F.F. Flint to Gen. Kibbe, July 12, 1859, Report of the Expedition Against the Indians in the Northern Part of This State, "Correspondence," p. 28, Bancroft Library, University of California, Berkeley, CA.

Gen. Kibbe's final report makes it clear that the California militia started out using the same method of attacking rancherias in the early dawn as that would be adopted by Jarboe's Eel River Rangers.

The imbalances of this so-called "Hoopa Valley and Trinity County Campaign," as well as the simultaneously fought Mendocino War, are crystal clear today. Muskets were issued to individuals in the California militia throughout the 1850s. These weapons had to be fired, cleaned, then reloaded with shot, which was rammed down the barrel. Next, powder was added and tapped close to a trigger and flint. After the hammer was pulled back or cocked, the weapon could be held up, and finally re-aimed for a second shot. Clearly, this took some time, and as I am reminded by Mr. Floyd Barney of Round Valley, this was one reason the Native Americans sometimes had the upper hand in close combat. They each usually carried at least two hundred arrows and could more easily re-aim and shoot.

At longer range, muskets were the far superior weapon when compared to the bows and arrows of the Native Americans. The new availability of more advanced rifles, such as the Hawkens, Sharps, or the St. Louis mountain rifles gave the Euro-American militia forces a distinct military advantage. All of these guns had greatly improved loading systems, more accurate sights, larger bores, and far more accuracy at long range than either a musket or the old Kentucky long rifle, which was too small in caliber for grizzly bears, buffalo, or elk. Perhaps the most favored weapon of the militia and the settlers was the so-called St. Louis rifle, made from 1820 to 1847. This .50-caliber rifle, made mainly in St. Louis, had a 36-inch octagon-shaped barrel and a plain maple stock.[78]

Beginning in about 1820 American armories had begun mass producing percussion cartridge rifles that were big improvements. By the 1850s older flint lock muskets were rare among the settlers and militiamen.

Still it is not entirely clear just how many Euro-Americans used these more accurate weapons. It may be that most, like the Asbill brothers in 1855, made do with older smooth-bore muskets which too often misfired, exploded, or were simply inefficient and inaccurate.[79] In any case, it is clear that the technological

---

77. This message was initially written to Governor Weller, yet by the time it was formally presented, the new administration of Weller's eventual successor, Governor John G. Downey, had already begun.

78. See Martin Rywell, *Fell's Collector's Guide to American Antique Firearms* (New York: Frederick Fell, Inc., 1963), 61. Mr. Rywell concluded his discussion of the St. Louis rifle: "It was designed for the needs of the trapper of the Far West."

superiority of the white militia was pitted against indigenous people armed with fewer, inferior rifles, bows and arrows, slingshots, or knives. Most of the Native American weapons could only be used at close range.

The Euro-Americans also held a great advantage by possessing centralized control and command. Other factors of their success included better communications, the telegraph, and an almost unlimited amount of munitions and ammunition, which many of the Native Americans lacked. A final Euro-American advantage, mentioned by Gen. Kibbe in his final report, was the cooperation of local predominantly Caucasian settlers. [80]

Only in close combat and in their more detailed knowledge of local terrain did California Native Americans hold a short-lived advantage. But even this was countered by the California militia's use of hunters, mountain men, or fur traders as guides. Between the years 1820 and 1858, these men and women had accumulated backwoods knowledge of trails, mountain ranges, weather conditions, and locations of wells and streams that in some cases was equal to the knowledge of the Native Americans. In 1858–1859, the Native American warrior bands had little chance of holding their ground, much less of attaining victory against the California militia.

---

79. See also Carranco and Beard, *Genocide and Vendetta*, 169–170 for a brief discussion of how Pierce Asbill bought a two-barrel Kingsley mountain rifle from George Kingsley, who employed L.C. Kersey, gunsmith, at his Red Bluff gun shop in 1855.

Of interest in this discussion may be the instructions given to immigrants about what to include on their journey West. The following list of recommended items was suggested by the Butterfield Company, a stage line connecting the eastern cities of Memphis Tennessee or St. Louis Missouri with San Francisco in 1859–1860:

> "One Sharps rifle and a hundred cartridges; a Colt's navy revolver and two pounds of balls; a knife and sheath; a pair of thick boots and woolen pants; a half dozen pairs of thick cotton socks; six undershirts; three woolen undershirts; a wide-awake hat; a cheap sack coat, and a soldier's overcoat; one pair of blankets in summer and two in winter; a piece of India rubber cloth, a pair of gauntlets, a small bag of needles, pins, etc.; two pair of thick drawers, three or four towels, and various toilet articles."

The quote above is from Robert Glass Cleland, *History of California: The American Period* (New York: The MacMillan Company, 1923), 145.

80. Report of Quartermaster & Adjutant General William S. Kibbe to Gov. John G. Downey, Jan. 16, 1860, p. 8. GP1:416, California State Archives, 4th Floor, 1020 "O" St., Sacramento, CA. Gen. Kibbe wrote this report as one military man to another: a general reporting on field operations to his commanding officer, the state's governor. The rough copy preserved and still on file at the California Archives is full of editorial hatch marks, with sentences added as afterthoughts. Words and sentences were scratched through and rewritten by the author. Obviously the author was in a hurry having no clerical help at the time.

In his expedition final report, Gen. Kibbe covered the number of enemy dead (two hundred), prisoners, and casualty totals for the Euro-Americans (one wounded, who recovered and could return to duty). He outlined the territory involved. It was vast, almost unknown virgin land, a lush empire that evoked the deepest human feelings of peace and plenty. There was almost all the great inland California valley above Sacramento. It included the foothills of the Sierras on the right and on the other side, first the Coastal Mayacama Range, valleys, and rolling farmlands. There were massive redwood forests and lengthy Pacific beaches from San Francisco with its beautiful Golden Gate outlet of Contra Costa and San Francisco Bays north all the way up to Oregon. All these facts were reported fully in florid prose before he got around to explaining anything about the actual monetary costs of the expedition.

Kibbe's report claimed that the results of the California militia's expedition in Northern California of 1859–1860 would be a permanent peace in this part of California:

> There is reason for gratulation ["congratulations" or possibly "gratification"] when the immediate benefits resulting from a conclusion of this war are considered; and its remoter favorable influences should also be taken into the account. It is a salutary lesson to the tribes, occupying territory contiguous to the scene of action, which they will not be likely soon to forget. It has taught them the certainty of the punishment which must sooner or later overtake them, for their hostile visitations upon the persons and property of the whites; ...[81]

Gen. Kibbe's report expressed a common Euro-American attitude of the time regarding Native Americans: if Native-Americans only could be "punished" sufficiently, somehow they would learn from the experience. Whether on expedition in North America, Asia, Latin America or Africa, the implication was the same: to "chastise," "punish," that is, shoot and kill enough of the "wild natives" or "savages," was the solution to all problems. In the moment of victory all Native American resistance would end. Gen. Kibbe and other leaders firmly believed that their better communications, the bravery of determined militiamen, and the apparently complete routs of the Native Americans in these cam-

---

81. "Report of the Expedition Against the Indians in the Northern Part of This State," Gen. William C. Kibbe to Gov. John G. Downey, p. 10, Jan. 16, 1860. See also "Appendix" and "Correspondence." F870 ISP2 no. 9, Bancroft Library, University of California, Berkeley, CA.

paigns would all work together to force the Native Americans to see things exactly as whites did.

But those who thought this were sadly mistaken. From a modern viewpoint Kibbe's errors are clear. Trying to make policy from 1851 to 1854 through the peaceful tactic of treaty writing had failed. Military force would now be used to subjugate and to relocate the Native Americans onto areas the whites did not want, onto remote places that were then called reservations. If the militia could kill enough Native Americans in a three-and-a-half-month period, all the other tribes would be so impressed that they would all immediately lay down their arms. They would not only surrender but they would become domesticated or "tame Indians." The roles of culture, family upbringing, tradition, and education were not even thought of, much less recognized as having any importance.

Kibbe also briefly told the governor and the California Legislature of his personal hopes for relocation of the Indian prisoners onto reservations. Indeed, even as early as September 1859, as the following report from Gen. Kibbe to Governor Weller indicates, this new problem was raising its ugly head: whom to charge with the transportation costs to relocate so many Native American prisoners?

> Tehama County, Sept. 19, 1859
>
> SIR—I have the honor to report, that the expedition under my charge, is now actively engaged against the Indians, and with tolerable success. We have taken upwards of one hundred and fifty Indians prisoners, and have killed less than ten. I arrived at Red Bluff on the seventeenth to make arrangements for the transportation of one hundred prisoners to the Mendocino Reserve. I shall leave here this evening for headquarters, and expect within ten days, to have a fight with a band of desperadoes, made up of Indians of every tribe within two hundred miles of this place, well-armed with rifles, and determined not to be taken alive. These number about sixty Bucks, and have committed many depredations, in connection with Pitt River and Deer Creek Indians.
>
> Mr. McDuffie, [in mid-1859, the utterly corrupt Thomas J. Henley was replaced by Superintendent James McDuffie] in reply to my note relative to prisoners, responded by saying that these would be received at Nome Lackee or Mendocino, but his department would bear no portion of the expenses of transportation....[82]

Another part of this message from Gen. Kibbe to the governor asked that he be authorized to send the Native Americans to Mendocino Reservation rather than to Nome Lackee. Gen. Kibbe believed that they would be less likely to return to the warpath in Mendocino County than at Nome Lackee, so close to Red Bluff and also to their original land.

Gov. Weller agreed with Gen. Kibbe. Almost all of the Native American prisoners first were sent to the Mendocino Reservation near Fort Bragg. One segment of this group, possibly some Concows and Pit River Indians, went by barge on the Sacramento River from Red Bluff first to Sacramento, then went southwest to San Francisco, and finally embarked by ship to the reservation. On Wednesday morning, Dec. 14, 1859, *San Francisco Herald* readers were informed:

> INDIANS IN SACRAMENTO EN ROUTE.—The steamer *Sam Soule* arrived in Sacramento, says the *Union*, about 2 P.M. Sunday, from Red Bluff, having in tow a barge containing between 400 and 500 Indians—the exact number of which we are not advised—including, however, about two hundred warriors from the Pitt river country—the prisoners taken by the volunteers under command of General Kibbe. They are in charge of Lieutenant Van Shull, *en route* for the Mendocino Reservation, and will leave for the Bay probably to-day, a vessel having been chartered at San Francisco by Gen. Kibbe for their transportation to the reservation....
>
> To remove them as far as possible from temptation, doubtless, they were permitted to build their camp fires on the Washington [West Sacramento] bank of the river, where they are under guard of the Rangers [probably, the Trinity Rangers made up of Trinity County volunteers]. Boats were plying till almost dusk, to and fro, and many visited the camp *via* the bridge. It is consented that they should be removed to the Mendocino Reservation, that being the only one in the State from which they would probably be unable to return to their old haunts. Should the Government afford them sufficient meat and drink, and treat them kindly, no danger may be apprehended from them.[83]

Returning to General Kibbe's final report, he took pains to describe, in as complete a way as he could, how terrible the Native Americans' "depredations" were, and how rugged and rough the area was which the soldiers of his command had had to operate in.

> Their depredations were chiefly confined to the white population ["who occupy a region" is lined out by the writer] of that tract of country extending from

---

82. "Report of the Expedition Against the Indians in the Northern Part of This State," "Correspondence." See the section at the front of this document, by General Wm. (William) C. Kibbe, published Jan. 16, 1860, dated September 19, 1859, p. 26, Bancroft Library, University of California, Berkeley, CA. See also an "Act for Payment of Expenses Incurred in the Suppression of Indian Hostilities, April 16, 1859," original at the State Archives; or a photostatic copy, Adjutant-General's Office, *National Guard of California*, 1940, Volume I, No. 88, "The Kibbe Rangers," p. 241, on file at the California Military Museum, 1119 Second St., Sacramento, CA. Thanks to its curator, Mr. William Davies, and his staff for their aid in locating this valuable WPA Administration historical document.

83. "Indians in Sacramento, En Route," *San Francisco Herald*, December 14, 1859, p. 3, col. 2, on file at the California History Room, newspaper microfilm room, at the rear of the room, 900 "N" St., Suite 200, Sacramento, California.

Butte Creek, on the South, to the head of Pitt River on the north—embracing an extent of more than one hundred miles square, with rugged and lofty mountains, intervening defiles, hidden valleys and secure fastnesses ^ [hatchmark in original] into which they would retreat for security, after having made a sudden and success- ful foray—...

During the last four years, between thirty and forty persons ["have been" lined out in original] were killed by these Indians. They had set fire to, and consumed entire fields of grain and grass, besides pillaging and afterwards burning the houses and cabins of the settlers.[84]

After naming the three officers in charge (Capt. Byrnes, Lt. Bailey, and Lt. Shull) of three thirty-three man detachments that together made up his com- mand, Gen. Kibbe described the modus operandi, which, as noted above, used the cover of darkness, and was similar to the pitiless means used by Captain Jar- boe and others:

These ["different" lined out in original] separate detachments were directed to approach and enter the Indian country at different points. The plan of moving upon and attacking the Rancherias of the Indians at night, I had learned by experience was the best and only one calculated to be attended with happy results notwith- standing the greater hazard of this mode of warfare,...[85]

Next, Gen. Kibbe described how the southern part of the northwestern California inland area of operations, which also included some parts of Mendo- cino and Tehama Counties, was cleared of Native American combatants.

II. As fast as a particular locality was cleared of Indians, a detachment was left for a limited period ["time" lined out in original], instructed to scout continually, with the view of discovering and preventing an attempt at return. In every instance, the object designed by this precautionary measure, was effectively secured. From time to time small parties of Indians were captured, until the southern portion of the country operated in, contained not a warrior to offer resistance. The intermedi- ate section was next visited,...[86]

This was a huge area. It included nearly the entire northern half of the state. Just as one might expect from any savvy staff officer in a report to his supe- riors, there is not a single word of criticism for anyone involved in the operation. Gen. Kibbe's report included mention of attempting to communicate to Native American bands in the field through an interpreter an offer of terms of surrender

---

84. General Kibbe's Report or the "Report of the Expedition against the Indians in the Northern Part of This State," Office of the Quartermaster and Adjutant General, Sacramento, Cal., January 16, 1860, To His Excellency John G. Downey, Governor of California, on file at the California State Library, 900 "N" St., Suite 200, Sacramento, CA and at Bancroft Library, University of California, Berkeley, CA.

85. *Ibid.,* 4–5.

86. *Ibid.,* 5–6.

before any action took place. Kibbe was careful to note that all the Native Americans refused to lay down their weapons and that they were determined to fight with his troops. In each area his units operated in, he claimed, only then did the militia commander issue an order to commence firing.

On page eight of this long, somewhat tedious report, Gen. Kibbe comes to the point of summarizing the results of the operation. Along the way he refutes possible critics with a disclaimer about killing any children:

> Suffice it to say, that the enemy were routed from every position, whether taken to elude their pursuers or for the purpose of defense, and were finally compelled unconditionally to surrender, out of the whole number of Indians fought, about two hundred ["from one hundred to" lined out in original, by author or some later critic?] warriors were killed, and twelve hundred taken prisoners, "no children were killed, and but one woman during the whole campaign") [*sic*; this statement has been added apparently in another hand, by someone trying to 'doctor' the record. It is written between the lines of Gen. Kibbe's report.][87]

As in the previous year, the report of the 1859 campaign made a strong case for complete funding of the entire campaign by the Legislature. Gen. Kibbe's Report finished with an accounting of a total cost of $69,468.43 to be paid by the state. Next comes the remarkable claim by Gen Kibbe:

> It will be ascertained upon consulting the vouchers on file in my office, and should be borne in mind, that nearly one fourth of this whole amount of expenses was incurred in the subsistince [*sic*] and transportation of Indian Prisoners captured by the Command. These Prisoners numbered over twelve hundred and were transported a distance of from two hundred fifty to seven hundred miles; the cost of which was $14,030.45. ...[88]

At the conclusion of Gen. Kibbe's War some Native American prisoners may have been transported south to the Tejon Reservation, which was about four hundred fifty miles from Tehama and Humboldt Counties or from the Chico area. One may question not only the charge of over fourteen thousand dollars but also the distance as was stated by Gen. Kibbe. One has to doubt how Native Americans survived such a long trip.

Great were the costs of transporting whole tribes of Native Americans in this era preceding railroads. As we have just seen with the Pit River tribe that went all the way from their homeland region east of Mt. Shasta on board barges down to Sacramento, then more travel over one hundred miles to San Francisco and finally by ship up the Pacific Coast- almost another hundred miles to the

---

87. *Ibid.*, 8.
88. *Ibid.*, 15.

Mendocino Reservation, the bill was very large. Some observers thought the federal government, in the form of the Office of Indian Affairs, should be billed for this charge.

Gen. Kibbe's Report maintained that the valleys his force controlled would soon support "at least one hundred thousand head of stock." It was a subtle public relations pitch to the California Legislature. In addition Gen. Kibbe's report concluded:

> Some twenty-five families of this year's emigration, have already taken up claims in these valleys. And this is the country which has been hitherto almost exclusively occupied by Indians—through which runs the great thoroughfare from the Sacramento Valley to the extreme North, and over which millions of dollars' worth of merchandize [*sic*] is annually transported; from a statement of which facts, the importance utility and necessity of the expedition can, I trust, be readily comprehended by citizens of all portions of the State.
>
> It affords me pleasure to state also that the Citizens generally residing near the field of operations have cooperated with the Expedition.
>
> Respectfully Submitted
> I have the honor to be
> Your Obt. Sevt
> Wm. B. Kibbe
> Quartermaster, Or Adjt. Genl., State of Cal.
> Army Expedition[89]

Gen. Kibbe's report was replete with euphemistic rhetoric. It was clear that the 1859 militia (or the "expedition," as contemporaries dubbed it) accomplished much of what some Mendocino County backers, men like George E. White and Judge S.C. Hastings, along with the campaign's other promoters in Humboldt and Tehama Counties, had most desired. It temporarily crippled most Native American resistance throughout Northern California, including most of Mendocino County. It also forced at least twelve hundred Native Americans from six or more different tribes to relocate from their traditional tribal areas onto faraway reservations.

This seemingly complete frontier victory was achieved through the use of military might, including forced marches through deep snow and setting up dawn ambushes of Native American rancherias. From the Euro-American settlers' viewpoint, the ninety-four soldiers fully deserved to be paid. By the end of 1859 both in Mendocino County, through Capt. Jarboe's operations (see Chapter

89. *Ibid.*, 16–17.

5), and to the east and north in Tehama, Humboldt, Klamath, and Trinity Counties through General Kibbe's "expedition," armed Native American forces had very nearly ceased to exist.

Kibbe's tactical victory over the Native Americans did not do what he hoped it would. Native American resistance in Trinity and Humboldt Counties for example had only just begun. Still it is remarkable because the only Euro-American militia casualty in Gen. Kibbe's Expedition, was a single injured soldier. He was injured when his weapon misfired. It is unknown how Gen. Kibbe arrived at his figure of only two hundred Native American dead. Gen. Kibbe did not include the large number of Native Americans who were wounded in action. Certainly there must have been many. Most of these Native American combatants probably died of their wounds.

From a Native American standpoint, almost all of these clashes ended in the wounding and deaths of many and also in forced removals of many tribes from their ancestral lands. However the conflict did not break their spirit nor end their resistance to the Euro-American invasion of the state. Unfortunately, there are few accounts extant, such as newspaper accounts or letters home written by soldiers, of this conflict. There were also relatively few government documents. Therefore the true Native American casualties in this frontier war actually were much larger than the small number recorded by General Kibbe.

Chapter 5. Vengeance and Taking the Land—Eden and Round Valleys, 1859–1860

"Captain Jarboe's orders to his men were to kill all the bucks they could find, and take the women and children prisoners."
—William Scott's deposition to the Mendocino War Committee, Cloverdale, March 2, 1860

The first, and an increasingly lethal, phase of the Mendocino Indian War in California began in the late summer of 1859. A single event started the first cycle of revenge that contributed to a war that ultimately affected the lives of almost everyone in Northern California: Native Americans living out in the wild in Eden Valley, a small mountain valley located a short distance south of Round Valley, killed three horses, including a prize stallion worth approximately $2,000. This prize racehorse was the property of the livestock dealer, real estate developer, jurist and Forty-niner, Judge Serranus C. Hastings.

Normally such an isolated event, as unfortunate as it must have seemed to the entire local ranching community, would not affect frontier life, start a war, or profoundly affect an entire state's history. Cattle and horses, like people, die every day for a variety of reasons. The Round Valley region's Native Americans did not suddenly start to slaughter Euro-Americans' livestock just because the Native Americans were hungry for meat or because they took a sudden dislike for Euro-American people. In this instance they killed one particular horse for a specific reason: to get revenge. They were sending a message about their human rights. However, this event would become a catalyst to the formation of militia groups that decimated the local Indian population.

Early in 1860, a state legislative investigation into this and other incidents of violence produced almost three dozen depositions. This investigation was designed with hopes of getting at the truth, from the Euro-American perspective, of what had been happening in the upper Eel River and, more specifically, northeastern Mendocino County. The depositions reveal even as they conceal the truth of this period.

Judge Hastings was a recent immigrant to California from another newly admitted state, Iowa. Unfortunately for the health of some local Native Americans in the Eden Valley and Round Valley areas, Judge Hastings was a wealthy and powerful person who also was savvy, ambitious and knowledgeable. Hastings had friends in high places, both in Sacramento and in Washington, D.C.: political allies who could help him. Few other Round Valley settlers with the possible exception of the Henleys could expect to have such profound political clout.

When Judge Hastings moved to California from Iowa in 1849, he must have brought along considerable funds from his law practice and from profitable previous real estate investments in the Midwest. As we saw before in Chapter 3, he bought up prime real estate in California including the deed to all of Eden Valley in Mendocino County as well as more property elsewhere in northern California.

As an absentee landlord, Hastings built for himself a comfortable house in Solano County. This was dangerous practice in frontier California, where local and personal ranch management was important. Nevertheless, his home was located within a comfortable riding distance of both Sacramento and San Francisco. He lived in high style with three Indian servants in a large and comfortable house.

Judge Hastings had imported a sizable herd of cattle to Eden Valley. There he planned to build and maintain an extensive ranch. His first act was hiring a ranch manager; a tough rancher named H.L. Hall. He later described this in his deposition to Assemblyman Lamar of the legislative investigative committee.

> I reside in Solano County; my age is forty-five years, and my occupation is that of a dealer in horses, cattle, and real estate. About the month of August, one thousand eight hundred and fifty-eight, I owned between three and four hundred breeding mares and colts. Desiring to find a place to graze them and raise horses and stock, I inquired of the Superintendent of Indian Affairs, Col. Henley, who recommended to me Eden Valley and the country between the Middle and South Forks of Eel River, then uninhabited, except by the Ukia Indians, who had been, and were then, hostile to white people, and had been committing depredations upon the stock in the vicinity of Round Valley; and, upon consultation with Col. Henley, I

believed that I could, by feeding one or two tribes, subdue them and make them useful, and have no difficulty with them, and, to this end, I placed my horses in charge of H.L. Hall; he was then a stranger to me, but was highly recommended to me from persons in Iowa. He took the horses to Eden Valley and established a ranch there at my expense, and supported a rancheria of Indians around him from the month of September to the month of January, one thousand eight hundred and fifty-nine, when I arrived at Eden Valley with a band of about three hundred cows and calves; I put them also in charge of Mr. Hall.[90]

Also in January 1859, the U.S. Army presence, long requested by some Round Valley settlers, finally materialized in the form of a platoon (seventeen soldiers and one officer) of the Sixth Infantry. The unit originated in Benicia by way of Fort Weller (near Willits), where it was snowbound during the winter of 1858. First under Major Edward Johnson's command and later under Lt. Edward Dillon, this platoon of regular cavalry soldiers resided in Round Valley for just over a year.

At about this same time, Judge Hastings and a number of other settlers began to suffer losses of livestock, some of which were probably caused by hungry Native Americans who may have killed some animals for meat. The Indians had also killed the livestock in response to unnecessarily excessive beatings of Native American ranch workers by Judge Hastings's ranch manager, H.L. Hall.

An interesting story was provided in this regard by a Round Valley settler named William Scott. In his deposition Scott told how H.L. Hall hired Native Americans as "packers," to carry or to "pack" heavy loads over the approximately sixty-five miles of treacherous trail from Ukiah City to Eden Valley. When the promised payment of one shirt for each worker was not forthcoming and the Native Americans complained about it, Hall responded by whipping two of them. It was soon after this that some of the settlers' stock started to disappear from the herds. Hall and others then began "killing all the Indians they could find in the mountains," and it was at this point, probably late in 1858, that the Hastings stallions were killed.

---

90. Deposition of Judge S.C. Hastings to California State Assemblyman Joseph B. Lamar, March 19, 1860 at Sacramento, CA, in *Appendix, The Senate Journal, 1860*, 30. Judge Hastings' deposition was the only settler deposition out of a total of approximately thirty-five taken at Sacramento. See also the Mendocino Indian War File, California Archives, 4th Floor, 1020 "O" Street, Sacramento, CA. Some Native American depositions were also originally recorded along with those of the settlers, military officials, and local reservation employees, yet all the Native American testimonies have disappeared from the Archives. It is possible the some of the Euro-American depositions have also disappeared.

Scott reports that Hall "believed that the Indians who had done the packing for him had killed the stallions because no other Indians would have known enough to have selected the most valuable stock."[91]

So it was in the spring of 1859, when his stallion and other livestock had been killed, that Hastings understood that unless he could kill or remove most of Eden Valley's Native American males, he could not permanently maintain any large herds of horses or cattle or probably any other livestock there. Unless he did something to change the pattern of events, soon his Eden Valley investment might become worthless due to losses of livestock.

Judge Hastings began thinking about using his close political contacts in order to get the military help he needed. He explained the situation later in his deposition to Assemblyman Lamar of the state's legislative investigating committee.

> On my arrival there [in Eden Valley or the Round Valley area] I learned the Indians had dispersed from the ranch to the valley and had killed seven breeding mares; this I learned from Mr. Hall and two or three other persons I found when I arrived there. I had no doubt then, nor have I at this time, that the reports were true.

> On my way home, about one day's ride from Eden Valley, my son, a young man of sixteen years of age, informed me that Mr. Hall had been out the morning previous to my arrival there and killed fourteen male Indians, in whose camp he found the remains of horses. This fact was concealed from me by Mr. Hall.

> In the month of April then following I drove into that country to South Eel River about a thousand head of cattle, intending to drive them into Eden Valley to join with the other stock. Previous to my arriving there I was informed by First Lieutenant Carlin, of Major Johnson's command, that the Indians had attacked my stock at Eden Valley and killed my black stallion, valued at over two thousand dollars, five fine American bulls, and also two or three American work oxen.[92]

At this point in his deposition, Judge Hastings described how he fired Hall after talking to both settlers and troops under Major Johnson's command about him. Nearly all these men had a low opinion of Hall and his methods. Hall had used force on uncooperative Native Americans and sometimes whipped them if they refused to work. The key to Hastings' actions throughout this period was not sympathy for the Native Americans, however, but fear for his property. Later on in his deposition, Judge Hastings charged that the amount just of his own

91. Deposition of W.T. Scott to State Assemblyman William B. Maxson, "Of the Assembly Committee," March 2, 1860, Cloverdale, CA, in *Appendix, The Senate Journal*, 1860, 23. At California State Archives, 1020 "O" St., 4th Floor, Sacramento, CA. Official documents including reports, laws, and speeches of the California Legislature were routinely printed in this publication.
92. Deposition of Judge S.C. Hastings to California State Assemblyman Joseph B. Lamar, March 19, 1860 at Sacramento, CA, *Ibid.*, 30.

personal losses alone amounted to more than ten thousand dollars from recent Native American thefts.

Meanwhile, only a few miles north of Eden Valley, at Round Valley, local residents were also having troubles that spring dealing with local Native Americans. In early June 1859, a group of thirty-nine Round Valley settlers, calling themselves "citizens of 'Nome Cult Valley,'" petitioned Gov. Weller. They requested the help of a volunteer company of militia:

> Ever since the settlement of this valley Indians have committed their depredations with a degree of success and boldness barely credible to one not cognizant with the facts.
>
> In several instances they have come to the very doors of our homes and taken away as many as 20 head of hogs out of the corral and driven them off. They have also killed stock in the valley in the daylight, and have committed innumerable depredations under cover of night.
>
> At first it was the policy of the citizens to treat them leniently in the hope of getting them to go on to the reservation and live peaceably....
>
> When the detachment of troops now here first came to this place, everyone was highly pleased at their presence, for we believed that we would then be relieved of the troublesome and unpleasant duty of guarding our property against the hostile Indians but so far from that being the case, the indifference manifested by the officers in command has encouraged rather than checked the Indians in their outrages.
>
> When Major Johnson came here he did not ask the cooperation of the citizens, but told them that he would manage the matter in his own way, though he kindly gave us permission, in case any stock was driven off by the Indians to follow them, if there was a chance to recover the property, but we were not allowed to molest the Indians.
>
> In view of the above facts we cannot rely upon the U.S. authorities for any assistance, and we are reluctantly compelled call upon your Excellence for protection of our lives and property.
>
> The Indians have already a good many arms among them, and they are growing worse as they become enlightened by contact with the whites.
>
> In regard to the memorial gotten up at this place, denying the truth of the statements made by C.H. Bourne, W. Robinson and others, we would simply say that it was signed by only seven citizens of the valley. The remainder of the signers are employees on the reservation, nonresidents of the place and soldiers.[93]

The complaint about Major Edward Johnson is telling. Almost from the start of the Sixth Infantry's presence in Round Valley in January 1859, there was a very large difference of opinion between the Army's officers and the Euro-

---

93. See "Petition from thirty nine citizens of Nome Cult Valley to Gov. John B. Weller," June 10, 1859, Round Valley File, Beard Collection, Held-Poage Historical Research Library, 603 W. Perkins St., Ukiah, CA.

American settlers as to what the Army should do about the settlers' charges of Native American "depredations" on their livestock. The officers, first Major Edward Johnson and later Lt. Edward Dillon, saw their tripartite duty as protecting the Native Americans, reservation employees as well as the settlers; their first priority being to protect the settlers. Acting as a police force to help stop thievery was another, distinctly secondary task, according to their own interpretation. Of course the settlers thought otherwise.

The claim that the Indians were well armed is also revealing. There were few Native Americans who had guns in 1859, and even fewer who actually could use them effectively. Yet it was becoming a serious concern to the settlers of Eden and Round Valleys, and certainly also a fear among all the whites in northern California, that they could soon be facing better armed Indians who would shoot better in the future.

The arrival of this petition for help in Sacramento caused Gov. Weller and legislators, like Assemblyman Joseph B. Lamar of Mendocino County, to be concerned about the safety of the settlers in Round Valley. Weller had initially appeared to be open to hearing both sides of the story. His first speech of the 1858-9 session in January 1858 complained mightily about how expensive it had been for the nation to take care of the Native Americans with its national reservation system. It had also decried how the whites seldom could or would establish the truth in their cases against Native Americans before they simply shot the first Native Americans they could find. Nevertheless, his partiality became clear now that it seemed possible that local settlers were being outgunned by Indians, or that the ranchers' livestock was being driven off and killed by Indians. Governor Weller would soon act decisively on the side of the settlers and ranchers to protect them.

As he struggled to make up his mind, Weller attempted to get the facts straight from the U.S. Army's local field commanders. After a wait, the information Weller received from the California militia's Adjutant General Kibbe was incomplete and inconclusive. As we saw in chapter 4, much of this information was slanted and blatantly exaggerated pro-settler propaganda. Although Gen. Kibbe's expedition generally took place far to the northwest of Round and Eden valleys, his reports seemed to Governor Weller to help corroborate everything Judge Hastings and others in Tehama County and in the Red Bluff region were charging about how damaging the Indian "depredations" had become.

According to Gen. Kibbe, Indians had attacked white settlers in Eden Valley and elsewhere. As time went on, new allegations about Native American attacks or "hostilities" were made to Gov. Weller. Next the Supt. of Indian Affairs for California Thomas J. Henley, endorsed the allegations made by some settlers that over seventy whites had been killed by the "Eukas" (Yukis).

We now know this charge regarding settler killings was grossly over-exaggerated. Seventy was about seven times the actual number of white dead. Another petition to Congress alleged that over $40,000 worth of Euro-American settler property had already been destroyed by Native Americans.

The final straw was the following appeal written in Eden Valley on July 11, 1859. Judge Hastings and sixteen other settlers met and signed a petition stating that further Indian depredations in Eden Valley had occurred. As the 1860 deposition of H.L. Hall, Judge Hastings' former ranch manager, attested, Judge Hastings was instrumental in authoring this petition and organizing the militia:

> Before this, about the first of April [1859], we found where the Indians had killed two horses and wounded another, which died afterward. Up to the middle of April there were missing five bulls, twenty-five head of horses, and twenty-five head of cattle. I went to Ukiah, and found Judge Hastings driving up six hundred and sixty-nine head of cattle, which he drove up and left on the same range at South Eel River, and then immediately moved the stock from Eden Valley to the same place. He remained there three or four days, and I proposed to him to get up a petition to the Governor for protection. We came to the conclusion it was best to form a company of twenty men and concluded on Mr. D. [Dryden] Lacock to command it. We got what signers there were there to a petition, which I think Judge Hastings drew up, and there were about ten who signed it. At that time myself and one white man resided in Eden Valley.[94]

It was impossible for Governor Weller to ignore this petition from Judge Hastings for long. Judge Hastings was not only a rancher but a powerful and widely respected jurist, politician, and former Congressman. While Weller and Hastings may not have known each other before meeting in California, the two

---

94. Deposition of H.L. Hall to Assemblyman Joseph B. Lamar, at Storms' Hotel, Round Valley, Feb. 26, 1860, (Mendocino) Indian War Files, California State Archives, 1020 "O" St., Sacramento, CA. As happened to Bear Flag soldier Patrick McChristian, foot soldiers in this era often went unpaid despite serving for months. For example McChristian, who enlisted at Sonoma, "for six months" under Fremont, eventually reached Los Angeles. "Our battalion was disbanded," and "...Having been cast to drift without a single dollar, I went on board the *Brig Primavera*, and I was granted the privilege of working my passage up to San Francisco, where I arrived about the first day of April, 1847 with a broken constitution and without a cent...." See R.A. Thompson's Nov, 1, 1855 typed recording of McChristian's statement," McChristian Narrative," Bancroft Library, University of California at Berkeley. A copy of which was loaned to this author in 1999 by Janis M. (Miller) Valderrama, great great granddaughter of the Hon. Sen. Jasper O'Farrell.

Democratic Party stalwarts had much in common: both had served as Congressmen in Washington, D.C., both were lawyers, both were trying to serve the public while trying to earn a living.

Hastings' ranch manager, H.L. Hall, explained that at first Round Valley's settlers had tried to get Dryden Laycock of Round Valley to head up the company. Laycock refused the assignment, claiming that he did not think the company would ever be paid. This was confirmed both by Judge Hastings and H.L. Hall in their depositions.

> Hastings: I then visited Round Valley for the first time in my life, called upon Dryden Haycock [sic, Laycock] whom Governor Weller had commissioned to raise a small company of volunteers, and found that Mr. Haycock would not serve without a private guarantee that his men and himself would be paid at a high rate. ...

> Hall: About this time the commission arrived for Mr. Lacock, brought by Mr. Frenley [sic, Henley]; said he was sent with it by Judge Hastings. I brought the commission to Round Valley to Mr. Lacock; he took it but refused to act under it; he took some steps to organize a company, but afterward abandoned it on account of the pay; about this time the stock was all moved out of Eden Valley. ..[95]

The petitioners requested Gov. Weller to name Walter S. Jarboe, another Mendocino County resident, as captain of the volunteer company. Soon after this Gov. Weller had to do this.[96] The offering of the post first to Laycock was also confirmed by Laycock in his deposition before the committee:

> I was not a member of the company; Mr. [Judge S.C. Hastings] Hastings wanted me to go on with it, saying that he would make good for it [Judge Hastings promised to pay Laycock if he joined the company or if he took command of it.]; I mean that he would see that the expenses were paid; he wanted me to start the company, and go with it and he would get my commission from the governor [Gov. John B. Weller.]....

> When I refused to accept the commission it was offered to Captain Jarboe by Judge Hastings and Mr. George Henley, who appeared the most anxious for the organization of the company; he accepted it;...[97]

---

95. Deposition of Judge S.C. Hastings to California State Assemblyman Joseph B. Lamar, March 19, 1860 at Sacramento, CA; Deposition of H.L. Hall to Assemblyman Joseph B. Lamar, at Storms' Hotel, Round Valley, Feb. 26, 1860, (Mendocino) Indian War Files, California State Archives, 1020 "O" St., Sacramento, CA.

96. "Proclamation of settlers in Eden Valley and vicinity," July 11, 1859. Ind. War Files. As quoted by Virginia P. Miller, U kom no'n: The Yuki Indians of Northern California (Socorro, N.M., Ballena Press, 1979), p. 65.

97. Deposition of Dryden Laycock to Assemblyman Joseph B. Lamar, Chairman, Select Committee on Indian Affairs, Feb. 28, 1860, at Storms' Hotel, Round Valley in Appendix, Senate Journal 1860, p. 51. California State Archives, 1020 "O" St., 4th Floor, Sacramento, CA.

Round Valley settlers William Pollard, Henry Brizendine, S.P. Storms, John B. Owens, Charles S. Bourne, and Dryden Laycock, had been employed at Nome Lackee in late 1855. Laycock had worked as a mason at that time.

Jarboe had participated in numerous raids before this. He had been wounded in one rancheria attack. This injury inflamed his eagerness to fight. As was noted by Professor Virginia P. Miller, Jarboe "had an intense, almost pathological, hatred of the Indians,"[98] and as Laycock testifies, Jarboe and his men began their work even before the official captain's commission from Gov. Weller arrived.

> Jarboe's company started about two or three weeks after this; it consisted of different men from those over whom I was offered the command; I think they were in operation over a month and a half before his commission arrived, and went on several expeditions against the Indians; I do not know how many; his company was formed from men from the vicinity of Redwood Valley, on Russian River. ...[99]

Many of the militia volunteers in Jarboe's Eel River Rangers came from the Russian River, a region over fifty miles to the south of Round Valley. Captain Jarboe also tried to enlist H. H. Buckles, a painter in Ukiah City. Buckles refused. Buckles said he did not like the character of at least one of the other militiamen in the company. He also doubted, as Dryden Laycock had, if the volunteers in the company would ever be paid. Like most other white settlers Buckles held a second job; he was "Deputy Assessor" of Long Valley, Mendocino County. Buckles's testimony suggests that, although the company's command was on the whole of good repute, the question of payment was a continuing issue of concern:

> "I am thirty-four years of age; I am a painter; I reside in Ukiah, have resided in this county, about two years, and in this place [Ukiah] about four months; I have been in Long Valley, during the last season, as Deputy Assessor, which office I now hold; two or three weeks after he had assumed the command of the company, Captain Jarboe and myself met in this place; he desired me to join his command; I then asked him under what authority he acted; he told me he had not at that time received a commission from the Governor; but expected one; he then said Hastings and Henley had become responsible for provisions, and they promised to get a bill passed through the Legislature to pass them; I mean Judge Hastings and Colonel Henley. I refused to join the command, from the fact that I did not believe Judge Hastings' promises could be relied on; as to Colonel Henley, I know nothing about; I said I thought the proper [procedure] would be to get a petition from the citizens,

---

98. Virginia P. Miller, *U kom no'n: The Yuki Indians of Northern California* (Socorro, N.M.: Ballena Press, 1979), 65 n 7.
99. Deposition of Dryden Laycock to State Assemblyman J. B. Lamar of the Select Legislative Committee, *Appendix, Senate Journal 1860*, 48-50, California State Archives, 1020 "O" St., 4th Floor, Sacramento, CA.

and get an appointment in that way; before he proceeded. About that time the commission arrived for Captain Jarboe. Kaskel, Mears & Co. showed me a letter from Judge Hastings, which I read, which, in substance, was a request to that firm to furnish Captain Jarboe supplies, for which he [Judge Hastings] and Henley would be responsible. Mr. Cohen, the Clerk of the firm, showed me the letter, and asked me if I thought the letter would be sufficient evidence to bind Hastings for the payment of the goods, if they were delivered to Captain Jarboe. I told him I thought it would; I talk [sic] him, that I thought he had rather pay the prior debt that he owed them, than have the letter exposed.

I knew some of Captain Jarboe's command; I knew some three or four; one of them, I think, was a man whose veracity was very good being one of the best fighting men of the company. The general reputation of the members of the company was fair in this community; they were men whom the people of this community relied on a great deal for protection. Captain Jarboe told me that after he had received his commission from the Governor, that Hastings and Henley had in a measure thrown him off, and owing to his (Jarboe's) [parentheses in the original] limited means, he was at his wits ends to furnish supplies for his men.

H.H. Buckles
Subscribed to and sworn to before me, this twenty-third day of February, one thousand eight hundred and sixty, at Ukiah City.

Jasper O'Farrell
Chairman Senate Committee[100]

Buckles was not alone in testifying that Supt. Henley and Judge Hastings had promised to provide the Eel River Rangers with supplies but then had reneged on the deal, leaving the state to pay for the militia. After exaggerating threats to their lives and ranches from the Native Americans in order to get protection, Hastings and Henley refused to help pay for it.

Whatever the problems were with getting the company supplied and paid, Jarboe wasted no time getting down to the business of killing Native Americans. Jarboe named his militia the "Eel River Rangers." The unit set out on raids on Indian rancherias even before Jarboe's commission from the governor had arrived. Jarboe's company continued its deadly raids on Native Americans from July 1859 until January 18, 1860 when the company was finally disbanded on the order of Gov. Weller.[101] As it turned out, money was not the main problem. The 1860 Legislature acted and paid the company over $9,000 for its many deadly

---

100. Deposition of H.H. Buckles to Sen. Jasper O'Farrell, on Feb. 23, 1860 at Ukiah City, *Appendix, Senate Journal 1860*, 28–29. California State Archives, 1020 "O" St., 4th Floor, Sacramento, CA.
101. Virginia P. Miller, *U kom no'n: The Yuki Indians of Northern California* (Socorro, N.M.: Ballena Press, 1979), 65.

raids on Native American rancherias in the Eden Valley and Round Valley vicinities.

It was at this time that one John Bland was killed under mysterious circumstances. According to the deposition of Lt. Edward Dillon, Bland had kidnapped two Native Americans from the reservation, claiming that they had stolen from him. After military personnel had brought one of the female Native Americans back to the reservation for protection, Bland came back and again took her by force. The woman escaped from him. A short time later John Bland's burned remains were found by some settlers. The settlers reacted in fear and rage. This incident destroyed any semblance of peace in Round Valley.

Some of the reports sent to Governor Weller show that Captain Jarboe's company used its own discretion. Jarboe had very little patience as he attacked and killed Native Americans. The Yuki tribe was most often targeted. After some cattle were reported killed on the Middle Fork of the Eel River, Jarboe went out on a murderous rancheria raid in Round Valley. On Dec. 3, 1859, Jarboe reported to Governor Weller:

> Birch [Jarboe's subordinate officer] immediately went in search of them and surprised a large rancheria about daylight and killed 9 Indians, but few making their escape. A lot of beef was found in their huts which established their guilt. On the 24th a man came in from hunting stock and reported that 5 horses were killed, and that he saw Indians then at work cutting them up. This was but 3 miles from the valley. Birch being encamped but a short distance from where the news was received was sent for and with his command started at night in the direction indicated by those who professed to know their haunts. The company came upon the Indians some 15 miles east of the valley in a deep canyon on the waters of the Eel River. This was in the night and the Indian spies discovered their approach. There was no time to lose and the attack was at once made. Several were killed and 9 squaws and children were taken prisoner.
>
> A tolerable interpreter being with the company the squaws were questioned, and revealed to them that the guilty party were one half mile distant in another canyon. They at once went as directed and found them in possession of the very horse flesh [identified by marks on the hides] that had been reported stolen. Of this party none escaped death. While the fight was going on the prisoners made their escape partly in consequence of the darkness and because the entire force being in the engagement. Total killed 18 all bucks, one little girl left by them in this fight was found nearly frozen to death and brought into the valley. This was a remnant of the same tribe that I had punished and severely thinned out on a previous occasion.[102]

102. Report of Capt. Walter Jarboe to California Governor John B. Weller, from "Headquarters, Eel River Rangers," Dec. 3, 1859, Round Valley File, Held-Poage Historical Research Library, 603. W. Perkins St., Ukiah, CA.

What is clear from this report is that this vigilante militia company carried on a deadly search and destroy mission in this area very near Round Valley. The total number of dead in this raid alone was at least twenty-seven persons, by the count of Captain Jarboe's own men. Those who made up the party acted as judge and jury to the Native Americans.

It is possible that the first rancheria was entirely innocent of any wrongdoing. In other words, nine innocent Native Americans may have been killed who were not even guilty of killing settlers' beef. Although the second party may have been the ones responsible for the theft and livestock killing, the first was simply in the wrong place at the wrong time.

The band of angry settlers led by Jarboe's subordinate "Birch" (probably Ben Burch, a local settler already mentioned who would later be described as a "loafer"), next used circumstantial evidence to condemn everyone in the second group. This is the kind of firefight sometimes referred to in press reports of battles as a "chastising of the Indians." In reality it was an official's contrived euphemism for the shooting or hanging of victims. This certainly was not the only incident of ethnic cleansing genocide that took place during the Mendocino War.

No mention at all is made in the above report of how hungry the Native Americans were or how unequal they were in the struggle they faced. There is no mention of how the attacks were laid out, how much time elapsed, or whether anyone was allowed to speak in their own defense before they were executed. Many other reports of such actions, such as Gen. Kibbe's Report cited above, made the point that before a fight started the Native Americans received some ultimatum and a chance to surrender before being shot down. It is significant that Jarboe made no mention of such a practice in this report of the battle. Almost simultaneously with this report, Governor Weller had written Jarboe a critical letter on December 4, 1859, ordering him to use more care in the future to be sure he was not killing innocent Native Americans.

Yet Jarboe would not be easily controlled. Later on in his report to Governor Weller, Jarboe described the "Ukas" (Yukis) "in that region ... [as] without doubt, the most degraded, filthy, miserable thieving lot of anything living that comes under the head of and rank of human beings."[103] Obviously just three months of killing had not been enough for the bloodthirsty Captain Jarboe. He made no bones about his disgust at and hatred of these Native Americans. Reading between the lines it is obvious that his true mission was to search and

---

103. *Ibid.*

destroy as many males or "bucks" as possible, regardless of their guilt or innocence.

There is little doubt here that many harmless and innocent people were killed. The overall purpose was clear: Judge Hastings wanted to clear Eden Valley of Native Americans so that his herds of livestock could be fattened for market in a peaceful place without obstacles. The goal of the Round Valley ranchers as a whole was the same as that of Hastings in Eden Valley or Long Valley: to remove the Indians who would go peacefully and use force whenever needed to kill or relocate the rest onto reservations.

As in more recent times, such as when Saddam Hussein or American troops use torture in Iraq, atrocities ultimately get attention. Newspaper reports of massacres by paramilitary groups like Birch's or Jarboe's soon began to disturb the public.

In January 1860, Milton Latham resigned his recently won post as governor of the state and became one of California's two U.S. senators. While Latham had won the popular election for governor the previous fall, in those days the Legislature chose senators to represent the state in Washington. So Lieutenant Governor John G. Downey, an avowed Buchanan supporter and middle-of-the-road democrat, stepped forward as Latham's and thus, ultimately, John B. Weller's real successor as the governor of California.

It was one of Gov. Downey's first significant duties as governor to pay for the costs of Gen. Kibbe's so-called "Expedition" of 1859, or of the War with the Win-toons. His administration also had to pay the bills submitted to the state by the primary Mendocino War unit, the Eel River Rangers. To many legislators and the public it was a shocking departure from a slower moving, generally more conservative past. It was a big crisis that the state suddenly had a seemingly huge pile of bills for wartime expenses when it also had many other unavoidable expenses to pay. It did not seem fair to simply pay for such expensive military campaigns out of the new state's limited treasury when the federal government had not yet even paid off all the expenses of the Mexican War.

In his initial report on Gen. Kibbe's expedition to the legislature, made in January 1860, Gov. Downey suggested that the issue be resolved using results obtained by an investigative committee made up of both state senators and assemblymen:

> While I admit the necessity which led to this expedition, and freely acknowledge the eminent services rendered by the officers and men composing the command, the expenses, so large in amount, would seem to demand a rigid scrutiny.

If it be intended to pay these expenses by direct appropriation of money, a few such will bankrupt the State Treasury. I recommend that the whole subject be referred to a committee, with power to send for persons and papers, with a view to a thorough investigation.

We have now a full treasury, and are enabled to pay all immediate demands upon it in cash.... Expenses of this nature are legally chargeable to the General Government [i.e., the federal government], and it would seem advisable to issue bonds as evidence of indebtedness against the State, instead of a direct appropriation of money.

JOHN G. DOWNEY, Governor.[104]

On January 17, the day after the governor's report, the *Sacramento Union* published a prominently positioned article entitled "Indian War Policy." The article complained:

If the volunteers took the field, it must be with the understanding that they must look to the General Government for pay. The terms were accepted; the service was rendered, and the bills of the expedition against the United States Government were audited as correct by the State Military Board of Examiners, consisting of W.C. Kibbe, G.W. Whitmore, and James L. English. The aggregate amount was $172,854.80. But the bill was not against the State; under no circumstances can she be held responsible. Upon a subsequent occasion, when $15,000 was appropriated by the Legislature to defray the expense of a company raised, we believe in Humboldt, Governor Johnson sent a special agent with the funds, clothed with the authority to accept the service of the company if necessary, and to disband it as soon as possible, consistent with the object in view. It was disbanded at the end of thirty days, and only about one-half of the appropriation expended.

Whilst disposed to afford all the protection required by his fellow-citizens, Governor Johnson had pursued a cautious and efficient Native American policy which did not involve the State in a heavy unusual expenditure. A very different line of policy was adopted by Governor Weller. Under his order the anti-Native American "expeditions" of the last two years were conducted at the expense of the State. The Quartermaster General was authorized to raise the forces necessary and prosecute the warlike expeditions upon the faith and credit of the State. They were thus made State wars, chargeable upon her Treasury—with the remote contingency of obtaining the amount from Congress. No money was allocated directly to California by Congress to help it pay for any of these 1858-9 Indian wars. But the State must first pay the expense.

To foot the bill of the Trinity and Humboldt expedition of last Winter, an appropriation of $52,000 was made by the last Legislature. We understand that the deficiencies claimed for that little war reach near $60,000 for which provision has yet to be made.

---

104. Governor John G. Downey's Message to the California Assembly, Jan. 16, 1860, "Report of the Expedition Against the Indians in the Northern Part of This State," 3, Bancroft Library, University of California, Berkeley, CA.

No reports of the cost of the expeditions of the past Summer have yet been made. The Quartermaster General's duties in the field have, so says ex Governor Weller, prevented him from preparing his report. But, judging by the cost of past expeditions, the bills to be rendered will exceed $200,000—they may reach a quarter of a million. Another campaign is now alleged to be necessary in the county of Mendocino, which, if entered upon, may consume the best portion of another hundred thousand dollars.

The policy of the State in relation to these Indian expeditions ought to be changed, unless the intention is to bankrupt the State Treasury. The Executive should go back to the position of Governor Johnson. If such large liabilities are absolutely necessary, let them be created directly against the United States. It is the positive duty of the National Government to protect the people of California from Indians who are under her supervision, and who are occupying public land or Government Reservations. If the policy pursued by the State is justified by the facts, the United States' agents and officials have been guilty of the most criminal neglect.[105]

Spurred on at least in part by the sentiments expressed in the *Union*'s article, the legislature followed the governor's lead and began a new investigation of the Mendocino War. The legislators were probably more moved by reports of how the Eel River Rangers in Mendocino County had mistreated the Native Americans than by similar killings carried out by Adjutant Kibbe's militia units.

In February and March 1860, state legislators in Sacramento formed a joint bicameral committee to investigate what was really happening in Eden and Round Valleys. The so-called "Select Committee on Indian Affairs" was made up of two state senators and three state assemblymen.

By the end of February, each member of this five-man investigating committee had made the long, arduous trip up to Round Valley from the state capital. The first sworn testimonies or depositions were made on Feb. 27, 1860. Eventually over thirty early Mendocino residents testified about the establishment of the militia and its activities. Those who testified included Judge Serranus C. Hastings, parts of whose testimony we have already read, Lt. Edward Dillon, and Nome Cult Farm's founder, former Subagent Simmon P. Storms. Other reservation officials and employees also testified, including the blacksmith and physician, laborers, and many others.

A reading of most of these depositions of Round Valley's settlers and employees at the reservation revealed a shocking profusion of vague allegations used to justify murderous attacks on Native American encampments. Nearly all the settlers were careful to record that livestock remains were found in the Native American rancherias after the murders of many of their Native American

---

105. See "Indian War Policy," *Sacramento Union*, 2, col. 2, January 17, 1860, California History Room, Suite 200, California State Library, 900 "N" St., Sacramento, CA.

residents. Still, on no occasion in any of the records I have examined in the State Archives did I find a case in which the inhabitants were removed peacefully, evidence examined dispassionately, or *any trial at all* held of the Indians *before* the sentence of death and executions were performed. Although we have no witnesses in the form of extant depositions made by the Native Americans, that of the whites is sufficient to condemn the raiders' actions as atrocities.

This is true even if we assume that Northern California Native Americans were driven by hunger to steal and kill cattle and other livestock. They knew that the whites considered this a serious crime punishable by death if they were apprehended. Their situation became more perilous each year as the invading whites, whether they were Army troopers or families struggling to begin farms, became more numerous and powerful. Steadily, the whole Native American way of life was being destroyed. Euro-American livestock grazing quickly destroyed native plants like clover, seeds, and edible roots. Such activity diminished whole populations of insects, small game and fish that the tribes traditionally had depended on to supply them with food. Hunger, degradation, disease and starvation were increasingly their lot.

There are many unanswered questions as to the causes of the precipitous decline in the Native American population in this mid nineteenth century era. Most contemporary historians stress the prevalence of new diseases as the main cause of the reduction of the California Native American population in the mid-nineteenth century. Lt. Johnson believed that nearly ten Native Americans died each day due to a lack of their accustomed diet. However complex the causes, what we see in these depositions was that the blame for the disruption of Indian life cannot be laid only at the feet of natural causes.

How can Native Americans be blamed for trying to survive in the wild when reservations developed into notorious death traps where numerous inhabitants were overworked and abused and many starved? Given that Native Americans in Central and Northern California, particularly those in the Round Valley and Eden Valley vicinities, came more frequently under attack by Euro-Americans after 1856, is it any wonder that by the second half of 1859 some of these local tribes, especially the Yuki and Wailaki, were driven to make occasional counterattacks?

Chapter 6. The Woes of the Settlers and Ranchers

"At another time I heard Mr. Hall say that he did not want any man to go with him to hunt Indians, who would not kill all he could find because a nit would make a louse. Mr. Hall said he had run Indians out of their rancherias and put strychnine in their baskets of soup, they had to eat."
— *William T. Scott's deposition to Assemblyman William B. Maxson, March 2, 1860.*

This and subsequent chapters contain more depositions by Round Valley's Euro-American settlers, Army officers, and reservation officials and employees given to the state's joint Investigating Committee on Indian Affairs in February and March of 1860. Whether a settler presently lived in Round Valley did not matter much to the committee of state lawmakers, two from the Senate and three from the Assembly. What mattered most was how knowledgeable the person was about the Mendocino War, from July to the last week of December 1859.

It is unknown whether there was a set of predetermined questions that each committee member asked the person giving testimony. What is clear from reading the depositions is that a number of the same subjects recur in these testimonies. For example, those who testified all gave their own names and how long they had lived in or near Round Valley. They also stated whether they thought they needed to be armed when they traveled and whether they had a claim to any payment from the state for participation as militiamen. Many also volunteered their opinion on whether or not they thought the Army platoon was doing a good job and whether or not they thought a militia unit should be raised and ready to go out if livestock was taken by Native Americans from anyone's herd. Thus it is possible, although no record exists of it at the California Archives, that there was some predetermined list of questions. What is certain is that the question of whether the Eel River Rangers should be paid was one of the main reasons for the investigation in the first place.

Especially to contemporary readers, the blatantly racial bias against the Native Americans of all of the depositions recorded here is offensive. However, the participants' contemporaries did not consider the statements to be even slightly prejudiced. One must look beyond such bias for the facts they tell us. Only then can we begin to benefit from these depositions that are like messages sealed in bottles long ago, still afloat on a vast ocean of ignorance and misconceptions. They clearly tell of dramatic situations that were tragic for many because of extraordinary acts of violence, crimes, and atrocities. Yet they also tell of acts of extraordinary personal courage made under great duress and devotion to duty and honor, and sometimes justice. One reads with fascination through one eyewitness account after another the story of a western way of life being created from the melding of two very different, and generally opposing cultures, almost constantly at war.

Immediately several things come to light in these depositions. Many of the settlers who described militia action began their accounts with some description of stock losses, including the value of the stock. Almost all of those who owned stock claimed to have lost it to Indian depredations, not by natural losses. Second, although the settlers had a variety of opinions about the efficacy of the Army's platoon in protecting settlers against Indian "depredations," the majority of them seemed to have thought that the Army was worthless in this regard.

Third, there were also a variety of opinions about the need for a permanent local militia. Although many, if not most, of the settlers and ranchers seemed to think this was a good idea, recommending some form of a local, permanent militia force of armed vigilantes ready to attack the Native Americans whenever they took livestock. Finally, in their descriptions of militia activities, the settlers presented a surprisingly consistent pattern: the raiding parties attacked in the early morning, they shot first and asked questions later, they tried to avoid killing women and children, and they almost always claimed to find evidence of stolen stock in the rancheria after the raid.

Of the following settler depositions, three are quoted next in their entirety: those of G.H. Henley, Jeremiah Lambert, and C.J. Small, et al. In the 1860 testimonies, generally each commentator was sworn upon a Bible to tell the "truth, the whole truth, and nothing but the truth," just as one would do today if he or she were testifying in a courtroom. In their depositions, rancher-settlers often used the term "stock raiser" or owner of a "ranchero" when describing what they did for a living.[106]

George H. Henley was one of Superintendent Thomas J. Henley's sons. At the time his ranch in southern Round Valley had become one of the largest in the valley. In his deposition, Henley describes the Indian "depredations," the June 1859 petition from the "citizens of 'Nome Cult Valley,'" and his agreement with Capt. Jarboe to supply provisions to the newly formed militia. His opinion is unmistakably clear: the presence of troops did little to protect livestock and a regular militia was mandatory for local law and order.

> I am 26 years old, and am a stock raiser. I reside in Round Valley, Mendocino County. And have resided here since the first of January 1859. When I came I bought stock in this valley, and I was told that the Citizens in the valley have been missing hogs that they supposed had been killed by indians, I was also told that the day before I arrived here the Citizens had been out chastising the indians [sic].
>
> I was a stranger here at that time and was not familiar with the habits of the indians, and not aware of their roguish disposition, and I was slow to believe that they were committing any extensive depredations. About two weeks after my arrival time here I was informed by a Gentleman here that he had seen the tracks of a band of horses that he supposed had been driven off by the indians.
>
> In a few days after I had revealed this information I went into the mountains myself southwest of the valley beyond the distance where stock usually ranged and discovered the tracks of about ten horses in one band that had been driven in the direction of the forks of the Eel River. And also in another place I found the tracks of another band of six or eight horses that had been driven in the same direction.
>
> I followed both of these tracks far enough to ascertain that the horses had been driven off by the indians.
>
> Mr. Storms was at that time in partnership with me and he owned about three fourths of all the horses in the valley.
>
> In November 1859 an Indian informed my brother [Thomas B. Henley. G.H. Henley and Thomas were sons of Supt. Thomas J. Henley, California's Superintendent of Indian Affairs][107] and myself, that some indians over in Eel River had driven hogs in their possession. The raiders a party of Eight, and went with the indian as a Guide to the place where the Indians were encamped, attacked their rancheria, and killed two of them, have supposed that we killed six of them and the rest of them escaped. Those killed were all bucks.

---

106. Not much is known about the origins or backgrounds of many of the Euro-American settlers who made land claims in Round Valley. Some "residents" whose depositions are extant were not permanent settlers, but vagrants. Unfortunately, some settlers did not testify, either in 1860 or in 1862. Some may have died or moved away. There also may have been other residents whose stories have simply been lost since they did not testify and unfortunately, no one in their families preserved personal letters or diaries.

We went into their rancheria and there found the heads of Seven hogs and portions of their carcasses. These hogs belonged to my brother [Thomas B.] and to Mr. Davis.

I had then sold out my interests in the valley to Mr. Storms, and did so because I found the Indians ever so troublesome, and was afraid that I would be unsuccessful in my enterprise.

Some time in the month of May [1859] there was some talk of raising a company of mountain men for the purpose of protecting the Stock of the Citizens of this valley from the depredations of the Indians.

The people have manifested an interest in raising this company in proportion to the amount of Stock they owned in the valley; several of the Citizens was at this place and a Statement was drawn up representing the Condition of things in this valley, and embodying a request that some one be commissioned to raise a company of twenty men to protect the property of the Citizens from the depredations of the indians, and this statement was sent to Governor Weller. I attended the meeting and drew up the statement myself.

Capt. Jarboe subsequently received a commission and raised the company and I made a contract with him to supply his company with provisions, I did so because he was not successful in making a contract Elsewhere or with Any other party, and rather than to have the Company not go into operation, I undertook to do it, but I stated to Capt. Jarboe that I did not desire to do so and was not prepared.

All the interest I had in the Valley at the time was a few pack mules and four or five horses.

I agreed to furnish him flour at $12 per hundred weight but as to other things I told him I could not fix upon a certain price as I did not know what they would ask me, and I should have to go to Tehama for them; but that I would furnish them as low as I could.

My bill against the State for Grains and flour furnished to Capt. Jarboe amounts to about Fifteen Hundred dollars, and this includes one beef which he got from my brother and which was charged to me.

In my opinion there is necessity for an armed force in this vicinity to protect the property of Citizens from the depredations of the Indians, I mean an armed force independent of the U.S. troops stationed here. From my knowledge of the Relations existing between the Whites & Indians in this vicinity and from the conduct of the Officers and troops in relation thereto I do not believe that the latter have had any benefit to the Settlers.

---

107. "G.H." (or George Henley) here referred to either Thomas B. Henley or "H.F." Henley, one of his four brothers. Deposition of G. Henley to Assemblyman J. B. Lamar, Storms Hotel, Round Valley, Feb. 27, 1860, *Appendix Senate Journal 1860*, "Testimony Taken Before the Joint Special Committee," 38–40. See also the 1860 Mendocino County Census, Microfilm #653, National Archives, Held-Poage Library, 603 W. Perkins St., Ukiah, CA. It included the names of approximately one hundred Round Valley settlers but no Native Americans.

The Officers have manifested no disposition to afford any protections to the Settlers, they seem perfectly indifferent to the depredations of the Indians. The people in this valley do not countenance the Killing of women and children.

I have been on speaking terms with the Officer in command at the Reservation till within the last five days. We are now unfriendly. There is an unfriendly feeling existing between the Citizens and officers, they are regarded in fact—as a nuisance.

I looked upon Mr. Bland as a quiet and peaceable, a temperate man. I have known him ever since I have been in the valley I have never known him to be guilty of any misdemeanor or disgraceful act.

When I sold out my interest in this Ranch, there was an Indian Boy named Jake who desired to go with me when I located again it was agreed between Mr. Storms and myself that he should go with me; he was an Indian that Mr. Storms had raised, and was not regarded as belonging to the Reservation; this Indian remained with Mr. Storms until some time in December last. And then went to the Reservation to be doctored, and remained there about a week; he then came to my house, without my solicitation, and said he had some to hire with me; three days after he came Capt. Reed [George Rees succeeded Storms as the reservation's Agent in charge], sent an order by one of his men for his delivery; I refused to give him in as I did not consider the Reservation had any control over him, Then next—Mr. Reed [George Rees], Lieut. Dillon and eighteen armed mounted men came down to my place and demanded The Indian. I informed Mr. Reed that the boy did not belong to the Reservation, that he had no control over him as I considered and I refused to give him up. The boy was not in the house and they did not take him. The Indian spoken of was about 21 years of age.

Mr. Hall's reputation with regard to truth and veracity with me is good, and generally so with this community.

Mr. Pollard's reputation for truth and veracity is not generally good.

I never knew but one white man who was killed in an attack upon the Indians, and he was a Soldier under the command of Lieut. Dillon. I know five white men who have been wounded in these attacks.

G.H. Henley

Subscribed to and Sworn to before me this 27th day of February, AD 1860 at Storms Hotel, Round Valley.

J.B. Lamar
Chairman of Select Committee on Indian Affairs.[108]

George Henley, Indian fighter and quartermaster to Captain Jarboe's Eel River Rangers, was willing to help supply Jarboe's men as long as he was well paid, according to H. H. Buckles and others. He must have given his deposition to the committee with a sense of self-satisfaction and pride. Henley went out of his way here to claim he was doing the right thing by forcing Jake, a young

---

108. George Henley's deposition, *Ibid.*, 39 and 40.

Native American man, to remain with him. This incident and Henley's comments about the military presence in the valley underline the split that developed and that lasted throughout 1859 between the Army's troops under Lt. Dillon and the settlers when it came to treatment of the Native Americans in Round Valley.

Again, one wonders how Henley himself thought he could be so sure that he and the others were killing the guilty Native Americans at the rancheria where they found hog remains after their attack. It was common practice for the Native Americans to remove and eat diseased dying or dead stock that they found on the valley land. White policy regarding this practice became gradually more restrictive as more settlers took up residence in the valley.

Also of note is the fact that Henley broke a subtle inter-settler code of silence when he went out of his way to attack the integrity of his fellow settler, William Pollard. Here it is clear that the settlers were deeply divided over the question of using force and having a permanent militia in the region.

William Pollard was an early permanent resident in Round Valley. Before moving there, he had lived further north, up above Red Bluff. According to Pollard's great-great-granddaughter, Ms. Janice Pollard Hague,[109] in 1860 he lived in Williams Valley, an area east of the present day location of Covelo. Covelo is the most significant town in Round Valley. According to Ms. Hague, her ancestor William Pollard originated in the Shasta area. Nome Lackee records note that Pollard was employed there. Many of Round Valley's early white residents came from the Red Bluff or the Sacramento Valley areas.

Mr. Pollard did not believe that Round Valley should have either California militia soldiers or U.S. Army soldiers stationed there.

> I am thirty-six years of age. I am a stock raiser in Williams Valley. I reside at the reservation. I have resided in this section about three years next August [1860?]. I was employed on the reservation by Colonel Henley, but am not now. I have not

---

109. Personal interview by author with Ms. Janice Pollard Hague, Jan. 6, 2000, at Held-Poage Historical Research Library, 603 W. Perkins St., Ukiah, CA. Ms. Hague stated that William Pollard married a Nomelaki woman "whose only name was 'Fanny.'" Ms. Hague's great-grandfather Enoch Pollard (William's son) married Mary Goodwyn, who was from a Euro-American family. Special Agent J. Ross Browne's Report to Commissioner Mix, cited earlier, also reported an interview Browne held with "a person named Williams." Williams testified that "in 1854 or 5, he signed a voucher for $2000 for his claim." But, according to Browne, Williams said he was never paid. When Supt. Henley finally talked with Williams, Williams became so frustrated with the government's delay that he lost his temper and stalked out of the interview. Nevertheless, his name remains on this small area near the southwest corner of the reservation. Browne to Mix, *Ibid.*, Round Valley file, 0193.

been employed for the last year on the reserve. I am acquainted with the character of the Indians in this vicinity. About the tenth or fifteenth of last September, I brought about one hundred and thirty head of cattle on to the North Fork of Eel River, about three or four miles from this place [Storms Hotel, which was about one-half mile southeast of Covelo] I get some two or three hundred sheep from Mrs. Storms [Sarah J. (Stevens) Storms, Simmon's wife. She listed her birthplace as "Massachusetts" and her age as "25" in the 1860 Census], and kept them in the valley. These sheep have been in Williams Valley about two or three months. My stock have been ranging within three or four miles of this valley, excepting some three or four head that were ranging in the forks of Eel River, some seven or eight miles from here.

About a month ago I went to the Sacramento Valley. Up to that time I had missed no stock, and on my way over I saw four or five head that were ranging in the forks of Eel River. I came back about a week ago and looked for these four or five head, and could not find them. I searched for them about one and half days. These cattle may be in the hills or the Indians may have got them, I cannot tell which. When I went to Sacramento Valley I took one man with me. I had a knife and he had a pistol. There are Indians in the forks of Eel River and on the head of Story Creek, but I saw none as I went over, or on the way back. If a man goes armed with a rifle or pistol, or anything of that kind, and goes along and minds his own business, I don't consider there is any danger, but I think there is danger if he goes alone unarmed. I have been more or less among the Indians for the last seven years. I never have been attacked by these Indians. I do not think there is necessity at present for any additional armed force in this valley to protect the property of the citizens other than that here, and I do not think there is any need of them. I have seen a great many cattle around in the hills this winter that have died a natural death, as there was no sign of their having been killed. The Indians eat these dead cattle, and the hides, and horns, and remains of these cattle, might be found in an Indian Rancheria, without being evidence that the Indians had killed the cattle. I have seen no dead horses or hogs. I have not seen the Indians gathering the carcasses this winter. But I have seen many times the Indians eating carcasses of dead animals that died a natural death. Men are constantly traveling through these mountains alone. Some go armed and some unarmed. I was not a member of Captain Jarboe's company, and have no claim, directly or indirectly, against the government for supplies furnished the company. I think there are about one thousand Indians between the North and South Forks of Eel River, and twenty miles northeast of this place [Storms Hotel]. Three years ago I think there were twice as many.

I live at head-quarters on the reserve and pay no board. I do the blacksmithing work there which is enough to pay my board. I am not employed there, but just stopping there.[110]

Mr. Pollard made the point that some cattle were dying of "natural causes," possibly due to drought or to other extreme weather conditions like snowstorms and early frosts present in the mountains. As other settlers testified before 1858,

---

110. Deposition of Mr. William Pollard, Feb. 27, 1860, Storms' Hotel, Round Valley, Mendocino County in *Appendix Senate Journal, 1860,* Chas. T. Botts, State Printer, 67–68, at the California State Archives, 1020 "O" St., 4th Floor

it had been common practice on the frontier to allow Native Americans to consume these dead animal remains.

William Pollard's deposition continued:

> I never had any stock killed on Eel River before I moved them to Williams Valley; I moved my stock from Eel River because the volunteers went up there and were fighting the Indians; an Indian came to me and asked me why the whites punished, and drove off, doing their devilments; the Indian said it was no use to behave themselves; I removed my stock because I was afraid that after the Indians were disturbed they would kill them;[111]

The kind of reasoning used by Mr. Pollard was remarkably similar to that used by many other observers, such as Lt. Dillon, Lawrence Battaile, and some of the other inhabitants of Round Valley. They concluded that the militia was making things worse, not better both for the Native Americans and for permanent Euro-American residents.

Pollard also included one of the few available examples of indirect Native American testimony, indicating that the militia activity was counterproductive. Instead of "chastising" the Indians into "better" behavior, the violence against the Native Americans led them to question their attempts to cooperate with or appease the Euro-Americans, as such attempts did not appear to satisfy the settlers or to improve the conditions of life at all.

Continuing his testimony, Mr. Pollard reported that it was the Native Americans who were killed first.

> I made no contract with any one to do the blacksmithing; I make no charge for it; Mr. Bowers is an equal partner with me in the stock; there was never any difficulty with the Indians between the forks of the Middle Fork of Eel River; this is on the trail to Sacramento Valley; I never heard of the Indians committing any depredations in Eden Valley until the white men commenced fighting them; I do not know of any expedition ever going out to Eden Valley against the Indians until these men were killed between Gravelly Valley and Eden Valley; I do not know the names of these men, but I heard they were hunters and were killed up there; the first I ever heard of being killed in this country, were Indians; I heard of Indians killing stock first, and about the same time I heard of whites killing Indians.

WILLIAM POLLARD

Sworn to, and subscribed before me, at Storms Hotel, in Round Valley, this twenty-seventh day of February, one thousand eight hundred and sixty.

J.B. LAMAR,

Chairman Committee on Indian Affairs[112]

---

111. *Ibid.*
112. *Ibid.*

Such testimony notwithstanding a second group of settlers felt that the actions of the militia were fully justified by the attacks by the Native Americans, not only on their stock, but on the settlers themselves. However exaggerated these claims may be the feelings engendered by the scattered deaths of settlers help to explain the brutal behavior of the militia. Conversely one might then also expect such behavior to come from the Native Americans, which was for the most part not forthcoming.

One settler to describe vengeance as a motivation for the attacks on rancherias is Charles H. Eberle, who, perhaps ironically, later became one of Mendocino County's first constables. In 1860 Eberle's job was known as the "magistrate." Sometimes the office of constable was the same as Justice of the Peace.

> Charles H. Eberle, being duly sworn, deposes and says:
>
> I am twenty-eight years of age; am a farmer; I reside in Round Valley;...I have resided in Round Valley since October, one thousand eight hundred and fifty-seven; I am a magistrate there; I think there are many Indians residing in that vicinity; I consider those Indians unfriendly to the whites; they manifest their feeling by killing stock, and our neighbors and friends; when I first went there the feeling was about the same; the Indians had killed a good deal of stock previous to my going there; three or four months after my arrival there the Indians killed Mr. William Mantel; Mr. Mantel was one of the party that volunteered to assist John Owens to drive his stock to Cold Spring Valley, and on his return, the water in Eel River being high, he undertook to drive his mare across the river prior to swimming himself, and while doing so he was shot by the Indians; these were Yuka [Yuki] Indians; John McDaniel was killed by them a year ago last September [1858]; I helped to bury his remains on the mountain; this was about twenty miles from the valley; he was a hunter; Mr. Mantel I knew personally; he was a peaceable man; I never knew him to molest an Indian in any way. ...[113]

In another deposition, a Long Valley rancher Jeremiah Lambert confirmed that George Woodman lost some of the first Mendocino county livestock that were taken by Native Americans. Woodman was one of the few Euro-Americans ever arrested and convicted for kidnapping Native American children. Elsewhere in the deposition, Mr. Eberle mentioned a raiding party under the command of Capt. Farley. Apparently unofficial raiding parties popped up like weeds throughout Mendocino County at this time.

> Jeremiah Lambert, being duly sworn, says:

---

113. Deposition of Charles Eberle to the Select Legislative Committee, *Appendix, Senate Journal 1860*, 34–35, California State Archives, 1020 "O" St., 4th Floor, Sacramento, CA.

I am forty-one years of age; I reside in Long Valley two years last fall; I have lost nine head of horses which I believe, to have been killed by Indians, and in some of which I have found arrowheads; I saw them in camp, and know them by the iron on the hide; I considered them worth four hundred and fifty dollars; they were killed during last fall, and the present winter; the Indians have killed stock recently.

Mr. Woodman has lost a good deal of stock; I have seen a good many of the carcasses where they were killed. About one year ago or a little more, I saw an Indian shoot an arrow into a cow belonging to Capt. Ford. I was hunting horses at the time; Captain Ford had about fifty head of cattle in the valley, which he took away in March last. There is a company there under Captain Farley; I belong to it; I went out and found two horses in a rancheria, and killed several of the Indians. Three or four times we went out, and found meat in the rancheria; I believe it necessary that protection should be afforded to the settlers in Long Valley; Mr. Farley, and a man he has with him, have lost eight head of horses to my knowledge. We tracked them to the rancheria. I saw Captain Jarboe and a few men in Long Valley, about two or three months ago.

HIS

JEREMIAH X LAMBERT

MARK.[114]

By the spring of 1860, forming of rancheria raiding parties by Euro-Americans and Hispanics had become almost a casual everyday undertaking. Note the breezy tone of the following deposition taken in Eden Valley.

C.J. Small, J. H. Hildreth, John A. Johnson, J. D. Hawkins, and Jose Maria, being duly sworn, depose as follows:

On the day before yesterday [Feb. 27, 1860] we started in pursuit of some Indians that had been stealing stock, having been informed by B. Burch [Burch, or Birch, commanded a segment of the Eel River Rangers in the fall of 1859] that he had seen the trail where Indians, had been stealing stock. We went to the spot where Burch had seen the tracks; (found them, the tracks) [parentheses in original] and followed in pursuit of the Indians; we continued to follow the sign until we came to the camp where we found signs of meat, which the Indians left; we then followed them until we found the rancheria and Indians—on the evening of the twenty-eighth, instant about fourteen miles south of Eden Valley—and attacked the Indians killing two bucks and wounding three Indians; one of the latter was a squaw, who was shot accidentally; the others escaped; there were about fifteen in camp. We took one child prisoner, it having been deserted by those who fled. We found in the rancheria remains of horses.

J. D. Haskins
John H. Hildreth

---

114. Jeremiah Lambert's deposition to Assemblyman J.B. Lamar, Feb. 29, 1860, in *Appendix, Senate Journal 1860*, 74–75, California State Archives, 1020 "O" St., 4th Floor, Sacramento, CA.

C .J. Small
John A. Johnson
  HIS
Jose X Maria
  MARK

Sworn to and subscribed before me at Eden Valley, the twenty ninth day of February, one thousand eight hundred and sixty.
  J.B. Lamar
  Chairman, Select Committee on Indian Affairs[115]

The settlers had started to become more efficient in their vengeful attacks on Native Americans. Note also in the above deposition that at least one Native American woman was gunned down "accidentally" by settler vigilantes.

Further, these ad hoc raiding parties had been active for several years before the commissioning of Jarboe's militia. In the testimony of settler John Lawson, for instance, such a party is described as active in 1856. Indeed, Lawson described the killing of Native Americans accused of stock depredation as "common practice." Lawson made no bones about his view of both the Army's lack of protection of Euro-American settlers and their livestock herds and changes in reservation management, especially the extension of fences, which he and other settlers claimed made life more difficult for the ranchers. Finally, note in particular Lawson's almost casual view of killing Native Americans in retaliation for their taking of livestock, in this case, hogs.

Lawson's deposition began:

> I am thirty-eight years of age; live in Round Valley; have lived here since the fall of one thousand eight hundred and fifty-six; am a farmer and stock raiser. In the winter of one thousand eight hundred and fifty-six I lost twenty hogs; I found the meat in the rancheria. We went after the Indians; we shot three; the balance, five in number, were tried at the reservation, found guilty, and hanged. I have lost ever since [sic, Lawson had stopped losing hogs four months ago] until the last four months; I had about three hundred head of hogs little more than a year ago; the Indians eat [sic] my hogs about as fast as I could raise them; I went out and killed one Indian. It is the common practice when the Indians kill stock to pursue them and kill them. About two years ago I hunted considerable in the mountains; did not consider it dangerous; I would not like to camp out alone without arms; one man alone, with arms, in the day time, could keep fifty Indians off; but at night they might crawl upon him and kill him; never have seen but one white man who was killed by

115. Depositions of Mssrs. C.J. Small, J.H. Hildreth, John A. Johnson, J.D. Hawkins and José Maria to Assemblyman J.B. Lamar, Feb. 29, 1860. Ind. War File or *Appendix Senate Journal 1860*, 75, California State Archives, 1020 "O" St., 4th Floor, Sacramento, CA.

Indians myself; I have heard of others being killed; I saw the body of William Mantle [or Mantal]; after he was killed; I do not know that Mr. Bland was ever employed upon the reservation.

I do not know that the settlers applied to the officers for aid against the Indians; I know that Lieutenant Dillon went out after Indians, and had a man shot.

I think the force here is sufficient to protect the settlers against the Indians, provided they would go out and look after the Indians. The troops have not been after the Indians but once or twice since they have been here; I understand that it is their business to protect the Indians on the reservation; I do not think the Indians are any worse than they were, or better than they were.[116]

Lawson's attitude toward the military presence in the valley was clear. He believed its real purpose was to protect the Native Americans, and so it was of little help at all to the settlers. It would have been helpful if the Army were to "go out and look after the Indians." Perhaps what Lawson really wanted to say was that he might have been happier if there had been more shooting and less fencing.

There has been some fencing done since Capt. Storms left; they are making fence now. Since Capt. Storms left the reservation there has been a pair of bars closed [perhaps a gate had been installed with "a pair of bars closed"?]; this [presence of the fence] has been an inconvenience to settlers going to the woods for timber; to some of the settlers the distance is double; I never seen any one pull down the fence on the reservation; I have seen an Indian lead a horse about fifty paces distant through the fence, which was then down; he did not put it up.

If the government would pay me for the stock I have lost I would give up my property and go away. I think the Indians are treated as well as they can be at the reservation.

On new year's day, one thousand eight hundred and fifty-nine, Mr. Brittinton and eight or ten others came to my house and killed three Indians; they shot them; they alleged that they had been stealing; I did not believe they were guilty; they were shooting them when I came home; I understood that ten or twelve were killed by the same men on the following day at the reservation, and one or two at Mr. Bowen's; at that time I lived where Thoms B. Henley now lives.

JOHN LAWSON.

Sworn to and subscribed before me, at Storms' Hotel, in Round Valley, this twenty-seventh day of February, one thousand eight hundred and sixty.

J. B. LAMAR,

Chairman Select Committee on Indian Affairs.[117]

---

116. Deposition of John Lawson to Assemblyman Joseph B. Lamar, in Round Valley, Feb. 27, 1860, in *Appendix, Senate Journal 1860*, 68–69, at California State Archives, 1020 "O" St., 4th Floor, Sacramento, CA.
117. *Ibid.*

Here one gets the feeling from this testimony that raiding parties were permissible as long as they were not carried out against one's "own" Native Americans. The more depositions one reads the clearer is the picture of a vicious cycle of revenge, essentially uncontrolled ethnic cleansing.

The testimony of settler and one-time reservation employee William Frazier provided further description of the "unofficial" raiding parties. According to Mr. Frazier, the raiding party he belonged to killed Native Americans in earnest and without hesitation once all the men got set in ambush. And once started, the genocide process was very difficult to understand and even harder to stop.

Unlike some other depositions in which the settler glossed over the unseemly graphic details, Frazier was not shy about spelling out his own role, clearly and without hesitation.

> We started on an expedition across Eel River, in the mountains between Round Valley and Long Valley. We left Long Valley in the evening. And traveled in the night before we saw the fire of an Indian rancherie [*sic*]. Which rancherie we surrounded when day was breaking. And waited until near sun up before we attacked and killed twenty, consisting of bucks, squaws and children. And also took two squaws and one child prisoners. Those killed were all killed in about three minutes. I took the prisoners to White & Simpson's Rancho, where there are some friendly Indians, and delivered them up to White & Simpson, who promised to take care of them. We found in this rancheria no signs of any depredation having been committed by these Indians. At White & Simpson's I procured an interpreter, through whom the two squaws said that they had lived on beef and horse meat for some time. We used no threats or promises to induce them to say so. They said that they had heard the Indians say that they had been killing stock longer than any white men knew anything about and that they intended to kill all the stock in the valley. They assigned no cause for killing the stock, and we could not induce them to do so. About a week afterward we went out on another expedition into the same section of country. On the first night we found two wounded Indians and one old squaw, all of which we killed. On our return home we found another rancheria, which we approached within fifteen feet before the Indians observed us. They then broke for the brush and we surprised them and killed thirteen bucks and two squaws. The rest escaped. Therefore I do not know how many there were in the rancheria. We took no prisoners. We found in this camp the carcasses of two horses. One of these horses belonged to Mr. Lambert. The other was not recognized. Mr. Lambert recognized his by the brand on the hide and color. We then went home.[118]

Frazier, who has just voluntarily confessed to murdering twenty men, women, and children in an apparently wanton slaughter, has also coolly related how his group then went out and murdered two wounded and one elderly

---

118. Deposition of William Frazier to Assemblyman Joseph B. Lamar, Storms Hotel, Round Valley, Feb. 27, 1860, *Appendix, Senate Journal 1860* P.B. Botts, State Printer, pp. 61–62 at California State Archives, 1020 "O" St., 4th Floor, Sacramento, CA.

Native Americans in cold blood. One has to wonder if he has not stretched the truth a bit in relating that they found the remains of Mr. Lambert's horses at the rancheria. Frazier continued his testimony with a blanket disclaimer that his group was organized and stood ready to provide only "mutual protection" to the other settlers.

> This company was organized for mutual protection, there being no regular force in that vicinity. There never has been [sic. a] company of United States troops stationed in Long Valley. This was the last expedition I was in the company. The company still hold themselves in readiness to act when necessity requires it. I never belonged to Jarboe's company. On the trail that led to this rancheria we saw signs of meat having been carried along. And that caused us to attack it. From that time up to three weeks ago last Monday, there was no fighting in Long Valley. I suppose, from what I have heard that there has been two hundred head of horses and cattle killed there since October last. They were worth at least six thousand dollars. They are a cowardly tribe of Indians. There are about three hundred Kaza-Pomas ["Pomos"]. There are forty or fifty Cahto-Pomas living on the rancho of White & Simpson, who are also friendly. In 1857 the different tribes in that vicinity of had a meeting and sent for me to be present. I was told by the friendly Indians that the Yukas encouraged the attempt to kill me. They surrounded me and one Indian drew his bow and arrow and held it on me. But I brought my pistol to bear on him before he could shoot and he cooled down. I then rode off. The only cause they assigned for it was that I made those around mind me. And sometimes whipped them, and they did not like me. There has been no white man killed in Long Valley that I know of. And no buildings burnt. I think there is a necessity for an armed force in that valley, for the protection of the lives and property of the citizens at present. I do not believe that the citizens have applied to the Federal troops for protection. The white population in that valley consist of about one hundred and twenty five.
>
> I know of no attack being made by the Indians either upon a white person or residence. I have often traveled through the region inhabited by these Indians, alone and without being molested by them. I know of no children being taken away from these Indians to be sent away. Among these hostile tribes which we attacked, we found no children. And I believe there has been a practice of abducting the children from them by some white men for the purpose of pecuniary profit.
>
> Before my company was organized, there has been a good many Indians killed in the valley by the citizens and Captain Jarboe's company.
>
> WILLIAM W. FRAZIER
>
> Sworn to and subscribed before me, this twenty-second day of February, 1860.
>
> B. LAMAR, Chairman of Select Committee on Indian Affairs
>
> EXAMINATION RESUMED
>
> In the camps of these hostile camps that we attacked, we found a plenty of acorns and such other food as they usually eat for their subsistence. Sworn to and subscribed before me, this twenty second day of February, 1860, in Ukiah City.
>
> J.B. LAMAR, Chairman.[119]

Added almost as an afterthought is Frazier's statement regarding the other food available to the Native Americans that seems to prove, by implication, that the Yukis killed stock for spite. One is also struck by the fact that almost every settler who described rancheria attacks in his deposition included at least a sentence or two about the remains of animals belonging to settlers that were found there. It is apparent that most settlers were using the presence of livestock remains as the justification for the shootings that had taken place at Indian homes or rancherias.

Recently, a Round Valley Wailaki gentleman told me that most Indians were not in real danger of starving because "they had all the deer they wanted."[120] Whatever the correct interpretation regarding the motivation provided by hunger or starvation may be, what is undoubtedly true is that Frazier clearly contradicted himself at least once in his above testimony. Earlier in his deposition he stated that at least one of the raiding parties he was with had killed children as well as adults. And yet now, at the end of his deposition to the committee, there were no children of Native Americans present when the whites attacked.

What we must conclude from the testimony of Frazier and others is that the settlers were eager not to condemn themselves regarding the treatment of women and children. The following account from the deposition of Charles H. Bourne makes this clear.

> I have been out on several excursions against the Indians since I have resided in this valley. There has always been a general understanding among all parties that I have been out with to chastise none but buck Indians; I never have seen, but in one instance, a squaw to have been shot, and that was accidental; I do not think that there is a man in this valley who would shoot a squaw, or child, or even an innocent buck, if he knew him to be so; I never have been on an excursion against the Indians but what I found more or less meat in their camp, either hare, beef, or sheep meat.
>
> CHARLES H. BOURNE.
>
> Sworn to and subscribed before me, at Storms Hotel, in Round Valley, this twenty-eighth day of February, one thousand eight hundred and sixty.
>
> J.B. LAMAR. Chairman Select Committee on Indian Affairs[121]

---

119. *Ibid.*
120. Personal interview of author with Mr. Emmett Simonin, August 22, 1999, Petaluma, CA. Mr. Simonin is a hardworking Round Valley Native American of the Wailaki tribe. Mr. Simonin (or Simmons) is the father of Ms. Cora Lee Simmons, Chairperson of "Round Valley Indians for Justice" (Ensuring Justice for Native Americans), a legal advocacy group that serves Round Valley Native Americans today.

Note in the last line of the above quotation that "hare" was found within the rancheria. It was certainly not against the law for Native Americans to shoot game, including "hare" or rabbits.

Captain Charles Bourne had another role to play besides that of working as a farmer. Like a number of the other settlers, Bourne became the leader of a settler raiding party that searched out and then did as much destruction as it could to a Native American rancheria. In the fall of 1861, Bourne would lead the party responsible for the locally infamous Horse Canyon massacre.

We can tell from Frazier's and others' depositions that most of the settlers were very well aware that kidnapping rings operated for profit. Desperadoes frequently attacked the Native American families and transported them to Sacramento, to the Bay Area or to southern California where they were resold for profit in slave auctions. Most of these Native American children then grew up with no sense of their own cultures and little of their own families.

An extremely revealing indication of the prevalence of this practice of kidnapping Native Americans for sale was provided by an outsider, George J. Clarke. Clarke was part of a party of hunters who sometimes went on vacation near Round Valley. He was deposed by Assemblyman Phelps, possibly when Phelps was en route back from Round Valley on the steamboat *Petaluma* to San Francisco. Clarke's deposition reads as follows:

> I am forty-two years of age. I am Purser of the steamboat Petaluma. Some time in the month of October last [1859] I was with a hunting party in the vicinity of Round Valley, and rented Capt. Jarboe's camp. I saw there a lot of about sixteen Indians, mostly squaws. They were in a building, by themselves, preparing food. There was a large quantity of meat hanging round the camp. They were supplied with it liberally. In the afternoon of the day of our arrival there were about sixty more Indians brought into camp. I saw flour and meat distributed among them in abundance. The next morning there was a large lot of meat brought in on mules, and given to the Indians. They were supplied with flour at the same time. The general conduct of Capt. Jarboe toward the Indians was uniformly kind. While I was there Capt. Jarboe discharged one of his men who had suffered another man to have intercourse with a squaw then a prisoner. While I was at Round Valley, or the vicinity thereof, there came into camp eight men, settlers from Round Valley. And stated that they had killed all the bucks they could, and taken two or three squaws prisoners. I heard the firing myself about a half an hour before they came up, and stated the facts above mentioned. These men said that they found dead hogs in the camp, or rancheria, and fired and killed all the Indians they could. Capt. Jarboe told me that he would not allow any Indian children to be taken away. Our party was desirous of

121. Deposition of Charles H. Bourne to the Select Legislative Committee, February 28, 1860, *Appendix Senate Journal 1860*, P.B. Botts, State Printer, 48, California State Archives, 1020 "O" St., 4th Floor, Sacramento, CA.

getting some, but he refused to let them have any, though they would have paid for them.

Neither myself or any one connected with me have, directly or indirectly, had any interest in any claim relating to Capt. Jarboe's expedition against the Indians.

GEORGE J. CLARKE

Purser of Steamer *Petaluma*

Sworn to and subscribed before me, this fifth day of March, 1860, on board the steamer *Petaluma.*

A. PHELPS,
Of the Assembly Committee.[122]

Jarboe carefully tried to cover himself from possible blame over the number of murdered Indians. He spread the rumor about the dead hogs to a visiting outsider, George Clarke, whom he knew could have no way of verifying the facts. Clarke described the prisoners as well taken care of, and claimed that Jarboe would not sell any Native American children to him.

Why Jarboe refused to sell children is unclear from the record. Possibly Jarboe opposed the practice of kidnapping Indian children. Perhaps he knew that he would probably lose his chance of being paid by the state if it was later revealed that he had made such a deal. Another less appealing interpretation is that Clarke's offer was not high enough so that Jarboe simply stopped the negotiation. Or perhaps Jarboe himself wanted to retain the Indian children for reasons of his own.

The other members of Clarke's party were probably interested in buying Native American children for various uses: concubines, field hands, mine workers, domestic servants. What is interesting is not the fact that members of this party wanted the children but that Clarke was so casual in mentioning the idea of buying them in this way, thus confirming the prevailing Euro-American attitude toward California Native Americans as chattel or at least free labor.

Equally telling is the angry and defiant tone of many of these testimonies. Almost all of the depositions carefully included a list of dead livestock, usually belonging to the person who gave the deposition. This list is usually presented prominently in the testimony so there can be no mistaking the cause of the

---

122. Deposition of George J. Clarke to Assemblyman A. Phelps, March 5, 1860 *Appendix Senate Journal 1860,* P.B. Botts, State Printer, 46, California State Archives, 1020 "O" St., 4th Floor, Sacramento, CA.

attacks on the Native American rancherias. These accounts present a biased, one-sided look at the situation in Round Valley.

William J. Hildreth was a rancher who worked on land belonging to Judge Hastings, possibly much like poor white sharecroppers did in the ante-bellum South. His deposition provided testimony about recent battles in Round Valley. Hildreth seems to have had a little different perspective on the causes of the conflict than other settlers. Hildreth stated that reservation Native Americans "were very poorly treated." He was frank and open in admitting that he could not be absolutely sure about which Native Americans were taking his stock.

Deposition of William J. Hildreth:

> I am twenty-five years of age; I am a ranchero; I am doing business for myself; I reside here [on the south fork of the Eel River]; I came here to live last April; I have resided in this county about eighteen months; I resided in Round Valley from May, one thousand eight hundred and fifty-eight, till I moved to this place; I have a ranch here; I keep stock here on the shares for Judge Hastings. When I went to Round Valley there were unfriendly relations existing between the whites and the Indians surrounding the valley. I have been in this business since last July. While I was there, there were from five hundred to one thousand tame Indians in the valley, including those who lived on the reservation. I heard that Mr. Lawson [left blank in original, "John" Lawson was another of the earliest settlers] lost, while I was in the valley, about eight or ten head of hogs. I think this was about July, one thousand eight hundred and fifty-eight, which loss was attributed to Indians who worked on the reserve; he had the prisoners with him, and took them to the reservation. The first depredations that I know of, of my own knowledge, being committed by wild Indians was committed in Eden Valley;[123]

Note the similarity of this account of these first so-called "depredations" with that of some others cited in this study, such as that of Judge Hastings. The first incidents in which hungry Native Americans, either from the reservation or "wild," may have killed stock for food occurred in Eden Valley and Long Valley. This makes sense when one considers that Round Valley is relatively closed in, so that any local Native Americans suspected of taking stock there were more easily apprehended and punished by settlers. Here the punishment was usually less severe than death. Several accounts state that Native Americans were beaten or locked up on or near Nome Cult Farm.

Hildreth described Judge Hastings' stock losses along with some of his own in the spring and summer of 1859. He continues to talk of the formation of his own ad hoc militia company, whose members included Jarboe.

---

123. This and subsequent quotes from Hildreth's deposition are from W.J. Hildreth's deposition to Assemblyman Joseph B. Lamar, Feb. 24, 1860. Ind. War File, California State Archives, 1020 "O" St., 4th Floor, Sacramento, CA.

... this was in July last. The mares, colts, and horses, of Judge Hastings, about three hundred and eighty in number; were delivered to Robertson and myself. I lived from July last to the first of September in Eden Valley, taking charge of stock running on that end of the range. I turned into my pasture all my riding horses, and one mule belonging to Hastings and Henley; after letting them run about a week, I sent my vaquero after the horses which were in the pasture; he came back and reported that some of them had been killed by Indians; I went down and found three of the three-year old colts, a mare, and the mule, dead; they were shot, and we found the points of arrows in them; I raised a party of six men and went in pursuit of the Indians, and tracked them to where they crossed the Middle Fork of Eel River, going in the direction of the reservation; I lost the trail at a point about three and a half miles from the reserve; Eden Valley is ten miles distant from this place, in a northerly direction; I have no means of judging what Indians committed this depredation but it was my impression at the time that they [were] reservation Indians. Those five head of stock I should think were [worth] four hundred and ninety dollars; I valued the mule at two hundred and fifty dollars. There are no other stock on this range but that of Judge Hastings, and there has been none. About a week after, there were four other horses killed in the same manner; we found them dead, with arrow heads in them; these animals were worth two hundred and forty dollars. I then turned my horses out of the pasture on the range for safety. About two or three weeks after this, I found three Indians skinning a yearling steer; I fired on them twice, and they ran down the cañon; I then raised a company and followed these three Indians to their rancherias; we attacked them, and killed seventeen; one of our party, Mr Jarboe was wounded;

This unit was the first recorded company of local militia. It carried out a bloody engagement in which at least seventeen Native Americans were killed. The only Euro-American wounded was Jarboe. None of the Euro-American militiamen were killed.

Judging from the way he later committed genocide, by attacking and slaughtering Native American at will, Jarboe was the kind of pioneer who neither forgave- nor often, if ever- forgot. Inferring from Hildreth's account, it may have been Hildreth who first taught Jarboe how to organize a group of settlers into an ambushing force to go out into the mountains, locate a rancheria, then just after dawn, attack without warning and kill Native Americans:

I led the party; one squaw was found dead, the rest were bucks; the squaw was shot by accident; we took one buck, four squaws, and three infants prisoners; we took them to Eden Valley, where the indian, through an Interpreter, confessed that his tribe had killed a great many stock, and would continue doing so as long as any stock ran loose; he also stated that if we turned him loose he would continue to kill stock, and he also stated that his tribe would kill white men; the Interpreter was a boy of the same tribe, who had been raised by white men, and belonged to Mr. Robertson; we court-martialed the man, sentenced him to death, and shot him; the squaws and infants were sent to the reservation. Since that time I have never seen any stock dead that were killed by Indians, but at various times have seen cattle and horses with arrows sticking in them.

Some of the Eden Valley settlers were not satisfied with the killing of seventeen Native Americans in this raid, probably because the only remaining live male Native American bravely spoke up to them. So they condemned him quickly and took his life as well.

Mr. Hildreth described further stock losses and the actions of the Eel River Rangers, of which Hildreth was a member. It is just as sad and depressing as Jarboe's account of his company's actions in Chapter 5:

> I have, since July last, missed seven or eight head of horses and colts that I cannot account for; the cattle I do not know how many are gone. Those that I have missed cannot be found on the range, which is almost sixteen miles square. Since I took charge, in July last, I estimate the damage to the stock to be not less than one thousand dollars; I have been acquainted with this stock since they were brought here; the first lot of stock, consisting of two hundred and thirty-five head of cows and seventy three calves, were brought here in January, one thousand eight hundred and fifty nine; in April, this lot was counted, and there were thirty-five or forty cows and steers, and two hundred calves, were brought; these also came from Judge Hastings, about the first of July, this lot was counted; and about sixty head of cows and steers were missing up to July last, was worth very near four thousand dollars. In the rancheria above referred to, we found the skulls and horns of two head of cattle, and also the hoofs of horses; also the crisped hide of a milch cow that I lost; and some jerked horse flesh, or beef. I belonged to Captain Jarboe's company, whom I joined after his commission arrived; the company was organized in Eden Valley; I joined when the company was organized—July and was with them until in October last.
>
> On one expedition we made to Long Valley we killed two men; and took thirty prisoners; the prisoners were all sent to Mendocino Reservation. On another expedition, in search of the body of John Bland, we killed eleven men, and took ninety-seven or ninety eight prisoners; most of these prisoners were tame Indians; about twenty of them were wild; we sent them to Mendocino Reserve. This was to the northwest of Round Valley, and about twenty-five miles from Nome Cult Reservation, or farm; George Henley furnished the provisions; we took beef, wherever we could get it. The above stated are the only successful expeditions I went on. I have a claim against the state for my service in the company.

Mercenary soldiers had almost never had it so good as did Hildreth and other members of Captain Jarboe's militia of 1859–1860. They were well paid, unlike some of the members of the Bear Flag Revolt in 1846 who had served to wrest the state from Mexico and were never paid. In part due to the legislative committee's investigation, the legislature paid the militia's main claim by June 1860. It is assumed that Captain" Jarboe and George Henley bought food for the militiamen.

Mr. Hildreth continues:

> The prisoners were always given plenty to eat; treated well, and given good advice through Interpreters. Strict discipline was maintained in the company; and

for an infraction of rules in regard to prisoners, one of the men was discharged; while I was with them. Captain Jarboe read instructions from the Governor, instructing him to be sure to always get the guilty Indians, and not punish innocent ones; Captain treated his prisoners kindly; he had two bucks and a squaw who were wounded, and always dressed their wounds himself.

Here Mr. Hildreth seems to be suffering somewhat from a conflict of interest. It would seem that he protested too well here in defending his boss in such an ardent manner. Quite possibly the governor's letter of caution in early December 1859 to Captain Jarboe came even as reports of this bloody massacre of Native Americans began to chide or embarrass the Weller administration. One has to ask what great skills in medicine did Jarboe possess that he could efficiently clean and dress the Native Americans his men had just shot? Did he wash his hands? Would any soldier want an angry enemy commander, who was once wounded in a battle, to play the role of a medic?

Mr. Hildreth concluded his deposition by commenting on the issue of the quality of treatment of Native Americans on the Nome Cult Indian Farm.

> I was employed on Nome Cult Reservation for one month, in one thousand eight hundred and fifty eight, and I resided five or six months within a half mile of the reserve, the Indians that worked were fed; and those that did not, were not fed; I worked Indians of the Yuka tribe. Captain Storms, was Indian Agent at that time, and these Indians were allowed no meat; and received six ears of corn per day; while I worked them—two ears in the morning; two at noon; and two at night. I worked then, on an average, eight hours per day. The Indians on this reserve, I think, were treated very poorly.
>
> W. J. HILDRETH
>
> Sworn to and subscribed before me, this, the twenty-fourth day of February, one thousand eight hundred and sixty, at Hildreth's Rancho, on the South Fork of the Eel River.
>
> J. B. LAMAR
> Chairman Select Committee on Indian Affairs.

There are no clearer statements or confessions of guilt anywhere on record of the maltreatment or abuse of Indians by Euro-Americans than this. Native Americans living on Nome Cult Farm, so-called "tame Indians," were being systematically starved by protein deprivation on a large scale at the reservation. It is small wonder that when federal inspectors like J. Ross Browne visited Nome Cult Reservation in 1859, they were told that most of the Native Americans were off in the surrounding mountains and hills hunting for acorns. Therefore, Browne had no way of accurately counting Native Americans on California's reservations including Round Valley Reservation.[124]

No adult human being, either of the mid-nineteenth century or of the early twenty-first, can survive on six ears of corn per day. And a Native American received this only if he or she toiled in the fields all day. One should recall that this diet was often supplemented by game that many male Native Americans hunted for during most of their daylight hours. The settler depositions tell in some cases an unwitting, horrifying tale of cruelty, insensitivity and neglect. Moreover as was revealed in another of Browne's reports to the Office of Indian Affairs, even Subagent Storms and some of the other reservation employees sometimes stole rations which should have gone to their Native American wards on the reservation, the people they were supposed to be caring for.

Another settler whose deposition provides insight into the beginnings of the Mendocino War and the actions of the Eel River Rangers is William T. Scott. His testimony began:

> I am twenty-eight years of age, am a farmer and stockraiser. I reside in Scott's Valley, Mendocino County and within five miles of South Eel River and Robinson's Ranch; having resided there one year.

> Those Indians in the surrounding years live there and trade backwards and forwards across Eel River with other Indians. They are like the Yukas in appearance. I have seen them on the north side of Eel River. I have had some seven hundred head of stock in my charge since the first of June last, and of this number I have never lost any to the Indians.

> These Indians have been in the constant habit of crossing the Eel River and hunting, in the surrounding country, until Captain Jarboe's company was started, when they were afraid to go there. I heard Captain Jarboe tell these Indians that if he ever caught them along the river he would kill them.[125]

Mr. Scott continued with an interesting hypothesis about the beginnings of the conflict:

> I know Mr. Hall, of Eden Valley, that some time in May last I had a conversation with him touching the Indian difficulties in that section of the country. Mr. Hall attributed the origin of the difficulty with Indians to the following cause. That a little more than a year ago he employed thirteen Indians in place of pack mules, to go and pack loads from Ukiah City to Eden Valley, and promised to give each one a

---

124. Special Agent J. Ross Browne to Secretary of Interior, September 4, 1858. Cal LR, Bureau of Indian Affairs, as quoted by William M. Hammond, "History of Round Valley Indian Reservation," unpublished MA Thesis, 1972, Roll 3, microfilm, 90, Chapter II, footnote 10, Sacramento State University Archives, Sacramento, CA.
125. This and subsequent quotes from Scott's deposition are from "Deposition of W.T. Scott to State Assemblyman William B. Maxson, Of the Assembly Committee," Cloverdale, CA., March 2, 1860 in *Appendix Senate Journal 1860*, 23–24, at California State Archives, 1020 "O" St., 4th Floor, Sacramento, CA.

shirt in payment. The distance, I think, is about forty miles. Mr. Hall said he did not get the shirts at the time to pay them. The Indians commenced complaining at not receiving the shirts. And he, Mr. Hall, whipped two of them to keep them quiet. He said he never gave them after he whipped them as they left them and never did not come back for them. Mr. Hall said previous to this time the Indians had never killed any of their stock. But soon after they killed some of their stock. Then Hall associated hunters with him and commenced killing all the Indians they could find in the mountains. When Hall met Indians he would kill them. Mr. Hall said the Indians had killed two fine stallions, one of which cost six hundred dollars and the other one thousand dollars. Said he believed the Indians who had done the packing for him had killed the stallions because no other Indians would have known enough to have selected the most valuable stock.

As we have seen, it was the killing of Judge Hastings' horses, and especially of the prize stallion, that angered and drove the judge to petition Governor Weller to commission a militia company. So it may be that this one particular depredation was in retaliation for the behavior of one overseer. This was the cruelty of H.L. Hall, once described by an admiring reporter as the "Texan Boy," and his contempt for the Yukis and other local tribes is clear in a number of the 1860 legislative committee depositions. Sadly, ranch manager Hall's abuse of the two Indians may have triggered this bloody phase of the Mendocino War.

Continuing with Mr. Scott's revealing deposition:

> At another time I heard Mr. Hall say that he did not want any man to go with him to hunt Indians, who would not kill all he could find because a nit would make a louse. Mr Hall said he had run Indians out of their rancherias and put strychnine in their baskets of soup, they had to eat.

All of these events transpired before Captain Jarboe's company was organized. Scott's testimony then went on to confirm the course of events that led up to the commissioning of the Eel River Rangers, making especially clear the motivations of Judge Hastings.

> A few days after, Judge Hastings drove a large band of cattle, some time in April last. He said he wanted the range for stock, that he could have the Indians removed and have them replaced by a volunteer company if the citizens would petition the Governor and that the citizens of Round Valley ought to do that. Said the soldiers were good for nothing in the mountains against the Indians. That the Indians would have to be removed by a volunteer company. Judge Hastings solicited me two or three times to sign a petition for a volunteer company. I told him it was nothing to do with me and that I did not think the Indians would be so bad if the whites would leave them alone.

> Before Captain Jarboe's company came there, Mr Robinson, who had charge of Hastings' stock, applied to me, and said if he could get five or six men to go with him, that there was about three miles down the river a rancheria. That they could kill off the old Indians and get the young ones, and make something of it. That he was afraid these Indians would kill his stock, if they had not already. Mr. Robinson

afterward told me that he had been to the rancheria above referred to, and killed some of the Indians, and took one Indian girl. That he would have killed them all if it had not been for a man named Howard, who went with him, who claimed some of the Indians, and prevented them from killing them. Robinson said Howard was as bad as the Indians, and that he meant to kill all the Indians on their side of the river they could find. This was prior to the formation of Captain Jarboe's company.

I resided at Scott's Valley, with my uncle. We had a large amount of stock. Never lost any and never felt any danger. I frequently hunted, slept out alone by a large fire and picketed out my horse, and was never disturbed by Indians. Camped within a half mile of Indians. I have lost about fifty head of stock from natural causes, but not from Indians, I believe some have died from getting into gulches, want of good food, some from disease. I know Indians eat the carcasses of animals found dead. I saw three head of Hasting's cattle dead from poverty or starvation, on his range, in August last.

This testimony stands in telling contrast to that of settlers who claimed that the settlers' stock losses were due solely or at least mostly to Indian depredations. Scott continues:

I was solicited by Captain Jarboe to come with him. Or join his company with two others residing with me. He, Captain Jarboe, said we could all three join and stay part of the time at home, and part of time with his company. And our pay would go on all the same. One man told him he thought that would be swindling the State. Captain Jarboe said the amount would be so small that it would never be missed. I told Jarboe, that I did not like, from report, the manner he was conducting the war. He requested me to go [out on patrol] a few days with him and see for myself. I went with him; remained for five days. Captain Jarboe's orders to his men were to kill all the bucks they could find, and take the woman and children prisoners. And if they got sight of an Indian, never to lose sight of him as long as they could follow the trail. The first we met while I was with Captain Jarboe were two Indians about a half mile distant. [They] appeared to be gathering acorns, unarmed. Captain Jarboe sent his men to surround them and be sure to get close enough to make good shots and kill them. One was killed and the other escaped. This was on the range claimed by Judge Hastings five miles from Eden Valley.

Here Scott notes how Jarboe planned to enlist more militiamen by promising them a "free ride" from the state. Note also that Jarboe's orders to his men were essentially to act as a death squad: to search out and destroy all male Native Americans wherever they might find them. Finally Scott states clearly how the militia set ambushes and shot Indians in cold blood.

A straight talking pioneer, when compared to some others, William T. Scott apparently told the truth as far as any one observer can when involved in an armed conflict with a hostile culture. Unlike more bloodthirsty, arrogant minority, Scott is not trying to influence other settlers, the governor, or the state's most influential politicians in his testimony. It is possible that Scott had a personal grudge to settle with Judge Hastings, H.L. Hall or others. Scott concluded:

> On the other occasion, a part of Jarboe's company pursued two Indians. The Indians hid in the rocks near the river. They surrounded the place, and Hall sent his dog after the Indian to drive him out of the rocks. The Indian shot the dog, dropped his bow and arrow and plunged into the river. And was shot in the water, while endeavoring to escape. The Indian was hunting, as he had the head of a deer stuffed, used by them while hunting.

California tribes in this era made use of deer heads to camouflage themselves while hunting. This was a good way to get close enough to a herd of deer to get a good shot at one without scaring them all off. Scott's account is clear evidence that Jarboe's men were shooting first without asking anybody anything or trying to determine innocence or guilt by searching for remains of stock.

The belief that the presence of an Army platoon was insufficient protection against Native American depredations was frequently expressed in the depositions of local settlers, many of whom would rather have a permanent local militia for protection. One such settler was an Irishman Martin Corbitt, whose land holdings were not as big as those of Storms, Henley or White, but who was often mentioned by others as having lost stock to the Indians. His deposition, that was somewhat more mature in tone than some, made clear the difference between the Army and the settlers when it came to "chastising" the Native Americans.

> I am forty-four years old, reside in Round Valley; I am a stock-raiser, have resided in this valley three years; my land joins the reservation, according to the last United States Survey; have had cattle killed by Indians; have lost, altogether, over twenty-four head of cattle—some were cows, yearlings, and calves; the cattle were killed, some in the mountains; am not afraid to travel through the mountains armed; I applied to Lieut. Dillon to aid me to hunt some Indians who had killed my stock; he sent five soldiers with me; we brought in eight or ten male Indians, and about twelve squaws and children; three Indians we brought in admitted they had killed stock; two escaped, and the other escaped; do not know of any stock that has been driven off by white men; have been out with some of the expeditions against Indians; there was thirty-five or forty Indians killed by us in the expeditions I was out with; these expeditions were before and after the troops came here.[126]

---

126. Deposition of Martin Corbitt given to Assemblyman Joseph P. Lamar at Storm's Hotel, Round Valley, Feb. 27, 1860, *Appendix Senate Journal 1860*, B.P. Botts, State Printer, 33–34, California State Archives, 1020 "O" St., 4th Floor, Sacramento, CA. Round Valley writer Mr. Floyd Barney, op. cit. stated that at this time Lt. Dillon was new to the valley. It is likely all the Native Americans might have died except for the soldiers' presence.

Although he had been present on expeditions where Native Americans were shot and killed, contrary to Army protocol, Corbitt's deposition mentioned that Lt. Dillon trusted him enough to send out five of his men with him on the occasion mentioned. He explained that this expedition took approximately twenty Native Americans "prisoners," yet apparently on this initial foray none were killed. As any responsible officer should do, Lt. Dillon was careful not to expose his troops to any unnecessary dangers. As Lt. Dillon is not mentioned as being present in this early raid on a Native American rancheria, one assumes that the five troopers and Corbitt were a sufficient force to handle the situation without killing any of the Native Americans. In spite of repeated settlers' claims about lack of help from the Army soldiers, in this case the settlers and troopers cooperated.

Corbitt continued with an often-heard formula describing militia raids:

> We always found bones and the remains of cattle in the rancherias, and once we found horse-meat; the Indians are not killing as much stock as usual; I am of opinion that we need an armed force for the protection of settlers; I do not think the troops here are any protection to settlers; when we could, we took prisoners and sent them to the reservation; have sometimes seen the Indians pull the fences down so that the squaws might get over easier, have sent them back to put it up; they pulled the fences down so as to let the cattle into the reservation; think the fence runs out of the valley one mile; there has been some byways closed up since Mr. Rees came on the reservation; the way we went through when I came here is closed; it is five miles further to the mills by the way we have to go now; after Mr. Storms left the reservation, these bars were closed.[127]

George Rees became Agent or Supervisor after Simmon P. Storms left in 1859 (see his deposition in Chapter 7). He also noted how some loveless settlers, especially the Wilsey brothers, sometimes trespassed onto reservation property to abduct Native American women.

Mr. Corbitt concludes:

> Had four cows killed during the last year; and there has been one missing a month; which I suppose the Indians have killed. I went out about four months since; we killed three Indians, and one at another time; did not make any application to the officers for aid, because I did not think they punished the Indians enough.

MARTIN CORBITT

Sworn to and subscribed before me at Storm's Hotel, in Round Valley, this twenty-seventh day of February, one thousand eight hundred and sixty.[128]

---

127. *Ibid.*
128. *Ibid.*

Here Corbitt articulated his fellow settlers' indictment of the Army in crystal-clear language: the Army is insufficient protection because they do not "punish the Indians enough." They did not ride off with the vigilante posses to kill Native Americans in retaliation for stock losses.

Another Round Valley resident, George Rees, became the second Agent at Nome Cult when Storms left (see his deposition in Chapter 7). He noted how some of the more lonely lovesick Euro-American settlers, especially the Wilsey brothers, trespassed onto the reservation to abduct Native American women.

H.L. Hall was the same rough character who first was hired and then later fired by Judge Hastings for whipping and abusing Native Americans in Eden Valley. Hall gave his deposition on February 26 at Storms' Hotel in Round Valley to Assemblyman Lamar.

> I am twenty-five years of age. I am farming and taking care of stock. Taking care of stock for myself, and Judge Hastings, and Col. Henley [Supt. T.J. Henley.]. I reside in Eden Valley. I have resided there since the latter part of August, one thousand eight hundred and fifty-eight. There were no settlers in Eden Valley when I went there. There were no inhabitants in Eden Valley when I went there. I took three hundred and twenty head the next month. They were mares, colts, and horses. In December, one thousand eight hundred and fifty-eight, my Indians told me that one mare had been killed, and before I went out after them they reported three or five killed. During that fall one hundred Indians came in and camped near my cabin. as far as I knew, these Indians were peaceable, and these are the ones I mean by my Indians. I went up to the rancheria with J.W. Smith, Charles McLean, and William Vaughn. We found some eighteen or twenty Indians, who ran away as soon as they saw us. I think eight or ten were killed and the balance escaped....[129]

Hall's testimony described how the reservation was limited to just four thousand acres. It was Hall's opinion that the reservation would support up to two thousand five hundred Native Americans with the right kind of management. Hall also thought that the Army troops were not

> of any benefit to the settlers. The officers have manifested no disposition to afford any protection to the settlers. They seem perfectly indifferent to the depredations of the Indians. The officer in charge, to my knowledge, never goes into the mountains to ascertain if any depredation has been committed by the Indians. The people in this valley do not countenance the killing of women and children.
>
> I have been on speaking terms with the officer in command at the reservation till within the last few days. We are now unfriendly. There is an unfriendly feeling existing between the citizens and officers, they are regarded in fact as a nuisance.[130]

129. Deposition of H.L. Hall to Assemblyman J.B. Lamar, Chairman Select Committee on Indian Affairs, February 26, 1860, Storms' Hotel, Round Valley, *Appendix Senate Journal 1860*, "Testimony Taken Before the Joint Special Committee on the Mendocino Indian War," 41, California State Archives, 1020 "O" St., 4th Floor, Sacramento, CA.

Hall's deposition contained some of the strongest statements against Indians on record anywhere, by common 1850s standards. Hall seems to have taken pleasure in killing:

> ...followed the trail of the two horses some two miles further, there we found where they had killed them, as evidenced by blood and hair. We took the trail where they had carried the meat off, followed about three quarters of a mile and found the Indians in a cañon; we attacked them; they jumped into the bush and commenced shooting arrows at us; there were about twenty-five or thirty Indians in the party; we killed ten or twelve of them and one woman....

George E. White made some of the grossest exaggerations in these 1860 accounts. Perhaps partly because of these strongly stated opinions, White became very influential in the events that took place after the committee's investigation was over. As will be clear later, politicians both in Sacramento and in Washington made use of White's deposition to attempt to bury the truth about the actual actions of the Eel River Rangers and other militia groups that operated in Mendocino County.

White was a very large man, "over six feet three inches tall, and weighed over 200 muscular pounds." According to a local legend reported by Estle Beard, before his arrival in Round Valley, George White had worked at Nome Lackee Reserve as a tavern-hand or laborer during the latter part of 1854.[131] By the 1860s White had amassed power. He gradually became one of the largest landholders and thus the most influential permanent Euro-American resident in the valley. By the 1880s, White would out-fight, bully and hire his way into becoming the largest landowner in Round Valley, eventually earning him the title "King of Round Valley." He was responsible for maintaining the western tradition of using terror and violence to gain and maintain personal power.

What follows is part George E. White's testimony in the spring of 1860 to the joint state legislative committee starting at the beginning:

> I am twenty-eight years of age. I am a stock raiser. I reside at Round Valley. Have for over two years. I lost stock by depredations of Indians when I first came, and have been losing stock at different times ever since. I have lost hogs, cattle, and

---

130. *Ibid.*, 40.
131. The information about George White working in a tavern, probably as a bouncer, came from a handwritten addition, which according to Held-Poage Curator, Ms. Lila Lee, was left at the Library by the historian Estle Beard. Beard wrote many of his comments in pencil in the margins of a copy of author Rena Lynn's *The Story of the Stolen Valley* (Willits, CA: L & S Publishing, 1977), 28, Held-Poage Library, 603 W. Perkins St., Ukiah, CA. This fascinating local history, now out of print, was the first modern Round Valley history of this period.

horses. I suppose the damage I have sustained from depredations of Indians to be from five to ten thousand dollars. It is impossible to tally exactly the amount, from the way in which stock ranges in this country. There is an ill feeling existing between the citizens and the officer in command. Just before the troops came in, I lost some of my hogs and other property, and I went in pursuit of them, and on the way, I met Major Johnson, to whom I had been previously introduced. Mr. Tobin was with him. Major Johnson asked me where I was going. I told him I was in pursuit of the Indians who had stolen them, and that I intended to kill them if I found them with stock. He told me if I killed any he would arrest me. I told Major Johnson that there had been some Indians encamped near my house, who had left the night before, and took with them some hogs and other property, leaving behind them a blind squaw, who told me that they had taken the property. He said that no Indians should be killed on such evidence as that. I also stated to him that I had been out about a week before, on an expedition against Indians, who had killed horses. I saw where they were killed, and we found the meat in the rancheria, but found no Indians. I also told him of several expeditions against the Indians, for killing stock, which we tracked to the rancherias, and where we had killed some Indians, and that I was glad he was coming provided, he would protect our stock. He said there must be no Indians killed, and he thought it was in his power to make the government pay for the stock killed. I told him that was all that could be asked, if he would do it. That was the first disagreement that I know of between the citizens and the officers.

I was not a member of Captain Jarboe's company. I have no claim directly or indirectly, against the government, arising out of the organizations of Jarboe's company. The troops stationed here have been of no benefit to the citizens, but on the contrary, have been a great disadvantage, because Indians who commit depredations, go there and receive protection.[132]

Ranch-builder George White was at his aggrieved best here. His description of events echoed what is apparent in many other depositions: there was no love lost between the Army and a narrow majority of the settlers in the region. White charged the Army with colluding with his enemy, "the Indians." He also claimed that the Native Americans got protection from the Army, which, unfortunately for many of them there, was also untrue. At the bottom of the enmity between the Army and the settlers was a disagreement over the function of the Army in the valley and, of course, also a major disagreement about what should be done about the Native Americans.

The Army's responsibilities were much more complicated than White or many other settlers appreciated. White could not have known all that the Army did to preserve the peace in Round Valley. No one settler did. This is one reason why the Legislature's committee took so many depositions. Also apparent here

---

132. Deposition of George E. White to Assemblyman Joseph B. Lamar, Feb. 27, 1860 at Round Valley, *Appendix Senate Journal 1860*, Chas. T. Botts, State Printer, 69–70, California State Archives, 1020 "O" St., 4th Floor, Sacramento, CA.

and in other depositions is the consistency of the Army's approach in these matters. Major Johnson stated the Army's position clearly for White and other whites hungry for ranch land: Indians were not to be summarily executed. The way to get satisfaction for loss of stock was by seeking reimbursement from the government. Unfortunately, neither the federal government nor the State of California was interested in setting up a stock reimbursement fund to repay the settlers for legitimate losses of stock killed off by the Indians; so, when it came to restitution or repayment for the value of their lost livestock, the settlers would have a very long wait.

White charged that the Native Americans cost him "five to ten thousand dollars" in damages. The situation was open for someone like White to charge almost anything he wanted to, with a better than average chance of receiving a favorable hearing by California officials. Like Storms, Henley and even Hastings, White was very much aware that the legislators could not have valid reasons to doubt his version of the facts. White also knew that, for the most part, other Euro-American settlers would be testifying with very similar depositions. In other words, he could be bold in his estimates of personal stock losses because he knew his view was being supported by the testimonies of many of his friends, fellow ranchers and other Round Valley settlers. He must have known also that depositions of this tone and viewpoint would make up the majority heard by the lawmakers.

Continuing now with George White's deposition,

> The evidences that are sufficient to satisfy frontier men, they do not consider sufficient, and would take no notice of it. I think the citizens derived benefit from the operations of Captain Jarboe's company. I think that an armed force is needed to protect the lives and property of the citizens in this section.[133]

Having established his own personal claim of losses, White then made a grossly inflated general estimate of $150,000 for the losses for the whole region.

> The Yukiah [Yuki] tribe are the worst Indians I ever knew to steal. On two or three occasions I have passed through the reserve fence, and found the stakes out, but I always put the fence up as I found it. While Captain Storms was there, there was a pair of bars for the convenience of settlers, but since he left, they have been taken away, and the passes closed up. The damage that I think the citizens of this and Eden Valley have sustained in consequence of depredations of Indians, is from one hundred to one hundred and fifty thousand dollars.

> GEORGE E. WHITE.

---

133. *Ibid.*

Sworn to and subscribed before me, at Storm's Hotel, in Round Valley, this the twenty-seventh day of February, one thousand eight hundred and sixty.

J. B. LAMAR,
Chairman, Select Committee on Indian Affairs.[134]

It is clear from reading such depositions that the settlers often relied on a kind of formula to describe their actions. First they described the number and value of the stock they had lost. Then they affirmed that the rancherias they attacked contained the remains of settlers' livestock. Therefore by implication all the Indians who happened to be present must be guilty of theft. All the settlers in this first group urged a permanent settler militia force be established in Round Valley to "punish" the Indians. In the next chapter other Euro-American eyewitnesses present another strong argument about Round Valley's crossfire of two cultures.

---

134. *Ibid.*

Chapter 7. The Employees' Depositions

It has been impossible to feed the Indians in that section of the country...
—James Tobin, ex–Nome Cult Farm special agent

The mentality and morality of individual settlers varied enormously. The majority of settlers, especially some like Frazier, Jarboe and others, apparently never hesitated in their killing frenzies to think about justice or whether they were even killing guilty parties. Others, like Battaile, Buckles and Lt. Dillon, deplored the massacres. Some probably tried to dissuade those settlers who reacted in mindless rage whenever there was a loss of livestock on the range, when there was a break-in of a settler's house or when settlers' possessions were reported stolen, supposedly by Native Americans.

Some Mendocino County settlers and many reservation officials sharply dissented from what Indian Affairs Department officials higher up the chain of command and in Washington thought.

James Tobin

James Tobin,[135] a San Francisco merchant and one-time special Indian agent in Round Valley, provided an interesting view of the causes of the Mendo-

---

135. All quotes in this section are from the Deposition of James Tobin to Assemblyman Joseph B. Lamar, Feb. 28, 1860, Storms Hotel, Round Valley, *Appendix Senate Journal 1860*, P.B. Botts, State Printer, 53–54, California State Archives, 1020 "O" St., 4th Floor, Sacramento, CA.

cino War. Tobin contended that it was a budget reduction that first caused problems to develop in Round Valley between the Native Americans and the white settlers. His deposition provides important insights, describing not only the relationship between Washington officials in the Office of Indian Affairs and reservation officials in California but also the relationship between the Army officers and the settlers in Round Valley. Quoted here are only those parts of his deposition that relate to the causes of the so-called Mendocino War.

James Tobin, being sworn, says:

I am forty years of age. I reside in San Francisco. Am a merchant. Have resided in California since 1849. I have been familiar with Mendocino County for nearly seven years. I have frequently been on the Indian Reservations. I have visited the places where the Indian Reservations have been established more than twice a year, for five years past. In consequence of the heads of the Indians Department in Washington, having curtailed the amount of the appropriation, for Indian purposes, it has been impossible to feed the Indians in that section of the country, to which our attention is now drawn. This fact is known to me personally. White people are permitted to settle in this region, and occupy the ground formerly occupied by the Indians, and the consequence is, depredations are committed on their stock by the Indians....

Tobin stated his opinion simply and openly. A federal cut in appropriations for the California Native American situation after 1857 was a primary cause of the Native American's need or hunger for settler livestock. Having highlighted the reduction in this vitally important aid from Washington, Tobin next stated another highly significant problem. At first, it seemed that all of Round Valley would be set aside for a Native American reservation. Instead of that, however, the increased numbers of Euro-American settlers created a situation that was ripe for conflict.

I have always treated the Indians well. Am well known to them and speak a little of their language. I turned my horses out in Eden Valley one night, leaving a rope on. This one they took, and led to a distance of a couple of miles, slaughtered, and eat [sic]. This is the first depredation that I know of my own knowledge. ...

Like many other early Californians, Tobin made a bit of room in his testimony to pat himself a little smartly on his own back.

The next passage reveals just who was responsible for sending Lt. Dillon's Army detachment to Nome Cult Farm in January 1859.

Over a year ago, Colonel Henley [Supt. of Indian Affairs], for the purpose of protecting property from Indian depredations, and to protect the Indians from the consequences, at the hands of white men, made an application to General Clarke, and had troops sent to Round Valley and Mendocino Reservations. I conducted the troops to these places. The day after their arrival in Round Valley, the officer in command [Maj. Edward Johnson], quarreled with the people, in my presence. That feud continues to this day.

This early split between the military and the settlers in Round Valley is an important key to understanding later events from 1859 through 1862. It is unfortunate that Tobin did not include more of the details here. The discord between the settlers and the detachment's commander was also noted by others, including Lt. Dillon.

Regardless of this initial lack of harmony among the Euro-Americans, Mr. Tobin related a fact that most historians seem to have ignored. According to Tobin, Goddard Bailey, a special investigator sent to California by the Indian Affairs Department in Washington to look at the new California reservations, made an important recommendation to his superiors that played a part in all the conflicts and bloodshed that lay just ahead.

> All these sad consequences are the result of the Department at Washington having acted as Mr. Bailey, [the Special Agent of the Indian Department (brackets in the original)] advised, reducing the appropriation, from a sufficient amount to feed the Indians, to fifty thousand dollars.

> Mr. Bailey stated to me, frequently, that he had not sufficient time to discharge his duty properly, being obliged to hurry so, that he could not spend more than two nights at each of the three places he visited with me.

> CROSS-EXAMINATION

> I know of my own knowledge that the Indians on the reservation in Round Valley are in want of the actual necessities of life....

Federal funding reductions in 1857–1858 took a fearful, and, as yet, uncounted, toll in human lives and suffering at the reservation level. More Indians were brought onto Nome Cult even as the number of immigrants increased into Round Valley with each year that passed.

Tobin continues to state that "some eighteen or twenty" white men were reported to have been killed by the Native Americans. According to a popular local history, Carranco and Beard's *Genocide and Vendetta: The Round Valley Wars of Northern California* (1981), this was about double the actual number of whites killed by Native Americans at that time in the Round Valley area.

Tobin continued:

> Round Valley contains about sixty inhabitants [presumably not including Indians]. I conducted a portion of the Sixth Regiment of Infantry, under the command of Brevet Major Johnson, Lieuts. Carlin and Dillon. About twenty-five men remained under the command of Lieut. Dillon. Thirty or forty conducted to Mendocino Reservation, who were under command of Lieut. Carlin. I conducted them there in December one year ago [1858–1859]. I was on close terms of intimacy with

these officers. I learned that they were not pleased with the order to go there, as they had just arrived from crossing the plains. Major Johnson is the officer referred to in my direct examination who quarreled with the people in my presence.... I have been in Round Valley three or four times since troops were stationed there.... There is a feeling of hostility existing between the citizens of Round Valley and the military. I have been employed as Special Agent by the Superintendent of Indian Affairs. I was so employed more than a year, ending July last [1859]. I am well acquainted with the nature and character of Indians in the northern part of California, and have had intercourse with them for about seven years. It is impossible for the Indians and whites to live together peaceably unless the Indians are fed.

The exact nature of Tobin's employment as "Special Agent" is not clear. Quite possibly he had acted as one of the Office of Indian Affairs agents following the treaty signings of 1850-51. However, it is clear that he had close contact with all parties involved: the Native Americans, the Army and the settlers. His testimony supports that of others in this chapter: "It is impossible for the Indians and whites to live together peaceably unless the Indians are fed."

I have spent about two months, for the last five years, in that section of the country, outside of the Indian Reservation. I think that there were upon an average upon the reservation in Mendocino County not to exceed 3,500 Indians for the six months previous to the first of July last [January through June 1859]. I do not know the amount appropriated for those Indians. The Indians confessed to me to taking and killing my horse. I went with Col. Henley and heard him make application to Gen. Clarke for troops.... When I first knew the Indians in Mendocino County I think they were hostile to the whites. I so thought because they presented themselves in large bands and endeavored to obstruct the passage of myself and others through their country. I know nothing more in regard to Mr. Bailey's duties excepting what he told me himself. I have no interest, either in stock or otherwise, in Mendocino County. I have no personal or pecuniary interest in any appropriation that has been or may be made for the suppression of Indians hostilities.

JAMES TOBIN

Tobin, a San Francisco merchant, mentioned that in the past he had been exasperated at being surrounded by large groups of Native Americans standing around and thereby preventing him from crossing their territory. This could also have been an unstated problem for others as well.

Tobin stated that he interpreted this action as a warlike act. From these depositions and others it is obvious that the Euro-Americans alone could not solve the problems caused by some of their own government's policies toward Native Americans. Removing them very often led to violence.

Tobin's testimony seemed to be that of a former Indian agent and merchant with no apparent land or stock raising ambitions in Mendocino County. He simply stated his perceptions and opinions based solely on his own observation about the reasons for the Native Americans' hunger at the reservation.

Tobin's position was in almost direct opposition to that of the so-called pioneers: George White, Judge Hastings, Supt. Henley, and others. They were men with a significant personal stake in the ranching industry and ambitions for much larger land acquisitions. They saw each and every loss of an animal as a revenge slaying or a mean, unnecessary outrage by evil and "savage Indians" who were nothing but a burden to white society and to the future of California.

SIMMON P. STORMS

In the fall of 1859, Subagent Storms reentered civilian life. In the 1860 Federal Census, former Subagent S. P. Storms humbly listed his occupation as "farmer." Storms was one of only two or three (out of approximately one hundred) Round Valley residents who declared anything under the "assets" category of the census form. Storms reported his personal assets to be "$35,000." No doubt that meant that he was already, at just "age 29," the wealthiest man in Round Valley on paper by the spring of 1860 when the depositions were taken. The census did not include Judge S.C. Hastings. Perhaps this was because Judge Hastings was not present in Round Valley when the census was taken. Hastings' holdings were in Eden Valley which was outside Round Valley.

Because he was now wearing another hat, that of private rancher, after his replacement as the farm's agent by George Rees during the fall of 1859, Storms took on a new role in California society. Whereas he had been hopeful or even gracious in June 1856 toward the Native Americans, now Storms sounded just like any other determined rancher bent on punishing and, if necessary, exterminating the Yuki and any other Native Americans who were not willing to become docile, "tame Indians."

> S. P. Storms, being duly sworn, says:

> I am twenty-nine years of age. I am a farmer and reside in Round Valley. I have resided there since June, 1856. I came here in the employment of Colonel Henley, Indian Agent and established Nome-Cult Farm. I remained on the reservation until September, 1859.[136]

---

136. This and the next few quotations are from Deposition of Simmon P. Storms to Assemblyman Joseph B. Lamar, Chairman, Select Committee on Indian Affairs, February 26, 1860, at Storms' Ranch, in Round Valley, *Appendix Senate Journal 1860*, 36–38, California State Archives, 1020 "O" St., 4th Floor, Sacramento, CA.

Knowing that most readers of his deposition would be strangers or state legislators not familiar with the local scene, Storms stretched the truth in claiming to be a farmer. Far from being just the agent-in-charge of Nome Cult Farm for the period between June 1856 and September 1859, Storms had also built a hotel and the main buildings of his own ranch south of Covelo in land that was off the reservation. Storms' hotel was listed as the location where a number of depositions were recorded by members of the Legislature's joint Select Committee.

Using his own hand-picked crew of Native American (possibly Maidu) workers, Storms developed his private ranch into one of the largest in Mendocino County by 1860. There is little doubt also that, when he needed them, Storms could count on using the reservation Native Americans to help him out with manual labor on his ranch.

Returning to Subagent Storms' deposition:

> The largest number on the farm was about two thousand, I mean Indians. In June, 1856 there were no settlers within thirty miles of the reservation. At this time the country was inhabited by Indians known as the Yuka tribe. The greater part of the Indians were Yukas. All the stock first brought to the reservation were a few milch cows and teams. The Indians at that time were thievish. The first loss was five American cows belonging to the Government; am not certain whether it was done by the Indians on the reservation or by others. There were about five thousand Indians who made Round Valley their home during the winter season when I first came there. The valley is round, contains about twenty five thousand acres. There were a few settlers came here in 1856. In the spring of 1858 most of them that are here came in. At the time I came here this valley contributed largely to the support of the Indians. As a consequence the Indians were deprived of a large portion of their support. The game driven back into the mountains as the valley became settled.

> Among the first settlers who came here was Messrs. Lanson, [*sic*, John Lawson] King, and [Charles H.] Bourne who brought stock with them, who suffered great damage that winter [1856–1857, probably] from Indian depredations on their stock.

Storms left it up to the imagination to work against the Native Americans. He described them as "thievish" but conveniently omitted all the labor the Native Americans put into building a stockade, cabins for both Native Americans and Euro-American reservation employees, a system of paths and roads, and the main reservation buildings, including a commissary, corral, barns, and warehouse. It is difficult to find any of the original records regarding the first reservation's structures. Storms seems on somewhat firmer ground in talking about the loss of Native American hunting and acorn-gathering ground during those crucial first two years of the reservation.

His deposition described the first Native American revolt at the reservation:

> This was before any expedition [he refers either to Gen. Kibbe's expedition of 1858–1859 or to those first of Farley and later of Jarboe] had been made against the Indians. In July, 1856, the Indians made an attack upon the reservation. Had it not been for the aid afforded by the settlers and a few mountain men, we would have all been exterminated....

Storms used the word "exterminated" with reference to the Euro-Americans' peril during the first two months after the reservation's founding. This was only a short time after his arrival and the beginning of Nome Cult Farm in Round Valley. In reality, it is almost anyone's guess how much actual danger there was.

On the contrary, by 1859 it was the Euro-American population that held complete power over the the northern California Native American population and especially the vulnerable Yuki.

Storms continued,

> There has not a week passed, but that stock has been killed. In the spring of 1859 there were sixty-eight head of sheep taken from my ranch in one night and the increase from one thousand head of sheep [here, Storms referred to the government sheep on the reservation.] was nothing in consequence of Indian depredations committed by wild Indians or those on the reservation. I did not have 750 that I could control, except the Yubas and the Nevadas ["Maidu"] from the other side [the east side of the Mayacama Mountains] of the mountains.

> In the fall of one thousand eight hundred and fifty eight there were about one thousand head of cattle and horses on this ranch; the ranch has about one thousand five hundred acres fenced in; the cattle range outside among the hills. To the best of my knowledge and belief there has been between four and five hundred head of stock killed, exclusive of sheep, on this ranch.

For the record, Storms apologized or explained his actions while agent-in-charge at Nome Cult Farm. His description of the Native Americans also seems to support the claims of the settlers against them. But his claim of "between four and five hundred head of stock killed" on "this ranch—the reservation—" ought to be taken with a grain of salt.

Most of the rest of the facts stated here are more reliable, but still suggest his new bias or conflict of interest. While he is correct that more land was actually fenced in, many fences were in poor condition and allowed stock to stray. One should note that the shrewd and careful Storms made no mention at all of how many Native Americans were currently starving or dying of other causes on the reservation.

The reserve in this valley contains about four thousand acres, and with proper management is capable of sustaining about two thousand five hundred Indians. Inducements were offered to these Indians to come on to the reserve while I had charge of it, but made no strenuous efforts, because I could not feed them all, and I believed they would be better off in the hills if they were not fed. Nome Cult Farm is a branch of Nome Lackee Reserve, and subject to the control of the Agent in charge of Nome Nome [sic] Lackee. I was not provided with clothing and provisions sufficient for all, and therefore I divided what I had among those I thought most deserving and worked.

Storms mixed fact and fiction like a modern-day talk show host or maybe even a campaigning politician. His claim that the reservation could support 2500 residents is doubtful, even with "proper management," in light of the subsequent bloody years of Nome Cult Farm. The other statement, about his inability to bring more of the Native Americans onto the reservation and his lack of provisions, is almost certainly accurate. It lays the blame squarely on those above him in the California Department of Indian Affairs.

It should not be forgotten that Storms had already made a great impact on all the groups involved in Round Valley. When he arrived there in the middle of 1856 to found the reservation, he no doubt thought he was very well prepared to follow through on all the promises he made to the local Yuki people on that first day in the valley. He had formed strong relationships with people like the Nisenan and Maidu before. This included personally taking on the burden of raising several from infancy in his own home.

In a later report Storms boasted that the ten or fifteen Native Americans he had with him "had been with me since one thousand eight hundred and fifty; I clothed and fed them, in a measure, at my own expense." The individuals he was speaking of were probably Maidu or possibly Nisenan from western Nevada or from Sierra County on the extreme eastern fringe of California. Other historians claim Storms' Indians were Nisenan. The bond between Storms and these Native Americans was profoundly strong. He had trained and worked closely with each of them as their overseer from 1854 to 1856 under Agent Stevenson at Nome Lackee Farm near Red Bluff. Most of them were very appreciative and understandably loyal.

Evidence of Storms' ties to individual Native Americans is also found in the testimonies of at least two other reservation employees. The deposition given by Dryden Laycock, who worked for Storms, included the following defense of Simmon P. Storms and his fair treatment of the Native Americans under his charge.

> In relation to the above statement of Captain Storms—the Indians mentioned in the statement—I know Captain has claimed as his own Indians for the last five or

six years, and that he has clothed and fed them at his own expense; I have seen him buy clothing for them, and said at the time, for whom he was buying them. Since Captain Storms left the reserve, the Indians living on this place would run and hide when they would see any of the employees on the reserve coming here, or passing by, for fear they would be taken to the reserve; and they have told me they would not live at the reserve, if taken there; and they would run away and go back to Grass Valley, if they were not allowed to live with Captain Storms.

DRYDEN LAYCOCK.[137]

Some of the reservation employees could have been critical of Agent Storms because he left reservation property to work on his own ranch. Charles H. Bourne, a longtime resident of the valley, echoes Laycock's defense of Storms almost word for word.

DEPOSITION OF CHARLES H. BOURNE, RESUMED.

In relation to the above statement of Captain Storms, I know the Indian he had here [the Native Americans whom Storms referred to as "Nevadas" or "my Indians"], some of whom lived on the reserve, came here of their own free will; others had never lived on the reserve; some five or six of them he raised from children, and clothed and fed at his own expense, and they always expressed a desire to live with him; they have, some of them, told me several times, that if they were taken to the reserve they would not live there; that if they were not permitted to live with Capt. Storms they would run away and go to their native land. ...[138]

Although we cannot know for certain that Laycock and Bourne were telling the whole truth, Storms was capable of equivocation, even, at times, of corruption. The fact that, since before his arrival in the valley, Storms had always employed Indians who remained loyal to him also tells us something about his good character. His role as the founder and the first Subagent, Agent or Supervisor of Round Valley Reservation deserves definite respect.

GEORGE REES

George Rees replaced Simmon Storms in late September 1859 as subagent in charge of the Nome Cult Farm, or what was soon to be Round Valley Indian

---

137. Deposition of Dryden Laycock to Assemblyman Joseph B. Lamar, Chairman, Select Committee on Indian Affairs, Feb. 28, 1860, at Storms' Hotel, Round Valley in *Appendix Senate Journal 1860*, 51, California State Archives, 1020 "O" St., 4th Floor, Sacramento, CA.

138. Deposition of Charles H. Bourne to the Select Legislative Committee, February 28, 1860, in *Appendix Senate Journal 1860*, 48, California State Archives, 1020 "O" St., 4th Floor, Sacramento, CA.

Reservation. Perhaps the long wet and cold northern California winters had exacerbated Storms' breathing problems due to his tuberculosis. Rees had worked his way up as an efficient workman and overseer under Agent Storms. Several settlers state in their depositions that he was somewhat more humane than Storms had been. However, the Native Americans at Nome Cult Farm were only slightly better off under Subagent Rees than under Captain, Major, Colonel, or Subagent Storms. Despite all the best efforts of its honest new Subagent, Native Americans on the reservation continued to have a very tough time of it. Not only did they die of disease, white settlers continued to raid rancherias and destroy reservation property, especially by damaging or removing fences. As the years rolled by the destruction of the Native American's habitat became increasingly serious.

Agent Rees' testimony appears balanced.

Deposition by Mr. George Rees, Overseer, at Nome Cult Farm:

I am forty-nine years of age. I am Overseer of Nome Cult Farm. I have resided there, and had charge, since the latter part of September last [1859]. I think there are five or six hundred Indians, all told, who remain on the reserve all the time. There are two hundred or three hundred more who go and come occasionally, but claim that as their home. These wandering Indians are furnished food when they are on the reservation. Food is given to those Indians who do not work, but not as regularly as those that work. Those that work are regularly fed. The food given to those who work consists primarily of corn, wheat, beets, pumpkins, and potatoes. About six or seven ears of corn per diem is the usual allowance of the work hands. When they are fed on potatoes we give them about six or seven pounds per day. Most of the land in the farm I think is susceptible of a high state of cultivation. This farm is dependent for what is not raised, upon the Agent at Nome Lackee Reserve. When Indians are brought in from the mountains we give them food and clothing, such as we have, to induce them to remain.

I think that under judicious management, the farm is capable of subsisting five hundred or six hundred Indians. I have found the fence in different places prostrated and stock within the inclosure, but I am unable to designate the parties that did throw it down; from the manner in which the fence had been thrown down, and the rails disposed, I could tell that it was torn down by white men. We found horses' tracks and wagon tracks, passing through the opening made.[139]

Rees' estimation of the potential of Round Valley as a reservation is much more measured than the earlier claims of Storms. He estimates that it could support five or six *hundred* Indians with "judicious management," not two or five

---

139. This and subsequent quotes from Rees' deposition are from Deposition of George Rees given to Assemblyman Joseph B. Lamar, Storms Hotel, Round Valley, Feb. 22, 1860, *Appendix Senate Journal 1860*, B.P. Botts, State Printer, 16–17, California State Archives, 1020 "O" Street, 4th Floor, Sacramento, CA.

thousand. We will see more about the fence destruction by the settlers in a later chapter.

Rees continues with an incident involving two women who lived on the reservation.

> We have a couple of Nevada squaws upon the place, who are good seamstresses, whom white men have been in the habit of inducing to run off from the reserve. Some two months ago some white men came and took them off and we brought them back; at this time, we found them at the home of Messrs. Wilsey.

From other accounts we know the Wilsey brothers had previously been reservation employees who also did general labor for some of the larger ranchers in Round Valley. They had now become Round Valley settlers and had abducted two young Native American women. Agent Rees' deposition continued:

> To punish the squaws, we locked them up in a warehouse, locked with a padlock on the outside; I think we had them locked a day and night; and the next night the lock was broken and they were taken away; we found one of them at Mr. Wilsey's, the other we have not found.

That the women should be "punished" for being unable to fight off their abductors was a crime and a significant miscarriage of justice. Even worse is the fact that they were taken off the reservation in a second abduction with the breaking off of the padlock.

One of the women was never again seen alive. From another settler's deposition, it seems that she may have been raped by white settlers other than the Wilsey brothers. It is possible that the second woman was murdered. I have found no further mention of her anywhere. Some Native American women doubtlessly went with white men as mistresses. Others became common-law wives of white men. In some cases, they went voluntarily because they had some prospects of being better fed.

Unfortunately, Mr. Rees' testimony is brief. He makes no further mention of the other "Nevada squaw:"

> These women speak and understand English tolerably well for Indians; one of them is about sixteen, and the other twenty 2 [*sic*, twenty-two] years of age; they are tolerably good looking. They appear to be contented on the reserve. I have good reason to believe that two white men took these squaws at the time the lock was broken. I know of one instance where Indians belonging to this reserve were harbored by Mr. George Henley, who refused to give them up, and it was necessary to use force to obtain them.
>
> GEORGE REES

Native Americans who had been conducted to the reservations often left during the day on hunting, fishing, or trading trips. According to ethno-historian Virginia P. Miller, in *Ukomno'n: The Yuki Indians of Northern California*, many male Native Americans spent almost their entire time hunting. And, as the above incident indicates, the settlers would not leave Native American women at reservations in peace. In fact, Native American women taken by white men were often unfairly punished by reservation officials for the crime of leaving the reservation property without permission.

OTHER RESERVATION EMPLOYEES

While many of the settler depositions asked for more militia protection from the state, other depositions present another side to the story. Some concluded that Round Valley was not in need of another armed force. Despite constant contrary pleas by some about Indian "depredations" of settlers' stock, an important group of residents, in an equal number to the more militant group, felt there had been more than enough outside intervention in the form of armed drifters and ad hoc militia companies.

Some of these residents provided a differing side to the story of the loss of stock. One such dissenter was Lawrence Battaile, a thirty-five-year-old Nome Cult reservation employee who listed his occupation as "at general work." Not much is now known of Mr. Battaile, where he was born or if he was educated, what he did before he arrived Round Valley, or even what happened to him after he testified to the committee in the spring of 1860. His name is not included in the 1860 Census, so perhaps he sickened and died or moved away from Round Valley.

One thing about Lawrence Battaile seems clear from his deposition: he had few, if any, ulterior motives. Judging from the facts he chose to relate in his deposition, this was a man who had no ax to grind, either with Native Americans or with other reservation employees, Euro-American settlers or ranchers. The tone and substance of his statement place serious doubt about one of the main points of many of the white settlers: that a militia force should be organized and paid for with state funds, trained at Round Valley and go out into the mountains and countryside to "protect" white settlers and to "chastise" Native Americans.

Battaile's deposition begins:

I am an employee on the Nome Cult farm and have been so employed since July 1858. I work at general work at the farm. When I came here Mr. Storms had charge of the farm. I first heard of indians killing stock in this vicinity in the Fall of 1858. I then heard of Martin Corbitt and some other losing cattle and hogs by the indian. From what I have heard of since I presume that the indians have killed more or less stock from that time to this, principally on the South side of the Valley. During the last two months I don't recollect of hearing of any stock being killed by them....[140]

This is in direct contradiction of Captain Storms' testimony. Storms had claimed that the Native Americans continued to kill stock belonging to the ranchers up until the early part of 1860. Mr. Battaile continues,

The number of indians which I suppose to have been killed by them, by white men in this vicinity since I came here from what I have heard in this valley is about 300 or 400. I base this estimate on what parties who have been out after indians have told me.

I cannot estimate the number [of] stock killed by the indians, because the accounts of stocks is frequently exaggerated.

The manner of attacking an indian camp is to attack the camp first and after the indians have been killed or run away, then to enter the camp and see if any evidence can be found against them. ...

Based on his own years of living and working in Round Valley, Battaile testifies that the raiding parties shot first before asking questions. Although this does not contradict other eyewitnesses to the attack, it is significant because Battaile seems to have had doubts of his own about the methods usually used by the Euro-American raiders. Battaile clearly admits in the second paragraph of the above quote that he thinks other Euro-Americans are deliberately exaggerating the numbers of stock reported killed.

I have seen during the past year several horses and cows that have died in this vicinity, some have been maimed and some had died from poverty, I think I have seen some fifteen or twenty that have so died. The indians frequently come and tell me that animals have died and ask the privilege of going and getting them to eat.

I generally go and look at the carcass, to see [illegible — "whether"?] the indians have killed it or not. Those I have examined I have usually found to have died by some other cause, than by indians. The indians when they take a carcass to eat usually cut it up and take the hide, head and all to their rancheria. If I should find these things in a rancheria far off from where cattle usually range I should think that they had killed the stock, unless the meat looked as if it had been diseased.

---

140. This and subsequent quotes from Battaile's deposition are from Deposition of Lawrence Battaile to Assemblyman William B. Maxson, February 28, 1860 at Nome Cult Farm, Round Valley, CA in the *Appendix-Senate Journal 1860*, B.P. Botts, State Printer, 26–27, California State Archives, 1020 "O" St., 4th Floor, Sacramento, CA.

The import of this testimony is clear. Livestock was vulnerable to disease, injury and starvation as well as to Native American "depredations." Native Americans used what they could of the carcasses when they found them. As we have seen, few settlers acknowledged this possibility. One of those who did was William Scott, who testified, "I have lost about fifty head of stock from natural causes, but not from Indians, I believe some have died from getting into gulches, want of good food, some from disease. I know Indians eat the carcasses of animals found dead. I saw three head of Hasting's cattle dead from poverty or starvation, on his range, in August last."[141]

Regarding the Army's platoon Battaile then states,

> There is stationed on this [illegible; ranch?] a platoon of a company of soldiers under the command of Lieu't. Dillon.

> They have been stationed here about one year. If any appreciation [*sic*, "application"] have been made by citizens to the officer in command for protection I should have heard of it. I think there has been two or three or possibly more applications.

Here he suggests that the settlers' complaints against the Indians were not corroborated by their appeals to the military. He continued,

> I am acquainted with the Ukia tribe in this ["Place" is lined out] vicinity. I do not consider it dangerous for a man to go alone to Eden Valley, Weaverville or Gihama [Tehama]. I have not travelled to Weaverville alone, but have been told so by men who have travelled the route. I think the Indians south of this place are disposed to steal stock. I should not call them hostile to the Whites. They subsist on roots grass acorns and Berries, some little subsistence from Game. The Game is scarce having been killed by the hunters. The primary motive is to get something to eat, although they kill some for spite—to spite some settlers who have been out killing them. Some indians [in Eden Valley] told me they would kill Mr. Hall's stock in Eden Valley because Hall killed the indians their woman and children. This was last spring....

This is the testimony of someone who had closely observed the Round Valley reservation and its practices there for nearly two years. Battaile explained that the "primary motive" for killing stock, like the motive for taking the carcasses of stock killed by other causes, was "to get something to eat." That the Native Americans both on and off the reservation did not have enough to eat seems clear from the evidence. Their once plentiful sources of nutrition were being steadily denied them. A recent account of these times by Nomlaki Native American Andrew Freeman states:

---

141. Deposition of W.T. Scott to State Assemblyman William B. Maxson, 'Of the Assembly Committee,' Cloverdale, CA, March 2, 1860 in *Appendix Senate Journal 1860*, 23, California State Archives, 1020 "O" St., 4th Floor, Sacramento, CA.

Men died every day from starvation. That was in Camp of Dark Canyon in the winter. Women would find a bunch of grass and eat it and would bring a handful back for their husbands. The women would have to chew it for the men. The man was too weak to swallow it. She would take a mouthful of water and pour it into his mouth. That was the way they saved a lot of them....

Garland on the present Oakes' place wouldn't let them take the Indians off of his land, and that's what saved them. When they took the Indians to Covelo [in Round Valley, on the Nome Cult Reserve] they drove them like stock. Indians had to carry their own food. Some of the old people began to give out when they got to the hills. They shot the old people who couldn't make the trip. They would shoot children who were getting tired. Finally they got the Indians to Covelo. They killed all who tried to get away and wouldn't return to Covelo.[142]

In the case of H.L. Hall, Battaile offers a secondary motive for taking the stock of Euro-American settlers: revenge. As we have seen, Judge Hastings in his own deposition referred to Hall as the first ranch manager of his stock in Eden Valley. If what Hastings and Battaile have testified is true, then we must also conclude that the Native Americans sometimes purposely killed animals belonging to whites who had offended them. Hall's abuse of the Native Americans, such as frequently beating them, and his even more hateful murders of Native American women and children, could have led to retaliation by the killing of cattle and horses under Hall's care (which happened to belong to Judge Hastings).

In this instance at least, they would not have killed for food but to take revenge for their lost loved ones. Almost certainly Hall was their intended target, not Judge Hastings, who was still a newcomer. Most of the Native Americans probably never even saw Judge Hastings. Battaile's deposition then described how settlers took revenge for the apparent murder of the Euro-American hunter, John Bland.

... some time (I think)] in October 1859 — on a sunday morning I did see ["and" is lined out] a dead Indian which upon examination I found he was killed by a bullet and I think his throat was cut—...

The dead Native American, known simply as "Bob," was a young coworker of Battaile's on Nome Cult Farm. He was an innocent victim of the Euro-American settlers' rage. Sadly, Bob was a worker on the farm who happened to be in the wrong place at the wrong time. A drunken mob of settlers killed Bob in retaliation for the killing of Bland. Which tribe actually murdered John Bland still is a mystery to this day. The Yuki were quickly judged guilty by the Eel River Rangers.

---

142. Andrew Freeman, Nomlaki, as quoted in Malcolm M. Margolin, revised 1993 edition, first published in 1981, *The Way We Lived: California Indian Reminiscences, Stories, and Songs* (Berkeley, CA.: Heyday Books), 164-165.

One of their rancherias was immediately attacked. Some observers of the time thought the real killers were Pit River Indians.

Battaile's testimony continued with his opposition to the formation of an independent militia to police Round Valley.

> I think there are over 200 working indians on the farm from my knowledge of condition of things [a word was inserted by Mr. Battaile, here, with a hatch mark to an area between the lines] at present. I do not think that there is a necessity for an armed force to be raised or sent here for the protection of the property of the Citizens—

> I think there is a sufficient armed force here now to protect the Citizens. If the Officers in command were applied to—The cattle range is so large on the hills that I do not think would prevent the Indians from killing [Inserted in the same way as above by Mr. Battaile] stock occasionally. Nor do I think that a regular organized Company would prevent the going out of small expeditions against Indians. The reason I think so is because that small parties did go out whilst Capt. Jarboe's Company was in operation—The fences on the farm have been pulled down often by the settlers evidently for the purpose of passing through and left down.

> I think that if this Ukee [sic; Yuki] tribe were all gathered in on the reservation that with proper treatment they would remain here. I think thus from my knowledge of their habits and characters, although they would frequently go in to the mountains—I believe such a course would conduce more to prevent depredations upon the stock of the settlers than the presence of any armed force or the occasional killing of the Indians except a total extermination of them—The settlers always told me when they did go to hunt the Indians—that the Indians had killed stock— and they Generally told me that they found meat in the Rancherias—I think sometimes they told me they did not find any.

As already noted, Mr. Battaile and numerous others testified that the Euro-American settler raiders usually surrounded the rancherias and attacked suddenly at dawn without warning. There was no time to gather and then to dispassionately sift through evidence. As Battaile notes here, sometimes after an attack the settlers did find remains of stolen stock. But sometimes they did not. He argued that the actions of the militia, as well as the unofficial raiders, only served to exacerbate the situation, which would be better handled by the "proper treatment" of the Indians and the presence of the Army platoon. He also seems to suggest that one should expect some occasional loss of stock as par for the course.

Mr. Battaile added:

> I am not conscious of having any feeling of prejudice or Bias against any of the Inhabitants of Round Valley.

Battaile's testimony concludes with another account of a kidnapping, and possibly, depending on one's interpretation in reading it, the rape of a Yuki or other Native American woman together with the abduction of four Native American boys:

> In coming into this valley on the first occasion I met a man with four (4) Indian boys taking them off and the third time I came on the trail I met a man taking of a Girl—she afterward returned home—I never knew any citizens of Round Valley taking Indians out of the valley to dispose of. I have heard parties residing in this valley say that they have gone in to the mountains and taken Indians and brought them in to stay with them and from circumstances I believe it was done without the consent of the Indians.
>
> I believe some of the Indians living with the settlers are better provided for than if they were on the reservation and some are not.
>
> Lawrence Battaile
>
> Subscribed to and sworn to before me this 28th day of February AD 1860 at Nome Cult farm.
> Wm. B. Maxson
> of Assembly Committee

Battaile's concluding remark about the adoption of Native Americans into Round Valley Euro-American settlers' households shows that the assimilation of Native Americans into employment in white households had already begun. For example, Storms, P. A. Wit, George Bowers, and other ranchers all had Native American household servants and/or cooks.

Reservation officials varied in their opinions regarding the need for a militia force in the valley in 1860. Even though he was not effusive in his praise of the U.S. troops in Round Valley, one reservation employee, the reservation's resident physician, Dr. John Burgess, like his co-worker Lawrence Battaile, made it clear that he felt more armed force was unnecessary. Dr. Burgess thought the Army was preferable to the use of a volunteer militia, like Captain Jarboe's Eel River Rangers.

Dr. Burgess's deposition contained one of the few records extant to relate what crops were grown on the reservation in the late 1850s and how the introduction of hogs depleted the Native Americans' food supplies and natural habitat for food like acorns.

> John W. Burgess, being duly sworn, deposes and says:
>
> I am forty years old. I am a farmer on Nome Cult Indian Farm. I have resided and been an employed on this farm since the sixteenth of October, 1858. I am well acquainted in Round Valley. From my intercourse and dealings with the Indians in this vicinity, I know their general character and disposition tolerably well. From information I received from parties themselves, that are in the habit of traveling in the mountains alone, and from them I learned that there was no danger of being

attacked by the Indians. From information, I did hear, I believe, that the Indians are in the habit of killing some stock. I do not consider the Ukias ["Yuki's"] a hostile or dangerous tribe. I do not think there is a necessity for a mounted volunteer company in this vicinity to operate against the Indians. Owing to the settling up of the valley by farmers, and the consequent retiring of the Indians to the hills, they have been deprived of the fruitful source of subsistence, such as roots, acorns, and clover. The hogs eat the acorns and roots, and the cattle take the clover, and, therefore, they kill stock to subsist upon.[143]

Dr. Burgess makes a special point of describing the Yukis as peaceful, albeit hungry, due to the loss of habitat. They were of no threat to Euro-American people. Could it be that those who knew the Indians the best, individuals like Battaile and Burgess, considered them less a threat than ranchers and other settlers were whose self interest was tied to stock raising?

Returning once again to Burgess' deposition:

> Upon this reservation, consisting of about five thousand acres, with proper management I believe five thousand Indians could be supported and well fed. On this farm all the Indians that work are fed three times a day, and those who do not work are fed two or three times a week, and the sick are fed every day. The Indians on this farm appear to be contented and satisfied with the manner in which they are treated.

Dr. Burgess' view of reservation management, like Storms', is perhaps a little too rosy. One can imagine how "contented and satisfied" a man might be with two ears of corn three times a day as sustenance while working as a field hand for eight hours a day. Further, his estimates of the farm's potential echo the caveat we have heard from Storms and others: "with proper management, I believe five thousand Indians could be supported and well fed."

Dr. Burgess continues to describe the impediments to such a positive outcome:

> The fences on the farm have been repeatedly pulled down by resident white men of the valley. And stock turned in on the reservation. Were it not for this, from my knowledge of the character of the Indians, I think they would before this have stopped killing stock. For I believe that for every beef that has been killed by them, ten or fifteen Indians have been killed....

Dr. Burgess also mentions the abduction of the two "squaws," the Native American seamstresses whom Rees discussed above.

---

143. This and subsequent quotes from Burgess's deposition are from Deposition of John W. Burgess to Assemblyman William B. Maxson, February 28, 1860, and March 2, 1860, *Appendix Senate Journal 1860*, B.P. Botts, State Printer, 24–26, California State Archives, 1020 O St., 4th Floor, Sacramento, CA. See also James J. Rawls, *Indians of California: The Changing Image* (Norman: University of Oklahoma Press, 1984), 171.

Sometime in August, one thousand one hundred and fifty-nine, and prior to the time Capt. Rees, the present Overseer, came here, I received of Captain Jarboe three squaws and two children. These are all the Indians received on this farm from Capt,. Jarboe's company. About the first of January a house on this farm, in which were confined two squaws, was broken open in the night and the two squaws were taken away. I afterward made a search for them, and found them in the house of Mr. Wilsay ["Wilsey"?]. she was under a bed in the house. She returned with me to the farm, And remained a few days, when she went away again. Mr. Wilsay stated to me that he did not want the squaws to come there, and I have reason to believe that he had no hand in taking them from the farm.

If not the Wilsey brothers, then who was responsible for the breaking and entering and the abduction of the two Native American women from Nome Cult Farm? In both incidents it seems the answers depend on whom you happen to ask. About the context in which the abduction occurred, however, Mr. Burgess is sure.

There always has been a prejudice on the part of the citizens of the valley against the farm. There is also a feeling of prejudice on the part of some of the citizens against the federal troops on the farm. There are some of the citizens who think if it was not for the troops the farm could not be sustained. And, that their presence is necessary to protect the farm from the aggressions of some of the citizens of the valley. And I think so too.

Dr. Burgess, a justifiably proud reservation employee and also a physician, went on to boast of the farm's success.

We harvested last summer about eight hundred bushels of rye, about twenty-five bushels of corn, and between five and six hundred bushels of potatoes. The wheat crop proved a failure, on account of the smut. We only had about four hundred and fifty bushels of wheat, about four or five tuns [sic] of beets, a large supply of pumpkins and melons, about twenty bushels of peas, and a variety of garden vegetables. We have already put in wheat and rye about two hundred acres; we intend to put in two hundred acres of corn, and if we can obtain the proper facilities we will put in three hundred acres; we will put in forty acres of potatoes; in beets, parsnips, pumpkins, carrots, turnips, peas, beans, and melons, we intend to put in a large amount; we have an abundance of seeds of various kinds on hand.

There is no better description anywhere of how wonderfully productive was the Round Valley Reservation's soil when it was put to productive use. Agent Rees was creating almost a Garden of Eden in this mountainous valley in north central California. Immediately after this, Dr. Burgess again revealed his positive feelings about the Indians:

From my knowledge of the Ukia [Yuki] Indians, their peculiarities, and habits, if the tribe were once placed upon the farm, kind and judicious treatment would induce most, if not all, of them to remain on it. I believe such a course would be most judicious in allaying their antipathies to the whites and the most effectual mode of restraining them from committing depredations upon the stock of the val-

ley. I think that the treatment received by the Indians from some of the white settlers has tended to exasperate them and caused them to destroy stock in a spirit of
revenge.

As Dr. Burgess explains, the settlers saw the Army as an impediment to the
possession and control of the valley by the settlers. Also important to many settlers was the destruction or the removal of the Indians by almost any means
available.

Settler and reservation employee William W. Frazier presents a contrast
to the views of Battaile and Dr. Burgess. His testimony, which we saw a little of
in the previous chapter, contradicts itself at times and is another expression of
the tension between the reservation and the settlers. Initially Frazier described
that there was some ambivalence about whether stock was taken by Indians or
not.

> ...the first stock I heard of being killed belonged to Woodman; and others,
> stated that they had lost a good many head of stock, but could not tell how many,
> because the grass was short and the stock strayed through the hills; Woodman, and
> others, employed by him stated that the cattle had come to his home with arrows in
> them, which afterwards died; some two or three head; I do not know of my own
> knowledge of any cattle having been killed by the Indians; ...[144]

Frazier, who, like Lawrence Battaile, had been a reservation employee, was
on the verge of contradicting many others' testimony. Regular settlers without
large herds or real estate interests, individuals like Frazier, seldom saw anything
that suggested that local Native Americans were carrying en mass "depredations" on the order of those that had been charged by others, like Judge Hastings,
George E. White, or H.L. Hall. Yet as we saw in Chapter 6, like many other settlers Frazier still got caught up in the predominantly Euro-American settlers'
hysteria against the Native Americans:

> ... the first serious difficulty that occurred between the whites and Indians, was
> one year ago, when the three head referred to, were killed; when Mr. Simpson, Mr.
> White, myself and others, hearing that the Indians had beef in the rancheria, in the
> valley went to the rancheria for the purpose, I supposed of chastising the Indians,
> when all fled but one, and we shot his head off, he tried to escape; some friendly
> Indians; these Indians were known as the Kaza-Pomos.[145]

The testimony of Mr. Frazier, as well as that of numerous other settlers,
described how raiding parties killed and wounded Native Americans. As we

144. Deposition of William W. Frazier to Assemblyman Joseph B. Lamar, on March 22,
1860 at Round Valley, Mendocino Indian War File, California Archives, 1020 "O"
St., 4th Floor, Sacramento, CA.
145. *Ibid.*

heard earlier, he concluded his deposition with another admission of Euro-American aggression against the Native Americans, describing how few Native American children there were because "there has been a practice of abducting the children from them by some white men, for the purpose of pecuniary profit."[146] Kidnapping rings run by desperadoes or criminals had operated very freely throughout much of Northern California since at least the early 1850s and probably before that.

Another Round Valley settler who was familiar with local Native Americans was Dryden Laycock, who had worked on the reservation under Subagent Storms. His deposition, partially quoted above, is particularly relevant to this study because he listed the names of some of the settlers who lost livestock. No one in the valley at this time knew more about the local Native Americans of the Round Valley area than Dryden Laycock.

His deposition began,

> I am thirty-five years of age; am a farmer; I have resided in this valley a little over three years; I have resided here nearly all the time I have lived in this country; I am employed by Captain Storms; when I came here I worked on the reservation with Captain Storms, until I came to work for him on his private farm; when I came into the valley there were no settlements in it but the reserve; at the time I came here this valley was inhabited by a great many Indians of the Yuca [Yuki] tribe; at that time there was about two thousand Indians on the reserve and under the control of the management of the reserve; at the time I came here the Indians were committing depredations on the government stock; they killed stock that was on the reserve; in one thousand eight hundred and fifty-six settlers began to locate in the valley; there are about fifteen settlers and stock raisers in the valley.[147]

Like Storms, Laycock claimed that when Nome Cult Indian Farm was founded in the summer of 1856, there were no settlers in the valley. In the absence of settler livestock, he claims, the Native Americans made "depredations on the government stock." A final misconception was that there were only fifteen settlers in the valley by 1860.

Laycock continues,

> ... from the time I first arrived in the valley up to the present time, the Indians have been committing more or less depredations; in one thousand eight hundred and fifty six the first expedition by the whites against the Indians was made, and have continued ever since; these expeditions were formed by gathering together a few white men whenever the Indian committed depredations on their stock; there

---

146. *Ibid.*
147. Deposition of Dryden Laycock to Assemblyman J. B. Lamar of the Select Legislative Committee, *Appendix Senate Journal 1860*, P.B. Botts, State Printer, 48 through 50, California Archives, 1020 "O" St., 4th Floor, Sacramento, CA.

were so many of these expeditions that I cannot recollect the number; the result was that we would kill, on an average, fifty or sixty Indians on a trip, and take some prisoners, which we took to the reserve; frequently we would have to turn out two or three times a week; these depredations were committed by the mountain Indians, and the Indians on the reservation;...

During the past year, Messrs. Storms, White, T. Henley, Wilsey, Corbett, Gibson, and Lawson, have had stock killed in this valley; I have seen fifty head of hogs, horses, and cattle, that have been killed by Indians, all of which belonged to Mr. Storms; I saw the bodies in the mountains and in this valley; there are about two hundred and fifty more head more missing that I have good reason to believe were killed by Indians....

The wild Indians in the vicinities above referred to ["in the vicinity of Eden and Round Valley, and North Eel River"], between North Eel River and South Eel River, I think number about ten thousand; they are divided up into small tribes, viz. the Numstruttes, Shumairs, and the Whistlers, and several other tribes; but they all go under the general name or the Yukiah [Yuki or Ukiah] tribe....

I know of nine white men who have been killed [by Native Americans] in this vicinity during my residence, and have seen the bodies of four.

DRYDEN LACOCK.

Sworn to and subscribed before me, this twenty-fifth day of February, one thousand eight hundred and sixty, at Storm's Hotel, Round Valley.

J. B. LAMAR,
Chairman Select Committee on Indian Affairs.[148]

From the quality of his testimony one can easily see why Hastings and many other important northern California residents recommended and preferred Laycock for the militia's captain's commission. Laycock had been a Tehama County Indian Agent between 1856 and 1858. No one knew the needs of the local Native Americans as well as the needs of the settlers.

Another reservation employee to discuss the cause and outcome of the Mendocino War was Alonso Kinsley. Kinsley was a long-term resident of Round Valley. Kinsley was a coworker of Subagent Simmon Storms.

I am thirty-two years of age; I have resided in Round Valley for over two years, up to the tenth of last September; I was employed as an employee on the reservation for about fifteen months of the time; I afterward had charge of a store in Round Valley. I have been satisfied, by reliable authority, that stock has been driven off and slaughtered by Indians. I think that this hostility is caused by the natural disposition of the Indians, and not by any aggressive act on the part of the whites; I never saw during my residence there any cruelty or bad treatment on the part of the whites toward the Indians; I wish to qualify that statement, if it may be called so— the remains of stock were found in possession of the Indians, and three or four Indi-

---

148. *Ibid.*

ans were shot. There has been war existing in Mendocino County between the Indians and the whites. There are about thirty United States troops stationed in Round Valley, and I was informed that they were there for the purpose of protecting the settlers from the Indians; I knew that the troops went out on an expedition to bring in some Indians who had been stealing some stock, and meeting with resistance, killed all the males at the rancheria they went to; so Lieut. Dillon told me....

I never knew any of the settlers to abduct squaws. I have no personal or pecuniary interest in any appropriation that has been or may be made for the suppression of Indian hostilities. I was employed by S.P. Storms, Sub-Agent, as Commissary a short time, and as Overseer the rest of the time; I was not the regular Commissary, but only acted in that capacity. The Indians who worked had sufficient rations issued to them; those that did not, had merely the privilege of gathering their natural food.

ALONSO KINSLEY. [149]

Kinsley's deposition stands in direct contrast to those of Battaile and Dr. Burgess in its characterization of Native Americans as guilty of theft. Alone among all the other depositions, it also charges that the U.S. troops may have set off the Mendocino War by slaughtering all of the male Native Americans in an earlier rancheria attack. Although there is no evidence that clearly disproves such an accusation, nowhere in all the extant official correspondence that I read have I read anything by Lt. Edward Dillon about the role of his troops in such an attack. Nevertheless, clearly there is nothing that disproves it. Martin Corbitt's deposition mentions the involvement of the Army troops in a foray against the Indians but listed no number of casualties. John Lawson's deposition, complaining that the Army's presence is insufficient, claims that Lt. Dillon "went out after the Indians, and had a man shot."[150]

Even if one reads just a few employee depositions, some key generalizations can be drawn from their eyewitness testimonies. First, most, but not all, would have supported increased funding for the reservation and also to increase the size of the reservation. Both recommendations were advocated by the *Majority Report of the Select Legislative Committee on the Mendocino War*, which accompanied publication of the depositions.

Second, there was no consensus of opinion about the need for the Army to be stationed there. Most who testified favored some local (or no) militia force as opposed to hiring a permanent state militia unit to "chastise" the Indians. Hav-

149. Deposition of Alonso Kinsley to the Committee, , *Appendix Senate Journal 1860*, B.P. Botts, State Printer, 53, California State Archives, 1020 "O" St., 4th Floor, Sacramento, CA.
150. Deposition of John Lawson to Assemblyman Joseph B. Lamar, Round Valley, Feb. 27, 1860, in *Appendix Senate Journal 1860*, 68–69, California State Archives, 1020 "O" St., 4th Floor, Sacramento, CA.

ing some force of armed men available for this purpose was supported by just one third of those who testified. One third opposed the idea. And one third was neutral about a militia force or indicated their neutrality about the question by not mentioning it in their testimonies. Thus there was not consensus of opinion among Round Valley's Euro-American residents in 1860.

Finally, there was a wide difference of opinion about how most felt the Native Americans were being treated on the reservation. Most did not even address the issue; and this question is still very much open to debate among historians and others today.

CHAPTER 8. DEPOSITIONS OF THE SOLDIERS

"For God's sake, how long are these things to continue?
"I have felt, and still feel greatly interested in this place, and those Indians; but
I am heartily disheartened at seeing these things, without the power to punish
the offenders.
　　　　　　　—*2nd Lt. Edward Dillon, Round Valley, Jan. 14, 1860*

Although Lt. Edward Dillon was the only Army representative to be deposed by the investigative committee, we can get some idea of the perspective of the military in Round Valley from the reports that Dillon filed in the course of duty. Some of these we have already seen in reference to the outbreak of hostilities. From these records we can imagine something of the Army's role in the development of Round Valley Reservation. The Army's uncomfortable position between the settlers and the Indians must have become clear soon after the arrival of Lt. Edward Dillon's company. Before the platoon's arrival in the valley in January 1859, no one could have anticipated how difficult a job it would be.

Lt. Dillon's reports describing attacks against the Indians are filled with a sense of shock and disgust, including this message to his immediate commanding officer, Bvt. Major Edward Johnson:

On the day before yesterday [March 21, 1859], Mr Battles [the 1860 Census for Round Valley Township listed "Lawrence Battle" as a resident there, with no age and no listing of income or assets] at the upper station, was out in the field and saw a man going towards the rancheria; shortly afterward he heard cries in that direction, and making towards it saw a man get on his horse and run off. The Indians then told him that this man had come up and forcibly taken a little squaw off behind some bushes, where Mr. Battles found her lying, her person torn and bloody. The Indians say this man drew a knife on some of them who attempted to interfere and that they knew him— I told Captain Storms that I could not do anything for the man lives off the Reservation. The victim is a Yuker [Yuki] girl some 12 or 14 years of age, perhaps younger.

2nd Lieut. Edward Dillon
6th Infy. to Bvt. Major E. Johnson
Fort Weller [near Willits, CA]
March 23, 1859.[151]

Native Americans had plenty of reasons to be resentful of Euro-Americans. The abduction and rape of their young females, some of whom were only children, was one oft-repeated crime. As Lt. Dillon points out, in many cases he could do nothing about such crimes because "the man lives off the Reservation."

The desperate conditions on the reservation were also described by Lt. Dillon's immediate superior, Brevet Major Edward Johnson. He commanded the U.S. Army's troops at the Mendocino Reservation near Fort Bragg on the Mendocino County coast. Major Johnson commanded the 6th Infantry's Company D that had marched from Suisun Bay up to the Russian River's headwaters during December 1858. There he'd established Fort Weller. In January 1859 Major Johnson accompanied Lt. Dillon and a platoon of Company D to Round Valley. One of Maj. Johnson's reports to Gov. Weller (August 21, 1859) read:

> I believe it to be the settled determination of many of the inhabitants to exterminate the Indians; and I see no way of preventing it. I have endeavored to collect them on the Reservation and several hundred are there now. but they have a great aversion to coming in doubtless owing in a great measure to the mortality at this time prevailing among them. Some eight or ten per day having died some days previous to my leaving the valley [Round Valley]. This mortality is attributable to a change of diet, scarcity of food, and the great prevalence of syphilitic diseases among them.[152]

As Bvt. Maj. Johnson described it, the Native Americans faced death by disease or by starvation on the reservation, or extermination by the settlers off the reservation. Just as Lt. Dillon had not created the conditions he noted in his report to Headquarters above, Major Johnson sadly reported the terrible dilemma that reservation Indians faced daily.

---

151. Message of Lt. Dillon to Bvt. Maj. Johnson, Fort Weller, March 23, 1859, Indian War File, California Archives, 1020 "O" St., 4th Floor, Sacramento, CA.
152. See letter by Major Edward Johnson to Governor John B. Weller, Aug. 21, 1859, Indian War Files, U.S. Archives, Washington, D.C., as quoted by Gary E. Garrett, unpublished M.A. Thesis, "The Destruction of the Indian in Mendocino County," 46–47, Sacramento State College (California State University at Sacramento), 1969.

Lt. Edward Dillon's deposition to the investigating committee, taken just before his men left the valley, is interesting throughout, yet to be brief, will only be quoted from in parts.

> I am twenty five years old. [I] am an officer in the United States Army. [I] hold a commission of Second Lieutenant of the Sixth Regiment of Infantry. And am stationed at Round Valley, in command of a detachment of twenty three men.
>
> I have been in this valley in command, since January, 1859. My head-quarters are on the Nome Cult Indian Farm....
>
> I had endeavored ["Two or three weeks" after his appointment and arrival in Round Valley] in the meantime, to make the citizens understand, that if depredations were committed, and evidence of the facts produced, I should punish the Indians myself, or turn them over to the civil authorities.
>
> About this time, Mr. Gibson informed me that the Indians had driven some hogs from his house, and satisfied me of the truth of this assertion. I went, accompanied by Mr. Gibson, for the purpose of punishing the Indians who had committed this theft, and took a portion of my command with me. I soon discovered signs of Indians going towards the forks of Eel River, but discovered no signs of hogs.
>
> I came to a rancheria which it seems these Indians must have entered. I told the Indians to come out, which they refused to do, and in consequence, it became necessary to fire the hut and to kill two Indians, one of my men having previously wounded by an arrow, shot from a hole in the hut; no sign of hogs being found about the rancheria ...[153]

The young second lieutenant had already discovered that his job defending Nome Cult Farm and maintaining peace in Round Valley would not be easy. Note also that Lt. Dillon's troops apparently 'took out' the wrong rancheria. Responding to Gibson's report of lost hogs, Dillon first tried to get the Native Americans to surrender. In the subsequent fire-fight one of his soldiers was wounded. We know from another source that this soldier eventually died from his wound. Lt. Dillon's deposition clearly stated there was "no sign of hogs" at the rancheria. Still, as related by Lt. Dillon, two Native Americans also were killed and their hut was torched. Yet, like many an American soldier assigned to "search and destroy" missions in South Vietnam in the 1960s, he knew that killing Native Americans would not accomplish the task the American military had been sent there to do in the first place.

---

153. This and subsequent quotes from Lieutenant Dillon's deposition are from Deposition of 2nd. Lt., Edward Dillon to Sen. Joseph B. Lamar, Feb. 27, 1860, Storms Hotel, Round Valley, *Appendix Senate Journal 1860*, B.P. Botts, State Printer, 56–60, California State Archives, 1020 "O" St., 4th Floor, Sacramento, CA.

2nd Lt. Dillon learned quickly from his period of Round Valley service. The following passage from Lt. Dillon's testimony gives some insight into the mystery of the Native American killing of the settler, John Bland.

> After Captain Jarboe had received his commission, he came into this valley about the time Mr. Bland was killed, and sent me a note, requesting my co-operation in chastising the Indians that had killed Bland, and some near the forks of Eel River, accused of having driven off two hundred head of stock from Long Valley. I was engaged at this time in examining the evidence in the case of Mr. Bland, and was far from being satisfied of what Indians had killed him, or that he had even been killed at all, nor had I any evidence of any stock having been driven from Long Valley. I therefore declined to co-operate with Captain Jarboe, for the above reasons.
>
> Since that occasion I have never been requested to examine into any case of Indian depredations, or been informed by any citizen that any had occurred....

This last sentence reveals much about Lt. Dillon's moral dilemma. By this time most of the settlers in the Round Valley region had already decided not to cooperate with him. Now he had only his own impressions of the facts to go on in reporting to this body of distinguished state legislators. Later on in his deposition, Lt. Dillon revealed additional information about Bland which made his case at once so important and yet simultaneously, so perplexing,

> Some time in the month of June last [June 1859] Mr. Bland, now deceased, came upon the reservation without the consent of the Agent, and took two Indians whom he accused of having stolen some articles of clothing from him. He carried them to Williams Valley, where he then lived, but before he had punished them a Corporal and party of men, sent by Major [Edward] Johnson, arrived at his house, causing Mr. Bland to leave precipitately.
>
> The orders of this Corporal were to arrest Mr. Bland, and to bring him, together with any Indians at the house, to Major Johnson. The Corporal found no one in the house, except a squaw, who he brought over. The squaw said she did not wish to return to Bland's house, and was placed by the Overseer for protection, in a house occupied by a sick white man, on the reservation, and Mr. Bland was told that he would not be allowed to take her away. One or two nights after this he came into the house and forced the squaw off. He took the squaw by the arms and pulled her out of the door. The house was about twenty yards from the Overseer's house. The squaw escaped from Bland, as he himself told me, and went to the mountains. I have never seen her since. This occurred some six weeks prior to the first rumor of Mr. Bland's death....

Bland was a frontiersman who was used to taking the law into his own hands. In the first incident, he had invaded the reservation and forcibly removed two Native Americans whom he judged to be guilty of a theft. Before he was able to carry out some form of punishment, the Army detachment arrived. Bland and probably also the Native Americans escaped. In a later similar incident, Bland abducted a woman from the reservation by pulling her by the arms from a house very near the "Overseer's house." He made his escape. Somehow, she then escaped from Bland "to the mountains." This had all occurred about six weeks before Bland's mysterious disappearance and murder.

It seems probable that in the interim time of six weeks there was plenty of time for the news of Bland's actions to become common knowledge in northeastern Mendocino County. Whoever may have killed John Bland certainly had plenty of time to think about how he might do it, to plan the crime and execute it. No one has ever solved the mystery of who did it. Vengeance may have played a part as some Native Americans, and this included many Yukis, were known to react fiercely to acts of known abduction or attack upon their women by whites.

Which tribe could have been responsible? The intriguing answer seems to rest with which settler version of the story one chooses to believe. The basic facts are these: Bland was a hunter and apparently even more of a loner than many were. Like Daniel Boone, Bland's preference for a life off on his own contributed to all the mysteries that surrounded his life and death. Bland had a cabin that was located in rugged high terrain well outside of Round Valley. Since Bvt. Major Johnson apparently had evidence against him, Bland might have been arrested. If he had, he could have been spared death if he had just stayed put or even turned himself in to the Army.

In the fall of 1859, one of the tribes, probably either the Wailaki, Yuki or Pit River, surrounded his cabin, abducted Bland and killed him. Jarboe's account reports that Bland was killed by Yukis. Elija[h] R. Potter reports that he died at the hands of Pit River Indians. Other historians, such as Professor Miller, report that it was the Wailaki who killed him. We do not know whether the woman who escaped his capture lived or died. Some group of Native Americans likely took the life of this irascible individual who was known to beat or abduct Native Americans as punishment for deeds he thought they had committed. He also forcibly abducted their women.

Later, Bland's body was burned at a stake, which was an almost unheard of act since the tribes in the Round Valley area rarely practiced cremation. Yuki who talked about it to Stephen Powers said they never scalped white men but that they did sometimes scalp other Native Americans. There is no evidence that Bland's body was scalped by the murderers. Euro-Americans soon recovered Bland's body. And so, partly as a direct result of this gruesome incident, Jarboe's party of angry rancheria-raiders made a very bloody attack on a Yuki rancheria.

Very quickly the news that Bland had died at the stake inflamed the most virulent anti-Native American prejudices and many more Native Americans, such as Bob, who was a hardworking reservation man, were murdered. More significantly, this incident played right into the hands of the most militant agitators against Native Americans such as Judge Hastings, H.L. Hall, Captain Jarboe and others. Near Round Valley's eastern edge, "Bland's Cove" is still in the adjacent national forest, recalling the strange life and violent death of the man who took the law into his hands once too often.

Lt. Dillon's deposition stated that he could prove that there were no serious depredations going on at Round Valley, at least not by the Native Americans.

> I wish to state, that the term "hostile" cannot be applied to these Indians; I have never heard of their having killed but one man in the last eighteen months; nor have I ever heard of their threatening to burn a house; I have never heard of their burning a man at the stake; nor have I ever, on all these various attacks on the rancherias, of one white man being killed by Indians in their defense. My orders, when I first came to this valley, were to arrest on good evidence any white man who interfered with the Indians or government property, and report the fact to my commanding officer.

> My orders now are, to arrest no citizen for any act for which one citizen of this State might not lawfully arrest another. In such a case my orders are to detain him in custody, and report the fact to my commanding officer. ...

The fact that Lt. Dillon's orders were changed is significant because some of his authority to discipline the settlers seems to have been taken away. He was forced to be more lenient toward the settlers later on in his platoon's tour of duty in Round Valley. Who may have pressured the Army to reduce his authority remains a mystery, but there is no doubt that it was someone with a good deal of authority, possibly Governor Weller, Judge S. C. Hastings, or someone at the highest command level at the Army's Department of the Pacific Headquarters in San Francisco. At the tender age of twenty-five, Lt. Dillon might have faced a long and bleak Army career if he had not acted in the spirit of his official orders at the reservation. Given that the Army could do little to restrain the settlers or to protect the Native Americans, Lt. Dillon suggested that no soldiers be stationed in the valley in the future.

In what was his final Round Valley report to Headquarters in San Francisco on Jan. 14, 1860, Lt. Dillon reported "continual" vandalism against reservation property, trespassing onto the reservation, and abduction of Indian women by local settlers, whom he called "rascals."

> Round Valley Cal.,
> Jan. 14, 1860

> I do not like to leave the Valley, while I see there is a continual disposition, on the part of the settlers, to annoy the Reservation. The fences are almost daily pulled

down, by persons taking pains to [illegible, possibly says "conceal their identities"] and it is a common occurrence to have Squaws taken by force from the place. About a week ago, some of the rascals came into the yard, broke open a door, and took off the Squaws that had been locked up by the Agent [George Rees]; this was done at night and was witnessed by no white person. Subsequently I can do nothing. For God's sake, how long are these things to continue? I have felt, and still feel greatly interested in this place, and those Indians; but I am nearly disheartened at seeing these things, without the power to punish the offenders. It seems to me a unheard of case, in which acts of this kind are committed on a Military Reservation without an inquiry, or attempt to bring the perpetrators to justice. XXXX [X's in the original.]

signed E. Dillon

A true copy:
ex Signed, W.T. Carlin
1st Lieut., 6th Infy. *Head Quarters Dept. of California*
San Francisco, February 1st, 1860
W.W. MacKall
(?) A.A. Saul[154]

After a full year of duty at Nome Cult Indian Farm by mid January 1860, Lt. Dillon was fed up with the laxity of regulations and the lack of power that the unit had had at Round Valley in protecting both settlers and Native Americans at the reservation. Tactfully choosing to use discretion as the better part of valor Lt. Dillon omitted mentioning the dilution of his orders from this his final report from Round Valley.

Some might even go so far as to say that he had become "burned out" by the stress of the long year of hard duty in this remote mountain valley. Yet he was equally concerned about the future welfare of the Native Americans he had labored so hard to protect. He appears loathe in having to leave them at the mercy of the settlers. At about this same time in early 1860 that the legislative committee began gathering its testimonies, Lt. Dillon and his platoon of regular U.S. troops were transferred out of Round Valley for duty.

Dillon's next assignment was to command the troops at Fort Bragg. As a native of Mississippi, Lt. Dillon must have already felt conflicted by the intensifying national debate over slavery's spread into the western territories. Nonetheless he continued his dedicated service to the nation as post commander at Fort Bragg from May 1860 until June 1861. National events then took control. Abraham Lincoln's 1860 election to the Presidency, the first purely sectional election

---

154. 1st Lt. Edward Dillon's final report before his transfer out of Round Valley to his commanding officer, 1st Lt. W.W. MacKall, copy on file in the Mendocino Indian War Files, California State Archives, 1020 "O" St., 4th Floor, Sacramento, CA.

in American history, caused eleven southern states to secede from the Union in early 1861. The Civil War began soon after. The nation's greatest war would rage on from 1861 until 1865. Yet just as Lt. Dillon had predicted about Round Valley, there were no immediate large, violent clashes between the Native Americans and the settlers of Round Valley.

Conflict between Euro-Americans and local tribespeople had been going on for some time when at last the U.S. Army was prevailed upon to step in and restore order. As is clearly illustrated by the deposition and reports of Lt. Edward Dillon, Army officers faced a situation that forced them to take actions and to make moral choices they were not professionally prepared for. In the end, it was the personal ability and the moral character of such military leaders as Lt. Edward Dillon and, later, Captain C.D. Douglas that partially altered the history of the valley. At least, they sometimes ameliorated the worst wrongs.

Partly because of lack of integrity of the regular reservation employees, but also due to the Office of Indian Affairs' lack of leadership, along with the lack of a workable plan for the operation of the reservation, civilian reservation leaders like Superintendent Henley and Agent Storms failed to fulfill their mission as reservation officials and advocates for the Native Americans. Nevertheless, the hard work that Lt. Dillon and his small platoon of Company D, 6th Infantry of horsemen attempted to do in conducting impartial and independent investigations and mediating between the two deeply divided racial groups should be admired by all who study Western history.

Chapter 9. Journalism of the Period and Round Valley in the 1860s

Almost everywhere in California from 1858 through 1862 there was a consistent pattern in the use of publicity. Newspaper accounts generally took the following format: a group of local Native American males bands together and begins to kill some of the settler livestock. A vigilante group of settlers is formed, searches for and then usually destroys some Indians at a local rancheria. There is mourning over the relatively small losses of the settlers' force as well as simultaneous celebration over the victory. The publicity then is often used by the state's Democratic Party politicians and other powerful citizens to assign an increased number of militia or regular U.S. Army troops.

Daily papers existed only in the state's largest cities like Marysville, Sacramento, and San Francisco. The editors of such dailies as the *San Francisco Bulletin* or the *Sacramento Union* relied on small weekly newspapers out in smaller rural Northern California towns and villages, like the *Mendocino Herald* in Ukiah, for example, for the latest stories about what was actually happening on the frontier.

Throughout the 1850s, many but not all newspaper reporters were biased toward the predominantly Euro-American settlers. Settlers and ranchers were an important part of the reporters' reading public. Almost all Euro-Americans tended to be unsympathetic to both the reservations and to Native Americans in general. The following example from the Mendocino War, 1858–1860, appeared in the *San Francisco Herald* on August 22, 1859. It was short on actual details while exhibiting an overt prejudice against California Native Americans in general.

> MASSACRE OF INDIANS IN MENDOCINO—Captain Jarboe's Rangers attacked an Indian ranch eight miles from Indian Vally, Mendocino county, lately, killing quite a number. Hall, the "Texan Boy," 6 feet 9 inches high, and weighing 278 pounds, who is the dread of all red skins, a week or two ago killed two Indians in a fair fight. A company is forming in Round Valley, under Captain Lacok, to go against the Indians. Round Valley races commence on the 22d. A lively time is expected.—*Napa Reporter*[155]

The article, quoted above in its entirety, neglects to report how many and how the Indians were killed. Imagine the public dismay today if the *CBS Evening News* were to report: "There was a costly battle" (in Iraq, the Middle East, Afghanistan, etc.) and that American troops ended up "killing quite a number," that one of our soldiers was "the dread of all red skins" or was "feared by all the Iraqi insurgents." No one would be very convinced.

One of the first community projects built in Round Valley was its racetrack. The article above neatly noted that the fall racing season in the valley would be starting on the same day this article was published, August 22, 1859. One might get the impression that the Round Valley race results might be more important that news on conflicts between settler militia and Native Americans.

Details in many of these reports were based mostly on hearsay, with a reporter getting his information from the leader of the vigilante group and then parroting back as truth what he had said happened at the scene of the rancheria or battlefield. The early California press simply did not have sufficient resources to send out reporters.

In another example, details of the action in August of 1861 are dependent on the witness of its leader, Charles Bourne, whose recollections are neither complete nor even necessarily accurate. Yet this kind of a news report was all that the public could go on:

> A party of ten white men, under command of Capt. Chas. Bourne, with 50 picked Indians—of the Pitt [Pit] River, Hat Creek and Concaw [sic] tribes-from the Nome Cult farm, followed the trail of the Indians about 14 miles, when they camped for the night. At intervals along the trail they found the bodies of 31 horses. The next morning, they left their horses at the camp and walked ten miles over a rough trail, crossing Eel River twice. On descending a steep bank, near the bed of the river, they all at once found themselves in the camp of the Wylackies, whose trail they had fol-

155. "Massacre of Indians in Mendocino," reprint from the *Napa Reporter* as printed in *San Francisco Herald*, Aug. 22, 1859, 3, col. 1, California History Section, California State Library, Suite 200, 900 "N" St., Sacramento, CA.

lowed. There appeared to be 400 or 500 Indians in the camp, and if the attacking party had been aware of their number they would probably have withdrawn, thinking 'discretion the better part of valor.'

When they found themselves in the camp, the Concaw [Concow] chief gave the signal, and at once arose the war whoop, startling the Wylackies and producing confusion among them. They appeared to have been feasting and gambling. Some of the squaws were cooking meat, while others were drying it. Two Mexicans were with the Indians. Capt. Bourne shot one of them, while the other escaped into the mountains upon a mule that was saddled, and which was stolen from a citizen of Round Valley a few nights before.

It was thought that more than 100 Wylackies [Wylackis] were killed. In their camp were found guns, hatchets, camp-kettles and clothing, supposed to have been taken from camps they had robbed and persons they had killed. There was also any quantity of horse flesh, beef and pork, in their camp.[156]

We know now that combat soldiers who have been the direct participants in any war in any era quite often cannot write objectively on battle events. This does not mean that Captain Bourne or the reporter deliberately exaggerated or lied about the actions described in the story; but sometimes journalists must rely on soldiers for details in their press reports. If such soldier-reporters are the only eyewitnesses available, one has to bear in mind the circumstances when they describe what happened at the scene.

Another example is the following article written by a jingoistic *San Francisco Herald* writer. He reported on an action by Captain Jarboe and the bloodthirsty Eel River Rangers.

MENDOCINO INDIAN DIFFICULTIES

A correspondent of the *Sonoma Journal* writing from South Eel River, October 1, gives the following information as to the Indian affairs in Mendocino county:

You are already aware that the settlers of this section have suffered greatly from Indian depredations upon their stock. In Eden Valley they have been compelled to remove their herds to other sections.

Capt. Jarboe, who with a small party has been employed to put an end to this state of affairs, is actively engaged. Last week he had a fight, near the forks of Eel River, with a large encampment of Indians. He surrounded them at night, and made the attack about day-break on the following morning. The fight lasted about one hour, and resulted in the killing of twenty-five bucks and the capture of fifty-five prisoners. Lieut. Wood passed here last Thursday, [October 10th probably] with the prisoners, who are to be taken to the Mendocino Reservation. Capt. Jarboe with ten men has started out toward the head waters of Elk Creek, where large numbers

---

156. "Indian War," a reprint from the *San Francisco Bulletin*, Oct. 15, in Ukiah's newspaper, *The Mendocino Herald*, Nov. 1, 1861, California State Library, Suite 200, 900 "N" St., Sacramento, CA.

of Indians are known to exist. Mr. Wall informs me that at the time the attack was made upon the Indians, they then had in their possession three horses belonging to a Mr. Woodman of Long Valley.

The citizens of Long Valley have petitioned Capt. Jarboe to visit that section with his Rangers, without delay, for the purpose of ridding them of the hordes of Indians infesting that region, and who are represented to be not only killing the hogs, horses and cattle of the settlers in large numbers, but also declaring their determination to kill the whites which threat they appear determined to carry into effect. It is much to be regretted that Capt. Jarboe's company is not more numerous. His entire force amounts to only twenty men. He is, however, doing wonders.

Notwithstanding affairs look bad at present, we hope with confidence for a favorable turn. After the winter sets in, the Indians will go into quarters and the Rangers will then be able to seek them out and capture them, after which life and property will be secure.[157]

The *Herald* writer finished with a paragraph that might well have come from a Chamber of Commerce brochure or a real estate promotional flyer.

To persons seeking good stock ranches, I would say, so soon as the Indian diffi-culties are disposed of, you cannot fail to find satisfactory locations in this region. The country is extensive, embracing about seventy miles square of first rate range, well supplied with deer, elk, etc., and at present but sparsely occupied by settlers. But I will close, promising that you shall again hear from me.[158]

There was no mention anywhere in this article of Nome Cult Indian Farm, or of any of the efforts of the Office of Indian Affairs or of the U.S. Army's efforts to bring peace to Mendocino County. There is also no mention of George Wood-man's Indian child kidnapping ring or of the intercultural conflicts then going on in northern Mendocino County and elsewhere throughout the upper half of the state.

As has been carefully studied by historian Robert Chandler, California did have a number of significant newspapers that consistently and valiantly champi-oned the Native American cause. These papers stand out in sharp contrast to the majority of papers. It must also be noted that the Democratic Party, the political party that prevailed in the State Legislature at Sacramento, maintained the widespread belief in the racial superiority of Caucasians or Euro-Americans over the Native Americans in society.

The public newspapers that were dedicated to helping the Native Ameri-cans to survive, as opposed to simply exterminating them, were: the San Fran-

---

157. "Mendocino Indian Difficulties," October 10, 1859, Monday morning, *San Francisco Herald*, 3, col. 4, California State Library, Suite 200, 900 "N" St., Sacramento, CA.
158. *Ibid.*

cisco *Pacific*, the San Francisco *Alta California*, the San Francisco *Bulletin*, the Sacramento *Union*, the San Jose *Mercury* and the Stockton *Independent*.

For example, on February 20, 1860, the San Francisco *Herald* stated that California Native Americans needed to be put on "reservations protected from their more savage antagonists with white faces and black hearts."[159]

Over a year later, the *Alta* pleaded to the dominant Euro-Americans that California's "Native Americans 'should be treated kindly,' as befitted a peaceful people."[160]

RESERVATION BUILDING, ROUND VALLEY STYLE

As the Euro-American militia units spread out across the northern third of the state in such widely separated regions as the eastern slope of the Sierra Nevadas west of Red Bluff and Redding, and the Humboldt Bay region, the Native Americans could not resist for long. In only about three months almost all of the tribes, the Pit River, Hat Creek, Wailaki, Yuki, Shasta, Concow, Yahi, Hoopa, and an almost innumerable number other small tribes were in trouble. The indigenous people here faced imminent defeat, subjugation, and a longer than forty-year period of deliberate cultural degradation at the hands of the Euro-American majority. Remnants of the defeated Native Americans began a process of forced removal followed by mandatory relocation onto strange, nearly uninhabitable areas that the white settler-soldiers called "reservations," "reserves," or "farms."

The year 1859–1860 was a critical turning point in California Indian Affairs Department policy regarding its Northern and Central California reservations. Making use of special investigators like Goddard Bailey and J. Ross Browne, the secretary of the Interior and the commissioner of Indian Affairs made some crucial and irrevocable decisions that affected the lives of both the Native Americans and the settlers in Round Valley.

Agent Vincent E. Geiger was an agent at Nome Lackee near Red Bluff who also wrote about Round Valley. Partly as a result of his recommendation the Indian Affairs Department decided to cut its losses. Nome Lackee was eventually

---

159. As quoted by Robert J. Chandler, "The Failure of Reform: White Attitudes and Indian Response in California During the Civil War Era," The *Pacific Historian*, 24, 3 (Fall, 1980), Footnote #7, 293, San Francisco *Herald*, February 20, 1860.
160. *Ibid.*, *San Francisco Alta California*, October 26, 1861.

to be closed. Nome Cult Farm or Round Valley Reservation would become one of the primary reservations along with the Hoopa and Mendocino Reservations of the northern and central regions of California. As many as possible of the vanquished Indians would be concentrated at the Round Valley Reservation.

In his report dated August 31, 1859, Indian Agent Vincent E. Geiger reported:

> . . . an Indian war [Gen. Kibbe's War], under the auspices of the State government, is now being waged against the Indians east of the Sacramento river. Some prisoners have been taken and sent to Mendocino, this place [Nome Lackee] not being considered sufficiently distant to prevent their return, unless a large force be kept to guard and watch them. In view, then, of all the circumstances, it is respectfully suggested that the Indians here, and those of the entire Sacramento valley, be removed west of the Coast range of mountains [the Mayacamas or the Coast Range], and the lands included in this reservation be thrown open to the occupancy of our citizens. The settlers of Round Valley still refuse to vacate their land claims. A small detachment of United States troops [Lt. Dillon's platoon] now located there, will, it is believed, be sufficient, for the present, to protect the government property from injury. If, however, it is the intention of the government to reserve the entire valley for Indian purposes, some immediate steps should be taken to secure it, as the longer the delay the more difficult it becomes to settle the conflicting claims.[161]

If Nome Lackee Reserve near Red Bluff closed, then Nome Cult Farm in northeastern Mendocino County would have to expand. It was an idea which James Y. McDuffie, the successor to California Supt. Thomas J. Henley, suggested. In his June 1859 annual report on the California reservations, Superintendent McDuffie describes Round Valley with the same nearly ecstatic appreciative language used by Storms and others had in earlier reports:

NOME CULT.

> This beautiful valley is embosomed in the coast range about sixty miles southwest of Nome Lackee... I have seen no where in California a spot so admirably adapted for an Indian reservation as this. With a soil of extraordinary fertility, a mild and equitable climate, an unlimited supply of every variety of timber and completely isolated by a belt of almost impassable mountains, if the reservation theory can ever be successfully worked out it can be done here. The wheat and rye had been harvested before my arrival, but there was a fine field of corn and some sixty acres of vegetables all growing with great luxuriance. There are a number of well

---

161. Report of Agent Vincent E. Geiger to the Commissioner of Indian Affairs, Nome Lackee Indian Reserve, August 31, 1859, as quoted by Stephen R. Holman, *Round Valley Indian Reservation: A Study in Ethnocentricity* (Committee of the Study of History, Amherst, Massachusetts: under contract with the U.S. Office of Education as EPDA Project #310511. *A Teacher's Manual*, 1970, 40, Jean and Charles Schultz Information Center, Sonoma State University, Rohnert Park, CA.

built log cabins on the reserve, and the cultivated portion is enclosed with a substantial oak fence. The place has a thriving, prosperous look, contrasting most favorably with the neglected appearance of Nome Lackee. The Yubas and Nevadas here, like those of the same tribes at Nome Lackee, have some little knowledge of agriculture and seem to possess some intelligence. The Yukas [Yuki] and other wild tribes are mere savages, the most degraded specimens of humanity I ever saw; I had no means of ascertaining their numbers as they were scattered in small rancherias all over the reserve.[162]

McDuffie's above description reminds us of some of the more positive reports on the reservation by Dr. Burgess and Subagent Storms. In his pleas to the Indian Affairs Department for more federal help in expanding the reservation and separating Round Valley's white settlers from the reservation McDuffie repeated Storms' recommendation to enlarge the reservation to include the entire valley. But McDuffie's eloquent appeal went completely unanswered both by state policy makers and federal politicians.

Returning to Supt. McDuffie's report,

There is one serious drawback upon the prosperity of the reservation. A portion of the valley has been thrown open to settlement and some ten or twelve settlers have taken claims there. The vicinity of the whites produces the usual effect upon the Indians; whiskey is sold to the men, the women are corrupted, and insubordination and disease follow as inevitable consequences. It is needless to enlarge upon this subject; the necessity of isolating the reservations from all contact with the whites is as obvious as it is paramount, and if Nome Cult [Round Valley Reservation] is to be retained for Indian purposes the white settlers there must be removed. The valley is not large, containing altogether only about twenty five thousand acres, and there can be no objection to retaining the whole of it.[163]

The annual reports from California's Indian Affairs officials to the Indian Affairs Department pleaded for more financial help and reforms. The terrible results of the Native American massacres of 1858–1860 are clear from both of the following excerpts from the annual reports of 1861 and 1862. The first was written by the new California Superintendent, George M. Hanson, who had replaced McDuffie in 1860.

The Republicans and the Lincoln Administration would belatedly realize some of the problems they faced in administrating California Native Americans in the far West.

I desire to call especial attention to the reports of the superintending agents of the two districts [northern and southern] into which, for Indian purposes, the State has been divided. From those reports it will be seen that a complete change in the management of our Indians relations is demanded. A change involving the breaking

---

162. Annual Report for 1859, *Ibid.* 37.
163. *Ibid.*

up of some of the existing reservations; the correction of gross and palpable wrongs upon others; the establishment of new reservations, as I trust will be the case, upon a far more ample scale than any heretofore established; and a thorough investigation, and, if possible, a correction of outrageous wrongs perpetuated, under color of law, against not only the property but also the persons and liberty of the Indians. To effect this change will require time, a considerable expenditure of money, and the exercise, on the part of all persons connected herewith, of great care, patience, and circumspection.[164]

The writer restates Subagent S.P. Storms' recommendation that the whole valley become the reservation. Here again California's superintendent of Indian Affairs calls for expansion of the reservation at the very time all politicians in the North tried to focus on raising money to equip and train the armies of the North in the Civil War. Superintendent Hanson must have seemed to them to lose all contact with reality with General Lee's and General Jackson's forces rapidly closing in around Washington, D.C.

In the passage that follows, the so-called "Mendocino War" and its disastrous effects upon both Euro-American-Native American relations and upon the health and welfare of the California Native Americans were being determined and noted by someone above the subagent, agent, or superintendent level within the Indian Affairs Department.

The Commissioner of Indian Affairs commented with chagrin, and obvious shock,

> The statement, as made by the Superintendent Agent Hanson of the causes which led to the employment of United States and volunteer forces against the Indians in the frontier portions of Humboldt and Mendocino counties, and of the crimes that are committed in the wake, and, as seems to be the case, under the *quasi* protection of those forces, presents a picture of the perversion of power and of cruel wrong, from which humanity instinctively recoils. This so-called "Indian war" appears to be war in which the whites alone are engaged. The Indians are hunted like wild and dangerous beasts of prey; the parents are "murdered," and the children "kidnapped." Surely some plan may be devised whereby the Indians may cease to be the victims of such inhumanity, and the recurrence of scenes so disgraceful impossible.[165]

Unfortunately for most California Native Americans, these words fell on deaf ears. The nation's attention was on the bloody battlefields of northern Virginia or on those of Tennessee and Mississippi, not on the West's Indian reservations like Round Valley in Northern California. With the North badly losing the

---

164. Annual Report on Indian Affairs-1861, *Ibid.*, 42.
165. *Ibid.*

Civil War, it is doubtful that this annual report for 1861, at the time of its writing, had much, if any, national political impact.

Official words in annual reports were one thing. Real life land policy and how it was implemented out on the California frontier was something quite different. Parts of Round Valley and many other valleys in Northern California for a number of months are transformed into floodplains by annual late winter and spring rains, or what would be called wetland habitats today. Taking advantage of a confusing situation, some white settlers made claims of these lands, even though they were technically on reservations. This made determination of the actual ownership of land such a painful exercise after the start of the twentieth century.

Despite the recommendations of many Office of Indian Affairs representatives, no funds whatsoever were allocated either in Washington or in Sacramento to buy out the Euro-American Round Valley settlers. Thus the witches' brew that was local politics in Mendocino County would simply get more concentrated and more bitter as increasing numbers of settlers moved into the valley and more Indians from as far away as the Pit River were forced to move away from their traditional tribal homelands.

The *Annual Report for 1862* included the following comments by Superintendent Hanson:

ROUND VALLEY.

Originally, as I am *now* informed by Colonel T.J. Henley, the old superintendent of Indian affairs, only a small portion of this valley was taken up and used by him as a farm, connected with the Nome Lackee reservation; and, as a matter of self-protection, he allowed, and perhaps gave encouragement to, persons to settle on the adjoining lands. The following year, however, he had the whole valley surveyed for an Indian reservation, and then gave notice thereof, forewarning further settlements and improvements of said valley lands. Nevertheless, regardless of said notice, many other persons thereafter made settlements thereon, and have entered upon the land enclosed for purposes of Indian pastures, taking the same up as "swamp and overflowed lands," and in this way have not reported and returned all the lands in the valley as belonging to the United States, but afterward sent in another report saying that this portion of the valley should have been returned as "swamp and overflowed land.[166]

The problem of maintaining the integrity of Nome Cult Farm's boundaries got worse, not better, with the passage of time. The number of Euro-American settlers in the valley increased from less than fifteen settlers in 1856–1858 to almost one hundred by 1860. This increased the power of the ranchers and settlers in

---

166. Annual Report on Indian Affairs-1862, *Ibid.*, 310–316.

their encroachments on Native Americans' rights and lands. The above quotation with its final "Nevertheless, regardless, etc." shows how wide the door had been opened for land-hungry profit-driven white pioneers to stride through. Most of the new resident Round Valley farmers ignored directives by the government. Later, some of the same persons openly led resistance to governmental notices about restrictions or bans on claiming more land for private farms or ranches within Round Valley. As we will see in the next chapter, the California legislature was no more successful in making reforms to the reservation system than was the Office of Indian Affairs.

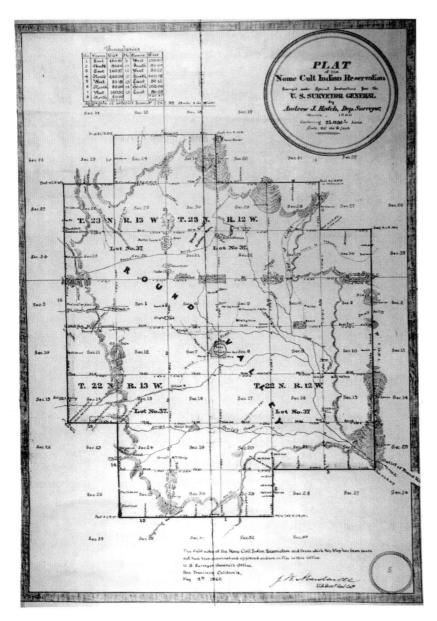

"PLAT of the Nome Cult Indian Reservation, 1860," the first official federal survey map of Round Valley. Source: Robert J. Lee Photo Collection, Held-Poage Library, Ukiah.

A

Subagent Simmon P. Storms, earliest known photo, ca. 1858. *Source: Robt. J. Lee Photo Collection, Mendocino County Historical Society, Held-Poage Library, Ukiah.*

Governor John B. Weller. *Source: Photo Collection, California History Section, California State Library, Sacramento.*

State Senator Jasper O'Farrell, Loaded for Bear Painting, ca, 1843, *Source: Gift to author by Janice M. Valderrama, O'Farrell's great-great-granddaughter.*

C

"Digger Indian Girl, stereo photo by Thomas Houseworth & Co., San Francisco. *Source: Photographic Collection of California History Section, California State Library, Sacramento.*

"Digger Indians at Ten Mile River, Mendocinio County,"John P. Soule photo. *Source: Bancroft Library, University of California at Berkeley.*

"Reportio de los M.SS., cartes, planos y dibujos relativow a las Californias, Existents en este Museo." *Source: Photo Collection, California History Section, California State Library, Sacramento.*

Three Mounted Settlers and an Indian," date and place unknown, *Source: Photo Collection California history Section, California State Library, Sacramento.*

"Indian Rancheria," Watkins Stereo #223, Stereo Collection, California History Section, California State Library, Sacramento.

'Nome Cult Native American Timber Cutting Party,' 1858, Subagent Storms standing 4th from left with arms on hips. *Source: Robert J. Lee Photo Collection, Mendocino County Historical Society, Held-Poage Library, Ukiah.*

CHAPTER 10. THE REJECTED *MAJORITY REPORT*, 1860

"History teaches us that the inevitable destiny of the red man is total extermination or isolation from the deadly and corrupting influences of civilization."
—*4ᵗʰ paragraph, Majority Report, 1860*

The Round Valley depositions in previous chapters were all recorded by a five-member select committee of the California Legislature composed of two state senators, Sen. William B. Dickinson (El Dorado County) and Jasper O'Farrell (Marin, Sonoma, and Mendocino Counties), as well as three state assemblymen, Assemblyman Joseph B. Lamar (Mendocino County), Abner J. B. Phelps and William B. Maxson. Assemblyman Lamar had been elected in 1859. One of his first acts was to write the bill that organized Mendocino County. As newspaper reports of Native American massacres and slaughters bombarded the public's consciousness, the California Legislature conducted a short but intensive investigation through the use of personal testimonies of Round Valley residents, Native Americans and Euro-Americans alike. Another important reason for the investigation was that the legislature needed to decide whether to pay militia soldiers who had volunteered and campaigned throughout the northern part of the state during 1858 and 1859 in Gen. Kibbe's Expedition. Mendocino County raids by the Eel River Rangers were but one part of this conflict. California and the nation as well had to face a moral question that shook everyone of whatever socioeconomic political or religious background: Would Californians continue killing Native Americans until they were all exterminated? Was genocide the only way of dealing with the problem of lost livestock on the open range?

Probably the most progressive leader of this "Select Committee on Indian Affairs" was State Senator Jasper O'Farrell, who represented Sonoma, Marin, and Mendocino Counties. A former surveyor (in 1843 the Mexican government had paid him one acre of land for every twenty acres he surveyed in Marin County), a professional cartographer, gold prospector, rancher and justice of the peace in Sonoma County, Sen. O'Farrell was probably nearly exhausted as he arrived in Ukiah in late February 1860. Sen. O'Farrell had been in the saddle for almost the entire past three days, starting off in Sacramento. It had been a long ride, especially for Sen. O'Farrell, who was about forty-five years old. Although he had led an active life as both a surveyor and a soldier, the assignment was not a simple one. Testimonies had to be heard and recorded, then reread, edited and published. Finally, a report had to be drafted with recommendations to the Downey Administration for Indian Affairs policy changes.

Late in February 1860 Sen. O'Farrell and his colleagues traveled first to San Francisco. From there they went by horseback or by steamer up to Petaluma. They rode north through beautiful rolling hills in Sonoma County to Cloverdale and on through more lush California ranchland crossing the Russian River to Ukiah City, about seventy miles south of the reservation. Finally they crossed smaller streams and passed through valleys into the more mountainous and rugged northeastern Mendocino County.

The long ride may have reminded Sen. O'Farrell in some ways of the 1844-1845 military revolt in favor of Alta California's Gov. Micheltorena against challenger Pio Pico; it had been a battle that was lost for control of the governor's office. O'Farrell had acted as quartermaster and guide for John Sutter's motley army, which included a Native American unit, that marched southward in support of Micheltorena over three hundred miles through the San Joaquin Valley southward from Sutter's Fort near Sacramento all the way to the San Fernando Valley just north of Los Angeles.

There Gov. Micheltorena's forces had lost a crucial battle to Pio Pico's forces. In the spring of 1845, Pio Pico became the new Mexican governor of Alta California, or what is today the state of California. The 1860 investigation may have also brought to Sen. O'Farrell's mind his job as the first chief surveyor of Alta California. O'Farrell studied civil engineering while still a young man in Ireland. In the early 1840s, he had plotted out many of the largest ranchos in northern and southern California.

Sen. O'Farrell may also have remembered how his only pay for a survey near Los Angeles in 1845 had been a large herd of tough Mexican cattle. With only the aid of one Native American vaquero, Tom, O'Farrell had driven this new herd back up the length of the state north into Sonoma County. His primary rancho was at Freestone in western Sonoma County. In 1847, O'Farrell had drafted the first accurate map of the future city of San Francisco, which included a wide and controversial thoroughfare that was called "Market Street." He was later nearly lynched by an ungrateful San Francisco mob for the map's large lot dimensions along Market Street.

A restful sleep in Ukiah might have restored Senator O'Farrell to health. He suffered from malaria, a disease he had contracted as a young apprentice-surveyor when working with a British surveying crew in Argentina before immigrating, possibly as a crewman on board a whaling ship, to California in October 1843.

During late February and early March 1860, the Legislature's Select Committee recorded personal testimonies or depositions of more than thirty residents, reservation employees, Native Americans and other residents of the Round Valley region.[167] When all the depositions were taken, the facts therein were compelling. Many Indians had been killed in cold blood. Even if one adds up all of the Native Americans reported killed in each of the thirty-four depositions now extant, it is still not possible to assess from them for certain how many Native Americans were killed by Captain Jarboe's company. The total was certainly well over four hundred. By Jarboe's own account the number was over three hundred killed.[168]

The methods used by the Eel River Rangers, the descriptions of conditions on the reservation and the reports of conflict between settlers and the Army- all these so impressed four out of five members of the Select Committee, the majority led by its Chairman, State Senator O'Farrell, that they concluded that the state urgently needed reform at Nome Cult Farm. Sen. O'Farrell and Sen. William B. Dickinson, together with two Assemblymen Abner J. B. Phelps and Will-

---

167. Unfortunately, all the Native American depositions were lost or deliberately destroyed. All of the investigating state lawmakers were from Northern California. Sen. Dickinson represented the town of Spanish Flat, El Dorado County. Assemblyman Phelps represented San Francisco and Assemblyman Wm. Maxson represented San Mateo. Rounding out the committee were Sen. O'Farrell from Sonoma, Marin and Mendocino Counties and Assemblyman Lamar also representing Mendocino County.

168. See Report of Capt. Walter Jarboe,"Headquarters, Eel River Rangers," to California Governor John B. Weller, Dec. 3, 1859, Round Valley File, Held-Poage Historical Research Library, 603. W. Perkins St., Ukiah, CA.

iam A. Maxson, wrote a seven-page report of their investigation, *The Majority Report of the Special Joint Committee on the Mendocino War*.

According the official record of the California Legislature in 1860, the *Journal, 1860* on p. 543, "Mr. O'Farrell, Chairman of Special Committee, appointed to inquire into the Indian difficulties existing in Mendocino County, made the following report: on motion of Mr. Dickinson, the reading was dispensed with, and nine hundred and sixty copies were ordered printed."

The report made several strong recommendations. The most significant was to enlarge the size of Nome Cult Farm, then a small reservation, from five thousand to twenty thousand acres. It also suggested increased funding so that all of Round Valley's Euro-American property owners would be bought out, eventually by the federal government. Round Valley would then be the primary northern California reservation, a suggestion that Simmon Peña Storms had made previously in an 1858 report to Supt. Henley, quoted above in this study.

This would have meant including in the reservation all but about a fifth of the entire acreage of the valley. In addition, more money would be spent by the state on improving the lives of Native Americans on the existing reservations. The Majority Report opposed the de facto policy of exterminating all of the state's Native Americans. The Report is a unique early statement for the record of the State of California's intention to support its Native American population.

The tone of the Majority Report is intriguing, even refreshingly modern. It pointed the finger of blame squarely at the Euro-American settlers who were in control of almost everything that happened in Mendocino County. It overstated its case only once, when it compared the record of Indian deaths under Hispanic rule up until 1848 to that of "the last four months." It thereby mistakenly concluded that there were more shooting deaths in that short period than over a period of more than one hundred years.

Still, the report's point of view is relevant.

> The scene of the original difficulties with the Indians was Round Valley. The many expeditions against them had driven them to Long Valley, distant about twenty-five miles, in which latter place and its vicinity they have killed some stock of the settlers. A most fearful retribution has been visited upon them by some of the settlers of Long Valley which place, as will be seen by evidence accompanying this report, an armed organization has been formed, of forty men, which is yet in existence, who go out at the call of their captain for the purpose of hunting Indians whenever they are satisfied that any stock has been slaughtered by the Indians, and, without ascertaining the guilty parties, shooting down indiscriminately, and afterward seek for the evidence of their depredations.

So much for the causes of the difficulties between the settlers and the Indians of Mendocino County. Your committee beg leave to submit the following remarks in relation to the Indian population of this State.

Accounts are daily coming in from the counties on the Coast of Mendocino of sickening atrocities and wholesale slaughters of great numbers of defenseless Indians in that region of country. Within the last four months more Indians have been killed by our people than during the centuries of Spanish and Mexican domination. Either our government or our citizens, or both are to blame.[169]

It was in these last few sentences of the *Majority Report* that the document went too far in its charges against the vigilantes of northeastern Mendocino County. Sadly, it was a fatal blunder. Some California legislators and, perhaps more importantly, most of the public were offended by this reckless, tactlessly broad allegation. Although typical of the rhetoric of the time, this exaggeration weakened the impact of the overall case that the pro-reservation authors were attempting to make.

As ethno-historian Sherburne Cook reported, many thousands of Indians more had died of various causes during the Hispanic era than had died during the American Period of the nineteenth and early twentieth centuries. One of the more obvious reasons is that the Hispanic era lasted much longer than a mere "four months" of 1859–1860. That point aside, from its first paragraph to its last the report confronted all Euro-Americans in California with the question of their failure to determine guilt in the relatively rare cases of Native American "depredations."

> *To the Honorable Senate and Assembly of the State of California:*
>
> Pursuant to a joint resolution passed by your Honorable Bodies, appointing a joint committee for the purpose of investigating and reporting the condition of Indian affairs in Mendocino County, we left the capital on the fifteenth day of February, A.D., one thousand eight hundred and sixty, and proceeded, *via* [Italics the original.] San Francisco, to Petaluma, Cloverdale, Ukiah City, Round Valley, and the Nome Cult Indian Farm in said valley, taking, in every place through which we passed, all the testimony which could be procured in reference to the object of our mission, and all of which testimony is hereunto annexed, and made a part of this report.
>
> Your committee find the same relations and condition of things between the white settlers and the Indians in Mendocino County as has always been the case from the first settlement of our country to the present time, whether on the frontiers or in the more thickly settled districts, where the Indian has been permitted to inhabit the same country with the white settler.[170]

---

169. See "Majority and Minority Reports of the Special Joint Committee on the Mendocino War," *Appendix Senate Journal 1860*, 4, California State Archives, 1020 "O" St., 4th Floor, Sacramento, CA.

The Report's next point was that, due to contiguous white settlements and Native American rancherias, much of the Native American's food supply had been removed and destroyed. This, in turn, had set up the condition of extreme hunger causing the Native Americans to attack and take settler livestock.

When livestock was lost, angry settlers were motivated by either the "an eye for an eye" vengeance or the "don't let the dog that bit you once bite you again" prevailing principles of the Western frontier. The great service that the California Joint Committee rendered society as a whole was to clearly show, through the publication of eyewitness accounts, what was happening as the logical result of the revengeful raids by Jarboe and others.

The idea of expanding the reservation as a solution to the "Indian problem" had been floating around for some time. Recall that one of Superintendent Henley's and Subagent Storms' earliest reports from Round Valley to superiors of the Office of Indian Affairs in Washington, D.C., had pleaded for expansion of the reservation limits to include the whole valley. But nothing had been done by the Office of Indian Affairs to implement it. As soon as possible Sen. O'Farrell's *Majority Report* was printed up and distributed, but unfortunately, the Legislature was in no mood to consider it seriously or to pass the requisite law to implement its recommendations.

The fifth committee member, Assemblyman Joseph B. Lamar from Mendocino County, filed a separate, dissenting and shorter *Minority Report*. This report stopped reform efforts dead in their tracks. Assemblyman Lamar believed that he was more in tune with how most Euro-Americans in Mendocino County really felt. Asssemblyman Lamar was determined to make his opinion known. Indeed, many in the valley, including Judge Hastings, Jarboe, and probably also, by now, former Subagent Storms and former Superintendent of Indian Affairs for California Thomas J. Henley, all strongly supported Assemblyman Lamar's position. That position regarding local Native Americans and control of the land in Round Valley was in direct opposition to the other members of the committee. Assemblyman Lamar considered all his Majority Report colleagues and many of the state's newspapermen as "Indian sympathizers." To Assemblyman Lamar and other Euro-Americans who thought the same way, they were almost traitors.

In his *Minority Report*, Assemblyman Lamar quoted George E. White, the Round Valley rancher with considerable landholdings who had made several bold claims in his deposition. White had implied that the Yukis were like insects

170. *Ibid.*

who, because they were merely pests, who "infested the region of [the] Reservation," and thus by implication should be eradicated from the land.

> From an estimate made under oath by a respectable citizen of Round Valley
> [George White], the property destroyed by the Indians of that Valley, and its vicin-
> ity, amounts in value to about one hundred and fifty thousand dollars. This con-
> sisted of different kinds of livestock—horses, hogs, sheep, and cattle. That species
> of property comprises the greater portion of the wealth of Mendocino County; and
> the time and energies of her people are devoted almost exclusively to the raising of
> stock. Upon such means they are almost entirely dependent for the support of
> themselves and their families, and however indifferently *Indian sympathizers* [italics in
> the original] may regard their losses, it is to the citizens of Mendocino a matter of
> serious import to suffer the ruthless destruction of their almost only means of sub-
> sistence.[171]

Assemblyman Lamar believed in this rugged looking Euro-American
rancher, George White, and completely ignored all conflicting testimonies of
numerous others. An ardent supporter of agricultural progress and development
for Mendocino County, Assemblyman Lamar decided to openly oppose all the
other members of the Joint Select California Legislative Committee based on his
belief in the reports of George White and others.

White's claim that one hundred and fifty thousand dollars worth of stock
had been destroyed by Native American attacks was unsupported in any of the
other depositions by white settlers, but this point seems to have been lost, not
just on Assemblyman Lamar, but almost on every other state lawmaker.

Despite the often-expressed hopes of Subagent Storms and others who
knew the facts about Nome Cult Farm, in the end the Legislature concurred
with Assemblyman Lamar, opting simply to ignore its own Joint Committee's
majority opinion and instead to fully fund the military expeditions of Gen.
Kibbe, Jarboe and others. Unfortunately, the Majority Report had received
almost no publicity. Whatever initial support it might have sparked soon was
quashed. In the still remote and even quite unknown regions like Round Valley
of northern California in 1860, the Report's recommendations seemed quixotic
and potentially extremely expensive. The public's mood in 1860 was increasingly
conservative and suspicious about spending public funds.

Many vocal conservatives at the time called for strict economy in government. Rumors of graft and corruption of the highest levels of government on
down made all lawmakers feel particularly vulnerable when it came to passing

---

171. *Minority Report*, by Assemblyman Joseph B. Lamar, Chairman of the Joint Committee,
Appendix Senate Journal 1860, 10-11, California State Archives, 1020 "O" St., 4th Floor,
Sacramento, CA.

any bills that increased spending allocations. Most decided instead in favor of simply continuing the status quo.

Indeed, at this time there were very few people, either in Washington or in Sacramento, who agreed with the idea of increasing aid to Indians by significantly enlarging the number or the size of the California reservations. Those who were in power were enjoying the unprecedented boom of prosperity begun by the gold rush, plotting out possible railroad routes and imagining all the implications inherent in the fulfillment of Manifest Destiny after 1848. Riding such powerful waves of prosperity while also facing the bitterly divisive issue of slavery of African Americans, California's political leaders definitely did not want to rock the boat by attempting to carry out such bold new and potentially costly policies.

The legislature was in no mood to take on large new responsibilities for Native Americans' welfare, or even their survival, when the possibility of being viewed as a "liberal" or "Indian sympathizer" meant certain political doom. Neither was the new governor, John G. Downey, eager to listen to the full Majority Report of April 1860. To Gov. Downey's opponents, almost from its first printing, the report seemed to be a crude attempt to quickly push the legislature into paying for both the Mendocino War and the War with the Win-toons. To implement its recommendation about quadrupling the reservation's size would take additional, significant appropriations.

Chances of the Legislature's adopting the Report's recommendations might have been significantly improved if there were any realistic chance that the federal government would step up to the plate and fund the new increased appropriations and also allocate money to expand Round Valley Reservation. Unfortunately especially because everyone had seen how absolutely Congress had rejected the eighteen California Native American treaties in 1853, there seemed little or no chance they would assist the state now.

Thus only one hundred copies of the report were ever printed. It may not have even been read aloud on the legislature's floor. Most lawmakers probably glanced at it and hastily discarded it with the rush of other business. To most legislators it must have seemed hopelessly impractical. The legislature quickly tabled AB 230, the accompanying measure that included the Majority Report's main points. The report was promptly forgotten both by state lawmakers and the California public.

Aside from politics, there were practical realities in the 1850s and early 1860s that strengthened the minority position. Settlers still generally lacked control over their California environment. It is sometimes forgotten by some that wire fencing was not an alternative until well after the Civil War. The fear of Indian uprisings was not the settlers' main concern. Losing livestock was a serious, omnipresent and especially nagging problem that affected both the so-called "stock raisers" and the farmers alike. Finding the actual Native American thieves who were responsible was an almost impossible problem as the Native Americans stole animals at times when no settlers actually saw it happening. Making matters worse there was a devastating statewide drought in 1860 and 1861.

> Cattle died by the hundreds for lack of grass and water; and the owners, anxious to save as much as possible from the wreckage, flooded the markets with such half starved animals as they were able to drive to the cities. The price of beef dropped to four, three, and even two cents a pound in the shops; and on many of the ranches the cattle were killed for what their hides, horns, and bones alone would bring.[172]

Given this new terrible problem that all the settlers faced, it is clear that many in the legislature thought it reasonable for some settlers to have slightly exaggerated the facts to the authorities in order to get the kind of military action everyone thought was needed. It really made little difference to the most powerful Euro-American politicians and state leaders if the 1859 petitions to Governor Weller were totally factual or not.

Finally, there was a general revulsion against the policies of the Office of Indian Affairs among the California public. It was a view based in part on newspaper accounts of Native American massacres. The former head of the Indian Affairs Department, Supt. Thomas J. Henley, had been a corrupt ex-head of the San Francisco Postal Department and Democratic Party hack. He was finally ousted from office as his corruption was made public in numerous shocking newspaper articles and equally damaging internal Office of Indian Affairs' and Treasury Department investigations and reports.

Tragically, the federal Office of Indian Affairs in Washington was unbelievably slow in getting around to surveying the limits of Round Valley and those of Nome Cult Farm. This eventually opened up a Pandora's box of legal differences, first, between individual settlers, and second, between settlers and the reservation officials over land claims. Many of these cases took decades of very expensive and bitter legal battles to finally resolve. Thus, settlers like John Law-

---

172. Robert G. Cleland, *History of California: The American Period* (New York: The MacMillan Company, 1923), 307.

son and others who may at first been willing to be bought out for merely the price of their small herds and improvements now dug in their heels. They were proud of their hard work in locating Round Valley, working their own farms and ranches, and building up the size of their herds. Those who could afford it decided to fight both against the reservation and any government attempt to force them off their land.

In California, and across America at this particular time, the Republican Party was coming into power. The public began to oppose liberals like Sen. O'Farrell and some of his old Democratic Party friends. Republicans opposed slavery for African Americans but were no more liberal than were the Democrats when it came to Native Americans. Even though he was well known to many, Sen. O'Farrell suffered politically from the fact that he was an Irishman and a Catholic who had spoken out against one of the leaders of the American side in the Mexican War, Captain John C. Fremont. In the fall of 1861, Sen. O'Farrell lost a statewide race for Lieutenant Governor. Any real hope of the legislature reconsidering the *Majority Report* and its liberal, pro-Native American recommendations had also died along with this defeat of Sen. O'Farrell at the ballot box.

As a revealing document on mid-nineteenth century thought regarding California Indians, the *Majority Report of the Special Joint Committee on the Mendocino War* is as heartbreaking as it is fascinating. State Senator O'Farrell and his three legislative colleagues hoped to make Round Valley Reservation the home for "about twenty five thousand Indians."[173]

The committee had realized the need. There were far more than this number of Native Americans living in the wild in California at this time. The actual Native American population at Round Valley could hardly be maintained at between two and three thousand. However Sen. O'Farrell's group, like Subagent Storms and other reservation officials had done before it, was simply naïve and too unrealistic. They did not have the support they needed of Gov. Downey or of the majority of their colleagues in the Legislature.

Meanwhile, a horribly high death rate continued to claim lives almost as quickly as the militia escorted California Native Americans onto Nome Cult Farm. Many Native Americans from almost every section of Northern and Central California entered there each month. No one counted them as they arrived. There is no record of their names, ages or actual tribes. No historians counted

---

173. "Majority and Minority Reports," *Appendix Senate Journal 1860*, 6, California State Archives, 1020 "O" St., 4th Floor, Sacramento, CA.

their deaths either. Not counting those shot by settlers, disease and starvation, due to inadequate or simply the wrong kinds of food, took a terrible toll in unnecessary deaths. In general the situation was particularly sad because the California public had almost no knowledge of this situation.

It did not help this grim reality to have such an overly sanguine report issued when there was no legislative support or executive leadership in Sacramento or in Washington, D.C. to make the needed changes. The nation stood on the verge of its great Civil War. Fierce debates over slavery's spread, fisticuffs, canings, and even duels dominated politics everywhere, even in the far Western states as California. As still happens today, whenever the American electorate becomes more deeply divided, most political leaders at all levels of government rush to abandon all of the more progressive plans for improving the lot of minorities, be they Native Americans, Hispanics or African Americans.

Occasional fighting between the Euro-American settlers and the Native Americans in Mendocino County and elsewhere in Northern California continued. Despite the over fifteen different sworn depositions from settlers that tell of how unfair the attacks were on the Indians, nothing was done to improve the situation. The California Legislature continued to ignore the Majority Report. Assemblyman Lamar proposed a single change by way of an amendment to the state's original 1850 law on the Native Americans. In June, the Legislature passed and Gov. Downey signed into law a provision that allowed Euro-American property owners like White and Hastings a more secure labor supply to work their ranches.[174] This amendment lowered the age at which Native American children could be legally adopted as so-called "apprentices" or indentured servants on ranches. It also included adults under this law for the first time. The 1850 law was finally abolished by the 1863 Legislature.

The new law allowed Euro-American ranchers and merchants to bond and thereby to enslave Native American workers to Euro-American landowners at an age of less than fifteen, simply by bringing them before a justice of the peace anywhere in the state. Unless supported by a very strong resistance by their own families, these youngsters were then enlisted as wards, or in reality, serfs for life on the ranches and estates of whites. Since a justice of the peace in frontier California was the primary, and in most rural counties like Mendocino County, the

---

174. See James J. Rawls' book, *Indians OF California: The Changing Image* (Norman: University of Oklahoma Press, 1984), 81ff.

only judge for a hundred-mile circumference, this further entrenched the Hispanic system of an enslaved Native American population.

State Assemblyman Lamar's true feelings on the subject can be inferred from an article he submitted to a newspaper. Of the California Native Americans, Assemblyman Lamar wrote:

> The most humane disposition that could be made of them, is, probably to reduce them to a mild system of servitude. Call them slaves, coolies or apprentices—it is all the same; supply them with christian masters and make them christian servants.[175]

Glumly, Senator Jasper O'Farrell and all the other members of the Select Committee on Indian Affairs had to return to their regular legislative duties, such as funding to build local roads, schools, and San Quentin State Prison, the first of many state prisons. After running and losing a race for Lieutenant Governor during the fall election of 1861, Senator O'Farrell at last had more time to look after his own land and family in western Sonoma County. Round Valley Reservation remained almost unknown to most immigrants as well as to many California residents. The Office of Indian Affairs continued to under fund and in some cases to poorly administer the northern California reservations.

In the end it was the predominantly Euro-American settlers who were daily gaining in strength in Round Valley, not the Office of Indian Affairs' Nome Cult Farm officials, the reservation and obviously not the Army. According to the 1860 Federal Census there were ninety-seven Euro-American settlers living in Round Valley in June of that year.[176]

---

175. See Assemblyman Lamar, cited in Rawls, *Indians of California*, 91, footnote 19.
176. See the copy of the Census of 1860, Microcopy 653, National Archives of the United States, Round Valley file, Held-Poage Library, in Ukiah, CA.

Chapter 11. "Arrant Fabrications": The 1860 Congressional Debate and Kidnapping Native-American Children

> In fact, all these tales of Indian hostilities, when sifted, are proved to be arrant fabrications. As to the stock said to have been appropriated by the starving Indians, (far less savage than their persecutors) [brackets in original], what does it amount to? Six hundred head taken by nine thousand Indians—driven from their lands and fisheries, and starving literally to death—were worth, at the outside, $12,000, let the State pay it, or double or treble the sum, and call upon the Federal Government to refund the amount.
> —Sen. Henry Wilson, R.-Mass., May 26, 1860, to the U.S. Senate[177]

Despite the recommendations of a majority of its own special Select Committee of the Legislature composed of four out of five of its members, the California Legislature as a whole had ignored the final report. As it had all along Round Valley Reservation had to struggle alone for existence. It was in a perilous position between the rock of the alarmed Euro-American settlers desiring ever more land and a hard place of the Office of Indian Affairs' inefficiency, lack of funding and mismanagement.

---

177. See the Senatorial debate on May 26, 1860 in *Congressional Globe*, 36th Congress, 1st Session, 2365–2369, as quoted in "Federal Effort to Transfer Indian Affairs to the State of California, 1860," 33ff, an article selected and edited by Robert F. Heizer, in *Federal Concern About Conditions of California Indians 1853 to 1913: Eight Documents*, Bellena Press Publications in Archaeology, Ethnology and History, No. 13 (Socorro, N.M.: Bellena Press, 1979). This book can be found at Held-Poage Historical Research Library, 603 W. Perkins St., Ukiah, CA.

News of the bloodshed and massacres of Gen. Kibbe's War and the Mendocino War eventually reached across the nation, to the Midwest, South, and East. Some newspapers reprinted reports from Mendocino County of Jarboe's and others' bloody raids on nearly defenseless Native American rancherias. In the climate of progress and a more enlightened and literate American society, such reports were not welcome. Even though Northern California landowners successfully stirred up hostility against the local Native Americans for killing stock, the general public in older regions of the nation like New England and Kentucky guessed correctly that most California Indians were not well armed. If they had known how peace-loving most of the indigenous people here were, they would have been even more upset by the obviously racist anti-Native American propaganda.

In the meantime, by the late spring of 1860, Congress in Washington engaged in an important debate which included discussion of the California reservations and the vigilante raids of the California militia upon Native American settlements in regions like Eden, Long and Round Valleys in remote Mendocino County. California's recently elected senator, Milton Latham, attempted to force a resolution through Congress. That resolution, H.R. 215, would have put the California state government in charge of all the Office of Indian Affairs' reservations in the state. In return for the state's taking charge of Indian policies, Senator Latham proposed that Congress would pay California $50,000 a year for the next twenty years, or $1,000,000 in total.

This action was adamantly and successfully opposed by a national coalition led by three of the leading senators of the period: Sen. Harry Wilson of Massachusetts, Sen. Robert Hunter of Virginia, and Sen. John J. Crittenden of Kentucky. We will read some passages from this debate below.

Speaking of what he viewed as a more efficient future for all Californians, Sen. Latham said:

> This is not a new project, for it has been discussed in California, and, as I said before, the Indians of California occupy a different relation to the Government from those of any other State of the Union. They have no lands there; you make no treaties with them; it's a mere matter of humanity for the Government to take care of them as its wards. ...[178]

---

178. This and subsequent quotes from the Senate's debate on May 26, 1860, are also from *Congressional Globe*, 36th Congress, 1st Session, 2365–2369, as quoted in "Federal Effort to Transfer Indian Affairs to the State of California, 1860" pp. 33 ff. an article selected and edited by Robert F. Heizer, Editor, *Ibid.*

Taking the floor after Senator Latham, Kentucky's Senator John Crittenden brought up the Humboldt Bay, or what some press reports referred to as the "Bloody Island," Massacre of 1860. The Senate and gallery were still agog over these details of gruesome murders of Native American women and children and mayhem when the next speaker, Republican Sen. Henry Wilson of Massachusetts, rose to speak. The Senate Chamber was hushed.

Sen. Wilson's remarks were a devastating and pointed attack both on Sen. Latham's proposal and the Office of Indian Affairs. What he said in his poignant speech of May 1860 brought out, at once, all the hypocrisy and falsity of California's Native American policy,

> These Indians have been neglected, and the evidence is in the Departments of the Government [the Office Indian Affairs and the Interior Department] to that effect—neglected by the persons appointed by this Government to care for them, who have grown wealthy by appropriating to themselves the money that should have been used to save the health and the lives of these Indians. It is a fact, to which the Senator from Kentucky [Sen. Crittenden] has just alluded, that great outrages have been perpetrated in the State [California]. I have upon my desk a report, made by Lieutenant Dillon to Major Johnson [Maj. Edward Johnson was then in command of Army troops at the Mendocino Reservation], of the doings of Thomas J. Henley that ought to disgrace that man forever; and I have here a letter from Major Johnson, referring to the action of that individual and to murders perpetrated under his observation.

Next, at Sen. Wilson's request, the Senate's clerk read to all assembled visitors in the gallery and the senators who were present,

> "The Jarboe Indian Massacres—Blood Money Wanted.—" The readers of the *Bulletin* are, perhaps, wearied and disgusted with the tales of barbarities upon the Indians, and it seems a thankless if not hopeless labor to attempt to excite a public sympathy for the fast decaying race; but if there is a Providence which regards and avenges the crimes of men, surely the people of this State are incurring a fearful responsibility, and are having a terrible retribution for the massacres and brutalities which they permit to be accomplished in their name. Another most dreadful chapter has been added to the damning record. Jarboe, who has been rioting in blood for the last year, in the Mendocino region, has just rendered his account of murders. The letter of this person to the Governor of the State [Downey], and which was by him submitted to the Legislature, on Tuesday, is a foul blot upon California. Here is an extract from it:
>
> On the 16th of September [1859], in Eden Valley, I mustered into service of the State of California, twenty men possessing the requisite qualification mounted on horseback, and armed with rifles and pistols. Up to that time the Indians had killed nineteen settlers and about six hundred head of stock in the region of the country spoken of, and were daily committing their depredations. I endeavoring to make a treaty of peace with them, and sent my interpreter out to their camp, who talked to them; he was a friendly Chumac [Chumash] Indian. They replied that they would kill every white man they could, and all the stock they could find—giving me reason

191

for it—and daring me to come out and fight. I did not attack them for some days afterwards, still hoping I might get along without bloodshed. On the night of the 20th of September, they came to Eden Valley and drove off some cattle. I followed and fought them with a detachment of ten men; and from the same date to the 24th of January, I fought them twenty-three times, killed two hundred and eighty-three warriors—the number of wounded was not known—took two hundred and ninety-two prisoners: sent them to the reservation [mostly to Mendocino but some also to Round Valley]. In the several engagements I had four men severely wounded, as well as myself.[179]

As shown by some of Jarboe's own testimony, this description of his actions as commander of the Eel River Rangers is, to put it mildly, in conflict with the testimony given in the depositions on all sides. He claimed that nineteen settlers were killed, when, at the most, two or three were killed over the course of several years. He stated that the Yuki Indians "dared" him to fight, promising to kill all the stock they could find. It is doubtful that any of this was true, as far as we can tell.

Senator Wilson, at least, was clearly aware of these facts. He continued,

> There is no excuse for any member of the legislature, or any citizen of the State, being deceived by the style of words which this man adopts in the narrative of his atrocities. He *fought* [Italics in the original] the Indians twenty-three times. Deliberate, cowardly, brutal massacres of defenseless men, women, and children he calls fighting! He killed nearly three hundred of these poor people. The *pretext* [again, italics in the original] upon which these butcheries were perpetrated is that nineteen settlers had been killed, and six hundred head of stock stolen. Now, we have the testimony of Major Johnson and Lieutenant Dillon that not one white settler had lost his life in that region at the hands of Indians during the past year—except a person [John Bland] who was killed in revenge for outraging an Indian woman. In fact, all these tales of Indian hostilities, when sifted, are proved to be arrant fabrications. As to the stock said to have been appropriated by the starving Indians, (far less savage than their persecutors), what does it amount to? Six hundred head taken by nine thousand Indians—driven from their lands and fisheries, and starving literally to death—were worth, at the outside, $12,000, let the State pay it, or double or treble the sum, and call upon the Federal Government to refund the amount.

The Senate's fiery debate over the reservation measure continued. When all of Sen. Wilson's sardonic yet colorful nineteenth-century rhetoric had finally ended, Congress decided overwhelmingly to scuttle Sen. Latham's proposed law. The fate of most of the California Native Americans was sealed: diminished numbers and more extermination to come. Like the California Legislature before it, the U.S. Congress simply continued to ignore reality. Nothing was done. No reforms were undertaken.

---

179. The piece read by the clerk was originally published in the *San Francisco Bulletin.* It was a part of the record contained in the *Congressional Globe, Ibid.*

The United States' Department of the Interior's relatively weak and tiny Office of Indian Affairs still had the immense and, at times, overwhelming task of trying to care for California's extremely numerous and varied Native American population- subdivided as it was into hundreds of small tribes or tribelets. All that Congress accomplished during the rest of the 1860 session was to split California in half into a Northern Division and a Southern Division. Congress continued to ignore all of the eighteen original treaties of 1851 with the California tribes.

None of the poorly funded reservations was increased in size. Worst of all, the conditions that had led Native Americans to take settler livestock prevailed just as they had done before the Mendocino War started. The Mendocino War and Gen. Kibbe's War as well as later ambushes left many more Indian families in misery—broken and in despair. They had to adjust to a future controlled by Euro-American settlers and by the employees of white landowners who sometimes acted violently against them for little or no reason.

For many Northern California Native Americans the daily high tide of abuses, rapes, and deliberate humiliations by some Euro-Americans would continue. Aside from continued violence, the decade of 1850–1860 was a period of little progress and much corruption in both state and national politics. Yet this decade was also a period of unparalleled growth in California and throughout the West. For in this same period the population of the nation increased by over one third; an astonishing 35.5 percent!

Just as astonishing was the fact that over sixteen percent of the entire U.S. population in 1860 was foreign-born, certainly due in large part to the lure of the gold rush. California had become a magnet for anyone who was less than satisfied with their circumstances and who had the wherewithal to come here. Fifty-five thousand flocked to California across the plains in 1859 alone. An unknown number of others immigrated by ship. Due in large part to the simple fact that few Euro-Americans could communicate with the local tribes and also because of the gigantic culture gap between whites and Native Americans, the Indians faced an uncertain and an increasingly difficult future for at least the next ten years.

Records of Native American numbers are virtually nonexistent. Although Indians in Mendocino were counted in both the 1850 and 1852 California Censuses, not a single Native American man, woman, or child was counted in the official U.S. 1860 Census in Round Valley Township found at Held-Poage Library in Ukiah. Doubtlessly some Euro-Americans also were not counted, but the fact was census officials verbally encouraged the settlers to participate. The same officials did not encourage Native Americans to come forward and be counted.

Although Round Valley's settlers denied that the Army had helped them much earlier, they were about to receive some more substantial help from the Army. Late in December 1862, following a series of bloody massacres, Company F of 2nd Infantry, a force comprised of over three times as many soldiers as were in Lt. Dillon's small platoon, arrived and established a new permanent military post called Fort Wright. The name was later changed to Camp Wright. Each of Company F's sixty-nine men carried a modern rifle, much more powerful and accurate than the Native Americans' bows and arrows. The company also had a mountain howitzer, which was, in fact, a cannon.

Before Euro-American mountain men and hunters came with muskets, pistols, and mountain rifles, the Native Americans were used to fighting out disputes in large one-day battles on open ground between masses of warriors armed only with bows and arrows, knives, and elkskin leggings. The fighting took place across open pastures or on gentle hills, much as Greek soldiers fought the armies of Persia two hundred years before the time of Christ. By the 1850s the evolution of long-range rifles like the Sharps rifle (ca. 1825) and the St. Louis mountain rifle (ca. 1843) made such battles not only obsolete but almost laughable.

With Congress' defeat of Senator Latham's proposed law that would have assured California Native Americans some federal recognition, their national case remained in same 'never-never land' that it had been in all along. Moreover, partly because of the new California law making Indian juveniles legal property of the highest Euro-American bidder, California Native Americans had entered a new period of virtual slavery.

SUPERINTENDENT HANSON AND THE KIDNAPPING RINGS

About a year after Congress decided to continue its hands-off policy regarding the California Native Americans, a newly installed Northern California District Superintendent of Indian Affairs, George M. Hanson, began his term of service to the state and its indigenous people. During the summer of 1861, racial tensions arose again between white settlers and the Native Americans in Mendocino and Humboldt Counties.

Regular Army soldiers and California militia like the Eel River Rangers reattacked Yuki, Pomo, Wailaki, Lassik, and other Northern California tribes and their children were made orphans as a result of the battles. Like the modern mafia, kidnapping rings made up of criminals and others operated freely throughout the headwaters of the Eel and Trinity Rivers in northwestern California.

In 1861, a Marysville newspaper reported,

Child Stealing

A day or two ago a couple of gentlemen of this city, were out near the tules in Colusa county, when they came across a party of men, who had in charge five Indian children about three or four years old, three of whom being girls, and two were boys: — The Marysville men were asked if they could not provide homes for these young heathen, their holders saying that their parents had been killed in battle and they were without anyone to care for them. The parties referred to said that they would see what could be done and went out again yesterday, having found homes for two, but the men who had them said that they must have some pay *for their trouble* [italics in the original article] and put the amount at which they would part with the children at $50, or such a matter. This, of course, showed that these men were selling the children....[180]

The article next described how this same group had had nine Native American children with them and the kidnappers "were seen coming out of the Coast Range [the Mayacama Mountains] with them." All three men were then arrested and charged. According to follow-up articles by the same paper two of the men, Laurie Johnson and James Wood, eventually went free after having to post $500 each as bail money. One man, James Freak, was released because the judge ruled that "the men were not legally held by the sheriff of Yuba County." Superintendent Hanson had been responsible for preferring charges in the case. It appears that he also deserves a lot of credit for trying to put such kidnapping rings out of business. The fact that someone was finally prosecuted for the kidnapping of Native American children must have eventually had a positive effect in bringing some justice and peace to Northern California.

Later, the same Marysville newspaper reported the following,

Provided For

The nine little Indians lately recaptured by Superintendent Hanson from the kidnappers, have all been provided with comfortable homes by the Superintendent,

---

180. See "6:9 Newspaper article, Marysville, 1861," in Robert F. Heizer, *The Destruction of California Indians*, with an Introduction by Albert Hurtado, Lincoln: University of Nebraska Press, 1974, 236.

who has assured himself that the poor little heathens will be cared for and well used by their guardians, most of whom reside in the city.[181]

Superintendent Hanson had begun his term of office by posting a bond during the spring of 1861. On July 15 he submitted a fifteen page report to the Indian Affairs Office in Washington recommending the closure of both the Mendocino and Nome Lackee Reservations. In so doing Superintendent Hanson made it very clear to Commissioner William Dole that he wanted to make real changes in the way the California reservations were operated.

For example, Supt. Hanson recommended removing all regulars as well as the less well trained California militia forces from the reservations. At the same time, he thought he could protect the Native Americans and the reservations themselves by arming and training reservation employees.

Yet again, things did not work out very well after Nome Lackee and Mendocino Reservations closed. Sadly, almost all of the Native Americans at the two reservations would eventually die along the way or be relocated onto other reservations, primarily the one at Round Valley or at Klamath Reservation. By 1864, both Mendocino and Nome Lackee Reservations closed permanently with the land sold to help recover the costs of all these changes.

One of the most noble of Supt. Hanson's seven objectives was to raise the pay of laborers to $75 per month in an effort to attract more married men with small families to what he described as "Indian work." He made the observation that too many white men were angering the Native Americans in Round Valley by trespassing onto the reservation property and forcing Native American women to leave with them, either to become concubines or common-law wives. Wisely Supt. Hanson realized that the Office of Indian Affairs would have to pay a little more than the minimum wage in order to attract high caliber men and women willing to give up private life to live on the relatively more isolated reservations in California.

Supt. Hanson believed that the new male employees' wives would make excellent teachers of the Native American girls and women. In this same remarkable report to Washington, Superintendent Hanson called for the re-survey of Nome Cult Indian Farm (or Round Valley Reservation) and for a special act by Congress to buy out Round Valley's white settlers so that the entire valley would become the reservation. In this Superintendent Hanson returned to Superintendent Edward Beale's principle of segregating or separating the whites from the Native Americans. On his next to the last page of this

181. *Ibid.*, "6:12, Newspaper article, 1861," 239.

long report to the Indian Affairs Office, Supt. Hanson listed the total cost of his new budget at $155,400.[182]

Unfortunately, perhaps because all of the Lincoln Administration's attention was required to raise troops and provide for their training and deployment in the Civil War, many of Superintendent Hanson's intelligent and perceptive recommendations were either totally forgotten or too long delayed. Despite the repeated recommendations of the Office of Indian Affairs, Congress never acted on Supt. Hanson's Round Valley settler-buyout plan. Therefore conditions at Round Valley became so bad that by 1862 most of the Concow tribe as well as other Native Americans attempted a long march back over the Mayacama Mountains to avoid starving to death during the winter of 1862-63. Regular Army soldiers returned to Round Valley in mid-December 1862 and remained there until 1875.

---

182. See the report from Superintendent of the Northern District of California George M. Hanson, July 15, 1861, Yuba City, California to the Commissioner of Indian Affairs William C. Dole, Washington, D.C., in Letters Received by the Office of Indian Affairs, 1821-1910, Microcopy 234, Roll 38, 1860-1861, National Archives of the United States.

CHAPTER 12. NATIVE AMERICANS RETALIATE

> *"Are we happy here? No, my brother. We have not been happy since we left our home!"*
> —Tom-ya-nem, Chief of the Concow, 1874.

Subagent Simmon P. Storms' overly optimistic first Nome Cult Farm report to his boss, Superintendent of California Indian Affairs Thomas J. Henley, described an almost idyllic valley whose resources surpassed any he had ever seen. This was a familiar refrain of incoming federal officials from Storms to Special Agent Goddard Bailey to, in 1862, the 2nd Army's Capt. Charles D. Douglas. Far too many newcomers ignored the racial turmoil and the many problems related to Round Valley's challenging geography.

In this and several subsequent communications to Supt. Henley and to the Office of Indian Affairs in Washington, Storms expressed his high optimism about the future of the reservation and its capacity to support a large population of Native Americans. Storms and Henley did not foresee that, once they had arrived and struggled for years to establish their businesses, farms and ranches there, the settlers would never allow themselves to be bought off their lands. The Office of Indian Affairs' own lack of organization and funding led to the critical failure to make the reservation the main business going on in Round Valley.

The ranchers and settlers wanted power. They needed to control the valley's lush range land. Finally they sought the right to construct their own community. Subagent Storms did not deliberately delude the inhabitants and the unknown chief of the Round Valley Native Americans whom almost certainly were Yuki. He either did not know about or hoped to be able to stop the abduction of Native American children by kidnapping rings or by a few settlers like George Woodman. His main job was to set down the structure for the new reservation. Storms named his enterprise "Nome Cult Farm." He also claimed Round Valley for the U.S. Government. Without a doubt Subagent Storms was successful in that.

The Mendocino War was a small part of a larger war won by California militiamen hastily organized under Gen. William C. Kibbe, Captain Isaac Messic, Captain Walter Jarboe and other officers. A kind of truce briefly prevailed by 1860 throughout the northern half of the state. The California legislature tried to study the conditions in Mendocino County, but its own committee's report was rejected and ignored by Gov. John G. Downey and other lawmakers. In June 1860 the legislature legalized the indenture of Indian youth as young as fourteen. It failed to take any moral position with regard to murders and exploitation of California Native Americans.

In the early years, and even as late as 1863, there were so many Native Americans in the valley that reservation employees at times had to rely on mountain men, hunters, and gunmen for protection. This was the other factor unforeseen by Storms and other authorities. Violence made it easier for the more aggressive Euro-Americans, particularly men like George White, Walter Jarboe, Dryden Laycock and others, to use vigilante-style tactics as the primary response and defense mechanism when livestock wandered off or was taken by the few aggressive Native Americans who lived in the vicinity. The result was that when Round Valley Reservation needed to expand and take over from Nome Lackee as the state's primary reservation in Northern and Central California, it was more dangerous for everyone than it had ever been before.

First of all, the Army, which had played a relatively conciliatory role in previous years, was now largely absent. When Lt. Edward Dillon and his platoon were transferred out of Round Valley the situation there was anything but peaceful. Although a few soldiers remained at the reservation, their small number emboldened settlers like G.E. White, C.H. Eberle, S.P. Storms, and the Henley family to work for the establishment of more private farms and ranches in the valley.

Reservation administrative changes did not help the situation. With the inauguration of President Abraham Lincoln in 1861 and the start of the Civil War back East, a new group of Western reservation officials took over California's

Indian Affairs Department. Under the incoming administration, George M. Hanson became the new Superintendent of Indian Affairs for Northern California. In Round Valley on October 1, 1861 Supervisor James ("California Jim") Short, formerly a friend of Abe Lincoln's and a farmer, replaced Agent George Rees as the head of reservation. In the 1830s Lincoln had temporarily worked as a surveyor.

James Short led, at best, a checkered career as supervisor.[183] Although he was undoubtedly a cut above Henley and some of the other settlers in honesty, Supervisor Short, like his two predecessors Storms and Rees, soon found that the constant pressure of supply shortages, settler-Native American hostilities and insufficient funds often led to deadly situations in which innocent lives were lost.

By 1860–1863, the number of Euro-American attacks on Native Americans in the Round Valley area became more common than in the preceding three years. This did not mean that all Euro-Americans hated and would murder any Native American they could, whenever they could. Many Euro-Americans never fired a bullet in anger, either at an Indian or at anyone else. Certain local tribes like the Wailaki or Yuki were particularly suspect. However, reports of the attacks after 1860 sound all too much like those of the previous years.

A MENDOCINO HERALD INVESTIGATION

On January 18, 1861, the following newspaper article titled "Troubles with the Indians," appeared in the *Mendocino Herald*:

> Indians in the vicinity of Round Valley and the country this side of there, are again likely to make a winter's troubles with the white settlers. Mr. Witt, deputy Sheriff, [P.A. Witt or Wit was also the second constable of Round Valley Township. With the Army's platoon absent, he was the sole peace officer for all of Round Valley] has just returned from Round Valley, and informs us that the whites have lately had a fight with them, in which 18 of the Indians were killed; one white man was wounded, but not dangerously. The unusual severity of the winter has doubt-

---

183. For a description of the Lincoln-Short relationship, see David H. Donald, *Lincoln* (New York: Touchstone Rockefeller Center, 1996), 55. According to Professor Donald, young Lincoln briefly worked as a surveyor about the same time of his first term as an Illinois state legislator. "Uncle" Short, "one of Lincoln's admirers", who later stated he was a "farmer for forty years," saved Lincoln's equipment by paying $120 in March 1835 at a sheriff's auction. Short "immediately returned it to him," according to Lincoln's biographer, Donald. Perhaps Lincoln repaid Short with the appointment as Round Valley's third Agent in Charge or Supervisor.

lessly reduced the Indians to a condition bordering on starvation, and the consequence is, they are committing serious depredations on the stock, great numbers of which range over the Eel River mountains.

The worst feature of these Indian depredations is, that when they commence killing stock, they do not stop when their absolute necessities are supplied; but kill, destroy and drive off large numbers, in many cases indicating a maliciousness they would avoid were they endowed with reason. A few winters more, with these unavoidable results, may convince our government and the enquiring world that the Indians cannot live in the midst of our settlements in peace, while guided by their own instincts and rude notions of government. Their rapid and almost immediate annihilation must be the consequence.[184]

This article is typical one-sided frontier journalism reporting on the killings of Native Americans. No thought is given to the welfare of the Native Americans aside from the almost callous mention of their near starvation. Rather the focus is on the need to protect settler livestock and agricultural enterprise. Starvation alone is not enough to explain stock depredations for this reporter, who explains this turn of events by pointing to the Native Americans' lack of "reason," their "instincts and rude notions of government." Note that the white settlers were allowing their stock to stray "over the Eel River Mountains." The article also includes Superintendent Beale's and Agent Storms' idea of separating Native Americans from settler population: the accepted theory of Indian Affairs by many educated and influential Euro-Americans of this time. At Round Valley, it never got any further than being talked about.

The next few sentences from the *Mendocino Herald* article are another example of the editor's personal biases. The writer seems to have forgotten his primary job of reporting the facts to the public,

Republicanism, or abolitionism, theoretically, or politically; may do well enough to operate on in a political campaign, and so far as the African race is concerned, has many sympathizers; but here, where the evil of contact between two races is always before our eyes, it is not at all unusual to hear even the most ultra antislavery men admit that a system of apprenticeship, making the Indians dependent on and subservient to the whites, is the only way that the almost immediate extinction of the Digger race can be avoided. In fact, many of them have already taken "apprentices," under our present imperfect State law who are again in some cases transferred to other parties.

It is contended that they are better off thus, than if they were running wild in the mountains. And so we think—Why not, then, have the Indians; turned over to the care of the State, and by bestowing upon the subject the care its importance

---

184. Unsigned article, "Troubles with the Indians," *Mendocino Herald*, 2., vol. 2, 11, Jan. 18, 1861, at Held-Poage Historical Research Library, 603 W. Perkins St., Ukiah, CA.

demands, have such laws enacted as will effectively protect both the Indian and the white. We may have occasion to refer to this subject again.[185]

So what we have here is the argument that somehow the servitude of the Indians is a compassionate solution, required to avoid their "immediate extinction."

After discussing this massacre with Deputy Sheriff Witt, a number of reporters led by the *Mendocino Herald's* editor E. R. Rudd [Budd], made the difficult trip over rough terrain up to Round Valley from Ukiah to further investigate this latest murderous incident. The article quoted below was published on February 8, 1861, and was signed only by a single initial "J." The entire article is found here, as it is preserved in the hardbound original copies kept in a separate outbuilding at Held-Poage Library, as a valuable eyewitness account of Round Valley events in early 1861.

> The reporters had finally reached the edge of the Middle Fork of the Eel River and: As we stopped and gazed upon its waters, rushing furiously past its rocky edges, foaming and dashing from side to side in all the fearful madness of a cataract, we thought of the many unwilling victims [Henry Stevens, who was Mrs. Storms' brother, drowned while attempting to cross the Eel River] it had engulfed. Yet this was no time for such reflections—in we plunged—Bill first and I following. The bath was a cold one and not altogether relished by our horses, who seemed to dread it as much as we did. The stream crossed and opposite bank gained, we ascended the long back bone of the mountain, and passing down the eastern slope soon found ourselves galloping over the broad bosom of the valley. A few minutes ride carried us to Henley's ranch where we found Barc and Tom awaiting our arrival. Here Bill and I separated, he passing further up the valley and I stopping for the night with my young bachelor friends. As we had brought with us the overland mail and pony express from Ukiah, with other interesting items of news, Bill hurried on to distribute it to the other residents alone. I would here remark that some of the papers contained the result of the late Presidential election [J. refers to President Lincoln's election of 1860]. Speaking of Mails and Mail facilities, reminds one that no portion of our country is so poorly provided for in this respect as Round Valley. It does really seem to me that some provision should be made to meet this important demand. Much has been said about this valley abroad and the people living in it; and I am satisfied even from the superficial knowledge I obtained, that but little is known either of its resources or the character of its citizens. From the fact of there being a Reservation here for the protection of the Indians, and because in times past supplies were high, and but few of the staples raised, the expense became enormous. Salaries, too, in those days for officers and attachees rated high, which added to other expenses, afford rich food for political capital among the discordant elements of office seekers and penny-aliners. Round Valley became synonymous with Reservation, and Reservation and corruption one and the same word. A few wild spirits scattered here and there, detracted somewhat, too, from the tone and respectability of the masses; and hence, the popular injustice so common towards

185. *Ibid.*

the people of this valley. It is a grave mistake that few save government officers, attachees and soldiers reside here. This class is small compared with the independent settlers or farmers.

The valley contains about eighteen thousand acres, whilst only five thousand are reserved for Government purposes. The farms which I passed were mostly well fenced and contained good comfortable houses. I do not know the exact population, though they polled about sixty votes. One thing, though, however, speaks well for them, the Under Sheriff informed me that every dollar of their delinquent tax has been paid.[186]

While possibly somewhat naive in tone, many of the writer's own observations are fascinating. Three facts that he reports need emphasis here. First, Round Valley's white residents probably did not know about the election of Abraham Lincoln until late January 1861, because apparently no telegraph line connected Round Valley to the rest of the nation. Second, this contemporary account speaks up for the honesty of the Euro-American residents of Round Valley. Like most pioneers in frontier California, it seems that almost all had paid their full share of taxes and had made few if any complaints about the amount. Here the number of voters is listed as "sixty," which is about two thirds of the ninety-seven listed in the 1860 Census for the valley's population. By modern standards this was a remarkable voter turnout for any election.

Third, "J.'s" observations about the reservation are telling. He describes it as somewhat of a political boondoggle, a government project that required heavy investment with little or no apparent return, rife with corruption and full of "rich food for political capital among the office seekers and penny-aliners."

"J." was invited to dinner at the Storms' family table:

> I saw but one lady while there—the estimable and accomplished wife of Captain Storms [Mrs. Sarah J. Stevens Storms]. Here I was invited to dinner, and could not help but feel the influence that one possessed of such rare qualities, must exert upon a pioneer settlement of this kind. Before closing my letter it may not be out of place to speak of the recent outbreak of depredations of the Indians in that vicinity; in which thirteen or fourteen [The number here is reduced from the original eighteen reported above.] were killed and one white man—Captain Lacock wounded, narrowly escaping with his life. The Yuka tribe are mostly within the valley, and immediately adjoining in the mountains. They number perhaps five or six hundred; whilst the Tlackees [Wylackies], a more warlike and unfriendly class, range within

---

186. See J., "Trip to Round Valley Number 2," February 8, 1861, *Mendocino Herald*, Held-Poage Historical Research Library, 603 West Perkins St., Ukiah, CA. The writer repeated the fact that Native American tribes like the Yuki and the Wailaki did not want to stay for very long on the reservation. Many historians, including Estle Beard and Virginia P. Miller, also record this as fact. Finally, as was the case for many attacks of one side by the other, accurate casualty figures remain lacking.

a scope of country some ten or twelve miles round, and number, perhaps, two thousand or more. There could have been no possible excuse for this last outbreak, as I was informed that Capt. Reese [Agent George Rees.], at the Reservation, has often supplied these very Indians with provisions and blankets, whenever they have asked for them. They have a great dread of the Reservation, and will not remain.[187]

The writer stated that the Wylacki ("two thousand or more") now outnumbered the Yuki ("five or six hundred"). This reversed the situation before 1856 as understood by most historians. The article concluded by praising Agent Rees for doing his job of distributing provisions and blankets.

It is possible that Mrs. Storms had been chosen by other settlers as the valley's spokesperson. Public relations was vitally important to the future progress of any frontier community. Both Mrs. Storms' political and her culinary skills were obviously very gratefully received by this young *Mendocino Herald* reporter.

THE HORSE CANYON MASSACRE

In late September 1861, there was another bloody Round Valley area massacre at Horse Canyon. Horse Canyon is located about twenty trail miles north of Round Valley in rugged terrain. During the late summer of 1861, a group of approximately thirty-five or forty Wailaki men had armed themselves with rifles. They had learned how to shoot accurately. This massacre eventually resulted in the deaths of up to two hundred and forty Wailaki Indians.

In a series of raids, the Wailaki concentrated on capturing Round Valley horses. In their rampage this sizable band of Wailaki warriors also killed a number of mules and other livestock that were kept in an isolated northeastern pocket of Round Valley. Some of the settlers began calling them "the gun Indians." That fall, many Round Valley settlers were away, busy elsewhere at various other tasks. When the crisis came, it was difficult for the settlers to raise and organize a vigilante force large enough to attack the Wailaki. Nine settlers, led by Charles Bourne along with a small number of hand picked Hat Creek and Pit River Indians, trailed the Wailaki band up to Horse Canyon. Along the way the vigilante party counted the remains of thirty-one horses.

Because the Wailaki were often aggressive, other Trinity and Mendocino County tribes, like the Nomlaki, Yuki, Lassik and others in the Round Valley locale, had a special respect for the Wailaki. There were nearly two thousand

---

187. *Ibid.*

Wailaki spread out in over twenty rancherias north of the valley. Like a great earlier Hispanic leader of *Alta California*, Gen. Mariano Vallejo, in Napa and Sonoma Counties, Round Valley's leaders decided to make use of such well-known, traditional Native American rivalries to destroy one of their most troublesome Native American opponents.

The Euro-American leaders pleaded with the Concow leader at Nome Cult Farm, an articulate chief named Tome-ye-nem, to help them to raise a large enough mixed Native American and white settler force to stop the Wailaki band of "gun Indians" who were picking off settlers' livestock.

The Concow originally came from an area just to the east and little north of Chico, in Butte County, a distance of eighty miles away from Round Valley. They had been removed from there to Round Valley Reservation in 1859. By 1861 the Concows at Nome Cult Farm and the Wailaki tribe north of Round Valley were neither strong enemies nor close friends. At first Tome-ye-nem was uncertain about whether or not to act. As neutrals, so to speak, the Concow were not strongly drawn to fight either for other Native Americans or for the predominantly Euro-American settlers.

Tome-ye-nem's eyewitness account of the Horse Canyon Massacre, as told previously in *Genocide and Vendetta: The Round Valley Wars of Northern California*, explained exactly how it happened.

> One day ... one of the Ad-sals [whites] came home and said that the bad Wailakis were killing all the Shu-min [livestock], and he asked me to come with my braves and help to kill the Wailakis. I shook my head and said no ... that they had done no harm either to me or mine.... I went to the headman [Reservation Superintendent James Short] on the reservation and asked him what to do but the other Ad-sals came to him, and he was prevailed upon, and he asked me to go.[188]

Since they had now become "reservation Indians," and perhaps more importantly, because the Indian agent asked him to, Tom-ya-nem decided to throw in his lot with the settler raiding party. With the Concows' help, Captain Charles H. Bourne now had a sufficient force to overwhelm the Wailaki warriors.

---

188. Lt. Augustus G. Tassin, "The Con-cow Indians," *Overland Monthly*, IV, (July 1884), 10–11, as quoted by Lynwood Carranco and Estle Beard, *Genocide And Vendetta* (Norman: University of Oklahoma Press, 1981) 11, footnote #25, in Chapter 6, "Subduing The Indians." The Ukiah newspaper reported: "One man, Henry J. Abbott, was dangerously wounded by an arrow, which passed in his breast and lodged below the ribs. Several others were slightly wounded." See "Indian War," *Mendocino Herald*, (Ukiah, CA) Nov. 1, 1861, 1, #52, 2, c. 2.

> So I took many of my warriors and some of the Yukas [Yuki] and Pitt-Rivers and we started on the war-path with nine of the Ad-sals.... The next morning we came to a creek [a branch of Hulls Creek, twenty miles north of Round Valley] at a place called Horse Canyon, and the Wailakis were there as thick as leaves, some singing, others dancing.... The trees were full of meat hanging in the sun to dry, and there were [so] many Indians that the Ad-sals became anxious and frightened; and did not know whether to go back or fight; and finally, they asked me to be chief during the battle.... I told my braves to be sure and not kill the women and little children, and I gave the war-whoop and we charged upon the Wailaki.[189]

Despite Tom-ya-nem's clear order to spare the lives of the women and children, the battle brought with it all the mayhem and confusion of other usual combat situations. The result was about ten to fifteen minutes of bloody fighting in which very few prisoners were taken alive. Many Wailakis either died or were wounded.

> Very soon the water in the creek became red, and the Con-cows and Pitt Rivers were wild and drunken with blood, and their tomahawks crushed the brain of the old and young alike.... One of the Ad-sals and myself gathered a great many women and children together, I told him that we would save them and take them to the Reservation, and he said, "yes," but just then one of the Yukas [Yuki] [was] wounded or killed; then the one with me turned around, and pointing to the women and children commanded to kill them all and they were killed; but we had a great many little children among the rocks. ...

> The dead Wailakis were strewn over the ground like the dead leaves in the fall, and for many days the sky was black with the ravens fattening on the dead; even now in the summer days, the white bones are bleaching underneath the wild flowers. And Wah-no-no-pem [Great Spirit] must have frowned upon his bad children, for we became after that, even more unhappy than before.[190]

This version of the story was unknown to most Euro-Americans until late 1874 or 1875, when Tom-ya-nem told it to Lt. Augustus G. Tassin, an Army scout assigned to duty at Round Valley who published it the *Overland Monthly*.[191]

Unlike many of the newspaper articles of the period, there is no tone of Victorian morality or racism against either race in Lt. Tassin's articles. Tom-ya-nem's account is eloquent, both in the simplicity of its metaphors and its graphic description of the Wailaki killings and ravens.

189. *Ibid.*
190. *Ibid.*
191. The *Overland Monthly*, a national geographical magazine, was a literary and news magazine that was published in the late nineteenth and early twentieth century by the *San Francisco News*. Interestingly, the *Overland Monthly* was also published in Chicago and New York. Lt. Tassin was assigned to scout in Mendocino County for the U.S. Army in 1874. He took a keen interest in the local Native Americans and interviewed both the Native Americans and the settlers.

THE LITTLE STONY CREEK MASSACRE

Meanwhile, times continued very tough for the Native Americans on the reservation throughout the following year, 1862. The settlers continued to harass them, including tearing down reservation brush and wood fences and sometimes even driving their herds of hogs, cattle, or horses over the Native Americans' freshly planted fields. As the spring of 1862 passed, conditions went from bad to worse on the reservation. Things got so bad then that the Army, as it had in 1856–1858, received many letters from Indian Affairs Department officials pleading for the dispatch of soldiers to Round Valley and to other California reservations. Perhaps because of the manpower required to fill the ranks of the Union armies in the East, the Army did not return to Round Valley right away. Any semblance of law and order disappeared there.

Violence and wrongful acts were committed both by the settlers and by Native Americans during the spring and summer of 1862. Just as the taking of their stock by Native Americans had infuriated individual settlers from 1859 through 1861, an Indian attack on Euro-Americans at Little Stony Creek brought about a new settler raid led by C.H. Eberle. He wrote the following newspaper article, which ultimately was printed on May 23, 1862, in the closest local paper, Ukiah's *Mendocino Herald*.

There was a ten-day delay in publication, as there was no telegraph service. This was well before the time of national news wire services like Associated Press. After it was written on May 13, a rider had to carry it from Round Valley to Ukiah. It was reviewed and finally set up and printed on May 23.

ROUND VALLEY—May 13, 1862

Eds. *HERALD*:

I take upon myself the sad task to chronicle an event which resulted in the death of two persons, one an esteemed citizen of this valley, Mr. Isaac W. Shannon, and the other a stranger by the name of Ford of Colusa county.

Mr. Shannon was one of the early pioneers of this section of the county, a man of enterprise, and his loss will be deeply felt by a large circle of friends.

Mr. J.B. Owens and Asa Bean, who arrived last evening from the Mountain House, Tehama county, are the bearers of the news, and from them I learned the following particulars: In the latter part of last month [April], some of the settlers of Little Stony Creek missed some of their stock, and found signs of some having been killed by Indians. A company of ten or twelve men was soon formed, and with a few domesticated Indians, started in search of the depredators. They tracked them through the hills a couple of days, when they found the body of Watson, who resided on Little Stony Creek. The body was found lying less than a mile from his house, pierced with five balls, and stripped of clothing.

Some of the party took the body in charge and the rest continued in pursuit. On the day following about four miles from the Mountain House [Mountain House was an overnight stopping place on the trail to Round Valley near Willits.] they found the body [of] an Indian boy of the Nome Lackee tribe, who had long resided in the family of Mr. Darling. The party then returned to Mr. Bean's on Thorn's Creek. The result of their discoveries was communicated to the neighbors, and several more joined the party, and among the number was Mr. Shannon, who was on the return from Red Bluff, and had been detained on that side of the mountain by the recent storm; also Mr. Bean [Asa Bean], Dryden Lacock, and several former settlers of this valley.

The party left Mr. Bean's last Saturday afternoon, and that night camped at Mr. Henderson's about five miles north of the Nome Lackee Reservation, at the foot of the mountain. Early the next morning they discovered the Indians about two miles from the Henderson's. The fight immediately commenced, the Indians standing their ground and fighting desperately, until they were nearly all killed. They were well supplied with fire arms and ammunition.

During the fight Mr. Shannon [Isaac W. Shannon] received a ball in the breast and expired immediately, as he was in the act of discharging his piece at an Indian. Mr. Ford was mortally wounded and expired about three o'clock the same day. It was a dear bought victory, and the little band returned in sadness, bearing their dead companions. Twelve Indians were found after the fight, and it is thought that many more were killed; but the country being rugged and brushy; they could not be found. Not more than five or six escaped. Several good rifles and plenty of ammunition was found in their camp.

Several squaws were taken, who were recognized as belonging to the Reservation in this valley. They are of the Hat Creek and Pitt River tribes, which caused our State volunteers so much trouble about two years ago.

The government, in its wisdom, saw fit to bring those Indians from their native wilds, and quarter them in the midst of our citizens, where their continued depredations are the sources of much vexation, pecuniary loss, and not infrequently the life of a valued fellow citizen is the consequence of their rascality. They are of a roving disposition, and are continually leaving the Reservation, and committing these depredations on their way to their old hunting ground. They will never be content with the drudgery and monotony of the Reservation.

C.H. EBERLE[192]

Eberle's name appearing at the end of the article is a departure from previous press reports that were anonymous or carried only an initial as a byline in the paper.

192. C.H. Eberle, article from "Round Valley, May 7, 1862," *Mendocino Herald*, May 23, 1862, 2, c. 2, Held-Poage Historical Research Library, 603 W. Perkins St., Ukiah, CA.

The tribe was not identified by the writer of the article. Possibly the raiding party had their own way of determining who was innocent or guilty. As in many newspaper articles of this period, the writer assumes that the raiding party attacked and killed only the guilty Native American party.

As in the case of the many letters and petitions of the 1858–1859 period, the writer blamed the government for first introducing the reservation to what he assumes was open land, or land that was free for Euro-American claims for private settlement. "The government ... saw fit to bring those Indians "...and quarter them in the midst of our citizens." There is no mention in the article about the federal government's establishment of Nome Cult Farm in 1856 or the fact that it predated almost all of the settlers Round Valley land claims.

Note that he blamed the depredations on more warlike tribes like the Hat Creek or Pit River tribes and not on the local Native Americans like the Wailaki, Wintun, Pomo or Yuki. This distinction, while it may seem insignificant to some, was a significant change from previous writings. Like the Wailaki of the previous Stony Creek battle, it appears that the Native American warriors were well-armed. Isaac Shannon was killed by someone who could shoot accurately in the battle. There seemed to be an almost grudging admiration in the final sentence from this writer who had lived in the valley for a relatively long time for a white man, almost five years.

The Concows Leave the Valley

By October 1862, Tom-ya-nem knew that the rain and snow of the often bitterly cold Northern California winter would soon arrive to isolate the valley for another three to six months. In winter the passes were so deep with snow that most of the trails in or out of the valley were impassable.

The so-called "reservation Indians" were also on guard due to the Upper Station Massacre of more than twenty Wailaki warriors on the morning of August 6, 1862. Due to poor farming methods, mismanagement by Supervisor Short, and unrepaired "slip gaps" in reservation fences, food stocks on the reservation were dangerously low. What happened next seemed to bear out Captain Eberle's judgment regarding the lure of the Native Americans' "hunting ground."

In his interview with Lt. Tassin the weary Concow leader described what he had decided to do, first explaining the situation in the valley:

The Ad-sals [Euro-Americans] were afraid that their Great Chief in Washington would keep all the valley for the Indians, and that the whites would have to go to some other home, and they hated us for it very much; often at night, in the springtime, some of the Ad-sals would steal around our fences and throw them down, and drive their shu-min [stock] into the fields, and the young corn and everything green would disappear in one night.[193]

The reason for the ongoing struggle was a war over turf, as it was so simply yet cogently stated by the Concow chief. By then the Euro-Americans had attained their required mastery of the land. Despite a general directive to the settlers from the federal Indian Affairs Office to leave Round Valley, most of the Euro-American ranchers there were determined to stay put. If need be, they would fight for their ranches and farms.

Tom-ya-nem continued:

One year [1862] there was nothing for us to eat, and I became very anxious for my Laukome [his wife], for the rains were coming fast with the cold winds.... and we would be shut in by the swollen streams, with starvation before and the Ad-sals behind. So I told my people to pull down their lodges and make ready to move. ... I went to the head man [Supervisor or Agent James Short] and shook hands with him, and told him that I must go, that I could not remain, that my people were starving and would have to kill the shu-min [stock] in the winter to keep from dying of hunger, and that the Ad-sals would kill them if they did. And in a long line, five hundred strong, we turned our faces toward ... the East ... and traveled onward to Wel-lu-da, our home.

Time had taught the Native Americans that they would be killed by the Euro-Americans if they continued to capture and kill the settlers' stock. The Horse Canyon massacre was sufficient proof to all that this was no less true now than it had been in 1859. Therefore, even though he may have sensed that their long trek over one hundred miles back to the Chico area would be pointless, Tom-ya-nem and his warriors were determined to try it anyway. Apparently Supervisor or Agent Short made little or no effort to stop the Concows from leaving the reservation.

Tom-ya-nem continued to describe the Concows' march after leaving Nome Cult Farm:

But when we got across the mountains into the valley of the Sacramento, the Ad-sals who lived there came towards us and asked Tome-ya-nem whither he was

---

193. This and subsequent quotes from Tome-ya-nem's story were taken from: Tome-ya-nem, Chief of the Concows, Nome Cult Farm (Round Valley Reservation) to Lt. A.G. Tassin, as quoted by Lt. Tassin in, "The Con-cow Indians," *The Overland Monthly*, IV, (July 1884), 11–12, as quoted by Lynwood Carranco and Estle Beard, *Genocide and Vendetta* (Norman: Univ. of Oklahoma Press, 1981), 115–116.

bound, and I told them, to ...my old home near Chico. And they sent the lightning [a telegraph message] to [California Indian Superintendent] Hanson ... and told him that I had left.

But one day long before I got there [to Chico], the white braves [soldiers] came down from Red Bluff, a great many of them with rifles and big guns [cannons], and they came up with us near a great river [the Sacramento River] that we were trying to cross, and we halted. Then Hanson came in a carriage and asked me why I had left Nome-Cult.... He wanted me to turn back to Nome-Lackee; but I said that we wanted to go to Wel-lu-da again for only one year. And he said that as we were good Indians we might do so, and that he would see that we had plenty of meat to eat.

By now it seemed pointless to Supt. Hanson to risk another destructive massacre of California Native Americans by trying to stop this isolated band of about five hundred Concows from reaching their destination. Hanson probably knew that he would be able to force them to return to Nome Cult farm by peaceful means later; so he said he was going to provide them with meat.

Tragically, the Concows had embarked on a kind of "long march" reminiscent in some ways of those made by the Sewanee, Creek, Cherokee and other tribes in the East before 1850. It was a long and treacherous trek eastward across Northern California over the Mayacama Range, then across the broad Sacramento Valley to their Butte County homeland in the Sierra east of Oroville and Chico in the late fall and winter of 1862. Once they arrived, the Concows found that they were not at all welcome.

Later on, in the summer of 1863, 461 Concows were forced to return the same way they had come: back across the wide Sacramento Valley and westward over the poorly marked and rugged mountain trails to Round Valley. Tom-ya-nem's testimony concluded:

> The Indians continued their journey onward until reaching their destination. So I went with my people and camped in a meadow some five miles from Chico, and my braves and my mi-hi-nas [women] went out and worked for the Ad-sals for a whole year. But many of them became very sick with chills [probably malaria as well as the flu] and when the time came for us to go back to Nome-Cult they were so weak that they could scarcely walk, and many died on the trail, lying down sick and dying all the way from Chico to this place [Nome Cult Reservation].

> And when we got here there was nothing for us to eat, and my people began to fall as thick and as fast as the acorns in the fall of the year ... and there was no one here to do anything for us— the White Chief Douglas [Capt. Douglas, commander of the Army troops at Fort Wright], who sent his medicine man to take care of my sick, and Ad-sals and mules all the way to Chico to bring my people left dying on the trail—and here have remained ever since.

> Are we happy here? No, my brother [Lieutenant Tassin], no we have not been happy since we left our home.

The same scene was also described, but from a somewhat different perspective, in *Genocide and Vendetta: The Round Valley Wars of Northern California*:

> When Captain Douglas at Fort Wright heard that the sick Concow Indians were dying along the mountain trail on their way back to Round Valley Reservation, he appointed Supervisor James Short to bring them in. Short took a pack train with food and some teams and wagons to carry the sick Indians. For thirteen days he worked to bring in a "portion of them."

> He later commented that "about 150 sick Indians were scattered along the trail for 50 miles.... dying at the rate of 2 or 3 per day. They had nothing to eat ... and the wild hogs were eating them up either before or after they were dead."[194]

> The long Concow ordeal ended when just two hundred seventy seven Native Americans returned to Round Valley. One hundred eighty four had either died or departed from the party before along the "Nome Cult Trail." It was a Far Western Trail of Tears of nearly one hundred miles.[195]

ANOTHER ATTEMPTED YUKI UPRISING

The Concow was not the only unhappy Native American tribe in the valley in 1863. Many of the Euro-American families inhabiting Round Valley then had not paid their Indian farmhands and domestic servants. In the early part of 1863, the Yuki attempted a final uprising that left a trail of burned farmhouses, barns and outbuildings. Fortunately only one settler, George Bowers of Williams Valley, was killed.

This uprising was led by three Yuki ringleaders: a teamster known as Pike, who worked for George White, another who worked for Mr. L. D. Montague, and a cook who attempted but failed to poison the Henley clan. Captain Douglas from Camp Wright immediately rode out against the Yuki band with a small force of fifteen soldiers. The raid ended in the deaths of six Yuki warriors and the capture of two elderly Indian women. Later a second group of soldiers went out

194. See Capt. Douglas to Lt. Col. Drum, September 27, 1863, *Official Records*, Part 2, 269 as quoted by Lynwood Carranco and Estle Beard, in *Genocide and Vendetta* (Norman: University of Oklahoma Press, 1981), footnote #37, and 116. The last Yuki uprising of the spring of 1863 is also reported in two previous local Round Valley histories: Rena Lynn, *The Stolen Valley*, Reprinted as a pamphlet from the series carried in *The Willits News* (Willits, CA: L&S Printing, 1977) p. 19, and in Carranco and Beard, Ibid., 116–117.
195. See the news article, "In their footsteps," Mike Geniella, *Santa Rosa Press Democrat*, Sept. 12, 2004, Section B, B1 and B3. Native American descendents of this long march, like Ms. Georgin Wright-Pete, a Wylacki Nomlacki Concow, along with about 150 others, have completed the same nearly one hundred mile trek from near Chico to Covelo in Round Valley each year since 1995.

and killed or apprehended more of the Native Americans thought to be responsible. After a brief trial, those found guilty were executed.

There is a divergence of historical opinion regarding the purpose of the
Army's presence at Round Valley. Prior to its arrival to the valley on December 11,
1862, Army headquarters in California at San Francisco received many appeals
from Indian Affairs Department personnel asking for the assignment of troops to
Round Valley. But the problem of remoteness and the lack of viable means of
transportation in and out of the valley loomed large. Troops assigned to Round
Valley could not come directly up from San Francisco. They had to travel by a
roughly semicircular route, southeast from Fort Gaston near the Hoopa Indian
Reservation on the Trinity River. According to the first entry to Camp Wright's
official records, called "Returns," dated Dec. 31, 1862, Company F started its
march to Fort Humboldt on Nov. 1, 1862. Fort Humboldt, where a young officer
named Ulysses S. Grant served, was far away from Round Valley, up north above
the rugged Pacific Coast near Eureka and close to the Oregon border.

Next, the company of seventy-one men ("two commissioned officers and
sixty nine enlisted men") made a long journey by land and sea to Fort Bragg, on
the Mendocino County coast. The men left Fort Humboldt on November 21, on
the schooner *Dashaway*, and landed at the Noyo River near Fort Bragg on December 1st. The last leg of the trip involved crossing through the dense Mendocino
coastal forest over a steep coastal range to Round Valley from the west. The company left the coast on December 5. The final leg of the march took another six
days. Captain Douglas' eyewitness description of this journey will follow in a
later chapter.

Company F of the Second California Volunteer Infantry under the com-
mand of Captain C.D. Douglas arrived in Round Valley on December 11, 1862.
Second in command and the author of the official records was 1st Lt. P. B.
Johnson. By the 1870s, this regular Army force swelled to seven companies.

Immediately upon the company's arrival, the valley was placed under martial law. Capt. Douglas closed up the valley's sole "whiskey shop," which
belonged to "Mr. Gibson." Protecting the reservation was not mentioned in Captain Douglas's report to headquarters. Initial orders of the troops called for them
"to grant protection to property" and to "punish all aggressive Indians."[196]

A later alternative understanding of the Army's purpose in returning to
Round Valley can be glimpsed in Lt. Tassin's account in the *Overland Monthly*:

> In the latter part of 1862, in view of the many complaints, made to the United
> States military authorities in California, by the Indian Department, against the

white settlers of Round Valley, Captain Douglas, with a company of the Second California Volunteer Infantry, occupied the valley on the 11th of December, 1862, and at once place it under martial law.

The Indian Department charged the settlers with killing Indians on the reserva-tion, running them out of the valley, destroying the Government fences, and turning their cattle and hogs into the fields and destroying the crops, and other Government property. They were also characterized as being a set of lawless men, and it was charged that all, or nearly all, were disloyal to the Government of the United States.[197]

Most of Round Valley's settlers were strong California Democrats. Some were native southerners while all thought of themselves as free and independent Westerners. Probably most, like many Californians, were ambivalent regarding which side they favored in the Civil War.

Although the Army's presence was possibly the result of complaints by the Office of Indian Affairs against the settlers, the attitude taken by the Army in Round Valley after the troops' arrival there was pro-settler in many matters. The post was "about one and a half miles northwest of the present town of Cov-elo."[198] This was almost at the actual center of Round Valley and was close to the reservation's headquarters.

By 1863, construction of permanent structures at Fort Wright sent a mes-sage to both Native Americans and settlers alike: the Army now assumed a peacekeeping and protective role for Euro-American inhabitants there, however poorly defined that role would be. By the end of 1864, log structures roofed with

---

196. Personal interview of the author with Mr. Floyd Barney, Round Valley local writer on Mar. 20, 2000, Ukiah, CA. See also Robert B. Roberts, *Encyclopedia Of Historic Forts* (New York: MacMillan Publishing Company, 1988), "Extract for the states of Oregon, Washington, California, Idaho, Nevada, Arizona, Utah, New Mexico," Fort Wright information, 99, at The California Military Museum, Mr. William Davies, Curator, 1119 Second St., Sacramento, CA. Camp Wright was originally called "Fort" Wright, as were others (Fort Seward, Fort Gaston, etc.) near Mendocino County but each remaining post became "Camp" after the Civil War.
197. Lt. A. (Augustus) G. Tassin, "The Chronicles of Camp Wright-II" *Overland Monthly* (August 1887) 169. Lt. Tassin described himself as a "scout" who was sent to Round Valley by the Army in 1874. While there, Lt. Tassin took many valuable personal interviews with Indians that make interesting reading to all students of Mendocino County or California history. *The Overland Monthly* was unique in American journalism in that it preceded *McClure's Magazine* and other national periodicals that were published at the same time in New York, Chicago and San Francisco. Bret Harte was an editor on *The Overland Monthly*.
198. From p. 3 of a three-page Round Valley timeline covering 1854-1864 provided to the author by Mr. Floyd Barney.

shakes were constructed to shelter two officer's quarters, enlisted men's barracks, a mess hall, bakery, hospital, guardhouse, storehouse, and stables. Federal soldiers remained at Camp Wright until they were eventually withdrawn on July 26, 1876.

With the Army's presence, manifestations of old vendettas between Euro-Americans and Native Americans, including assault and rape lessened somewhat. During 1860, at least four white babies were born in Round Valley, with two more in 1863. In 1862, Andrew Gray built the first water-driven sawmill, which was improved by 1864 so that it could grind wheat into flour.[199] In 1863, for the first time since the start of the American Period, some semblance of law and order, at least for Euro-American settlers and reservation employees, began to prevail. The settlers did not pursue and summarily execute warlike Native Americans like Chief Lassic and his warriors, but some Native Americans were convicted of murdering white settlers, and then executed. Adherence to law and order helped make the entire community more self-reliant, prosperous and independent from the rest of the state. A permanent Euro-American presence in the valley was now almost beyond question.

About the same time, the permanence of the reservation was confirmed in September 1863, when Nome Lackee Reservation closed forever and disappeared. Round Valley became the foremost reservation of the north central region of California, including the Pacific Mendocino County coast, the Sacramento River region, and northern Sonoma County. In the same year Supervisor Short was dismissed. Dr. William Melendy replaced Short in the office. The former residents of the Nome Lackee Reservation were forcibly marched by the Army across to Mayacamas from the Sacramento Valley to Round Valley Reservation.

Shortly thereafter, in October 1863, Superintendent Elijah Steele visited Nome Cult Farm.

> On Monday, the 5th of October, I started over the mountain for Nome Cult [or Round Valley] reservation. I found the mountains very high and precipitous and the trail a very hard one to travel. The evening of the 6th instant I arrived at Round Valley headquarters, and found everything in a state of confusion.[200]

199. This and subsequent quotes from Superintendent Steele's report are from "Annual Report on Indian Affairs-1863," footnote #6, 399–406, *Ibid.*, 42–44. This report was headed, "October 31, 1863, San Francisco." Although written slightly after the period of time covered in this present book, the comments are still relevant to Round Valley's story. The post of "California Superintendent of Indian Affairs" was eliminated by the Office of Indian Affairs when the state was divided into a northern and southern district.

Small wonder that conditions appeared to be so bad at Round Valley to the superintendent. One cannot begin to understand the strain it must have been for a reservation employee trying to work with so much violence, tension, anxiety, sickness, and dying among the Native Americans consigned to live there.

Superintendent Steele's report counted as patients, like a doctor on his rounds through an epidemic ward, the Indians he saw on the trail between Nome Lackee and Nome Cult Farm. Many of the Indians on this forced march to their new home were starving.

> On passing over the trail, I passed over sixty six sick Indians and squaws at the different watering places, who had been left at the "Mountain House" by Captain Starr, on his passage with the Indians from Butte county to the reservation. I examined their condition; found Mr. Eddy, who had been appooined [sic] by Mr. Hanson [former superintendent of Indian Affairs in California] as special agent with them attending as well as he could to their wants. They had about three days' stock of provisions on hand. Upon interrogating him as to the cause of keeping Indians in as reduced a condition as many of them were, moving daily on the trail, I was informed that Mr. James Short, under orders from Captain Douglas, of Fort Wright, had charge of their passage, and the orders were to move all in as fast as possible.

> I inquired for Mr. Short, and was informed he was ahead on the trail. Soon after meeting with him I learned that the mules had strayed off the night before from the camp-ground, and that he had, with the Indian packers, just removed all but two, which he termed the Henley mules, which he presumed had returned to the ranch, and that he would be in the next day for a supply of provisions. The next evening he came in with a part of the mules, and I ordered the necessary supplies to be prepared for him for the following morning, which was done, but he did not call for them. I inquired if he had found the Henley mules, and was answered in the negative, but said, as they had strayed from their grazing ground, he presumed they would find their way into the valley. That night they came in, each with a sick squaw lashed upon its back, and the squaws almost in a dying condition. How long they had been lashed on I could only learn from an Indian boy who was helping Mr. Short with the train, and he said "two days and two nights" that the mules got into the brush when they were unpacking them, and they did not see them or miss them until next morning. One of the squaws, I was informed, died soon after coming in.

There is a stark contrast to be seen in the brash optimism of Supt. Henley's reports from the relatively better days of the reservation of 1856 to the compelling realism of this later superintendent's report:

> I remained at Round Valley eight days, during which time I made a careful examination of the affairs of the reservation, the situation and number of Indians subject to its discipline and the state and character of the country and inhabitants immediately contiguous thereto.

---

200. *Ibid.*, 42–44.

The reservation I found in a very dilapidated condition, the buildings constructed of logs, with oak shakes for roofing, very ill arranged, incommodious and uncomfortable, and fast falling to decay. A portion of the fencing was likewise rotted down, and has to be renewed this winter. This is being done by aid of one white man and a squad of Indians.

Here was a case where the reservation's fencing had not been deliberately torn down, either by Native Americans or by Euro-American valley settlers. It simply was rotten and had been allowed to fall into disrepair.

As we will see in a later chapter, the poor condition of the reservation fences eventually led to tragedy. It was a ritual to repair the fencing each winter. Steele's report was written in October, before the fence repair work for the year was due to begin.

Finally, returning to Supt. Steele's report,

The Indians were very poorly clothed—in fact, many of them with nothing but a breech-clout, but a small amount of clothing or blankets having been distributed to them of the supplies forwarded to Mr. Hanson this summer, and none coming to my possession....

I ordered Supervisor Melendy to immediately distribute the blankets among the sick, and what clothing there was to the naked. The supply was quite inadequate to their extreme necessities.

I held a talk with the Indians; told them I could make them no promises, other than, that if they were industrious, obedient, and peaceful, they should be protected, and what was raised on the reservation should be devoted to their support. I told them also that there was a short supply of provisions this year for so many, and that as there was a very large crop of acorns on the surrounding hills, their native food—I desired them to be industrious and lay in and cure a large supply, enough not only for this season, but for the next also, to provide for the contingency of a failing crop. ...

The military company stationed at Fort Wright, under the present commander, Captain C.D. Douglas, are of no use whatever.

To make matters worse, more raids and massacres of the indigenous people were about to begin in the vicinity of Round Valley. The situation was complicated by the relocation of faraway tribes: like the Concow from the mountains of Butte County, the Shasta from up near Redding, and the Nomelaki from near Fort Bragg, to Round Valley. Northern California Native Americans were essentially prisoners of war or possibly even refugees within a land that a short time ago had been their homeland for uncounted centuries.

In the end, all the Euro-American institutions, like the reservation, family farm, local tavern, store, mine, and ranch, its banks, churches, lawmen, courts, and even its local race track not only survived, but prospered in Round Valley and Mendocino County. The greatest casualties were to the California Native

Americans: Yuki, Wailaki, Wintun, Nomlakis, Pomo, Miwok, Yani, and all other hundreds of small local Central and Northern California tribes. It took the same kind of courage, patience and endurance displayed by the African Americans in the late 1950s and early 1960s for Round Valley's Native Americans to remain nonviolent and to work toward maintaining the peace and for a brighter future.

CHAPTER 13. TENSION MOUNTS BETWEEN NATIVE AMERICANS AND SETTLERS

We went to Kill them for stealing stock and for other depredations.
—Martin Corbitt's testimony to the General Investigation of
Indian Affairs by Capt. Douglas, Dec. 19, 1862.

With the end of strong Native American resistance in the Mendocino War by January 1860, the number of open conflicts between the Euro-American settlers and Native Americans had temporarily decreased. Shortly after the end of the Mendocino War there was an uneasy pseudo-truce. In reality, although the Native Americans could not have realized it at the time, their final chance to mount any organized resistance to the complete invasion and conquest of the state was over.

Peace came and went like the wildflowers in June along the treacherous trails from Round Valley through the mountains and down to either the Sacramento Valley, Fort Bragg, Ukiah City or Weaverville. The same point might be made about many locales on the far western frontier at this same time. Technology and new inventions were starting to improve the lives of most Americans including some Native Americans. Railroads were well on the way to revolutionizing travel over vast reaches of the present-day Midwest, Southwest and Far West. In 1844, Samuel F.B. Morse had perfected the telegraph. In 1846, Elias Howe invented the sewing machine. Another invention in the fall of 1859 was the elevator. In his report to Gov. Downey on the war that had been fought in 1859, Gen. Kibbe stated that California Native Americans had found a way to follow California militia's troop movements during the War with the Win-toons by secretly analyzing militia telegraph messages. And by 1861 the transcontinental telegraph flashed into service, thus instantly making the Pony Express obso-lete.

In California's remote Round Valley, far away from California's largest towns and cities, peace depended entirely on whether or not the nervous Euro-American settlers could coexist with both the local tribes of Native Americans and the other greatly different tribes being forced on the reservation by the Army or by local militia units.

As we have seen from the tone of their depositions in 1860, many settlers were obsessed by the fear that local Native Americans were about to kill their livestock or commit thefts of their personal property. As they struggled for some sort of psychological balance, many of these same settlers looked to the United States Army or the California militia for protection.

The year 1860 had also brought on a vacuum due to the end of the initial one-year period of the presence of an Army platoon near the reservation in Round Valley. California's state legislators had failed to promote or maintain the peace, even while tensions increased between well armed settlers and more numerous yet poorly armed Native Americans. The Legislature chose to com-pletely evade its duty of making a comprehensive statewide reservation policy.

During 1861, occasional violent incidents nearly reopened the Mendocino War in full measure. During the fall of 1861, at least four violent incidents took place. Reports from reservation employees to both Congress and the Office of Indian Affairs in Washington, D.C. described the destruction of reservation fences by unknown Euro-Americans. A second problem was the abduction of Native American women from the reservation by white men for either sexual or forced labor purposes. Twice during the summer of 1862 two unemployed white men, Pat Ward and Slade Lamb, abducted Native American women from Round Valley Reservation. Despite an order by the supervisor against these Native American women leaving the reservation and in spite of the supposed security offered to the Native Americans while on reservation property, such abductions continued.

A third incident involved two shots fired late one evening near James Short, Supervisor of Nome Cult Farm. The incident took place at Supervisor James Short's house on the reservation. At least one rifle ball passed all the way through the structure. Even though the Supervisor was not injured, news of the incident reignited public concern.

The Headquarters of the Department of the Pacific in the San Francisco Bay Area sent Captain Charles D. Douglas, commander in charge of the regulars in Round Valley, a letter and three initial orders setting the new rules for government on the reservation. According to the Army's first month's Returns for Fort Wright (January 10 to the 20, 1863), "Do" [document] November 15, 1862, received December 17, directed Capt. Douglas "Not to use harsh measures, when the proper time for the removal of settlers arrives, as long as they behave properly."[201]

A brief Army investigation began on December 18 and 19, 1862 into Round Valley's "Indian Affairs" or the recent violent incidents that took place in early October on the reservation. It brought to light many serious violations of Native American human rights. As described here by Green Short, one of Supervisor James Short's two sons, the apparent theft of two personal settler items broke the tenuous peace between settlers and Native Americans during the summer of 1862. It led to the murder of an innocent Native American man by a bloodthirsty group of Euro-American vigilantes and the flagrant violation of a reservation employee's (Green Short) trust by the armed party of settlers.

> During last summer [The summer of 1862] the house of Mr. Montague in the Valley was robbed and a pistol & Blanket stolen. He said it was done by Yukees [Yukis]. Messrs. Montague, Arthur, McWilliams and others came to the Reservation hunting one of the suspected Yukees. They wanted to take and frighten the Chief and some of the head ones of the Yukees being at my place to make them give up the Yukee that stole the Articles. I told them they could do so if they would promise not to hurt them. They promised they would not hurt them. They violated their promise and killed one of the Indians. They cut his throat. I did not see him killed nor did anyone else. The Yukees said so. But we saw his body. This was on the 21st of July last [July 21, 1862].
>
> They have since found the Articles. I believe they were found at Mr. Witt's [Wit's] Rancheria. McWilliams. Montague. Ben Arthur and Birch were the men who came to my place.
>
> I think Birch is a loafer, Montague is a Settler. Arthur is a Settler. McWilliams has no fixed residence.[202]

---

201. See Post Returns of Fort Wright, Round Valley, Microfilm 617, Roll 1467, November 1862 document from Head Quarters Department of the Pacific, received by Company F on December 17, 1862, to Capt. C. D. Douglas, National Archives, Washington, D.C. This document along with the other five communications from Department of the Pacific Headquarters to Capt. Douglas during the first month of the Army's occupation of the valley make it clear that the Army was supposed to be both peacekeeper in the region as well as "to exclude from the Indian Reservation all intruders." (Document of November 5th 1862). Obviously, by this time the Office of Indian Affairs had finally decided to begin the process of buying out the Euro-American settlers, whether ranchers or farmers, in Round Valley so that the entire valley might be used for the federal Indian reservation.

The settlers had pledged to Supervisor Short that they only wanted to question the Yukis on the reservation. According to the above quote they pledged they would not hurt anyone only threaten them. Green Short, the son of Supervisor James Short, took them at their word.

Without any evidence against the Yukis other than hearsay, Green Short abnegated his responsibility for the welfare of the Native Americans on the reservation. If he and his father had had previous administrative experience with Native Americans of the West they probably would have realized how quickly things could get out of hand. Apparently without any apology or even an explanation, Short stated the items had been at "Witt's [or Wit's] place" all along.

Small wonder then that the level of fear of the Yuki at the reservation went up astronomically at this point. From the Native American viewpoint, the Army had just ignored another deliberate and cold-blooded killing by the settlers. Another crime that affected relations between the settlers and Native Americans was the kidnapping of a young Yuki man by a settler by the name by Peter [or James] M. McWilliams.

P. A. Wit was born in Virginia. Wit was one of the earliest settlers to Round Valley. He was also fluent in the Yuki language. Mr. Wit (or "Witt") had become one of the more influential leaders of the Round Valley settlers. As noted previously Wit later became the second Sheriff ("Constable") of Round Valley Township.

Wit's testimony provided some of the key facts needed to understand the nature of Round Valley society during the early 1860s. A few of the more experienced, frontier-toughened veteran hunters, traders, and frontiersmen, men like P.A. Wit, S.P. Storms, former Superintendent Henley, and Judge S.C. Hastings, held *ex-officio* positions of great influence over other Euro-Americans, and especially over the less experienced latecomers or recent immigrants to California like the Short family and others. These men were often fluent in several of the California Native American dialects, as well as English. They could interpret for others. They understood what most of the Native Americans were saying. Such men were critically important persons who made possible everyday trade and necessary commerce between the settlers and Native Americans.

---

202. Testimony of Green Short to Captain D.C. Douglas, Commanding Officer, Camp Wright at the General Investigation of Indian Affairs, December 19, 1862. Camp Wright Post Letter Book, RG 393, Part 5, Entry 1, 1, 27–28, National Archives and Records Administration, 700 Pennsylvania Ave., N.W., Washington, D.C.

Like Simmon P. Storms before him, Wit had attached a number of local Native Americans who were probably from the reservation to his own ranch. During interrogation on December 18, 1862, the first day of the hearing, Wit described the part he played in the transfer of a young Native American man. Note the price as settled upon by the buyer, McWilliams.

Ques: Do you know a man by name of Peter McWilliams?

Ans: I know a man that goes by that name. It is a kind of nickname. His name as he signs it is J.M. McWilliams.

Ques: Do you know of his taking an Indian child out of the valley?

Ans: I know he started with one. I did the interpreting for him. I talked with the mother and made the bargain for the child and paid what she asked. I do not think the child belonged to the woman. It was I think in October last [1862.]

Ques: What was the bargain?

Ans: To give a Blanket for the child.

Ques: What did McWilliams intend doing with the child?

Ans: I understood that McWilliams wanted the child for Mrs. Kirkpatrick to raise. I know the folks or I would not have done the interpreting. McWilliams is a good man. He has worked for me a good deal. He stops with me when in the Valley. He is now in the valley. The child belonged to the Yukee Tribe. I have a large number of Indians bound to me. The child was raised about my Rancheria. Mr. McWilliams is not a *bona fide* [underlined in the original] Settler.[203]

On the Native American side, most of the peaceful, large local tribes, like the Yuki, Nomlaki or Pomo, had already begun to adjust to life on the reservation. A few tribes had even begun to speak English. Just after the end of the Mendocino War in late 1859, other tribes from northern California, such as the Mad River, the Concow, Shasta, Pit River and some of their more warlike neighbors like the Wailaki and Wintoon (or Wintun) arrived on the reservation.

A third group including some of the original Nevada and Nisenan were bilingual. Moreover, many of the Native Americans worked at trades. For example women who were seamstresses or men who were drovers, horsemen, vaqueros

---

203. Significant here is that there was a definite "pecking order" among Round Valley Euro-Americans. It might best be understood as: #1. Settlers (those who had land claims which were generally recognized by other settlers and even by the reservation officials). #2. Upper-level reservation or Office of Indian Affairs employees; the California Superintendent of Indian Affairs and the agent or supervisor of the reservation. #3. Newcomers and regular employees like blacksmiths, farmers, general laborers, or even servants in settler households. P.A. Wit's testimony to Capt. C.D. Douglas, December 18, 1862, Camp Wright Post Letter Book, *Ibid.*, 18.

or cowboys had very useful skills that made them valuable members of early California society. Their specialized abilities assured them a place in future California society.

Between some tribes there were strong traditional tribal antipathies. For example, the Yuki and the Wailaki and the Yuki and the Nomlaki had always been bitter enemies. The so-called "reservation Indians," especially the Yuki, kept bothering Euro-Americans, both the settlers and reservation employees, with fears about how the Wailaki were armed and dangerous. Because these issues were repeated the charges came to be believed by the settlers. From a modern perspective these fears may appear to have been mostly groundless. Yet to the Yuki and even to many of the settlers and reservation employees in the fall of 1862, such fears were real.

Suddenly, during the late summer of 1862, a large group of between eighty and one hundred Wailakis had appeared on the Upper Station, the northwestern part of Round Valley Reservation. To those Yuki living on the reservation and also to Supervisor Short and son Green Short and his family who lived on an isolated part of the reservation, this potentially hostile band of Native Americans must have seemed particularly dangerous. It was rumored that most of this group of Wailakis were single males (or warriors). The fact that most of the newcomers had left their families, their wives, children, and elderly, somewhere outside of the Round Valley vicinity made the group appear even more menacing to the Euro-Americans, especially, given the bad reputation of the Wailakis (i.e., the "Gun Indians" of Horse Canyon notoriety) just about one year before this. No one knew what would happen next.

Fears of the Yukis trying to survive on the reservation and fears of settlers for the future of their livestock herds suddenly coincided. Such apprehensions led to the organization of a force of more than twenty Euro-American men who attacked and killed twenty-three Wailakis at the Upper Station Massacre on the morning of August 6, 1862.

Martin Corbitt, an Irishman and Round Valley settler since July 1857, who like the Asbill brothers came to California "from Missouri," stated on December 19, 1862 to the Army's "General Investigation of Indian Affairs":

> ... Lives about two miles from the Reservation Headquarters. My boundary lines joins [sic] the Reservation on the North side. Never let down any of the Reservation fence. Has put it up when down. My hogs were in the Reservation field and I threw down the fence, drove them out, and sent my Indian Boy to put it up again. I believe he did so. It is a poor fence.

Was present at the Killing of Indians on the Reservation last August. There was at least twenty of us, some of them settlers. D. K. Dorman, Owens, Moore, Montague, Otis Wilsey, Arthur and others. We went to Kill them for stealing stock and other depredations. We also supposed they were the same ones that Killed Mr. Shannon, [recall that Isaac Shannon had died at the Little Stony Creek Battle] an old resident of the Valley. A year ago they took horses and hogs from Mr. Owens. I think 30 horses and at least 30 hogs. Last winter Messrs Dorman & self lost some 75 or 80 head of cattle that ranged on the Northwest side of the valley and hills near the Wylackee [Wylacki] country. The Indians Killed were Wylackees. They had bows and Arrows. Don't know of any Ammunition being found in their camp. The Reservation employees knew that the Indians were to be attacked. Mr Owens & Self told Green Short of the proposed attack. He said something should be done. That they came for no good, that they came without families. There were about 80 Indians in the Camp attacked. Mr Green Short loaned me his Pistol. He knew what I wanted it for.[204]

During the past five years of his life in Round Valley, like a number of other settlers, Martin Corbitt had lost cattle, hogs, and horses by Native American attacks. The Wailaki was thought to be the tribe mostly responsible. Regardless of how he may have felt about Native Americans before he came to California, by 1862 Corbitt had acquired a deep dislike for wild Indians.

Other settlers' fears of the Wailaki were also high before the attack. As he had nursed a grudge against the Wailaki, Martin Corbitt joined the party that attacked and killed twenty three Wailakis at Upper Station on August 6, 1862.

On the day after the battle, August 7, a small party of five led by Supervisor James Short including Dr. Melendy went out to the site of the massacre to count the dead. Other testimonies confirmed the Wailaki dead as twenty-two men and one woman. An unrecorded number were also wounded some of whom must have died as the Wailaki retreated back into the mountains. Supervisor Short stated in his testimony to Capt. Douglas' hearing that he made no effort to find out who had done the shooting.

On the Round Valley settlers' side reports listed the settler dead at just one: Slade Lamb. Lamb was a drifter who had once gotten into trouble before by abducting two Native American women when he and his partner Pat Ward were supposed to be repairing reservation fences. Ironically, Lamb and Ward were also the same two men who had angrily shot at Supervisor Short's house on the

---

204. Testimony of settler Martin Corbitt to the General Investigation of Indian Affairs, December 19, 1862. Camp Wright Post Letter Book, RG 393, Part 5, Entry 1, vol. 1., 30–33, National Archives and Records Administration, 700 Washington Ave., N.W., Washington, D.C. Even Supervisor James Short criticized the condition of the reservation's fences.

reservation. A report of this incident was one reason for Company F's transfer down to Round Valley from the Humboldt Bay region.

The bad news from Round Valley caused some staff officers at Department of the Pacific Army Headquarters to think it was almost time to force the settlers completely out of Round Valley. The only other Euro-American casualty at the Wailaki (or Upper Station) Massacre of August 6, 1862 was George Montague. Montague was wounded in the hip in the melee.

CHAPTER 14. COMPANY F OCCUPIES ROUND VALLEY AND DECLARES MARTIAL LAW, AUGUST 1862–SPRING 1863

> *"Sir, I have the honor to report for the information of the General Command-ing that all I have met so far of the Settlers in Round Valley they appear to be peaceful and law abiding men. I have only seen about twenty or so and these tell me that they are entirely willing to live under any law the Government pleases to Set over them. There is no doubt there are some disloyal men here but so far they have been very quiet, on my march into the valley..."*
>
> — *Captain C. D. Douglas, 2nd Infantry, Commanding,
> Dec. 15, 1862.*

A Wailaki group arrived on a mostly uninhabited portion of the reserva-tion in late summer 1862. They may have been seeking rest and refuge. Led by some who carried a grudge, the settlers decided to take justice into their own hands. At an impromptu meeting on August 5 in a field that belonged to Messrs. Shannon and Grey, twenty-seven settlers planned to attack the Wailaki before sunrise. By now the procedure must have become routine for those settlers who participated. Reacting to a rumor that the Native Americans might soon be leav-ing the area and that they might kill some of the settlers' stock, the settlers, to use a currently common military term, made a "pre-emptive strike" against the Wailaki camp. The reported fact that two children and one woman also died indicates that the Wailaki group were not all warriors.

In the attack the drifter Slade Lamb died when he was shot in the heart with an arrow. One of the planners of the attack George Montague received a serious hip injury. These two were the only white casualties according to several contemporary sources and also to the historians Carranco and Beard, *Genocide and Vendetta.*

In both the Horse Canyon defeat of the Wailaki in the fall of 1861 and the Little Stony Creek fight of the following year, settler-led bands of vigilantes had enforced the only order that existed in Northwest and Central California. The head of the Office of Indian Affairs in Washington, D.C., Commissioner William Dole attempted to pressure General George Wright, the Army's commander in chief of the Department of the Pacific in San Francisco to dispatch troops to Round Valley. In September, 1862 Col. Francis Lippitt from Fort Humboldt near Eureka visited Round Valley on an inspection trip. His visit may have been the Army's response to the Upper Station Massacre in early August. Today his duty there might be called a "fact finding mission."

Col. Lippitt spent enough time there to assess the situation and to come up with some perceptive personal conclusions. He noted that the Pit River Indians were the most numerous on the reservation. His report also noted a female chief of one of the tribes who was very intelligent. He talked to reservation employees and interviewed settlers as well as to some of the Native Americans. Colonel Lippitt stated that,

> eighty or ninety [settlers] in number are evidently determined to break up the reservation. Four of them have squatted upon 1080 acres of it and refuse to go off. The settlers generally are constantly threatening the Indians, that they will kill them if they do not leave.[205]

In part at least as a result of Col. Lippitt's reports, the departure of the Concows and the Upper Station Massacre of the Wailaki group, in November 1862 General Wright ordered a company of soldiers into Round Valley. An allegation that most Round Valley settlers were disloyal to the Union was another reason Gen. Wright ordered in troops. Until 1876 from one to six companies remained on station near the reservation at the post, that the first commander there, Captain Douglas, founded and named after his commanding general, General Wright: "Fort Wright."

This new influx of regular troops was an escalation of the Euro-American side's presence as well as the US Government's pro-Union strength in Round Valley. There had always been a number of pro-Southern sympathizers such as the Wilsey brothers there. Since its start as a Euro-American settlement Round Valley had always been a Democratic Party stronghold. Pro-Unionists greatly outnumbered pro-Southern sympathizers. Because the Army was known to

---

205. Col. Lippitt to Lt. Col. Drum, October 13, 1862, *Official Records*, Part 2, 169 as quoted in Carranco and Beard, *Genocide and Vendetta*, footnote #41, 358.

respect law and order the introduction of Army troops may have actually given the more peaceful group of settlers more confidence in their relations both with the most violent settlers and the Native Americans in the Round Valley vicinity. As was noted above Company F of the 2nd Infantry originated at Fort Gaston, a fort on the Trinity River northeast of Eureka.

In his initial report to Headquarters, Capt. Charles D. Douglas, Company F's Commanding Officer, had fears about safely crossing the snow and rain swollen Eel River before it became impossible to ford.

> Fort Bragg
> December 2, 1862
> Sir:
>
> I have the honor to report that my Company "F," 2nd Inf. C[California].V[Volunteers]. embarked on the schooner "Dashaway," at Bucksport near Fort Humboldt at 10 o'clock am on the 21st November 1862 and landed at Nove [sic; Noyo] Creek near this Post at noon yesterday. We were at sea over ten days. This slow passage and great delay was occasioned by the calm and foggy weather which prevailed during the entire passage. Exceedingly regret this delay.
>
> There where I was led to expect means to transportation to Round Valley some seventy five miles distant. But I find upon examination that the AAQM [Assistant Adjutant Quartermaster] is unable to transfer to my AAQM [Lieut. P. B. Johnson] at this Post not to exceed twenty three (23) mules and fourteen (14) incomplete old and dilapidated pack saddles. Lieut. Johnson has been or rather will be able to put them in serviceable condition by tomorrow night at a slight expense for new material [Capt. Douglas was making it clear in this paragraph why his arrival was delayed as well as why he had had to spend more than had been expected].
>
> Tomorrow or next day I shall start with from Twelve (12) to fifteen (15) pack animals belonging to a citizen and the means of transportation it has been possible to employ. With these and the fourteen Government Packs in hope to be able to transport to Round Valley the Company property. Ammunition and supplies, mountain Howitzer and ammunition and AC stores for at least thirty days for Command numbering Sixty-nine men and two commissioned Officers before the Fifteenth of the present month.
>
> It is absolutely necessary to use the utmost dispatch and every available means to hurry along the supplies of the command. Because the rain will so greatly raise the waters of Eel River as to prevent its being crossed, in fact quite impassable and at the same time obstruct the tract over the Mountains to such an extent, I am informed as to prevent *the passage of a Pack train* [emphasis in the original].[206]

Obviously Lt. P. B. Johnson, Captain Douglas' second in command, was a man of a great many talents: observer and writer, official recorder of most of the

---

206. Col. Douglas, Ft. Bragg to Lt. Col. Drum Dept. of the Pacific, Dec. 2, 1862, Camp Wright Post Letter Book, RG 393, Part 5, Entry 1, vol. 1, National Archives and Records Administration, 700 Pennsylvania Ave. N.W., Washington, D.C.

company records, quartermaster, second in command, trail guide, leather worker, and even blacksmith (to repair the "old and dilapidated" pack saddles). He also left us a detailed and impeccably handwritten military daily log of Round Valley's most important events as the Camp Wright Post Letter Book.

On the first day after arriving at Round Valley, Capt. Douglas reported to headquarters.

December 12, 1862

Sir: I have the honor to report the safe arrival of my Command in this valley late yesterday evening....

The next sentences discussed the various difficulties in travel and a severe rainstorm that caused yet another day's delay in the company's trip at Long Valley. Capt. Douglas described the Eel as "a bad stream to cross," even when its level was low or normal.

Next, the captain added information on how he chose the site and named the new post:

Today [Dec. 12, 1862] I have reconnoitered the Valley. I have been unable to find a suitable place for a Camp and the Erection of Winter Shelters in the immediate vicinity of the Head Quarters of the Nome Cult Reservation. The best place and the one I have selected as near the Centre of the valley on a gravelly ridge, never overflown, handy to wood and water and convenient to building materials. It is less than a mile and a half from the Head Quarters of the Nome Cult and in a Military and every other point of view is by far the most desirable place in the whole Valley for a Military Post. I have taken the liberty of naming this Post Fort Wright [For General George Wright, the Commander in Chief of the Pacific Department, or of the U.S. Army's forces in California.] and trust that my choice will be approved.

Very respectfully,
C.D. Douglas,
Capt. 2nd Inf.
Commanding[207]

To Lt Col R.C. Drum
Asst Adj Genl
Dept of the Pacific

Interestingly, on the same two days that Company F's soldiers first explored Round Valley's grassy expanse to locate a spot for their headquarters (Thursday and Friday, December 11 and 12, 1862), approximately two thousand five hundred miles southeast of Round Valley, General Lee's and General Burn-

---

207. *Ibid.,* 3–4.

side's regiments marched into position to begin the costly Battle of Fredericksburg. Although it was almost a victory for the North, Fredericksburg ended in yet one more early Civil War victory for the Confederacy. While some readers may well question what relevance Fredericksburg had regarding events at Nome Cult Farm, we must recall that federal money paid salaries for all American soldiers wherever they served in 1862. In other words, one reason why there was less money to spend to aid the Native Americans at Nome Cult Farm was that most of the money raised from taxpayers went to paying American servicemen, most of whom were on duty attempting to stop the South from seceding in the Civil War.

In his next report to Headquarters Capt. Douglas described his first impressions of Round Valley while downplaying the issue of the settlers' loyalty. Douglas acted to forestall conflicts between his troopers and some of the local settlers by closing the only bar or "whiskey shop" in the valley:

> December 15, 1862
> Sir:
>
> I have the honor for the information of the General Commanding that all I have met so far of the Settlers in Round Valley they appear to be peaceful and law abiding men. I have only seen about Twenty or so and these tell me that they are entirely willing to live under any law the Government pleases to Set over them. There is no doubt there are some disloyal men here but so far they have kept very quiet, on my march into the valley. Yesterday I passed the only Whiskey Shop in the valley and I ordered it closed forthwith. The order was obeyed without a word. I had information that this was the Headquarters of the disloyal men of the Valley. And to prevent trouble between my men and them just now I thought it was best to close up the house. I have had no time to investigate Charges against the Settlers of this Valley such as destroying fences on the Reservation and running off the Indians and little misdeeds. The men that it is supposed shot at Mr. Short (the Supervisor of Nome Cult Farm) were two men named Lamb and Ward both since dead. I will hold an investigation of all these matters as soon as Mr. Short returns from San Francisco.
>
> I have the honor to be
> Very respectfully
> C.D. Douglas
> Capt. 2nd Inf.Co
> Commanding[208]
>
> To Lt Col R.C. Drum
> Asst Adj Genl
> Dept of the Pacific

The next few quotations cover Captain Douglas' two-day investigation on Indian Affairs December 18 and 19, 1862. This investigation at first focused on

---

208. *Ibid.*, 4.

events that happened nine months earlier. There had been a number of clashes with Native Americans that preceded the Upper Station Massacre. The first incident in March, 1862 began with a rumor spread by a Native American woman. Angry settlers visited the reservation forcing the Native Americans to disarm and give up their bows and arrows.

According to Supervisor James Short:

> The Indians on the farm did a year ago dread the Wylackies. I don't know whether they do or not. My son [Green Short] never left his place to my knowledge through fear of the Wylackies.
>
> At the time the settlers took the Arms away from the Indians, the Wylackies and Yukies ran away. They said they were afraid of being killed. I sent my son after them and he brought most of them back. Squires Eberlee [Eberle], Battail [Battaile], Lamb and Howard with a number of others [here, Short named some of the settlers who were in the party that had coerced the Native Americans into surrendering their arms]. Some twenty or thirty of the Settlers came to the Reservation Headquarters last March.

> Ques. What did they do?
>
> Ans. They took all the guns, bows and arrows and ammunition from the Indians.
>
> Ques. Did you see them do so?
>
> Ans. I did.
>
> Ques. Did you object?
>
> Ans. I objected to their destroying the Articles but not to their taking them away. They were not destroyed.
>
> Ques. What cause did the Citizens assign?
>
> Ans. They claimed that the Indians had killed an Ox for [belonging to] Mr. Battle. They said a Squaw had told them so.
>
> Ques. Did the Citizens say anything to the Indians there?
>
> Ans. They told them that if they were caught off the Reservation with Arms they would be killed.
>
> Ques. Is this the only reason you had to believe the Indians had cause to fear the Settlers?
>
> Ans. Yes.[209]

While the settlers denied knowing if any of their peers had torn down the reservation fences, Col. Lippitt had charged them with doing it in a report to Headquarters (September 1862). He also said that settlers had threatened the

Native Americans, saying they would be killed if they did not leave the reservation. Again, the Army had ordered Col. Lippitt to go to Round Valley because of the Concows' departure from the reservation.

These charges were strongly denied both by the employees and settlers in their testimonies. Captain Douglas was shocked to learn that Supervisor Short had not done anything to try to stop the settler vigilante band that carried out the Upper Station Massacre of the Wailakis on the morning of August 6, 1862.

The official hearing on Round Valley's Indian affairs took place at the reservation's headquarters on December 18 and 19, 1862. This was a two-day collection of reservation employee and settler testimonies made under oath before Captain Douglas and his second in command of Company F, First Lt. P.B. Johnson. It was Lt. Johnson who wrote Camp Wright Post Letter Book, like a daily log, at Captain Douglas' dictation. Ten settlers or reservation employees testified. The hearing's format also allowed Capt. Douglas to cross examine many permanent Round Valley settlers. A formal notice through Supervisor James Short summoned certain settlers to appear as the two officers prepared to take down their formal testimonies.

As he witnessed and then later read back over the written testimonies, Capt. Douglas was struck by Supervisor Short's gross mismanagement and lack of competence in running the reservation. He made this same charge the subject of a later, separate report on his investigation to the Department of the Pacific Headquarters. Other observers of Supervisor Short's tenure reported conditions they saw on the reservation at this "starving time," to borrow the term used by other historians to describe a food shortage in colonial New England.

One of the newest employees, J. M. Robinson, was the second man to testify on December 18, 1862. Mr. Robinson, like Supervisor Short, had been a farmer in Illinois before coming to California.

> He was employed on the Reservation. From Illinois. Have been on the Reservation since the 14th of August last [Or about one week after the Upper Station Massacre]. From Illinois. Have not been longer in the valley.

---

209. Supervisor James Short's testimony, Dec. 18, 1862, *Ibid.*, 8–9. Short denied that the reservation Native Americans had been threatened yet he also maintained he knew of the food shortage. He claimed he had notified California's Superintendent of Indian Affairs, George M. Hanson, about the food shortage. Later in his testimony to Capt. Douglas, Short said, "they [the Native Americans] could not live unless they stole from the Settlers. That if they stole they would be killed." *Ibid.*, 9.

Ques. Do you know of any Indians leaving the Valley since you have been on the Reservation?

Ans. I do.

Ques. How many left?

Ans. I don't know. I judge upwards of four hundred.

Ques. When did they go?

Ans. They went in the month of October I think.

Ques. What caused them to go?

Ans. I don't know more than their own assertion.

Ques. What were their assertions?

Ans. They did not think there was provisions enough to keep them and that they had been told they would be killed if they did not go.

Ques. How long before they left did they make these assertions?

Ans. I think on the morning they left. They left in the evening. I had heard some 'chatting' about their leaving some day before. But did not think it amounted to anything.

Ques. On what terms did they part with the Supervisor Capt Short?

Ans. I saw him shake hands with some of them and bidding them goodbye. I suppose from that and other things that 'it was a cordial feeling.'

Ques. What is your particular duty on the Reservation?

Ans. Pretty much everything. I superintend the farming sometimes. *It is the worst managed place or concern I ever saw* [emphasis in original].

Ques. Do you know of any threats having been made against the Indians?

Ans. I do not. They have said that if the Indians did so and so 'they would all be killed.' That there was not provision for them, that they would kill stock to eat, and then the Settlers would have to kill them to save themselves. *There is nothing for them to eat. I know there is very little stuff that should not be preserved for other purposes such as seed.* [Again, emphasis by Lt. Johnson or by him at the direction of Capt. Douglas.]

Ques. Who spoke to you in that way?

Ans. I think Mr. Steven Smith spoke that way. Robinson you know there is nothing to feed them and there will be a fuss this winter in spite of everything. I don't care whether the Government takes the Valley or not. All I want is for the Government to feed the Indians who are here.'[210]

One cannot escape being struck by the greater sense of humanity of a few of the lower ranking reservation employees, such as Mr. Robinson, and a few others like Steven Smith. According to another settler's testimony, Smith helped

---

210. Testimony of J.M. Robinson, December 18, 1862, *Ibid.*, 12–13.

the Native Americans by agreeing to sell a supply of corn to the reservation despite its lack of credit. Unfortunately, Smith did not testify at this hearing so there is no record of his views.

Another settler, Randall Rice, talked about the condition of the reservation's fences in the fall of 1862, just before the massacre. Rice testified that he had arrived in Round Valley in 1858 and was "a farmer and a stock raiser." Rice also said his land was "about two miles from the Reservation Headquarters."

> ... Was in the valley in August last. I have heard of Indians being killed in the Valley during the past summer. I heard that some of the Indians left the valley last Fall. I saw them after they had left. I was going out of the valley a few days afterwards overtook them on the Road. Had no conversation with them. Do not know of any threats having been made in the valley to kill the Indians and if they did not leave.
>
> Knew Pat Ward. He was not what I would call a settler. He was a good deal of a loafer. Did not own anything to my knowledge. Do not know of any person taking down Government fences. A piece of land I purchased this fall adjoins the Government fields on the South side. The fence is a Rail fence. Part very good part bad. Most of it new fence put up last summer. It would not I think turn hogs. It would other stock. Do not know of any" Slip gaps" in the fence. Have seen the fence near the Lake. It would not in my opinion turn stock. In September it was not up for a quarter of a mile. There was no fence there. The Government fence would not do for me. I would not trust a crop of grain to it myself. Have had a claim in the Valley since 1859. Had one in 1857 but sold it to Mr. Wit, a resident of the valley.[211]

Rice must have made a good impression. Soon after the hearing ended, Captain Douglas named Rice justice of the peace. Captain Douglas acted swiftly to replace Smith Gamble for the rest of the approximately two-month martial law period.

Another hearing participant, Green Short lived with his wife and child out on Upper Station both before and after the Wailaki Massacre on August 6, 1862. He had moved to Round Valley "about 15 Months" before December 19. A group of settlers that included Martin Corbitt and J. B. Owens rode up to his home just before the massacre and warned Short that there was going to be some kind of confrontation with the new Wailaki party. On his own initiative the supervisor's son quickly moved his family to the relative safety of the reservation headquarters on August 5.

In the following words Green Short described how the massacre started.

> There were 22 killed I believe. Don't know who killed them. They were killed about 150 yards form my house. I was at the Reservation. I went there the night

---

211. Testimony of Randall Rice, December 18, 1862, *Ibid.*, 16–17.

before the killing. We went back a day or two after. I heard something about the Indians to be killed the day before. I heard a couple of men say they were to be killed, and that I had better take my family away. I took my family away. This was in August last, I think. I was told by Mr. Owens & by Mr. Martin Corbitt. Was not present at the killing. Mr. Corbett borrowed my pistol. I did not know what he wanted, but supposed it was to kill the Indians with. Did not make any objection to the Indians being killed. Did not tell them to go ahead. Don't know as I told them anything. Don't think I told them. I was glad they were to be killed. I was at Headquarters when told. I believe I informed my father that night what I had been told. I don't know as he made any objection. He did not to my knowledge try to stop the Indians being killed. I pointed out the Indian camp to Mr. Corbett a day or two before. The Indians that had been killed had been there only a day or two, some of them a week. none to exceed two weeks, save one that was killed that I had known for a year. I only saw this one living on the Reservation before Some twenty five came in the day before the fight. There were Seventy five or Eighty of these Indians. I don't know what Indians they were but supposed they were Wylackees.[212]

In an earlier incident in the spring of 1862, Owens reported the loss of twenty-five or thirty head of horses from his ranch. Whether or not this particular group of Native Americans, over twenty-three of whom were killed in August, 1862, were in any way connected with this earlier incident will, almost certainly, never be known. Other sources list the number of Wylackis in the camp at about one hundred on the day of the attack. Many more, probably including at least some women and children, must have been wounded.

James McHenry was a blacksmith from Indiana. McHenry's version of events may be one of the most reliable because not only was he present at the massacre, but also because he seems to have had a relatively unbiased mind. As a new employee and also a recent immigrant to the valley, McHenry may not have yet had time to form the kind of hardened prejudiced opinion against Native Americans some of the valley's older settlers, like Owens, Arthur, Otis Wilsey, or Corbett. At the same time McHenry was no tenderfoot. He said he was "in the Valley since 1858." In addition his credibility was attested to by P.A. Wit, who also testified in the hearing. Wit called McHenry "a good man." For such a relative newcomer to be called that was pretty high frontier praise for someone who, unlike some of the others to testify, did not even have a land claim yet.

McHenry stated on Dec. 19, 1862:

Was present at the Killing [capitalized in original] of Indians on the Reservation last summer. They were killed about the first of August last. I believe, don't know how many were killed. There were a good many Killed. There were a good many these besides myself. Mc Lain, Otis Wilsey, Montague, Duell, Hugh Glenn, Novel, Hiram Henley, Slade Lamb, Griffin Grey, Nutingham, and Several others.

---

212. Testimony of Green Short, December 19, 1862, *Ibid.*, 25–26.

There was at least 27 or 28 of us. It was before day. I suppose the Reservation folks knew about the proposed killing. I was stopping at the Reservation at the time with Capt Short Supervisor. I suppose Capt. Short knew about it. When I came in from the mountains that evening he asked me what luck we had hunting Indians. I told him we had not had any luck and we had not found any. He then said he did not see the use of men going into the mountains to hunt Indians when they were in here on the Reservation. He said they had been coming in bands of from ten to fifteen since we had been out. We had been out six or seven days. He said they were coming in for 'no good.' About a 100 had come in. He said, "that placed in the position he was, he did not like to sanction any act, but he thought something ought to be done with them.' ...

According to the testimony above Supervisor James Short appears to have acted as a kind of *agent provocateur*. McHenry continues,

We had been hunting the Wylackees. They had driven off cattle from the Williams Valley and been stealing wheat. The Indians killed were Wylackees. I borrowed Capt. Short's Pistol the evening before the attack. I did not tell him what I wanted of the Pistol. I don't know whether he knew what I wanted of the Pistol.[213]

A final version of the Wylacki Massacre of August 6, 1862 was left on Dec. 18, 1862 by Stewart Short, Supervisor James Short's second son:

Ques. Where was you about the first of August?

Ans. I believe on the Reservation....

Ques. Did you know that the Indians were to be Killed?

Ans. I heard the day before that there was to be an examination or something of the kind.

Ques. How many Indians were Killed?

Ans. I believe 23 Squaws, a small child and some 19 bucks. *Some of the Killed, one or two had been there eight or ten months. The rest had been coming for two or three weeks back. Therefore came in together a day or two before* [emphasis in original]. They were Wycackees. They have a bad reputation. They are accused of Killing stock and other like depredations. . . .The Wylackees are considered as wild Indians. They come and go once in a while as they like. The Indians living around the Upper Station (Witness their residence) [parentheses in original] are afraid of the Wylackees. They frequently alarmed us by asking for help. *We had once to take my Sister to Headquarters on account of the Wylackees kicking up a fuss* [emphasis in original].[214]

One could go on quoting more and more charges by valley settlers about how troublesome and warlike was this one tribe, the Wylacki. As in the depositions made to the Mendocino War Legislative Committee in 1860, the term "wild

---

213. Testimony of James McHenry, blacksmith, to the hearing, Dec. 19, 1862, *Ibid.*, 28–29.
214. Testimony of F.S. Short, Dec. 18, 1862, *Ibid.*, 15–16.

Indians" was often a code for "enemy." There was often no onus of blame if a Euro-American took the life of such a Native American.

After this two day hearing by the officers of the Company F, held in the waning chilly December days of 1862 at the reservation, there was no prosecution or subsequent trial of anyone involved. There would be no verdict, no judge, no jury, and no punishment meted out to the few who had planned and carried out this vicious slaughter. The primary purpose of the hearing was to find out what the settlers and employees swore were the facts surrounding the Upper Station Massacre, the decision by the Concows and some other Native Americans in October to leave the reservation and to determine if it was necessary to continue martial law in Round Valley.

One of the most serious charges made in news reports and rumors about the settlers was that they had threatened the Native Americans on the reservation with death unless they left the valley. Another reason for the introduction of the troops and for holding the hearing was the rumor about pro-southern sympathies and lawlessness of Round Valley's white settlers.

In his initial summary and report of his findings to General Wright and to The Headquarters of the Department of the Pacific at San Francisco on December 23, 1862, Capt. Douglas stated:

Headquarters Fort Wright
December 23, 1862

Sir,

I have the honor to transmit a copy of the testimony taken at a General Investigation of Indian Affairs held in Round Valley by myself on the 18th and 19th Inst. The examination was conducted with reference to certain charges preferred against the Settlers of this valley Such as Killing the Indians on the Reservation, driving the Indians out of the valley, destroying the Government fences and turning their cattle and hogs into the fields, and destroying the Crop and other Government Property. Also, that the Settlers of Round Valley were a set of lawless men and that all or nearly all were disloyal to the Government of the United States.

The General commanding will see by the testimony given under Oath by the Employees on the Reservation that they entirely fail to prove any of the above charges. They swear positively that they never saw any Indians Killed on the Reservation [obviously, Capt. Douglas refers to the time period earlier in 1862, before August 6, the date of the Wailaki Massacre.] and never heard any of the Settlers threatening to Kill the Indians if they did not leave the Reservation and valley.

It is shown that Capt. Short the Supervisor parted with the four or five hundred Indians [the Concows primarily but also some "Kenshews, some Pit River and a few Yukees and Wylackees"] that left the Valley last October in a very 'Cordial Manner.' [Capt. Douglas paraphrased here from J.W. Robinson's testimony on Dec. 18. Rob-

238

inson used the words "cordial feeling" to describe how the Concow leaders shook hands with Capt. Short in October before leaving on the deadly trip back to the Sacramento Valley during which the Native Americans died in scores from exposure and starvation.] It is now certain that the Indians did not leave through fear of the Settlers nor on account of any threats they had made....

Capt. Douglas stated that the real reason that the over four hundred Native Americans had left the reservation was that they feared that they would starve to death if they stayed. In fact,

> No matter which way the Indian turned a cruel death stared him in the face. Now the Question is which of the two parties is to blame for this wild and disorderly state of Indian affairs, the Government Agents or the Settlers? Without question the Superintendent Mr. Hanson and the Supervisor Mr. Short are the parties guilty of the whole trouble. Through their misrepresentations, they have caused it all. The Interests of the Government and of the Indians have been grossly and shamefully neglected in this valley. The entire Reservation is in a most ruinous Condition, rendered so by neglect. There is no fencing on the Reservation that will prevent Stock from breaking in anywhere they try. Nothing hardly to protect the Crop put in to feed the Indians from the depredations of large band of Stock grazing in the Valley, belonging to the Settlers and the Government. ...

It is unnecessary here to cite all of Capt. Douglas' report to understand the main trends in his thinking. In addition to holding the two day-hearing Douglas had had enough time to conduct his own personal inspection of the reservation including its fences, weed-infested fields, and the headquarters building that Supervisor Short left locked whenever he went off for a visit to San Francisco or elsewhere. Despite his repeated negligent acts as the reservation's chief administrator, incredibly, the Office of Indian Affairs retained Short on duty in the office as supervisor (or "agent") of Round Valley Reservation. Perhaps here the Commissioner may have had to defer to President Lincoln's high opinion of Short. The terms 'supervisor' and 'agent' were interchangeable until May 1863.

The unforgivable human rights abuses that Captain Douglas found out about when he considered the ten settler testimonies shocked and disgusted him once again. There is a tone of incredulity, even of shame, as he reported to his superior officers at what he had heard and all that the written record, its entirety now before him, showed.

> I have myself rode around and all over the entire Reservation and have seen enough to convince me that Government interests have been most shamefully neglected. Even had the Supervisor saved all of the Crop put in last year there would not have been enough to feed one third of the Indians. The greater portion of the Crop was put in a field full of weeds of all Kinds, indeed the field has not been ploughed for two years or more. It could not be expected that seed cast on such ground would yield a good Crop.

As Douglas noted above, seeds planted among weeds do not produce a crop. The Concows were right in thinking they faced starvation by remaining. There were a number of other settlers and reservation employees who testified as to the poor nature of the fences. In fact one large section had been washed out in a flood. Nobody had tried to replace it.

Apparently Capt. Douglas assumed that it was a waste of time to interview any Native Americans to see what they thought were the reasons for the Upper Station Wailaki Massacre. Maybe he knew that under current California law and therefore in practice, Native Americans had no legal standing.

Perhaps because he had many often demands on his time, he absolved the settlers of blame for the massacre.

> This same son [Green Short] testifies under oath that all the Whites on the Reservation and the Settlers in the Valley were in fear of this Band of Wylackees. From all the testimony taken in this matter I am convinced that the Settlers Killed these Indians in self defense. I would not say so much about these Indians but that it has been reported that they were a peaceful tribe and living on the Reservation. But as the whole testimony on the subject is before the Department Commander [General Wright] he is the proper Officer to judge whether or not the Indians were Killed by the Settlers in Self defense....

Supervisor Short's administration of the reservation had been so lax that the federal government's normally good credit had been negated with almost all of the local Round Valley farmers. There was so little food for the reservation Native Americans that Short now had to buy an emergency supply of corn from local farmers, an amount totaling about twenty-five hundred bushels. Capt. Douglas' report continued:

> I will here state that the mismanagement of Indian Affairs in this valley has brought the Government into discredit. So much so that the Settlers of the Valley will not sell a pound of provisions to the Indian Department without the Cash in hand. The Superintendent & Supervisor notes or bonds are held worthless. And the Settlers justify themselves under the plea that the Office, or any of the Reservations to their best knowledge and believe [that] He has not paid for anything in this valley. Since my coming into the Valley the Supervisor bought of Mr. Steven Smith about twenty-five hundred bushels of Corn to feed the Indians on. And for this small amount M. [Mr.] Smith would not take the Notes of the Superintendent or Supervisor and to keep the poor Indians from starving a private Citizen went security for the payment of the Amount.[215]

The last sentence of Captain Douglas' report on the hearing indicates that there was a Good Samaritan among the settlers who "went security of the

---

215. Captain C.D. Douglas to Lt. Col. R.C. Drum, Asst. Adj. Genl Dept. of the Pacific, Dec. 23, 1862, *Ibid.*, 41.

Amount." This act of kindness or of compassionate philanthropy by an unknown person saved many Native Americans lives that winter.

Along with the quarterly reports and other regular records of events, such as deaths or disciplining of soldier that one might expect to find in the official records from a US Army company on long assignment in the field, there were the testimonies of reservation employees, settlers, and general laborers.

Reports like this by Capt. C.D. Douglas rest like nuggets of truth in a vein of historical ore. Martial law over the Round Valley lasted for only a short, approximately two-month duration until February 11, 1863. However, the ban against selling liquor remained in effect for an unknown period after that date.

In actuality, the Army's primary official purpose for Company F's presence in Round Valley was simply to protect the settlers and their property. It was also charged with protecting the reservation and the Native Americans that lived on it. However the Army records from 1862-63 did not address the status of the reservation's property or of its inhabitants, the Native Americans, or whether they were prisoners of war, indentured servants, slaves or war refugees. Sadly nor is there any listing of numbers, names, ages, births, deaths or even tribes of the Native Americans who lived there in early 1863 in this record.

Meanwhile settlers came and went freely on reservation property. They moved almost completely at will. Most of the Native Americans on the reservation needed arms or bows and arrows for hunting for meat. The fact that Supervisor Short depended on the settlers, at least in part, to keep track of the level of arms possession on the reservation revealed the Indian Affairs Department's internal weaknesses and disorganization at the nearly every level.

In a month's time Captain Douglas had reflected sufficiently on Supervisor Short and the poor conditions on the reservation. In a two-page report dated January 19, 1863, meant to be read by General Wright through official channels (Lt. Col. R. C. Drum was between Douglas and Wright in the chain of command), Capt. Douglas articulated his observations against Short, just as he had on Dec. 23.

> I consider that it would be gross neglect of duty in me not to report the entire want of zeal and gross mismanagement of Indian affairs in that Nome Cult Indian Reservation under the present Supervisor and the management will not be better unless he is *removed* [emphasis in the original]. The Supervisor seems to be determined to ruin the Reservation under his charge. His assistant Mr. Robinson was engaged erecting and putting up fences in a proper state to protect the crop but the Supervisor interfered and forbid him to make fencing until he was ordered to do so by him and that order was not given until the weather rendered all attempts at

improving the fence quite impossible. This man Robinson has used his best endeavors to put in a crop and to protect it....

The next event led Supervisor Short to fire Robinson.

> Mr. Robinson was turned out of doors [a] few days ago by the Supervisor for declining to feed the Indians after his hard days work in the field, this is very hard unmanly treatment of the only man on the Reservation that does any thing or seems to know that they have any duty to perform. It is held to be the duty of the Supervisor to feed the Indians. This feeding consists in giving the Indians their daily rations, which is from two to three ears of corn to each Indian big or little; all this can be accomplished in one hour or less. If prompt and vigorous measures are not at once taken to stop this dangerous and wicked trifling on the part of the Supervisor very little if any crop will be harvested this year. And the consequences are easily foretold. The pangs of hunger will make the Indians desperate and dangerous a bloody conflict will ensue resulting of course in the extermination of the poor being seeking to satisfy an empty stomach.
>
> Round Valley is better adapted by location[,] soil and extent for a large Indian Reservation that any place I have ever seen in California.
>
> To enter the valley from any direction it is necessary to cross high mountains and Eel River, and at the present season this stream is impassable. The valley contains as surveyed Twenty-Five thousand (25,000) Acres of as fine a land, that can be found in the state were the whole valley taken for a Reservation the Settlers claims (their improvements) bought and they removed with their Stock. A capable energetic man placed in charge thousands of Indians could be maintained in peace and plenty. When a few hundreds are now basely subsisted at the daily risk of outrages being committed. Whites and Indians cannot and will not live in peace and quietness so near and the sooner either party is removed the better.
>
> The Citizens are very quiet and orderly in fact they have been so since my arrival in the valley. If I have considered it my special duty to report the entire neglect of duty in an officer of another Department of the Government I have had ample grounds on which to base such report.
>
> Very respectfully
> Your Obedient Sert.
> C.D. Douglas
> Capt. 2nd Inf C.V.
> Commanding[216]

Capt. Douglas made almost the same recommendation that the other two had made (Subagent S.P. Storms' first report to Supt. Henley in June, 1856 and

---

216. During the brief two-month period of martial law, Capt. Douglas removed Justice of the Peace Gamble Smith from office for "drunkenness and quarreling with soldiers." Randall Rice, a settler from Vermont, replaced Smith temporarily in the office. Despite the presence of Company F, another settler, George Bowers, was murdered by a Native American servant in early April 1863. Capt. D.D. Douglas to Lt. Col. R.G. Drum, *Ibid.*, 49–51.

the *Majority Report of the Select Committee on the Mendocino War* in 1860): to incorporate the entire valley's twenty-five thousand acres for a federal reservation. At the behest of Superintendent Hanson, Congress tried passing a bill to pay the Round Valley settlers to relocate elsewhere. But few actually ever moved away.

The passage of seven years from 1856 to 1863 made this solution increasingly impractical and unlikely. No one, with the possible exception of President Lincoln himself, had the requisite authority to carry out this recommendation. The idea continued to be suggested by outsiders throughout the 1860s in the face of fierce resistance by private ranchers and settlers.

The Upper Station Massacre of "more than twenty Indians"[217] happened on reservation property in early August, 1862, about four months before the Army's arrival. The number of dead reported by one of Supervisor Short's sons, Stewart Short, was twenty-three, including one woman and two children. According to a 1870s article by Lt. A.G Tassin: "it is more than probable that many more were killed in the retreat and rout, who were never accounted for besides many who were severely wounded and died in the mountains."[218]

While it is clear that the Wailaki Massacre had been in General George Wright's mind when he made his decision in early November to order Company F to Round Valley, it is doubtful that Captain Douglas was ordered by Gen. Wright to declare martial law. The settlers' testimonies at "A General Investigation of Indian Affairs", made it clear that the evening shots fired at Supervisor Short's home near the headquarters of Nome Cult Farm was probably another reason for Gen. Wright's decision to call in the troops. A third reason was the departure of the relatively large party of from four to six hundred Indians from the reservation in October. Rumor was that they had been threatened with death by the settlers unless they left the reservation. Most of these Native Americans were Concows who made a fatefully wrong decision in October to leave on an endless march back to their home territory in the Oroville and Chico region.

All these events had made the federal Office of Indian Affairs authorities appear suspect to the outside world. The Army decided to commit Company F to Round Valley. The investigation's findings were so shocking that Capt. Douglas wrote an unusual series of alarmed reports to the Headquarters of the Department of the Pacific. One can assume that anything Capt. Douglas wrote to

---

217. Carranco and Beard, *Genocide and Vendetta*, 314–315. See also Carranco and Beard, op cit., footnotes Nos. 32 through 34 which describe the massacre.
218. Carranco and Beard, *Ibid.*, footnote #32, 238.

"Lt. Col. R. C. Drum, Asst. Adj. Genl., Dept. of the Pacific," was also meant to be read by General George Wright, the commander in chief of all U.S. Army troops in California. General Wright was the only officer with enough authority to commit or withdraw regular Army troops.

Writing in 1877 in his classic ethno-historical book *Tribes of California*, Stephen Powers commented on the code of warfare between Native Americans and Euro-Americans as a form of almost inevitable "extermination." The following quote comes just after Powers' description of the murders of the Euro-American Commissioners who had been sent by the government to negotiate peace with the Modoc of extreme Northern California:

> ...In fact, the plain and painful truth is that, since the day of Miles Standish, the "code of warfare" has been broken very many times on both sides, for the simple reason that when civilized men are arrayed against uncivilized men in a struggle for life, it ceases to be civilized warfare, or any other kind, except a war of extermination. Disguise it as we may, that is what the war has practically been on both sides from the settlement of the continent to this hour.[219]

Due to the lack of written records from the Native American viewpoint and the general view that the California Native Americans were below Euro-Americans in status and intelligence, much of that record is either unclear or absolutely unknown.

While tragic for the Native Americans, the Round Valley events of early 1862 through January 1863 were defended by Euro-American participants and their spokespersons, such as Assemblyman Joseph Lamar or Judge S. C. Hastings, as an economic necessity. A few at the local level thought they were losing livestock they perceived as invaluable to their own survival. Rather than wait for help from either the Army or semi-professional militia, the settlers formed an attack force and even borrowed two pistols from Supervisor Short and his son Green to carry out the massacre of the Wailaki. It is doubtful whether this particular party of Wailaki, which possibly numbered as high as one hundred to two hundred, had any intention of taking anything from anyone. Neither side in the conflict, and least of all, the reservation employees had control of the situation.

Yet another aspect of the tragedy lay in unrealistic plans made by the Office of Indian Affairs naively and arrogantly so far away in the nation's capital. The department erred drastically in thinking it could merely create reservations

---

219. Stephen Powers, With an Introduction and Notes by Robert F. Heizer, *Tribes of California*, (Washington, D.C.: Government Printing Office, 1877), 264.

in remote California areas like Round Valley and, overnight, expect them to be efficiently and humanely run. Add to that the general lack of will for any purposeful follow-through on this naive policy by some of the most corrupt officials in all of American history, men of little integrity like Thomas J. Henley and James Short.

What began as a relocation order, in early-1850s frontier California, led first to the creation of reserves, farms, or reservations like Mendocino, Nome Cult Farm, Nome Lackee in Tehama County, or Klamath or later of the Hoopa Reservation in Northwestern California. Some of these reservations closed down. Nome Lackee closed in 1862. Nome Cult Farm developed into a place where hundreds of Native Americans suffered greatly. Many residents died of starvation or slow deaths as a result of alcoholism, communicable diseases like smallpox or from venereal diseases. Yet, in at least some cases, these deaths were not deliberately planned and carried out by the Euro-American people in local control.

Nearly a hundred years later Nazi Germany under Adolph Hitler made the fateful and terrible decision to kill its Jewish population as well as millions of others perceived by Nazi leaders as "undesirables." Euro-Americans may not have acted in such a cold-blooded manner to kill off the Native Americans and yet the results in terms of ruined lives and extermination of a people may have been just as painful in the long run of history. Weapons such as starvation, consigning victims to lives of abject poverty, and venereal disease were slow but just as deadly, if not more so, to the Native American population as the poison gas in the Nazi death camps.

Settlers sometimes fought each other bitterly for the security of a deed for land. Deals for land ownership were of much greater concern to many settlers than other pressing situations, such as the local Native Americans' welfare. However, one should beware of judging the settlers in Round Valley too harshly. It should also be recalled that there was no such thing as one type of settler. Some, like Mrs. Dryden (T. A. Porter) Laycock, probably were devout believers in the Christian gospel who tried hard to be peacemakers or bridge builders between Euro-Americans and Native Americans, and not murderers. Others were more like Hall, Jarboe, and Woodman, or anywhere in between.

When the California relocation policy for Native Americans began in the early 1850s, many leaders including Governor John B. Weller and many in the Office of Indian Affairs hoped that all California Native Americans somehow would adapt and learn to care for themselves on the reservations. To the everlasting shame of the California Legislature and of the state's highest office hold-ers led by Gov. John G. Downey in 1860, the *Report of the Special Joint Committee on the Mendocino War* became a dead letter. Its primary proposal, to expand Round Valley Reservation to include the entire valley, never came close to becoming a reality. The bloody pre-1860 period of death and brutality toward Native Ameri-cans continued on through 1863.

James Joyce's famous remark is applicable here: "History is a nightmare from which we are all trying to escape." For many, if not most, Northern Califor-nia's Native Americans of this mid-nineteenth century period, 1854–1863, life itself was mostly an inescapable nightmare.

Changes were taking place in California with such rapidity after the first gold strikes of 1848 that it is hard for even the most knowledgeable historians of this period to describe it. As noted economist John Kenneth Galbraith once reported with incredulity, "In but one year, 1850, following the rush of the adventurers, fortune seekers and optimists of the world to the Mother Lode, the new state of California produced as much gold as the whole world had in an average year of the preceding decade."[220]

Is there any wonder that immigrants rushed to join wagon trains and board ships to get here? As we have just seen, Euro-American leaders, whether they were politicians, soldiers, miners, shopkeepers, ranchers, or settlers them-selves, believed that they needed to force the Native Americans off the best lands as soon as possible.

According to Elizabeth Renfro, one of the primary historians of the Pit River tribe of the Shasta area, far to the northeast of Round Valley,

> The history of the American Indian peoples is—across the entire continent—a story of exploitation, deception, and outright extermination. That the holocaust was of greatest proportions in California can be explained by two basic facts.
>
> First the frontier process in California was highly accelerated compared to the settling of the East and Midwest....

The primary reasons for this were: first, the "greed for gold" of the (prima-rily white) immigrants. And,

> The second major difference between the situation in California and that of the rest of the continent was that the California Indians were among the most gentle and "primitive" of North America's aboriginal peoples. Most were generally at peace and in harmony with their environment, and that very harmony—exemplified in

---

220. John Kenneth Galbraith, *Money: Whence It Came, Where It Went* (Boston: Houghton Mifflin Company, 1975), 52.

their view of nature and themselves as parts of a whole and their acceptance of what life offered them—branded the California Indians as hopelessly ignorant, lazy, backward, and ignoble in the eyes of many of the whites.[221]

As was noted by contemporary Euro-American observers such as Stephen Powers, Lt. A. G. Tassin and others like the *Mendocino Herald*'s reporters and editors cited above, in general the California Native Americans appeared to them to be "lazy" or "ignoble." Such was not necessarily the case at all. It is simply more likely that these reporters, at least in part, were ignorant of the depths of knowledge and deeper wisdom of these people and their subtle but real relationship to their environment and to nature in California.

221. Elizabeth Renfro, *The Shasta Indians of California and Their Neighbors*. (Happy Camp, CA: Naturegraph Publishers, Inc., 1992), 89–90.

CHAPTER 15. FURTHER INJUSTICE, 1863-1864

"Now the Question is which of the two parties is to blame for this wild and dis-
orderly state of Indian affairs, the Government Agents or the Settlers?"
—*Captain Charles D. Douglas, Commander of Company F,*
2nd Inf., Round Valley Cal., to Headquarters

Some Native American religious practices, such as the belief in the supremacy of the earth, and a number of their cultural practices were important factors in their rapid decline and their loss of position as the dominant race of California and the West in general. Elizabeth Renfro clarified this point.

> Native Americans, as is reflected in their stories and mythology, did not see themselves as having dominion over the earth and its creatures. They were not ambitious to make their marks upon new lands or to change the world "for the better." That, to them, would not only have been a foolish waste of time, but would have demonstrated a lack of understanding and respect for the balance of nature, for the interdependence, among all living things.[222]

Few if any Round Valley settlers had the time to think about the "balance of nature" in the 1850s and 1860s. Like the Shasta tribe over a hundred miles northeast of the valley, they could not at first grasp what the Euro-Americans were capable of doing. When they finally began to realize what they were up against and tried to ally themselves with other local tribes to fight the onslaught, it was already far too late.

All the Native American tribes in northwest California may have had a common ancestor. The following information applies as much to Round Valley's indigenous people as it did to the Shastan people. As Ms. Renfro noted,

---

222. Elizabeth Renfro, *The Shasta Indians of California and Their Neighbors* (Happy Camp, CA: Naturegraph Publishers, Inc., 1992), 24.

Naturally, such a value system left them unprepared for the actions of the whites. Not only did the Shastan peoples themselves not consider abusing the rights of the land and of the creatures who lived in it, but they could not conceive of anyone else wishing to do such a thing. They did not have the imagination much less the experience, in purely psychological terms, to help them to grasp what the whites were capable of—what they were actually doing—until it was too late. Their lands were taken, their villages broken up, their families torn apart, and their social system undermined.[223]

In the five short years from 1857 to 1862, as noted above, great changes occurred at Round Valley both on and off the reservation. When Captain Douglas and Company F declared martial law in December 1862, he made at least four sudden alterations to the status quo. Life immediately changed for all the valley residents, of whatever race.

The first was that "the Government," or in other words, the North (as opposed to "the South," the birthplace of some of Round Valley's prominent white settlers) imposed control by banning pro-Southern toasts, flying the Confederate flag and singing most Southern songs, especially "Dixie," in public. As a way of emphasizing this change Captain Douglas, in December 1862, replaced Justice of the Peace Smith Gamble with Randall Rice. Gamble had had some disagreements with some of the soldiers in Captain Douglas' command. And, according to Capt. Douglas, Gamble was also a hard drinker who often neglected his duty. Rice was a Vermont native and a valley settler since 1858. This was a pointedly public and deliberate act, meant to emphasize to all Round Valley residents that any defamation of the North or the United States Government and any act which could be construed as unpatriotic and anti-government also would be grounds for arrest and probable prosecution.

Captain Douglas prohibited the selling of alcohol in the valley. As well as closing Mr. A. J. Gibson's liquor store, Captain Douglas demanded the removal of all spirits entirely from the valley. After a short time any liquor found either on Euro-Americans or Native Americans or in their homes or rancherias would be destroyed. Suddenly Round Valley had gone from being wide open and "wet" to strictly proper and "dry." If the opinion of the average Round Valley resident had been polled at the start of 1863, this change would probably have been mentioned most often as the most significant.

The intrusion of this U.S. Army company of troops changed the general tone of Indian-Euro-American relations in several ways. No longer were settlers able to ride roughshod over Native American rights. Even though martial law

---

223. *Ibid.*, 24.

was in effect only from December 18, 1862 until February 11, 1863, it caused some of the settlers concern over their future position of control in the valley. When martial law ended, Euro-Americans would resume oppressing and sometimes murdering Native Americans without fear of being prosecuted by the civil authorities. But now, if they committed such acts, the Army might well arrest them.

Early 1863 was a time when all the Native Americans in the Round Valley region had to be especially careful. Just as some of them may have thought they could relax a little because Army troops were there, news arrived of the brutal murder of the Williams Valley settler, George Bowers. There were a number of possible causes of this murder: a Native American's fear of Euro-American violent abuses, the immaturity of a normal male adolescent and possibly revenge over an interracial love affair.

Bowers had been a long-time Round Valley resident. Like many frontiersmen, Bowers was a loner. He lived by himself with the help of a young male Yuki servant about four miles east and north of the reservation's southern border in Williams Valley. Before this, Bowers and a Yuki woman had had a child together. When she left him with a party of Native Americans, Bowers became infuriated. He coerced his servant to pursue and watch as Bowers shot and killed a number of Native Americans he thought he had tracked into the mountains. These killings alarmed the young Yuki man. He attacked the settler rather than risk becoming another one of his victims: late one evening as Bowers sat resting in his cabin, he killed Bowers by hitting him in the head with an ax.[224]

The murder brought out a detachment of Company F soldiers. It left Fort Wright and went on a long cold and fruitless march after the suspect through deep spring snows in April 1863. In his report to Headquarters on April 11, 1863, Capt. Douglas related the following:

Fort Wright Round Valley Cal
April 11, 1863

I have the honor to report that in Consequence of the murder of Mr. George Bowers of Williams Valley [four miles north of Round Valley] by Indians, I left this Post 7th inst with a detachment of fifteen men in pursuit of the perpetrators of the murder.

---

224. For further details on Bowers' killing see Carranco and Beard, *Genocide and Vendetta: The Round Valley Wars of Northern California,* (Norman: University of Oklahoma Press, 1981), 117.

Captain Douglas' report was handwritten, and in a much less clear hand, with more internal corrections than any of the very neatly written reports from December 12, 1862, through March, 1863. Unlike most, this was probably written by Captain Douglas himself in the Camp Wright Post Letter Book. Capt. Douglas and his men had been under considerable stress. He almost certainly wrote his report hurriedly, just after his return to the valley.

As was very often the case during this period, by the time Captain Douglas discovered that his detachment was in pursuit of Native Americans who had nothing to do with the crime, it had already killed six innocent Native Americans in the mountains.

I marched in the night into the Mountain Country they inhabit, so as to Conceal my movements from the ever watchful enemy. Soon after daylight on the morning of the eighth my Indian guide found their trail, which we followed as fast as the Snow storm which was then raging would permit us to travel. About dark we captured a Buck and one Squaw, which fell behind their party; Soon after their Capture I Camped [under the Shelter of large trees, having no tents] as the snow-storm was so severe that traveling in the night in such a rugged and broken Country was found intensely impracticable. I left the Camp at day-break the morning of the 9th and about 9 O'Clock AM we found a small Camp of the Indians we were in pursuit of which Could not Keep up with their Band. I endeavored to make them all prisoners but Could not as they would not Surrender but fight. I therefore gave the order to fire and the entire party were Killed except two old Squaws that gave themselves up. Six bucks were here Killed, not one of the whole party getting away. I then gave up the pursuit as my men had no rations to go any further. My men in the detachment carried three days rations and one blanket, and the three days rations being exhausted and no means of replacing them, I could not do otherwise than return to this Post.

I have Indian Scouts in the mountains hunting for the main Camp of those Indians who murdered Bowers and when they find it they will guide me to it. The Squaws we Captured are on the Reservation.

Very Respectfully
Your Obdt Servt.
(signed) C.D. Douglas,
Capt. 2nd Inf CV
Comdy. Post

To:
Lieut Col. R.C. Drum
Asst. Adjt Genl
Dept. of the Pacific[225]

Captain Douglas was unable at first to find the young man, despite his troops' search of the mountains. Initially, the captain mistakenly believed that a number of other Native Americans were responsible for Bowers' killing. Then the authorities took a number of Yuki Indians as hostages and held them until other Native Americans finally produced the young man responsible for the murder.

For obvious reasons, news of Bowers' killing had caused quite a commotion throughout Round Valley. It wasn't until late in 1864 that the Yuki youth was arrested. The youth reported his whole story to witnesses just before his execution at Fort Wright on December 7, 1864. In some ways, this incident shows how unprepared many Native Americans of whatever tribe were when faced with the invasion and complete subjugation of California after 1848.

Time and time again, Round Valley's Euro-American residents proved that no one could force them to abandon their own vision of an independent and prosperous agricultural region under private control. Whenever a new group of reservation officials challenged this vision, there was immediate and overwhelming united settler opposition.

For determined stock raisers and ranchers like Martin Corbitt, Randall Rice, P.A. Wit, J.B. John B. Owens, William J. Hildreth, S. S. Davis, John Lawson, William Pollard, George E. White, James M. Wilsey, Jackson Farley and others anything that obstructed the economic progress of the ranching industry was looked upon as a serious threat to their present and future existence. The valley's one main industry was, and still is, agriculture. Due in part to the unique geographical nature of this large and level valley, ranching was the favorite kind of settler agriculture or industry. By "ranching," one means raising sheep, hogs, cattle and/or horses for sale or for food. While later federal officials worked to try to buy these settlers ranches so that the land could become part of the reservation, almost all of the above settlers were steadfast in their determination to hold onto their properties, either for themselves or for their own families.

On the other hand Captain Douglas' entries in Camp Wright Post Letter Book give us a sense of the key events that affected everyone in Round Valley, from December, 1862 to the spring of 1863. He did not write daily entries or reports as this would have been time-consuming and more than what his supe-

---

225. Capt. C.D. Douglas, April 11, 1863, to Lt. Col. R.C. Drum, Dept of the Pacific, *Ibid.*, 60–61, RG 393, Part 5, Entry 1, vol. 1, National Archives and Records Administration, 700 Pennsylvania Ave. N.W., Washington, DC.

rior officers considered necessary. He wrote reports on many subjects he thought were important, or when he thought that Headquarters should be informed. Many reports were routine. Others, such as the twenty-six page word-for-word testimonies of ten different settlers and reservation employees, of the two-day "Investigation of Indian Affairs," were unique one time documents.

In addition to making such ad hoc reports, Douglas was required to keep up a regular reporting format. One name for these regular 1860s Army reports is "The Returns of Camp Wright." For each quarter of the year, the number of active duty soldiers and the number of officers as well as how many soldiers were sick was listed. During the approximately four month period of December, 1862 through April, 1863 Captain Douglas also made a detailed review of food stocks, ammunition, equipment and supplies at the post.

The Upper Station Massacre of the preceding August had not ended conflicts over the killing of settler livestock. In the following report to Headquarters, Captain Douglas noted how missing horses belonging to Messrs. Owens and Eberle had the settlers forming vigilante parties once again to hunt down other Wailaki warriors.

> Fort Wright, Cal.
> February 8, 1863
>
> Sir,
>
> I have the honor to report for the information of the General commanding the Department that the band of Indians known as the "Wylackees" had killed a large number of horses and cattle on [sic, of] the Settlers of the Valley in the last month. They killed eight or nine head of horses the property of Mr. Owens a few days ago. And I have seen myself a number of cattle in the Valley wounded by their arrows. Messrs Owens & Eberlee [Eberle] came to me a few days ago and reported that the Indians had killed the above number of horses. I sent one of my Sergeants with them to Investigate the matter and he reported that he saw the remains of what he supposed to be 8 or 9 horses. He also reported that he followed the Indian's trail from where the Killing the horses [the place where the horses were slaughtered] to within a short distance of Eel River and he said there was about 40 Indians in the Band.
>
> I have just been informed by Col. Henley that five or six of the Settlers followed this band of Wylackees last week Said he believes that a few of the Band were Killed. He did not inform me of the names of the Settlers that went out. I request to be instructed as to my duty in this matter whether these men that Killed the Indians should be arrested or let alone.
>
> I do not consider that I have any power to send out any troops from the post to capture Kill or in any way punish these Indians as I was not sent here for that purpose.

But these Indians should be punished as they are and according to all reports always were bad Indians.

Very respectfully
Your Obdt Servt
C.D. Douglas
Capt. 2nd Inf C.V.
Commanding Post
Lt. Col. R.C. Drum
Asst Adj Genl.
Dept of the Pacific[226]

It is doubtful if Captain Douglas had received any instructions from General Wright or from his subordinate staff officer Lt. Col. R. C. Drum regarding his authority to intervene. Just as Lt. Dillon had been frustrated on many occasions in 1859 due to his lack of authority, now also Captain Douglas faced the same dilemma. Should the soldiers go beyond protecting the lives of the settlers, their families, or the reservation employees and their families? If there were dangerous, or so-called "bad Indians" attacking settlers, why should not regular troops go out to "punish" them? Should the Army also intervene if settlers' livestock was being lost to Native Americans living outside the valley? Conversely how much should be done to protect innocent Native Americans? Just as Lt. Dillon had been forced to do before him, Captain Douglas now faced terrible dilemmas that Headquarters, located far away, over two hundred miles south from Round Valley, never fully recognized and thus could not begin to help solve. Here was a vast gray area which would remain a source of trouble.

Another problem which could not be avoided as the spring of 1863 slowly replaced the hard cold months of winter was the question of the settlers' loyalty to the Union. Even before the Mexican War started, horse racing had already become a much-loved California pastime. James Wilsey owned a racehorse. His horse had just won a race held at the Round Valley racetrack.

The following letter to Headquarters by Captain Douglas presented a humorous side to the Army's duty of suppressing pro-Southern sympathies.

Fort Wright Round Valley Cal
Colonel,

---

226. Capt. C.D. Douglas, Feb. 8, 1863, to Lt. Col. R.C. Drum, Asst Adj Genl, Dept of the Pacific, San Francisco, CA, *Ibid.*, 53–54.

I have the honor to report that I arrested last Sunday the 19th of April James M. Wilsey of Round Valley for uttering treasonable sentiments against the Government of the United States. The said Wilsey did in my presence at the Race track in Round Valley hurrah for "Stonewall Jackson" this on the 19th inst, he has taken the oath of allegiance to the United States and also gave bond I herewith enclose for the action of the Department and Commander. And I may respectfully request to be instructed what further proceeding is required in this case. The only excuse Wilsey made to me for his conduct was that his horse being named "Stonewall Jackson" and the horse winning the race he thought that he had a right to hurrah for said "Stonewall Jackson."

James M. Wilsey has a very good name in the valley and this is the first bad conduct he has been known to be guilty.

Very Respectfully
Your Obt. Servt.
C. D. Douglas
Capt Inf Cal. Vol
Commanding

To

Lt. Col R.C. Drum
Asst Adjt. Genl.
Dept. of the Pacific
San Francisco
Cal.[227]

James Wilsey was no average settler. He and Supt. Thomas J. Henley were longstanding ranching business partners. Despite Captain Douglas' belief that Wilsey was innocent of being a pro-Southern sympathizer, Wilsey was soon in trouble once again with the Army authorities. This time the alleged crime was much more serious.

This case showed how much the power of the military was circumscribed in late April 1863. Part of this power vacuum stemmed from the state's restriction preventing Native Americans from testifying against Caucasians in civil courts. Although there were Native American eyewitnesses to Wilsey's murder of a Native American man on the reservation in broad daylight, Captain Douglas quickly had to release the two suspects. The report indicated clearly that he thought that he had no choice but to release the men even though his feelings were obviously aroused. No trial was held because of the lack of legal evidence.

227. Capt. C. D. Douglas, date unknown, to Lt. Col. R. C. Drum, Asst. Adj Genl, Dept. of the Pacific, San Francisco, *Ibid.*, 63–64.

One must recall that the nearest accessible town, Ukiah, was over sixty miles away. Captain Douglas' report began:

> Fort Wright Round Valley, Ca
> April 28, 1863
>
>
> Colonel,
>
> I have the honor to report that on the complaint of Jas Short Supervisor of the Round Valley Indian Reservation I arrested George W. Gaffney and James M. Wilsey & kept them in close confinement three days & nights. I then released them as there was no testimony but that of Indians of killing one of them, when said Indians were specifically engaged in packing fresh Beef to the Supervisor's house. Said Beef being killed by the Supervisor's order & for issue to Indians without Cause or provocation whatever.
>
> It is not known that these men shot at the Indians [here noted as in the original] killing one.
>
> JM [James Wilsey] did well assureth that they killed the Indians as charged by the Supervisor but unfortunately for lack of white testimony I am very unwillingly compelled to set them at large hoping that my proceedings will meet with your approval....
>
> Very respectfully
> Your Obdt Servt
> C.D. Douglas
> Capt. 2nd Inf C.V.
> Commanding Post[228]

This report, like the report that Capt. Douglas made on his detachment's chase after Bowers' murderer, was made in a shaky, hastily written script. It is clear from the vantage point of some 150 years later that the Army's Department of the Pacific, the federal Office of Indian Affairs and the state's government had all laid down far too few guidelines for the military to follow. Although it was against the law to kill a Native American in cold blood anywhere in California, the law was rarely enforced. In other cases lynch mobs simply acted on the spot and executed suspects of whatever race. Lack of understanding of proper procedures also sometimes allowed murderers to go free.

---

228. Capt. C.D. Douglas, April 28, 1863, to Lt. Col. R.C. Drum, Asst Adj Genl, Dept of the Pacific, San Francisco, *Ibid.*, 64–65.

THE LEGACY OF THE MENDOCINO WAR

Storms' so-called "Nevada Indians," who were possibly either Nisenan or Maidu, became his coworkers. They were diligent people who had accompanied him throughout the hard early years of reservation building. Those who remained were stranded at Nome Cult when Storms left the valley on business in the early 1860s. Rather than stay in Round Valley among other reservation employees they considered strangers, without the relatively high rank that their long association with Agent Storms had given them, they left Mendocino County and tried returning to their homelands, either in the Sacramento Valley or in Nevada County. There is no record of what happened to them.

Euro-Americans in Ukiah later rewarded Captain Jarboe with the post of Justice of the Peace. The term meant something very different then. Before the 1860s anyone in early California who held this office had extensive authority, up to and including, the power to order a condemned prisoner to be executed. In most rural California areas the Justice of the Peace was the only judge in the only kind of court up to that time that existed there. Charles H. Eberle became the first Justice of the Peace in Round Valley.[229]

While ranchers often cooperated, in Round Valley one rancher alone, George E. White, after 1875 won out in the long, brutal battle for control of the valley's prime grazing land. Using hired thugs who were not above poisoning their victims, White managed to bully his way to the top. Similarly, Judge Hastings in Eden Valley became a wealthy cattleman and a statewide political kingmaker. Both men's political paths were littered with corpses as well as the ghostly spirits of defeated opponents.

All the Native Americans from Nome Lackee Reservation near Red Bluff, which was located over thirty miles to the northeast of Round Valley, had to relocate to Round Valley in 1864. The Army forcibly marched them through deep snowdrifts and treacherous snow-clogged passes across the Mayacamas. The early Indian reservation of Nome Lackee, the large forerunner of Nome Cult Farm, was completely closed before the beginning of the final year of the Civil War.

---

229. For more details about the early constables and justices of the peace in Mendocino County see the early twentieth century local history by Aurelius O. Carpenter and Percy H. Millberry, *History of Mendocino And Lake Counties* (Los Angeles: Historic Record Company, 1914), 93.

Starting with a single building erected by Benjamin Arthur and T. Murphy, the predominantly Euro-American community of Covelo became the only real town in Round Valley. Sanders Hornbrook and D.M. Dorman built the second structure there, which became a saloon. Eberle named the town Covelo after a Swiss fortress.

Local leaders such as Captain Charles H. Bourne were rightfully revered by later generations for their bravery and their services to other settlers. Today Bourne's remains, along with those of some other early Round Valley settlers such as Frank M. Asbill, Benton Burch, Barton Jackson Davis, W.G. Gibson, Supt. Thomas J. Henley, Thomas B. Henley, John Laycock, T. Murphy, and George E. White, lie at Valley View Cemetery in Round Valley, according to a recent local photo history *Families* by Elmer A. Bauer and Floyd E. Barney.[230]

As was reported by witnesses and participants alike, there was a campaign to clear or exterminate all those whom the Euro-American majority commonly called "Indians," from the best lands in Northern and Northwestern California. A pattern of using armed bands of Euro-Americans led by mountain men who knew the habits of local Native Americans as well as the terrain began in 1858 and continued throughout 1859. The genocidal and vigilante type of violence lasted throughout the 1860s. In the mid-1870s, during the Grant Administration, the Methodist Episcopal Church took over local control at Round Valley Reservation and this period of lawlessness and vigilante rule finally came to an end.

There were no treaties, no declarations of war, no period of tension or preparation, no truces, and no respect for the opponents who were almost always referred to merely as "savages." At once, this robbed California's Native Americans of their heritage, their most sacred memories and history and any hope for any decent quality of life in the short term. Lies, exaggerations and innuendoes were deliberately foisted on a naive and unsuspecting public and manipulated by a few leaders whose names have been repeated often to create an unreal poisoned climate of fear and racial hatred.

Mendocino County, like the Eureka and Red Bluff areas in the late 1850s, was a temporarily wide-open region completely without law and order, or any local or state police. The Asbill brothers shot first and asked questions not at all. Their sole code was, "the only good Indian is a dead Indian."

---

230. See Elmer A. Bauer and Floyd E. Barney, *Families: A Pictorial History of Round Valley, 1864 To 1938* (Covelo, CA: Friends of Round Valley Public Library, 1997), printed in Hong Kong, 318.

One cannot help but wonder how history might have been changed if certain factors had been different. The removal of funding and the reduction of interest by Congress in implementing an adequate policy from the Native Americans' viewpoint were disgraceful acts. The California Native American tribes gave up the titles to their ancestral lands on the promise of the Indian Office's Commissioners in 1851–1852 that they would provide for their needs. When they arrived on the reservation, they were subjected to more degradation, poverty, starvation, and exploitation from self-serving employees.

If Round Valley had been surveyed, as was recommended, most of the settlers, who increased in number from about sixty in 1856 to almost one hundred in 1860, might have been restrained. This could have given the more honest element within the reservation's officials and settlers, led by men like Samuel S. Davis, Battaile, Laycock, and Rees more power and influence locally. Instead, the balance of power tipped toward men like Judge Serranus C. Hastings, George E. White, the Wilsey brothers, and the Henley clan, whose corruption and graft proved they had no qualms about solving problems with the Native Americans by using military force, whether private vigilante bands or the California militia.

A third factor was the withdrawal by the U.S. Army of most of Lt. Dillon's platoon of about twenty soldiers early in 1860. This was like a red flag for the settlers in the valley inciting them to attack the reservation. The reservation's fences were habitually pulled down and rebuilt. The abduction of women from the reservation continued. Settlers drove their livestock across borders of the reservation, destroying the crops in the fields. There were more murders of Native Americans that are undocumented.

In 1873, Stephen Powers wrote about an suicidal incident at "Bloody Rock," a bluff that is located in Potter Valley, in Mendocino County. He made no reference to the date it occurred.

> After the whites became so numerous in the land that the Indians began to perceive they were destined to be their greatest foes, the Chumaia began to abandon their ancient hostility to the Pomo, and sought to enlist them in a common crusade against the newly-come and more formidable enemy. At one time a band of them passed the boundary-line in the defile, came over to the Pomo of Potter Valley, and with presents and many fair words and promises of eternal friendship, and with speeches of flaming, barbarian eloquence and fierce denunciation of the bloody-minded intruders who sacrificed everything to their sordid hankering for gold, tried to kindle these "tame villatic fowl" to the pitch of battle. But the Pomo held their peace and divulged the matter, telling them all that the Chumaia were hoping and plotting. So the Americans resolved to nip the sprouting mischief in the bud, and fitting out a company of choice fighters went over on Eel River, fell upon the Chumaia, and hunted them over mountains and through cañons with sore destruction. The battle everywhere went against the savages, though they fought heroically, fall-

ing back from village to village, from gloomy gorge to gorge, disputing all the soil with their traditional valor, and sealing with ruddy drops of blood the possessory title-deed to it they had received from nature. At last a band of thirty or forty—that was as near the number as my informant could state—became separated from their comrades, and found themselves fiercely pursued. Hemmed in on one side, headed off on another, half-crazed by sleepless nights and days of terror, the fleeing savages did a thing which was little short of madness. They escaped up what is now called Bloody Rock, an isolated bowlder standing grandly out scores of feet on the face of the mountain, and only accessible by a rugged, narrow cleft in the rear, which one man could defend against a nation. Once mounted upon the summit the savages discovered they had committed a deplorable mistake and must prepare for death, since the rifles in the hands of the Californians could knock them off in detail. A truce was proclaimed by the whites, and a parley was called. Some one able to confer with the Indians advanced to the foot of the majestic rock, and told them they were wholly in the power of their pursuers, and that it was worse than use-less to resist. He proffered them their choice of three alternatives: Either to continue to fight and be picked off one after another, to continue the truce and perish from hunger or to lock hands and leap down from the bowlder. The Indians were not long in choosing; they did not falter, or cry out, or whimper. They resolved to die like men. After consulting a little while they replied that they would lock hands and leap down the rock.[231]

If this incident took place in the fall or winter of 1859, the Euro-American force of "choice fighters" probably held a state commission from Governor Weller to shoot to kill male Native Americans, especially any who advocated armed resistance to the policy of relocating all Native Americans onto reservations.

Powers noted in his introduction to the story that this particular Yuki group had tried to incite another tribe to help them resist white settler forces.

> A little time was granted them to make themselves ready. They advanced in a line to the brow of the mighty bowlder, joined their hands together, then commenced chanting their death-song, and the hoarse, deathly rattle floated far down to the ears of the waiting listeners. For the last time they were looking upon their beloved valley of Eel River which lay far beneath them in the lilac distance, and upon those golden, oat-covered and oak-dappled hills, where they had chased the deer in happy days forever gone. For the last time they beheld the sweet light of the sunshine down on the beautiful world, and for the last time the wail of his hapless children ascended up to the Great One in heaven. As they ceased, and the weird, unearthly tones of the dirge were heard no more, stout hearts of those hardy pioneers were appalled at the thing which was about to be done. The Indians hesitated only a moment. With one sharp cry of strong and grim human suffering—of the last bitter agony—which rang out strangely and sadly wild over the echoing mountains, they leaped down to their death.[232]

---

231. Stephen A. Powers, *Tribes of California* (Berkeley: University of California Press, 1976), originally published in 1877, 138.

232. *Ibid.*, 138.

This account is a near-perfect Victorian period example of the "noble savage" idealization of the "tragic" Indians, full of language that at once glorifies and vilifies their way of life. After singing their death song and taking their last look out over their beloved Mendocino County, now "forever gone," together they leapt to their death. Their death stands as the tragic requirement for Manifest Destiny, that the Red Man must cede his place to the white.

We might be tempted to read the story of the Win-toon and Mendocino Wars, recalling them as the dirge of an old way of life, now forever gone. However, real human beings on both sides were lost during these so-called "Indian Wars." The sacrifice both of Euro-Americans and Native Americans should be remembered as the price of the transfer of Northern California from one culture to another.

Despite the fact that Capt. Douglas's company performed other important tasks such as leading and protecting pack trains through the mountains surrounding Round Valley and manning an Eel River barge across a ford in the river, the soldiers were also important to the safety of valley residents. During the summer of 1863 a small group of Yuki burned a Round Valley barn in July. Capt. Douglas's troopers immediately sprang into action.

> One patrol killed four or five Indians who were routing settlers from their homes. Two Indians, including the principal chief, were killed while trying to murder a settler. With the aid of testimony of both settlers and Indians, Douglas was able to identify the five leaders of the plot. In the presence of all Indians in the valley, the five were hung at the new Army post on July 21, 1863.[233]

As 1863 ended, there was still a large gap separating the Army from the Office of Indian Affairs. As many more Native Americans came onto the reservation, the Office of Indians Affairs and the Department of the Pacific's Headquarters in the San Francisco Bay Area still had not agreed upon what was the Army's duty.

---

233. See the Internet article, "Historic California Posts- History," Colonel Herbert M. Hart, USMC (retired) Executive Director, Council on America's Military Past, at The California State Military Musuem's website at http//www.militarymuseum.org/FtWright.html.

CHAPTER 16. CONCLUSION: "JUSTIFIABLE CONQUEST"?

> *"[I]t is perhaps well to remind ourselves that the best and gentlest of them [the pioneers] did not question their right to appropriate land belonging to someone else, if Indian—the legal phrase was 'justifiable conquest.'"*
> —*Theodura Kroeber, Ishi, 1961.*

The story of Round Valley Indian Reservation is one that makes for grim reading. Its original residents, various "tribelets," or nearly ten segments of the Yuki tribe, were slowly and inexorably exterminated. Settlers took Yuki tribal lands and other tribes of Northern California Native Americans were "relocated" (driven) onto the reservation. Beginning in early 1859, a war between Euro-American resident militia and Native American warrior-soldiers broke out that led to the destruction and the eventual defeat of many of the Native Americans in this region.

In Round Valley, California, as well as in numerous other frontier settlements throughout the West, many Native Americans lived out their lives working to help build Euro-American farms and ranches that were the forerunners of the agribusiness corporate giants of today. Unfortunately, there is almost no documentary evidence of these people's lives. In most cases, even their names are lost.

The Native Americans retained their dignity and self-respect in spite of all; and they passed along their culture to their progeny.

It is instructive to consider at some length how one of the important early anthropologists, Theodura Kroeber, felt about the treatment of Native Americans by the now-dominant white immigrants. In 1961, Kroeber wrote of the situation in California in her classic biography of the famous Yahi survivor, Ishi:

Forced migrations account for some hundreds of Yana deaths; but death by shooting and particularly by mass-murder shooting interspersed with hangings were the usual and popular techniques of extermination. The Yahi opposed to this mass murder a courageous and spirited opposition, raiding when they could, killing when they could, and killing where it hurt as they were being hurt. But the taking of a horse, a mule, a cow, or a sheep; a bag of barley; even the firing of a barn now and then and the occasional murder of an innocent child or woman appear in the totals a puny revenge. The story is not a pretty one. It seems proper, at this distance, to confront the facts and the judgments which flow from the facts. Many of us in California number among our ancestors a grandparent or a great-grandparent who came from somewhere in the "east," either with the Forty-niners or in the later waves of immigration following close upon them, family units these later ones, burdened with wagons and horses and cattle and oxen: men and women moving out from their country's earlier centers, homeless, but looking for a home. We have been taught to regard with pride the courage and ingenuity of these ancestors, their stubbornness in carving out a good life for their children. It is neither meet nor needful to withdraw such affectionate respect and admiration; it is perhaps well to remind ourselves that the best and gentlest of them did not question their right to appropriate land belonging to someone else, if Indian—the legal phrase was "justifiable conquest." However broad and real governmental and popular approval was, this invasion was like the classic barbarian invasions—a forced intrusion on a settled population, and its replacement by the intruders. Such invasions have occurred many times, and continue to occur in the history of mankind, but also as well in the history of all forms of life; they are a part of the biological urge of each plant and animal to make or to take a place for itself and its descendants. Invasion, then, is a necessitous act in the Darwinian sense of struggle and survival; it is instinctive, primitive, and in itself inhumane. ...[234]

Whatever we might now think of Kroeber's version of social Darwinism, her concern that we avoid over-generalizing is entirely valid. Many of the settlers' depositions revealed strong feelings and prejudices against Native Americans. However, this does not mean that most, or even that nearly all, settlers hated Native Americans. Quite to the contrary, the records reveal a number of positive efforts on the part of the settlers to help Native Americans in specific instances, particularly in cases of outright and unexpected starvation or other disasters. For example, in the middle of the winter of 1862–63, when there was little food available at the reservation to feed the Native Americans, an anonymous settler donated enough money to the reservation's supervisor, James Short, and to Captain Douglas, to buy five thousand bushels of corn. The corn saved the lives of many Native Americans. Settler depositions also tell stories of cases in which Native Americans helped Euro-Americans to survive harsh frontier circumstances; or they asked individual settlers for advice. Then, as now, it could be enormously difficult to make gestures of understanding across the racial

---

234. Theodura Kroeber, *Ishi in Two Worlds: A Biography of the Last Wild Indian in North America* (Berkeley: University of California Press, 1961), 47.

divide and to invest in peace. It took the greatest personal courage to go against the trend, refraining from violence and killing.

So, why did this bloody conflict, which many Euro-Americans by the middle of 1859 had begun to call "The Mendocino War," occur? That is the question this book has attempted to present and to answer. The conflict was certainly avoidable. Looking back at the sparse yet very poignant records left by the participants, we find clues as to where and when the Euro-American leaders in this isolated valley made tragic errors.

One important clue as to why the region's policy-makers, including governors, senators, and other state officials made many mistakes in the establishment of Native American policy came out in a report to the Office of Indian Affairs in Washington, D.C., on August 14, 1858. Subagent Storms, the reservation's founder, repeated a recommendation that he had clearly made at least once earlier. The Buchanan Administration, the Office of Indian Affairs, and Congress totally ignored this proposal for the next two years:

> To secure the complete success of this place [the reservation] the whole valley should be set apart for a reservation. Past experience shows that it is not for the benefit of the whites, and much to the disadvantage of the Indians, that they are allowed to mingle together.
>
> If this valley be taken as a reserve there will be nothing to induce men to settle within sixty miles east, seventy north, thirty west and forty south. For five months of the year communication is cut off from the Sacramento Valley by deep snows on the mountains. I think the improvements in the valley may have cost the settlers from twenty-five and thirty thousand dollars. None of the land has been surveyed.[235]

A prompt land survey might have made all the difference. It might have brought Congress' attention to the crisis that was about to explode. Subagent Storms also said here that, for only about thirty thousand dollars, the federal government could buy all of the remaining land and settlers' "improvements." After selling their claims, the settlers would leave Round Valley. According to their depositions, some had already sold out and left. The entire valley could have been set aside and devoted for the sole use as California's largest Indian reservation.

---

235. Letter Number 109, Major Simmon P. Storms, Overseer of Nome Cult Reservation to Special Agent Interior Department Goddard Bailey, Indian Affairs Department, August 14, 1858, microfilm copy by Mr. John J. Thomas, P.O. Box 446, Weaverville, CA., Estle Beard Box, Held-Poage Historical Research Library, 603 W. Perkins St., Ukiah, CA.

The fact that the Office of Indian Affairs chose to ignore this recommendation is proven by the date on the original federal Surveyor's Department Map, performed in March 1860 by federal Deputy Surveyor, Andrew J. Hatch. This map, or "PLAT of the Nome Cult Indian Reservation," was finally registered according to the inscription at the bottom of this document, in San Francisco on May 4, 1860. While this twenty-month delay may seem insignificant now, to Round Valley's 1858–59 residents this long delay in making the official federal land survey was critically important. Clearly, the government took far too long in following Storms' advice. With the passage of time, the settlers were saved from a possible government buy-out.

As has been discussed, another factor was how much Indian policy changed due to unforeseen events. The Office of Indian Affairs' naive plan for a peaceful Native American farm to be expanded into a full reservation of 25,000 acres within Round Valley did not take into account the presence of the rancher-settlers. The escalating arms race between the settlers and some Native Americans (like the Wailaki, the so-called "gun Indians") was unforeseen; and the increasingly divisive debate over slavery before the Civil War kept Washington from focusing on matters in the far West as the situation evolved.

Another serious mistake by the Office of Indian Affairs was simply to crowd too many different tribes onto reservations with a vague idea that they would all soon become self-supporting. Unfortunately, at most reservations, including Round Valley, hard natural realities such as drought were exacerbated by the actions of angry vigilantes pulling down reservation fences, driving livestock across newly planted fields, and committing murder or rape to prevent accomplishment of this goal. Another reality that slowed reservation progress was the fact that most Native Americans, especially males, could not bear the thought of spending most of their daytime hours within reservation boundaries.

The most significant key to the war's outbreak was the tentative hold that most of the settlers had on their land and profits: what settlers sometimes called their herds' "annual increase." In settler deposition after deposition, the most prevalent theme was how very hard ranching was in Round Valley. There is an ever-present concern over lost livestock. There is also a nearly omnipresent obsession with so-called "Indian depredations." It was such concern for their common future livelihood, even more than fear for their lives, which caused some Round Valley's settlers to plead for a state militia intervention.

Captain Walter Jarboe's Eel River Rangers committed overt rancheria attacks and bloody massacres, which eventually broke the back of the Native

Americans' resistance. After formal war ended in early 1860, there was another short period of armed neutrality, followed by more massacres at Native American camps: Horse Canyon, Little Stony Creek, the Wailaki Massacre of 1862, George Bowers' murder, and Company F's bloody reprisal attack of the spring of 1863.

From the modern perspective of relatively safe workplaces and peaceful homes for most Americans in California, it is easy to forget that such domestic peace, or what the Declaration of Independence called "domestic Tranquillity," was generally not the rule at Round Valley California from 1856 through 1863 and even until the mid 1870s. In reality, a safe house for a settler or an unmolested rancheria for a Native American family was the exception rather than the rule.

Early in 1859, when the 6th Army's small platoon of soldiers and two officers took up residence near the reservation's boundary, the unit's eventual commander, Lt. Edward Dillon, thought that settlers who committed acts of violence and possible crimes like whipping Indians or molesting their women should be arrested by the military, held temporarily, and then eventually prosecuted by civil authorities. Unfortunately, neither Mendocino County nor the California State Government had any funds or sheriffs, constables, magistrates, and courts to handle the many cases of offenders. There was no local level of impartial law enforcement.

When the Mendocino War broke out in full fury during the autumn of 1859, the role of this Army platoon changed and focused more on protection of the actual settlers or of reservation property and less on sheltering the Native Americans. With the Army's absence from Round Valley for nearly three years from January 1860 until late December 1862, the settlers had time to gain complete and unchallenged control in the power struggle there.

Another important clue as to why policymakers made the decisions they did is found in one of Governor John B. Weller's speeches to the California Legislature on January 5, 1859. Gov. Weller began the first speech of his second and final year as Governor by referring to the most important single measure passed by the U.S. Congress with reference to the California's Native Americans:

> Senators and Assemblymen:
>
> The Act of Congress of 1852, authorized the President to select five Military Reservations, in or near this State, upon which the Indians can be placed....
>
> The settled policy of the federal Government, for many years, had been to remove the Indians from the States where they were found, to the immense region,

then unoccupied, west of the Mississippi. This policy in a few years transferred most of this population beyond the white settlements, and placed them where they could follow their accustomed occupations (hunting, fishing, and fighting) unmolested....[236]

Gov. Weller continued his history lesson to the Legislature by explaining how the discovery of gold in 1848 began "a flood of immigration to our shores." Next, to appear prudent and thrifty to all of the just-assembled state legislators of the new term, Gov. Weller presented some research by reading off the listing of expenditures of the Office of Indian Affairs, for the pay of officers, employees, traveling expenses, etc.

Office of Indian Affairs Expenditures

1853	250,000
1854	225,000
1855	358,000
1856	202,000
1857	179,000
1858	252,000
Total	1,446,000

The total, he observed, was:

near a million and a half of dollars expended in six years upon them. From the most reliable information I can obtain, there are not, upon all these Reservations, more than three or four thousand Indians, and upon the one which gave the greatest promise of usefulness, (Sebastian) [or "Tejon,"] there are not more than two or three thousand.[237]

Governor Weller's focus on the high costs inherent in operating the reservations over the previous six years made it all the more unlikely that this Legislature would spend any more than it absolutely had to on the reservations. Many Euro-Americans and, one would suspect, almost all of the lawmakers on January 5, 1859 in the State Capitol opposed spending more state funds to support or educate Native Americans. Moreover, the assembled legislators were not given any direction or leadership.

Governor Weller turned next to the subject of the conquest of California and how it had profoundly affected relations between Native Americans and the

---

236. Speech of Gov. John B. Weller, to the California Legislature, January 5, 1859, *Senate Journal 1859*, 34, California Archives, 1020 "O" St., 4th Floor, Sacramento, CA.
237. *Ibid.*, 35.

immigrants to the state. The following remarks followed some general personal observations about how the federal government had transferred Native Americans "across the Mississippi" beyond where any Euro-Americans had yet moved.

> In 1848 we acquired an immense territory on the Pacific, and the discovery of gold produced a flood of immigration of our race.... Here we found (in California alone) [parentheses in the original] some 75,000 Indians, scattered over the territory in every direction, and the work commenced of pushing them back toward the East.[238]

The state might have been better served if John B. Weller had decided not to continue his political career by taking office as Governor of the huge new state. Weller's personal ambivalence towards Native Americans is clear in every line of this speech. The California assemblymen and senators must have been disappointed by this rambling display of whining about spending and the utter lack of policy to address the needs of the state's large Native American population. There was not even a vague plan to lead the state forward.

Weller, the Ohio politician turned temporary-Californian, obviously did not have any inkling that almost fifty more years of fighting would continue, until 1900, between the two opposing cultures before the Native Americans would finally be defeated everywhere in California. Nor did Gov. Weller and other state leaders realize how heroically and with what great personal courage the Native Americans would be willing to fight and die for their freedom.

It is slightly ironic to read a later story about some of the Eel River Rangers. On October 26, 1907 the Mendocino *Beacon* printed a story about six ex-volunteers, W. J. Hildreth, D. C. Crockett, L. M. Ruddock, J. A. Jamison Sr., Wiley English, and F. M. Burke. All six had served under Captain Walter S. Jarboe during the fall and winter of 1859. The headline of the story read, "The Unrewarded Eel River Rangers." In many cases these men had been cruel and relentless in their killing of the Native Americans. According to the article, the men were paid "$5,074.67 by the State of California for their services and for their supply bills another $4,129.98." Despite the fact that the federal government was supposed to reimburse the state, the treasury department reduced the men's pay to the regular Army's pay level. Each of the men gave personal depositions to Commissioner A. J. Doyle of the Court of Claims in Ukiah. Their depositions were then sent to Washington. It is not clear how much more money, if any, the men eventually received. It is possible that other men who served as Eel River Rangers had been paid but, for some reason, these six men's pay was omitted.

---

238. *Ibid.*, 35.

Turning from the pay of the Mendocino War soldiers to Round Valley land ownership in 1867, several surprising facts are clear. By this date the Office of Indian Affairs was at last pressuring Congress to buy out the settlers in the valley. In 1867, according to an official report by Robert J. Stevens to the Commissioner, 26 Euro-American settlers held farms or ranches of forty acres or more or in Round Valley. The following listing of "Round Valley settlers and the land they have enclosed" is excerpted from Amelia Susman's 1937 study, *The Round Valley Indians of California:*

Geo. E. White- (W. P.) Agent	1,600 acres
The four brothers Henley –farm	1,200
S. M. Smith	2,000
Samuel S. Davis	640
William H. Witt, Johnson	560
D. C. Dorman	320
W. M. Johnson	320
M. Corbitt	320
J. A. Owen (s and o)	320
Chandler	320
Parnell	320
Gray (grist and sawmill)	320
C. H. Bourne (s and o)	
J. A. Wiltsey [Wilsey]	240
J. H. Thomas	180
Hornbrook	160
Antone Leger	160
Griffin	160
Updegraff (Wiltsey's ranch)	
Morrison (quartersection)	160
S. O. Moore	160
R. Rice	160
C. H. Eberle (inside res. Limits)	150
H. Schenck	100
S. N. Gambrel	80
S. C. Lawrence	40[a]

a. *Special commissioner Robert J. Stevens to Commissioner of Indian Affairs L. V. Bogy, Jan. 1, 1867 as quoted by Amelia Susman-Schultz (Schultz was Susman's married name), "The Round Valley Indians Of California An Unpublished Chapter in Acculturation In Seven [or Eight] American Indian Tribes," 31, 1976, Contributions Of The University of California Archaeological Research Facility, Addenda #7, Settlers 1867," 104. Special Commissioner Stevens remarked in another report to Comm. Bogy: "The Indians are the only things in the valley not pleasant to contemplate." Susman, 87.*

Freedom from strife in Round Valley finally arrived in 1875. The Army withdrew and Fort Wright closed its doors in 1876. Lumber from the buildings was sold to nearby residents. Mendocino County had by then become a generally more peaceful place to live.

POSTSCRIPTS OF ROUND VALLEY'S MAIN CHARACTERS

The story of what followed for the leaders who shaped Round Valley's early history is almost as interesting as the history was. As was noted in Chapter 3, California's Senators Gwin and Broderick appealed to U.S. Army's Commander, Maj. General James Wool to assign troops to California's far-flung Indian reservations. Sen. David G. Broderick, who was a brilliant and controversial orator, potentially a presidential candidate in 1860, died in a duel with his former friend and political ally, Judge David S. Terry. It was the last formal duel between two important politicians on the North American continent. Broderick's unnecessary demise—like many killed in "Bleeding Kansas," put him among the first Americans killed-in-action in the Civil War. The background cause of this duel had to do with a struggle for political power within California's dominant Democratic Party and Sen. Broderick's progressive views.

Dueling had already become unpopular. The two angry men had trouble finding a place to hold their duel. When Santa Clara County authorities first rejected the idea of holding it there, Judge Terry and Sen. Broderick, along with a few attendants and members of the press, met on the morning of September 13, 1859 on the shores of San Francisco's Lake Merced. According to the accepted version (Bancroft), Sen. Broderick was thought to be the better marksman of the two.

Sen. Broderick was the first to aim and fire his weapon. Perhaps he was sick with the flu or with some other illness. Possibly because he was too weak to lift his pistol up high enough, his shot fell short and hit the turf just in front of Judge Terry. Another possible reason for Sen. Broderick's poor shot could have been that he had some personal problems on his mind that early fall morning. A third reason might be that he purposely wasted his shot with the expectation that his opponent would do the same.

But Judge Terry aimed carefully and did not miss. The bullet hit Senator Broderick in the chest, a little below his heart. After suffering in severe pain for two days, Broderick died. It was a sorrowful end for a very popular and promising young national leader. Senator Broderick had been such a beloved popular figure that there were public funerals held simultaneously on both coasts. In a public outpouring of grief, mourners lined up by the hundreds to pay their respects to him.

After leaving the governor's office early in 1860, John B. Weller served as one of the first post-Mexican War American ambassadors to Mexico from 1860 to 1862. When the long Civil War finally concluded in April of 1865, former Governor Weller returned to private law practice moving to New Orleans, Louisiana. Weller lived out his life there until his death in 1876.

California's second Superintendent of Indian Affairs Thomas J. Henley retreated to Round Valley after being fired from his position in May 1859. He lived there the rest of his life with his nephew and two sons. He helped to work the family ranch. He is buried along with a son, Thomas B. Henley, at the Valley View Cemetery in Round Valley.

Judge Serranus C. Hastings continued playing a major role in California politics. Other than his role as a ranch-builder, possibly his greatest contribution to the state was to donate what was a very large sum of money, about $1 million, to establish Hastings Law School of San Francisco. Certainly this was a noble and generous act. Hastings was the first and, for many years, the only law school in the state. It is now a part of the University of California.

Lt. Edward Dillon, Commander of the 6th Infantry's platoon of just twenty dragoons who honorably served Round Valley and the reservation from Jan. 1859 to Jan. 1860, like many southerners who had served in the West, resigned his U.S. Army commission and joined the Southern forces. He served with General Lee's Army of Northern Virginia throughout the Civil War. Eventually he became a farmer back in the South after the Civil War before passing away there during Reconstruction.

George E. White, whose uncle was Gen. Thomas B. (Stonewall) Jackson, continued to increase the size of his ranch by both fair means and foul. He hired a number of armed thugs or outlaws who terrorized other valley ranchers. Many Round Valley ranches started by other settlers became part of White's spread from 1865 to 1900. White became known as "The King of Round Valley." His large Victorian home was the largest and most elaborately furnished house in the valley and one of the largest and most ornate in Northern California.

Perhaps the oddest postscript of all was the life of Simmon P. Storms after his replacement as agent of the Reservation by George Rees in the fall of 1859. He suffered from tuberculosis. It probably contributed to his early death at about thirty-five in 1865. Nome Cult Farm's founder, Storms was on a business trip far from California on the eastern coast of Central America. The rugged reservation agent's mission may have been to transport a new breed of cattle to California. The difficult route across Central America often led to travelers' deaths from diseases like smallpox, typhoid or tuberculosis. "Greytown," now known by its Hispanic name of "San Juan del Norte," Nicaragua, is located on the extreme southeastern corner of that country, almost on the border with Costa Rica. In June 1865, as he rested in the community then called "Greytown," "Major" Storms began to have trouble breathing.

The only published news of his passing was brief, and it was also slow to reach readers in faraway Mendocino County, California. In between mundane news items about state political appointments and the appointment of one "Dr. Scudder" as "Pastor over Mr. Kittredge's congregation in San Francisco," on August 11, 1865, the following short obituary appeared in Ukiah's paper, *The Mendocino Herald*:

> S.P. Storms.—S.P. Storms, formerly SubIndian Agent At Round Valley, and well known to the people of this county, died of consumption at Grey Town, about the 10th of June, as we learn from H.J. Abbott, who passed through the place on his way to California a few days after his death. [239]

Senator Jasper O'Farrell's life also ended on a sad note. The colorful California pioneer, surveyor, map maker, 49er, ranchero, benefactor of San Francisco through a home for orphans and of Bodega Bay through a Catholic church, had continued to influence Northern California events despite political setbacks. Perhaps because his mind had been affected by a lifelong struggle with malaria, a disease he possibly contracted during his early years as a surveyor in South America, in the early 1870s Senator O'Farrell got involved with a corrupt group of urban politicians when serving as one of San Francisco's harbor commissioners. Powerful Republicans sued the Democratic board for fraud. The California State Supreme Court finally decided against ex-Senator O'Farrell and the harbor commission. Although Sen. O'Farrell never committed any serious crime, he had to resign.

The effort to clear his good name as well as a prolonged, exorbitantly expensive legal battle to retain his family title to land holdings in Sonoma and

---

239. See obituary of SubAgent S.P. Storms, Aug. 11, 1865, *The Mendocino Herald*, Ukiah, CA, 3, c 2, on file in the newspaper storage building, Held-Poage Historical Research Library, 603 W. Perkins St., Ukiah, CA.

Yolo Counties eventually led to his death at a friend's San Francisco bar in 1876. The bold, humane *Majority Report of the Select Committee on the Mendocino Indian War* that Sen. O'Farrell co-authored was never adopted nor used. In Round Valley the Yuki, Wailaki, Pomo, and the remnants of the Shasta, Concow, Pit River and many other tribes continued to decline both in size and influence throughout the nineteenth century.

Probably the nation's foremost nineteenth century literary figure, Mark Twain left an unforgettable vignette on John B. Weller. In "A Notable Conundrum" (October 1, 1864, a piece describing San Francisco's Mechanic's Fair), Twain wrote:

> The fair continues, just the same. It is a nice place to hunt for people in. I have hunted for a friend there for as much as two hours of an evening, and at the end of that time found the hunting just as good as it was when I commenced....There is a handsome portrait in the Art Gallery of a pensive young girl. Last night it fell under the critical eye of a connoisseur from Arkansas. She examined it in silence for many minutes, and then she blew her nose calmly, and says she, "I like it—it is so sad and thankful."
>
> Somebody knocked Weller's bust down from its shelf at the Fair, the other night, and destroyed it. It was wrong to do it, but it gave rise to a very able pun by a young person who has much experience in such things, and was only indifferently proud of it. He said it was Weller enough when it was a bust, but just the reverse when it was busted. Explanation: He meant that it looked like Weller in the first place, but it did not after it was smashed to pieces. He also meant that it was well enough to leave it alone and not destroy it. The Author of this fine joke is among us yet, and I can bring you around if you would like to look at him....[240]

On a reservation record page on National Archive microfilm dated "December 1855," the following names of future Round Valley residents appear: John B. Owens, D. [Dryden] Laycock, S. Henry Brizendine, Wm. Pollard, Charles S. Bourne, and Patrick Farley. This dusty record was from Nome Lackee Reservation. In other words, these six individuals had been employed as reservation employees in the Sacramento Valley near Red Bluff the year before Nome Cult Indian Farm. Each of these six Euro-Americans played a significant role in first establishing and then building Nome Cult Indian Farm or Round Valley Indian Reservation.

---

240. Mark Twain, "A Notable Conundrum," originally published October 1, 1864, *Californian*, as quoted in Bernard Taper, 2003 reissue, *Mark Twain's San Francisco*: Berkeley, Heyday Books, 1963, 54 and 56.

Sometimes such reservation records had a special section that listed the duties and the rate of pay for each individual. It is not without interest in today's fast paced world of video-conferencing, cell phones, shorter and shorter attention spans, and, for some, seven digit annual incomes to note that in the last quarter of 1855, two persons, Samuel and Mary Ann Jenison worked on the Nome Lackee Reserve. For the three-month period of work as a laborer Samuel earned $50. Mary Ann (they were either husband and wife or father and daughter) earned a total of $40. For the same quarter, Mary Ann's duty was officially described: "to teach Indian girls to serve."[241] Finally, the Nome Lackee register also noted S. P. Storms' name along with the simple job listing: "farmer."

The modern-day California controversy over Indian gaming would have seemed very odd to Mark Twain and also to that small party of Euro-American reservation employees and Native American guides that rode away from Nome Lackee Reservation on a chilly early June morning in 1856 to cross the Mayacama Mountains to found Nome Cult Indian Farm. There may be a little poetic justice in the recent success of Native American tribes through the legalization of casino gambling.

---

241. See "A Statement of Mechanics, Laborers, Etc. on the Nome Lackee Military Reservation, Ending 31st December 1855," Roll 234, 3, Superintendency of Thomas J. Henley, California, National Archives of the United States.

APPENDICES

During the fall of 1858, the Office of Indian Affairs sent the Special Investigator G. (Goddard) Bailey to California to conduct a fraud investigation of the California Superintendent of Indian Affairs Thomas J. Henley. Bailey made a tour of Northern California Indian reservations that included Nome Cult Farm and the Mendocino Reservation.

Bailey recorded the depositions of numerous individuals during his investigation. Charges made against Henley centered mostly upon a lumber mill that had been built on the northern edge of Mendocino Reservation near Fort Bragg on the Pacific Coast. It had been charged by former clerk of the Mendocino Reservation G. Canning Smith that Native Americans were used as workers in this new mill even though it was owned by a settler. Profits from the mill were not being shared with the federal government even though the lumber came from the reservation's land.

Another charge involved the high price paid for potatoes and other goods that Superintendent Henley paid San Francisco merchants that he personally chose. It was discovered and proven that such goods could have been bought and supplied to the Mendocino Reservation more cheaply if they had been bought in either Mendocino County or in Bodega in Sonoma County. A third charge was that Henley who was in a partnership with the Wilsey brothers had overcharged the government for a herd of cattle and horses that had been driven from Round Valley to the Mendocino Reservation and sold there.

Another Special Agent, J. Ross Browne, accompanied Special Agent Bailey during the course of his Northern California visit. Even though Browne and Bailey were unable to completely prove that Supt. Henley was guilty as charged, there was more than enough evidence to prove that Henley was at least over-charging the Office of Indian Affairs in an inefficient way. As a result the government dismissed Henley in June 1859.

The following is Simmon P. Storms' deposition made to Special Agent Bailey in August 1858.

1. Deposition of S.P. Storms, Overseer at Nome Cult

About six months ago a man named Brizantine settled in Eden Valley. When Col. Henley was up here last he said there was a man named Hastings who had a lot of horses, who was looking for a place to take them to. I told him that Eden Valley was a very good place, but that it was nearly all taken up. He told me if I could buy Brizantine's place for Mr. Hastings to do so. I bought the place in the month of July last [1858], and paid $400.00 for it out of my own funds. Have not been refunded that money. Look for repayment in the first instance to [from] Hastings, and if he fails to pay it to Col. Henley. This money was not placed in my hands by Col. Henley to buy this claim referred to. I expressed the opinion to Col. Henley that it would be advantageous to the reservation to have Eden Valley settled by some person known to those in charge of the reservation, who would bring stock into it. Eden Valley is a small valley twelve miles distant from Nome Cult. It was at the time I expressed this opinion that Col. Henley informed me that Judge Hastings wanted a place for his horses.

Know Dr. Ames [Dr. T. M. Ames had been Mendocino Reservation's physician since March 1857]. He also testified in this investigation. First saw him when he came over from Mendocino, about three months ago. He said J.R. Browne had made charges in reference to the Mendocino reservation. Amongst others that the Indians were not furnished with a sufficiency of food. I understood him to say that he had furnished Mr. Browne with the information upon which some of the charges were based. He told me the same thing as he did Dr. Burgess, vis.: that when he got food enough to feed the sick Indians under his charge he cured them; and when he did not he turned them loose.

Simmon P. Storms

In presence of

Thos. J. Henley

J. Ross Browne

Sworn to and subscribed before me at Nome

Cult this 11th day of August 1858-

G. Bailey

Special Agt. I.D. [Indian Department]

Source: *Letters Received by the Office of Indian Affairs, on the Superintendency of Thomas J. Henley*, Microcopy 234, Roll 36 (1858), National Archives and Records Administration, College Park, MD.

2. INDIAN POPULATION IN THE WESTERN STATES AND TERRITORIES, 1860

Table No. 3.— (Bottom of the 1860 Census, p. 136) Excerpts from: "Indian population in the States and Territories and enumerated in the Census and retaining their tribal character"

State or Territory	Indian Population
West of Arkansas	65,680
California	13,540
Oregon	7,000
Colorado	6,000
Dakota Territory	39,664
Nebraska Territory	5,072
Nevada Territory	7,550
New Mexico Territory	55,100
Utah Territory	20,000
Washington Territory	31,000
Total	294,431

Author's note: The federal estimate above was less than one twentieth of what most California historians now believe to have been the correct total for the entire state. Perhaps the low federal estimate was one reason California's Indian reservations were inadequately funded and poorly planned.

Source: Preliminary Report of the Eighth Census, 1860. Jos. (Joseph) C.G. Kennedy, Superintendent, Washington (Washington, D.C.), p. 136.

3. ROUND VALLEY NATIVE AMERICANS

As estimated by Kroeber and Merriam

	Population as of 1770	Population as of 1910
Nongatl, Sinkyone, Lassik	2,000	100
Wailaki	1,000	200
Yuki	2,000	1,000
Huchnom	500	
Coast Yuki	500	
Pomo	8,000	1,200
Maidu	9,000	1,100

Note: According to historian Amelia Susman (1937) "... over 800 Indians are on the rolls of the Indian Office as living in Round Valley." See Amelia Susman, The Round Valley Indians of California, An Unpublished Chapter in Acculturation In Seven [Or Eight] American Indian Tribes, p. 15, No. 31, 1976, Archaeological Research Facility, University of California, Berkeley, CA. Editor: Robert F. Heizer. Note also that Pit River, Shasta, Nomlaki were not herein included.

Bibliography

Newspapers and other sources of government documents, letters and reports and personal sources of the author are listed after the secondary sources, which appear first in alphabetical order. Not all works consulted are listed.

Books and Articles

Hubert Howe BANCROFT, *BANCROFT'S WORKS HISTORY OF CALIFORNIA*, Vols VI (1848-1858)& XXIII, San Francisco, The History Company, 1888.

Elmer A. BAUER and Floyd E. BARNEY,, *Families: A Pictorial History Of Round Valley, 1864 TO 1938.* Covelo, CA: The Friends of Round Valley Public Library, 1997, published in Hong Kong.

Stephen Dow BECKHAM, *Requiem for a People: The Rogue Indians and the Frontiersman*, Norman, University of Oklahoma Press, 1971.

Anthony J. BLEDSOE, *Indian Wars of the Northeast A California Sketch.* San Francisco, Bacon, 1885. Reprint Oakland, CA, Biobooks, 1956.

Carl BODE, Editor, in collaboration with Malcolm COWLEY, *The Portable Emerson.* New York, Viking Penguin Inc., 1946, copyright renewed 1974 by Viking Penguin, Inc.

Dee BROWN, *Bury My Heart At Wounded Knee.* New York, An Owl Book. Henry Holt and Co., Inc. 197

Vinson BROWN and Douglas ANDREWS, Edited by Albert B. Elsasser, *The Pomo Indians of California and Their Neighbors.* Happy Camp, California, Naturegraph Publishers, Inc., 1969.

Vinson, BROWN, *Native Americans of the Pacific Coast.* Happy Camp, California, Naturegraph Publishers, Inc., 1985.

Aurelius O. CARPENTER and Percy H. MILLBERRY, *History Of Mendocino And Lake Counties.* Los Angeles, CA. HISTORIC RECORD COMPANY, 1914.

Lynwood CARRANCO and Estle BEARD, *Genocide AnolVendetta: The Round Valley Wars Of Northern California.* Norman, Oklahoma, University of Oklahoma Press, 1981.

Robert CHANDLER, "The Failure of Reform: White Ates and Indian Response in California During the Civil War Era," *The Pacific Historian,* Vol 24, No 3 (Fall, 1980), 284-94.

Robert Glass CLELAND PhD., *History Of California: The American Period.* New York, The MacMillan Company, 1923.

V. A. CHESTNUT, *Plants Used By Indians of Mendocino County Califronia,* Reprinted by Mendocino County Historical Society as first published in Contributions from the United States National Herbalism, Volume VII Mendocino County map and preface added 1974.

Robert Glass CLELAND, *HISTORY OF CALIFORNIA: THE AMERICAN PERIOD,* New York, The MacMillan Company, 1923.

Sherburne F. COOK, *The Conflict Between The California Indian And White*

Civilization. Berkeley, University of California Press, 1976.

Christopher CORBETT, *ORPHANS PREFERRED, THE TWISTED TRUTH AND LASTING LEGEND of the PONY EXPRESS,* New York, BROADWAY BOOKS, A division of Random House, aInc., 2003.

Owen Cochran COY, *GOLD DAYS.* San Francisco, Los Angeles, Chicago, Powell Publishing Company, 1929.

William Heath DAVIS, Harold A. Small, Editor, *Seventy-Five Years In California.* San Francisco, John Howell Books, 1967, originally published in 1889.

Ron DEMELE, *People Of The Pit River Nation.* Golden State Printers, for the Johnson-O'Malley Program, Shasta County Schools, no date but circa 1980, Raitha Amen, Researcher/Consultant. Elder Consultants-Joy Johnson (Astarwawi), Edna Townsend (Isatawi), Neva Barlese (Hawesidawi), Leo James (Achomawi), Lucian Williams (Achomawi), Ramsey Blake (Aporige), Ruth Wolfin (Ilmawi), Edna Webster, Rile Webster (Madesi), Lela Rhoades (Isatawi).

David Herbert DONALD, *Lincoln.* New York, Touchstone Rockefeller Center, 1995.

Dolan H. EARGLE, Jr., *CALIFORNIA INDIAN COUNTRY THE LAND AND THE PEOPLE,* San Francisco, Trees Company Press, 1992.

William H. ELLISON, "The Federal Indian Policy in California, 1846-1860" *The Mississippi Valley Historical Review,* Vol 9, No 1. (Jun., 1922), 37-67.

George M. FOSTER, *A Summary of Yuki Culture.* Berkeley and Los Angeles, University of California Press, 1944.

John Kenneth GALBRAITH, *Money Whence It Came, And Where It Went.* Boston, Houghton Mifflin Company, 1975.

Lilburn GIBSON, *Eden Valley, An Epic Of Yesteryear*, Fort Bragg, Mendocino County Historical Society, 1966.

Edward W. GIFFORD, *The Coast Yuki*. Sacramento Anthropological Society, Spring, 1965.

Pliny Earle GODDARD, *The Habitat of the Wailaki*. Volume 20, No. 6, pp. 95-109, UNIVERSITY OF CALIFORNIA PUBLICATIONS IN AMERICAN ARCHAEOLOGY AND ETHNOLOGY, Berkeley, University of Califronia Press, 1923.

Pliny Earle GODDARD, *Habitat of the Pitch Indians, A Wailaki Division*, Volume 17, No. 4, pp. 217-225, UNIVERSITY OF CALIFORNIA PUBLICATIONS IN AMERICAN ARCHAEOLOGY AND ETHNOLOGY, Berkeley, University of California Press, 1924.

Marion GOEBLE, Editor, *Lake County Indian Lore*. Lakeport, Lake County Pomo Bulletin, Lake County Historical Society, Aug., 1977.

Bonni GRAPP, *Footprints An Early History of Fort Bragg, California and The Pomo Indians*. no publisher, published privately, 1967.

George HEIZER, *Gibbs' Journal Of Redick McKee'S Expedition Through Northwestern California In 1851*. Edited and with annotations by Robert F. HEIZER, Berkeley, Archeological Research Facility, Department of Anthropology, University of California, Berkeley, 1972.

George HEIZER, *They Were Only Diggers A Collection Of Articles For California Newspapers, 1851–1866, On Indian And White Relations*. Romona, CA BALLENA PRESS, 1974.

Robert F. HEIZER, *THE DESTRUCTION OF CALIFORNIA INDIANS A Collection of Documents from the period 1847 to 1865 in which are described some of the things that happened to some of the Indians of California*, Lincoln, University of Nebraska Press, 1993.

Robert F. HEIZER, Editor, *Collected Documents On The Bloody Island Massacre Of 1850*. Archaeological Research Facility, Dept. of Anthropology, Berkeley, CA. University of California, 1973.

Robert F. HEIZER, *The Eighteen Unratified Treaties of 1851-1852 Between the California Indians and The United States Government*. Berkeley, Archaeological Research Facility, Department of Anthropology, University of California, 1972, Fascimile Reprint by Coyote Press, Salinas, CA.

Robert F. HEIZER, *FEDERAL CONCERN ABOUT CONDITIONS OF CALIFORNIA INDIANS 1853 TO 1913: EIGHT DOCUMENTS. Selected and Edited by Robert F. Heizer, Congressional Globe,* 36th Congress, First Session, pp. 2365-2369 and *FEDERAL EFFORTS TO TRANSFER INDIAN AFFAIRS TO THE STATE OF CALIFORNIA, 1860,"* pp. 25-50, Ballena Press, Socorro, NM, 1979.

Edward E. HILL, *The Office Of Indian Affairs, 1824–1880 Historical Sketches*. New York, Ulearwater Publishing Company, Inc., 1974.

The author was the "Assistant Director of General Archives Division, National Archives and Records Service General Services Administration.

Stephen R. HOLMAN, *Round Valley Indian Reservation: A Study In Ethnocentricity*. Committee on the Study of History, Amherst, Massachusetts, under contract with the U.S.

Office of Education as EDPA Project #310511. A Teachers Manual, 1970, at the Jean and Charles Shulz Information Center at Sonoma State University. Rohnert Park, CA.

Albert L. HURTADO, *Indian Survival On The California Frontier.* New Haven, Conn., Yale University Press, 1988.

A.L. KROEBER, *Elements of Culture in Native California,* Berkeley, University of California Press, University of California Publications In American Archaelogy and Ethnology, Vol. 13, No 8, pp. 259-328, November 21, 1922, ttimile Reprint by Coyote Press, Salinas, CA.

Alfred L. KROEBER, *Handbook Of The California Indians.* Berkeley, The California Book Company, Ltd., 1953.

Theodura KROEBER, *ISHI In Two Worlds A Biography of the Last Wild Indian In North America.* Berkeley, University of California Press, 1961.

Peter M. KNUDTSON, *The Wintun Indians of California and Their Neighbors,* Happy Camp CA, Naturegraph Publishers, 1977.

Donovan LEWIS, *Pioneers of California True Stories of Early Settlers in the Golden State,* San Francisco, SCOTTWELL Associates, 1993.

Robert M. LUMIANSKY, Concise Dictionary of American Biography, Volume 1, 5th Edition, New York, Charles Scribners Sons Macmillan Library Reference USA-Simon and Schuster, Prentice Hall International, 1986.

Josephine Short LYNCH, [Edited by Katherine B. and Herbert A. Elliott], *SHORT An Early Virginia Family,* Richmond Virginia, Whittet & Shepperson, 1970.

Rena LYNN, *The Story Of The Stolen Valley.* Reprinted from the series carried in *The Willits News.* Willits, CA, L&S Publishing, 1977, out of print, at Held-Poage Historical Research Library, 603 W. Perkins St., Ukiah, CA.

Malcolm M. MARGOLIN, *The Way We Lived: California Indian Reminiscences, Stories, And Songs.* First published in 1981, Berkeley, CA Heyday Books, rev. ed. 1993.

Marc McCUTCHEON, *The Writer's Guide to Everyday Life in the 1800s,* Cincinnati, Ohio, Writer's Digest Books, 1993.

Clement W. MEIGHAN and Francis A. RIDDELL, *The Maru Cult of the Pomo Indians-A California Ghost Dance Survival,* Stephen Powers, Overland Monthly, Vol. 9, pp. 498-507, and Stephen Powers, *The Northern California Indians,* No. VL, [The Pomo and Cahto], pp. 53-63. Autry Musuem Papers, No. 23, Autry Museum of Western Heritage, 4700 Western Heriiage Way, Los Angeles, CA 90027-1462. Autry Museum Highland Book, 1972.

C. Hart MERRIAM, *Ethnogeographical And Ethnosynonymic Data From Northern California Tribes,* Subtitle, *Contributions To Native American Ethnology From The C. Hart Merriam Collection* Number 1, November 1976. Publication supported by the Mary W. Harriman Foundation, Anthropological Research Facility, Berkeley, California.

Virginia P. MILLER, *Ukomno'n: The Yuki Indians Of Northern California.* Socorro, NM, Bellena Press, 1979.

Marz and Nono MINOR, *The American Indian Craft Book*, Lincoln, University of Nebraska Press, Bison Books, 1972.

Doyce NUNIS, Jr., *Josiah Belden: California's Overland Pioneer*, Georgetown CA, The Talisman Press, 1962.

Lyman L. PALMER, *History Of Mendocino County California*. San Francisco, Alley Bowen & Co., Publishers, 1880.er

George Harwood PHILLIPS, *Indians and Indian Agents The Origins of the Reservation System in California, 1849-1852*. Norman, University of Oklahoma Press, 1997.

George Harwood PHILLIPS, *INDIANS AND INTRUDERS IN CENTRAL CALIFORNIA, 1769-1849*. Norman, University of Oklahoma Press, 1993.

Stephen POWERS, *Indians Of California*. With Introduction and Notes by Robert F. Heizer, July 13, 1975, "Reprinted from *Contributions to North American Ethnology*, Volume III, Department of Interior, U.S. Geographical and Geological Survey of the Rocky Mountain Region, J.W. Powell, in charge (Washington: Government Printing Office 1877) new Copyright 1976, by The Regents of the University of California, Los Angeles, University of California Press.

James J. RAWLS, *Indians of California—The Changing Image*. Norman, University of Oklahoma Press, 1984.

Elizabeth RENFRO, *The Shasta Indians Of California And Their Neighbors*. Happy Camp, CA, Naturegraph Publishers, Inc. 1992.

Robert B. ROBERTS, *Encyclopedia Of Historic Forts Of The United States*. New York, MacMillan Publishing Company, 1988. Extract for states of Oregon, Washington, California, Idaho, Nevada, Arizona, Utah and New Mexico.

Fred B. ROGERS, "Bear Flag Lieutenant," (Henry L. Ford), *California Historical Society Quarterly*, XXX, (June 1951), pp. 157-175.

Fred B. ROGERS, "Early Military Posts of Mendocino County," *California Historical Society Quarterly*, XXVII, (Sept. 1948), pp. 215-28.

Joseph G. ROSA, Robin MAY, *An Illustrated History of Guns and Small Arms*, London, Peerage Books, Hennerwood Publications, Ltd. 1984 [first published in 1974].

Ralph J. ROSKE, *Everyman's Eden: A History Of California*. New York, The MacMillan Company, 1967, 2 volumes.

Martin RYWELL, *Fell's Collector's Guide To American Antique Firearms*. New York, Frederick Fell, Inc., 1963.

William B. SECREST, *When the GREAT SPIRIT Died, The Destruction of the California Indians 1850-1860*. Sanger, CA, Fquill Driver Books/Word Dancer Press, Inc., 2003.

Oscar T. SHUCK, *Representative And Leading Men Of The Pacific*. San Francisco CA, Bacon & Company, Printers and Publishers, No. 536 Clay St., betw. Montgomery and Sansome (Streets), 1870. 702 pp., "JOHN B. WELLER by the Editor" pp. 515–521. At Bancroft Library, University of California at Berkeley, Berkeley, CA.

Ted SIMON, *The River Stops Here- Saving Round Valley, A Pivotal Chapter in California's Water Wars*, Berekely, University of California Press, 1994.

Eric Krabbe SMITH, *Lucy Young or T'teotsa Indian White Relations in Northwest California, 1846-1944.* Santa Cruz, University of California at Santa Cruz Press, 1990.

Kenneth M. STAMPP, *AMERICA IN 1857- A NATION ON THE BRINK*, New York, Oxford University Press, 1990.

Robert Louis STEVENSON, *The Silverado Squatters.* San Francisco, Mercury House, 1996, originally published by Chatto &Windus, 1883, follows the text of Grabhorn Press Edition 19542 "with a small number of editorial corrections."

William F. STROBRIDGE, *REGULARS IN THE REDWOODS The U.S. Army in Northern California 1852-1861.* Spokane, WA, Arthur A. Clark Co., 1994, 283 pp.

Amelia SUSMAN, *The Round Valley Indians of California An Unpublished Chapter In Acculturation In Seven (Or Eight) American Indian Tribes,* Edited by Robert F. Heizer, No. 31- 1976, Archaelogical Research Facility, University of California Berkeley California.

Bernard TAPER, *MARK TWAIN'S SAN FRANCISCO*, Berkeley, CA, Heyday Books, 1963, reissued 2003.

Clifford E. TRAFZER *California's Indians and the Gold Rush,* Sacramento, CA, Sierra Oaks Publishing Co., 1989.

Veronica E.V. TILLER, *American Indian Reservations And Trust Areas .* Albuquerque NM, Department of Commerce, 1996.

John B. WELLER, *Remarks Of Hon. Mr. Weller, Of California On The Mexican Boundary Commission—The River And Harbors Bill—The Fugitive Slave Law, And California Land Titles.* Delivered in the Senate of the United States Monday, Aug. 2, 1852.

Who's Who in American History, Historical Volume, 1607-1896, Revised Edition, 1967, St. Louis, Von Hoffman Press, Inc., 1967) p. 641 on John B. Weller.

Del WILCOX, *Voyagers to California.* Elk, CA, Sea Rock Press, second printing, 1993.

James WILSON, *The Earth Shall Weep A History Of Native America.* New York, Atlantic Monthly Press, 1998.

NEWSPAPERS

"CALIFORNIA LEGISLATURE ELEVENTH SESSION THIRTY SEVENTH DAY Monday, Feb 13th", *Sacramento Daily Union*, Sacramento, CA, Feb. 14, 1860.

"INDIAN WAR," *Mendocino Herald*, Ukiah, CA, Nov. 1, 1861, Vol. 1, #52, p. 2., c. 2.

"In Their Footsteps," Mike Geniella, September 12, 2004, *Santa Rosa Press Democrat*, Section B, p. 1 and p. 3.

"INDIAN WAR POLICY," *Sacramento Daily Union*, Sacramento, CA, Jan. 17, 1860, Editorial, p. 2., c.2.

"Late And Important Intelligence From Mendocino County—Indian Difficulty, &C. &C," *San Francisco Daily Alta California*, San Francisco, CA, June 4, 1858, Friday morning.

"'MENDOCINO WAR' EXPOSURES," *Sacramento Daily Union*, Sacramento, CA, Monday, April 16, 1860, p. 2, cols. 1 through 4.

"Eds. HERALD—Round Valley, May 7, 1862," *Mendocino Herald*, Ukiah, CA, May 23, 1862.

(Lt.) A.G. TASSIN, "'Chronicles of Camp Wright." *The Overland Monthly*. Parts I and II (July, August, 1887) *San Francisco News*, 'on the Pacific Coast,' 415 Montgomery St.

"TRIP TO ROUND VALLEY—NO. 2, Eel River." by J.(A writer known only by this single initial.), Editor of *Herald, Ukiah Mendocino Herald*, Ukiah, CA, Feb. 8, 1861, Vol. 1, No. 11, p. 2, c. 2.

"The 1870 Ghost Dance and the Methodists: An Unexpected Turn of Events in Round Valley," Virginia P. Miller, *Journal of California and Great Basin Anthropology*, Vol. 3, No. 2.

WEBSITES AND ARTICLES

"Round Valley Indian Tribes," a website listing current "Tribal Resources" includes the names of all seven of the current (December, 2004) members of the 'Round Valley Indian Tribal Council.' It is dated 2001. **www.covelo.net/tribes/pages/tribes.shtml.**

"Round Valley Indian Reservation History." A three page summary that includes the following statements regarding the multi-tribal makeup of the current community there: "From years of intermarriage, a common lifestyle, and a shared land base, a unified community emerged. The descendents of Yuki, Concow Maidu, Little Lake Pomo, Nomlaki, Cahto, Wailaki, Pit River npeoples formed a new tribe on the reservation, the Covelo Indian Community, later to be called the Round Valley Indian Tribes...." Alesso at **www.covelo.net/tribes/pages/tribes_history.shtml.**

"Historic California Posts: Fort Wright (Camp Wright, Fort Right)," A seven page description of the influence of Camp Wright on Round Valley's history. The section titled "History" was written by Col. Herbert M. Hart, USMC (retired) Executive Director, Council on America's Military Past. This includes two photos, a map of Camp Wright from a textbook titled *Pioneer Forts of the Far West*, 1965. This short but interesting history written from a military perspective can be found at **www.militarymuseum.org/FtWright.html.**

FEDERAL OR STATE OFFICIAL REPORTS AND RECORDS:

Congressional Globe. 36th Congress, First Session, pp. 2365–2369. Senatorial debate held on May 26, 1860 as quoted by Robert F. Heizer, Editor. *Federal Concern About Conditions Of California*

Indians 1853 TO 1913: Eight Documents. Selected and Edited by Robert F. Heizer (1-152) (Socorro, NM, Bellena Press, 1979). *"Federal Efforts To Transfer Indian Affairs To The State*

Of California, 1860" pp. 25–50. Anthropology Room, Held-Poage Research Library, 603 W. Perkins, Ukiah, CA.

Interior Department Appointment Papers, Microcopy #732, Roll #20, The California Superintendent of Indian Affairs, 1852–1862, Supt. Agent: Northern District, 1858–1863, Southern District, 1858–1866. Letter # 44 Maj. Gen. John E. Wool to Senators D.C. Broderick and Wm. Gwin, 9pp. Estle Beard Box, Held-Poage Library, Ukiah, CA.

Letters Received By The Office Of Indian Affairs, 1824–1880, M-234 and Letters sent by the Office of Indian Affairs, 1824–1880, Rolls 35 thru 38, (1856-1861), and M-21-(Microfilm) Roll 55 1856. Rolls 55 thru 58 are available on microfilm from 'NARA' and can be ordered via the Internet and also located at National Archives Building, 2nd. level, 1000 Commodore Dr., San Bruno, CA.

"Majority And Minority Reports Of The Special Joint Committee On The Mendocino War," *Senate Journal,(Appendix), 1860.* CHAS. T. BOTTS, State Printer. "Majority Report," pp. 1–6, "Minority ReporMt," pp. 7–11 and 18. *Testimony Taken Before The Joint Special Committee On The Mendocino Indian War,* depositions, pp. 13–74. California State Archives, 1020 "N" St., Sacramento, CA.

No author, U.S. Works Progress Administration, *National Guard Of California.* Units 1 to 100, Volume 1, #79. Kibbe Guard, 6th Div., 2nd Brigade, Weaverville, Trinity County. September 27, 1858, #88. Kibbe Rangers, Unattached, Red Bluff, Tehama County, Aug. 18, 1859. 1940. (Note that no record exists in this book for the "Eel River Rangers."} At the California Military History Museum, basement, 1119 Second St., Sacramento, CA. William Davies, Librarian.

Elija(h) Renshaw Potter, "Partial Transcript of Historical Events of Round Valley," copy by K.C. Dennis, Held-Poage Research Library, 603 W. Perkins St., Ukiah, CA.

"Report No. 103." E (Edward) A. Stevenson, Nome Lackee Agent to Supt. Thomas J. Henley, July 31, 1856, p. 250, Estle Beard Box, Held-Poage Research Library, 603 W. Perkins St., Ukiah, CA.

Report Of The Expedition Against The Indians Of This State, "Appendix" and "Correspondence," by Gen. William C. Kibbe, California Quartermaster, Jan. 16, 1860, pp. 4–33. Gen. Kibbe's handwritten report to Gov. Downey summarizing the War with the Wintoons, 1858–1859. Bancroft Library, University of California at Berkeley, Berkeley, CA. One copy can also be found at the California Archives, 1020 O St., Sacramento, CA.

Special Agent J. Ross Browne to Commissioner Hon. Charles E. Mix Sept. 4, 1858 San Francisco to Washi inclungton, D.C., "Report of J. Ross Browne Special Agent or in relation to Indian Affairs in California," National Archives Microfilm Publications, Microcopy No. 234, *Letters received by the Office of Indian Affairs 1824–1880,* 1858, National Archives, National Archives and Records Service, General Services Administration, 1958, (0187 to 0236).

Letter of Simmon P. Storms to Hon. Thomas J. Henley, Nome Lackee Reserve, June 29, 1856, as photocopied by John E. Keller, 3191 Acalanes Ave., Lafayette, carbon copy from National Archives, Microfilm Series 234, Frames 47–76, in the Estle Beard Box, Held-Poage Historical Research Library, 603 W. Perkins St., Ukiah, CA.

Letters Received by the Office of Indian Affairs 1824-1881, Report of Superintendent George M. Hanson, California's Northern District Superintendent of Indian Affairs, Microcopy 234, Roll 38, Page Numbers 0141 thru 0161. Contains Supt. Hanson's 1862 plans and reports on his personal visits to the four Northern California Indian Reservations (Klamath, Mendocino, Nome Cult Farm (Round Valley) and Nome Lackee. In order to consolidate operations and stop duplicate spending on the Northern California's Indian reservations, Hanson recommended closure of Klamath and Nome Lackee. The Office of Indian Affairs followed this advice by closing Nome Lackee and Klamath. Native Americans at Klamath were marched to Mendocino while those at Nome Lackeea were "driven" (language used by the Army) to Nome Cult (Round Valley).

CENSUS REPORTS

California Census Of 1852. Volume III Accession number 156713 at California History Section of the California State Library, Sacramento, CA.

California Census Of 1860. Mendocino County Census, Round Valley Township. National Archives, Microfilm, #653, Roll #60 at Held-Poage Research Library, 603 W. Perkins St., Ukiah, CA.

Preliminary Report of the Eighth (Federal) Census, 1860, Joseph G. Kennedy, Superintendent [of the Federal Census Department], Washington, Government Printing Office, 1860. Source: Robert (Bob) Buchanon.

UNPUBLISHED THESES, DISSERTATIONS OR OTHER SCHOLARLY ARTICLES

Gary E. GARRETT, "The Destruction of the Indian in Mendocino County 1856–1860" unpublished MA Thesis, History, July 22, 1069, Sacramento State College, now CSU or California State University at Sacramento, Sacramento, CA.

Edward W. GIFFORD, "The *Coast Yuki,*"Sacramento, CA, Sacramento Anthropological Society, Spring, 1965 pp. 97 GN4 S1593 No. 1–2 ANTH at Foster Library, Kroeber Hall of Anthropology, University of California at Berkeley, Berkeley, CA.

William Marion HAMMOND, "History Of Round Valley Indian Reservation," Unpublished MA Thesis, Jan. 5, 1972, Roll 3—on Microfilm at Sacramento State University Archives, was California State College, now California State University at Sacramento of "CSU", Sacramento, CA.

Gary HELM, "The Round Valley Reservation School: An Experiment in Assimilation," Unpublished MA Thesis, pp. 1–108, at California State University at Sacramento or CSU, 1990.

Lisa Ann (A.) MERTZ, "Let the Wind Take Care of Me; The Life History of Lorin Smith, a Kashaya Pomo Spiritual Leader," Unpublished PhD dissertation in Anthropology, The Graduate School of Union Institute, September, 1991.

Jeffrey MAWN, "Jasper O'Farrell: Surveyor, Farmer, and Politico" Unpublished MA Thesis, History, 1968, University of San Francisco, in San Francisco, CA, copy lent to the author by Janis M. (Miller) Valderrama, Fall 1999.

SPECIAL COLLECTIONS

John B. WELLER papers, T.W. Norris collection, "Philosophical statement," May 5, 1854. Bancroft Library, University of California at Berkeley, Berkeley, CA.

John G. DOWNEY papers, Bancroft Library, Ueiversity of California at Berkeley, Berkeley, CA.

PERSONAL INTERVIEWS

Mr. Emmett SIMONIN, Mr. Simonin (or Simmons) is the [father of Ms. Cora Lee Simmons, Chairperson, Round Valley Indians for Justice "Ensuring Justice for Native Americans", Covelo, CA], Aug. 22, 1999, Walnut Park, Petaluma, CA.

Ms. Janice Pollard HAGUE, Jan. 6, 2000, Held-Poage Research Library, 603 W. Perkins St., Ukiah, CA

Mr. Floyd BARNEY, of Covelo, March 20, 2000, Ukiah, CA.

Mr. Robert J. LEE, "Historical Photographs," 730 Grove Ave., Ukiah, CA 95482.

Mrs. Lila LEE, Director, HELD-POAGE HISTORICAL RESEARCH LIBRARY, 603 W. Perkins St., Ukiah, CA 95482, 1999-2002. I made numerous trips from my Home in Sebastopol to Ukiah for materials. The Lees were of great asistance with unfailing words of good humor and directions as to where to Sources on Round Valley's history. Two more gentlemen who worked at Held-Poage Library are Mr. Ed Bold and Mr. Phil Carnahan.

Donna J. HOWARD, Curator, Lake County Historical Courthouse Museum, 255 N. Forbes, Lakeport, CA 95453, late Fall 1999.

INDEX